Handbook
of
CHURCH MANAGEMENT

WILLIAM H. LEACH

Editor, *Church Management*

Englewood Cliffs, N. J.

PRENTICE-HALL, INC.

OTHER BOOKS BY WILLIAM H. LEACH

PUTTING IT ACROSS
HOW TO MAKE YOUR CHURCH GO
CHURCH FINANCE
CHURCH PUBLICITY
CHURCH ADMINISTRATION
COKESBURY MARRIAGE MANUAL
IMPROVED FUNERAL MANUAL
TOWARD A MORE EFFICIENT CHURCH
SERMON HEARTS
SERMON HEARTS FROM THE PSALMS
SERMON HEARTS FROM THE GOSPELS
HERE'S MONEY FOR CHURCHES
PRIZE SERMONS (EDITOR)
THE ALTAR IN YOUR CHURCH
PROTESTANT CHURCH BUILDING

Co-authorship with Marcus Bach

VESPER DRAMAS

Co-authorship with J. W. G. Ward

SPECIAL DAY SERMONS WITH WORSHIP OUTLINES
THE TRAGEDY AND TRIUMPH OF EASTER

Fifth printing . . . . *January, 1963*

©—1958, by
PRENTICE-HALL, INC.
ENGLEWOOD CLIFFS, N.J.

LIBRARY OF CONGRESS
CATALOG CARD NUMBER: 58-12327

PRINTED IN THE UNITED STATES OF AMERICA
37720-C

IN APPRECIATION

Special appreciation is due my wife and daughter, who have been of invaluable assistance in the assembly and preparation of the material for this book.

W. H. L.

Cleveland, Ohio

CONTENTS

1. THE VALIDITY OF CHURCH ADMINISTRATION   1

Good Church Administration, 5. Working with People, 9. The Place of the Minister in Church Administration, 10

2. DIVERSITIES OF OPERATIONS 12

Organization for Executive Procedure, 16. Remedying the Situation, 18. Why Departments? 22. Established Churches, 22

3. THE CHURCH AS A CORPORATION 25

Relics of Establishment, 26. Types of Incorporation, 28. Membership Incorporation, 30. Responsibilities of the Trustees, 31. Powers of the Religious Corporation, 32. Further Steps Toward Unity, 32. Legal Liabilities of Churches, 33. Taxation of Real Estate, 35. Special Assessments, 37. Exemption of Parsonages, 37. Other Taxes, 40. Churches and the Sales Tax, 40. Some Areas of State Control, 41. Contrary to Public Policy, 43. Church Liability, 44. Regulations Which Protect Churches, 45. The Federal Government and Church Taxation, 47

4. LOCATING & ESTABLISHING NEW CHURCHES .   48

Cooperative Action, 53. Working Through Church Federations, 54. Independent Churches, 55. Chicago Church Federation, 56. Subnormal Communities, 60. Zoning Laws as They Affect Churches, 60

5. INTEGRATING THE CONGREGATION 65

Using the Mail, 67. Registering Guests, 71. Organizing the Parish for Administration, 71. Geographical Organization of the Parish, 74. Typical Plan, 74. The Talent Ballot, 77. Integration of New Members into Church, 77

6. THE CHURCH WITH A MULTIPLE MINISTRY .   81

Division of Work of the Clergy, 83. The Heart of the Matter, 85. The Minister, 85. Conclusions for the Minister, 87. The Minister of the Parish, 87. Relationship to Others in North Church, 88. Conclusions for the Minister of the Parish, 89. The Minister of Education, 90. Staff Problems, 92. The Lay Staff, 93. Secretary to the Minister, 94. Office Secretary, 96. Book-

6. THE CHURCH WITH A MULTIPLE MINISTRY (cont.)

keeper, 97. Records Secretary, 98. Conclusions for Secretaries, 99. Custodian Job Analysis, 99. Director of Food Services Analysis, 101. The Business Manager, 102. Employee Staff Meetings, 103. Duties of the Church Manager, 104. Basic Function, 104. Conditions of Employment, 104. Duties and Responsibilities, 105. Membership Records, 105. Church Property and Equipment, 106. Personnel, 106

7. ORGANIZATION FOR A NEW BUILDING . . . 108

Who Shall Decide the Site? 112. The Finance Committee, 112. The Construction Committee, 113. The Financial Campaign, 115. Getting Mortgage Money, 122

8. THE ERECTION OF NEW BUILDINGS 126

The Five Point Church, 128. Some Basic Plans for Building, 129. Building for Worship, 130. Rooms for Choir, 138. Other Areas in the New Building, 139. Air Conditioning, 140. Bells and Carillons, 140. Using the Out-of-Doors, 141. Good Educational Rooms, 142. School Organized by Departments, 143. Economizing on Assembly Rooms, 145. Orderly Arrangement of Space, 147. Equipment, 148

9. CARE OF THE CHURCH BUILDING 151

Church Maintenance Check List, 151. Heating and Air Conditioning, 155. The Parsonage, 156. Church Building Insurance, 157. Recommendations, 158. Other Building Insurance, 160. Care of Floors, 160. Other Floors, 161. Fire Safety Check Sheet, 162

10. THE MINISTER AS AN EXECUTIVE 165

The Tools for Program Making, 169. The Minister and His Official Board, 171. Some Techniques, 175. The Minister as an Executive, 177. A Program for the Official Board, 181. Check List for Making the Year's Program, 185

11. THE ADMINISTRATIVE CENTER 190

Study Equipment, 192. Care of Books, 193. Dewey Decimal System of Library Classification, 194. Card Index, 197. Study Records, 198. In-Church Consultations, 198. Equipping the Office, 199. Duplicating Machines, 201. The Addressing Machine, 205. Folding Machines, 206. Stampers and Sealers, 207. Relationship of Study and Offices, 207

12. FINANCING THE LOCAL CHURCH 208

The Mechanics of Fund Raising, 210. The Making of the Budget, 210. Local Church Budget, 212. Annual Expenditures of $15,000 Budget, 213. Publicizing the Budget, 215. A Plan for the Every Member Canvass, 219. Compo-

12. FINANCING THE LOCAL CHURCH (cont.)

nents of the Plan, 220. Organization of the Solicitors, 221. Publicity Helps, 222. The Dinners, 223. Instructions to Solicitors, 224. Variations and Substitutes, 227. Accounting, 228. Budget Control, 230. Annual General Budget, 231. The Functional Sheets, 232. Some Operating Principles, 235. Wills and Endowments, 235

13. CHURCH PUBLIC RELATIONS 243

The Out-Door Bulletin Board, 247. Bells and Chimes, 247. The Printed Word, 248. A Church Paper, 250. The Community Newspaper, 253. The Denominational Press, 254. Projected Materials, 254. Radio and Television, 255. Force of Total Impact, 256. Administering the Program, 256. Space Advertising, 257

14. THE SERVICE OF WORSHIP 258

Building Facilities, 258. Front Entrance, 259. Timing, 259. Preparation of the Building, 260. Tips on Good Ushering, 261. The Service of Worship, 267. A Progressive Service of Worship, 271. Minister and Choir, 272. Check List for the Evaluation of Public Worship, 273

15. THE MUSIC OF THE CHURCH 278

Director and Organist, 279. The Position of the Choir, 280. Choir Rehearsal Rooms, 281. The Entry of the Choir, 282. The Organization of the Choir, 284. Financing the Music Program, 286. Enlisting Choir Members, 287. Necessity for Rehearsals, 288. Suggestions for Small Churches, 288. The Minister and the Choir, 289

16. CHURCH SCHOOL ADMINISTRATION 291

Organization for Religious Education, 296. Board of Education, 297. The Director of Christian Education, 297. Department Organization, 301. Organizing the Departments, 303. The Primary Department, 304. Double Services, 309. Audio-Visual Aids, 310. Equipping the Classroom, 312. Graded Pictures, 315. Other Activities, 318. Vacation Bible School, 318. Religious Drama, 318. Summer Camps and Conferences, 319

17. USING THE CHURCH YEAR 322

The Use of Seasonal Colors, 328. The Minister's Executive Calendar, 330

18. MINISTERIAL ETHICS & PRACTICES 335

Ministerial Ethics, 337. The Man, 337. How Many Hours? 339. Place of Reading, 341. Personal Finance, 342. Ministerial Discounts, 344

19. THE ETHICS OF THE PARSONAGE 348

Essential Qualities, 350. The Family in the Parsonage, 351. Family Privacy, 353. Entertainment in the Parsonage, 355. Compensation of Family Love, 356

20. THE MINISTER & HIS CHURCH 358

The Minister Owes Time to His Church, 359. Minister without Portfolio, 361. Good Use of Time, 361. Use of Parsonage, 364. Things the Church Must Do, 365. The Minister as a Candidate for a Church, 368

21. THE MINISTER IN HIS PROFESSION 371

Predecessor and Successor, 372. What the Minister Owes His Successor, 374. His Brothers in the Community, 376. Ten Commandments for Ministers, 379

22. THE PASTORAL MINISTRY 380

A Department of Pastoral Work, 383. Home Visitation, 383. Help for the Minister, 387. Lay Help in Pastoring, 388. Emergency Calls, 389. Prayers in Emergencies, 390. The Minister as a Counselor, 392. Preparation for Counseling, 395. Pastoral Techniques, 396

23. THE MINISTRY OF MARRIAGE 402

Variations in the Service, 409. A Second Minister, 409. A Minister Officiates at Wedding of His Daughter, 410. Use of the Engagement Ring, 410. Local Church Check List, 410. Informal Weddings, 413. Integration of the Communion Service, 414. Minister at the Reception, 414. The Post-Marriage Ministry, 414. The Golden Wedding Service, 416

24. MINISTRY TO THOSE WHO MOURN 420

The Pre-Funeral Conference, 422. Funeral Trends, 423. Minister and Mortician, 424. The Funeral Service, 425. The Committal Service, 432. The Post-Funeral Ministry, 433

25. THE CHURCH & ITS YOUNG PEOPLE 436

The Program in Operation, 440. Sunday Evening Program, 443. The Weekday Session, 444. The Leadership of Youth, 447. Qualifications for a Youth Counselor, 448

26. WOMEN IN THE CHURCH 458

Women's Organizations in a Local Church, 461. Organizing the Program, 466. Planning, 466. Educational Program, 467. Work Program, 468. Money-Raising Plans, 469. Budgeting Receipts, 470. Constitution for Women's Association of Lakewood Congregational Church, 471. An Installation Service for the Officers of the Women's Organization, 476

27. EVANGELISM IN THE LOCAL CHURCH . . . 479

Pastoral Evangelism, 480. The Pastor's Personal Evangelism, 484. The Communicant Class, 486. Lay Evangelism, 488. The Community Survey, 488. The Evangelistic Visit, 490. Sunday School Evangelism, 494. The Place of the Revival Meeting, 495

INDEX 500

THE VALIDITY OF
CHURCH ADMINISTRATION

"YOU ARE LUCKY TO BE WORKING IN THE CHURCH," SAID A friend. "It is the only field I know that has not undergone terrific changes in the fundamentals and practices."

He was a good churchman but how little he really knew of what has been taking place in church life since 1900! Jesus Christ doubtless is "the same yesterday, today and forever." But his church does not enjoy this permanency. In the years of our century, there have probably been more changes in church practices than in any other century of this Christian era, nor have changes been limited to techniques of administration.

After 1900 theology took a turn toward liberalism. For a time it seemed as if the new learning would control the future. Then suddenly the new authoritarianism rose with strength. Its spirit has definitely influenced theological leaders. The lay-controlled Sunday school is being replaced by the denominationally-controlled church school with serious graded curricula. It hasn't been achieved as yet but it is on its way. The new church architecture is so different from that of the last century that unless a cross is placed conspicuously, a passerby has difficulty recognizing it as a house of God. The minister's tasks have been doubled and tripled. Church offices have become a common practice in the parish. Collections have given way to church finance. Pulpit announcements have been succeeded by good programs of church public relations.

Pastoral counseling has increased the burdens of pastoral calling. Inter-church activities and interdenominational activities as demonstrated in local church federations and the National Council of the Churches of Christ in the U.S.A. has become influential. Denominations have learned the art of direct mail publicity and

1

are pouring their information onto the desks of local ministers. As buildings have become larger, custodial staffs are replacing the church sexton. The minister and his family have found a new freedom. They no longer face the restrictions of colorless dress, simple amusements, and social contacts.

Stunts and tricks to fill pews have developed into recognized techniques of church administration. A new profession—that of the church business manager—has started its growth with a specialized field in the larger churches. Denominational offices in the nation, state and local cities have doubled and tripled their staffs. Chairs of church administration have made their appearance in many of the theological seminaries.

It is quite a change from the early years in the life of *Church Management* when a lecturer on parish administration was a curiosity. In one seminary in which I was a chapel lecturer, I noticed the absence of faculty members. The reason given was that "our young men are bright enough to know how to stand on their heads without bringing in an expert on the subject."

It is too bad that a fiction has been permitted to develop which divides the tasks of the church into two classifications: (a) the spiritual and (b) the organizational. Under this fiction the preaching of the sermon, the conducting of prayer meetings, and the leading of a confirmation class are spiritual tasks of the ministry. The direction of a committee seeking a new site, the organization of an every member canvass, or the installation of a new organization is organizational. In the line of quality the church usually assesses the spiritual as a little higher than the organizational. Hence those laymen who excel in uttering public prayers or who are qualified to teach Bible class have a higher rating than those who direct the financial canvass or arrange the mortgage at the bank.

It is a question just how far the instructions of the New Testament should influence our church organizations of today. If, however, we give them any validity at all, we must concede that the ministries of the early churches were varied; they followed the pattern of a leader. Saint Paul organized, Apollos administered (watered), but God giveth the increase.

Following the Resurrection of Jesus the apostles scattered themselves around the then-known world. They preached the word and made converts to the faith. This was immediately followed by the organization of local churches. The organizations were not as simple as some people have supposed. In the book of Acts we have the account of the church at Jerusalem which found its members in economic difficulties and organized a communist-like group with a common treasury. To meet the criticism of partiality they elected deacons by casting lots. These men were given the task of administering the funds held in common. Other churches took some lessons of this and the relief of poverty was a constant part of the program of the early churches. Yet they had their individual differences.

By the middle of the third century the church in Rome possessed such a complex organization that readers are puzzled. Cornelius, a writer of the time, says that in Rome there were forty-six Presbyters, seven regional deacons, seven sub-deacons, forty-two acolytes, fifty-two exorcists, lectors and doorkeepers, and some fifteen hundred widows who were recognized in some formal capacity of service. In addition, we find the following terms mentioned—bishops, deaconesses, virgins, grave-diggers, ministrants, and others.

These are mentioned with no intention that they supply the pattern for the local church of today but to show that the early church was a much more complex organization than some of us think. When later Christianity became incorporated into the Roman Empire the development of many additional offices in the local church was inevitable. The point is that the local church as a corporation has all the tradition of history.

Saint Paul likened the local church to the human body; (I Corinthians 12:12-31). No better parallel has ever been made. The early church pictured the local organization as a ship. This symbol has appeared often in Christian history. A Christian novelist writing about 225 A.D. gives this picture:

For the whole business of the Church is like a great galley, bearing through a violent storm men of many places, and who desire to inhabit the one city of the good Kingdom. Let, therefore, God be your captain; and let the pilot be likened to Christ; the lookout man to the bishop; the sailors to the Presbyters; the overseers of the rowers to the deacons; the stewards to the catechists; the multitude of the brethren to the passengers.

It is evident that these early church leaders thought of the local church as an organization with a division of duties. They had their systems of church organization and the growth of the kingdom was dependent upon competent organization and qualified leaders.

The over-simplification of the local church which followed the Protestant reformation gave great emphasis to the task of the preacher. The preacher-prophet was exalted high above every other activity in the church. Church organization was simple. The pastor served as priest, prophet, pastor, and director of activities. The care of the offerings may have been placed in the hands of a competent person but the early churches (in this country at least) had no recognized trustees which the law requires in most states today.

As churches grew larger and budgets became of considerable size the need for organization became more apparent. Many clergymen resented the newer methods and preferred keeping their churches merely preaching stations rather than enlarging the programs. The real conflict between the old and the new is simply this: "Is the church a preaching station on the way of life?" or "Is it a community through which, in worship and practices, the communicants seek to build for their lives on earth the Kingdom of God?" The prophet soul who still sees the minister as an Amos in the wilderness may vote for the preaching station; the person who believes that the working organization is the way to save individuals and build the kingdom will want the second. We believe that historical precedent as well as world evangelism is on the latter side.

There were so many forms of local church organization

among the first century churches that there can be no agreement as to which may be the real form of local church organization. Indeed we can question whether or not there are any set patterns which need to be minutely followed. We do try, however, to follow their dreams and intents, supplying techniques which meet the modern challenges. Our church departments might sound strange to apostolic ears; our emphasis on efficiency might not be appreciated by the early church fathers but the end sought—the Christianization of society—is identical with the apostolic vision.

Good Church Administration

Good church administration is based on the principle that the best methods of local church organization are those which best accomplish the purpose of the church. At times these may challenge the traditional practices; at times, they may parallel them.

Historically this has been pretty much practiced through the ages. The differences in church administration ideas have come about because of differing situations. Sometimes these have been national, sometimes economic, sometimes political.

Good church administration requires that the techniques used in the program of the churches should be the most effective ones available for reaching the ends sought. The fact that Saint Paul wrote his letters to the churches in a large, bold hand is no argument why the modern minister should not use a typewriter. The end sought is the composition, not the machinery of production.

The nineteenth-century church in America was led by a pastor who had a study but no office. He did not own an automobile, he did not use a telephone. The minister of today uses these conveniences and they increase his capacity.

Good church management insists that when you build a new church building, you erect it to fit your program—not merely to follow tradition. Churches, doubtless, have always done this and probably always will. The cruciform church did not spring from the mind of the apostles. The additions which made the arms of the cross were first erected to secure needed additional space. Then some one noticed that unconsciously the builders had erected a church in the form of a cross.

Modern church buildings are about one hundred per cent functional as they should be. For a period in England it was customary for the clergy to have the responsibility for the erection and maintenance of the chancels of the parish churches; the laity had the responsibility for the nave. The clergy built the chancel to fit the needs of prayer, sermon, and song. The laymen built for a place to stand or sit for worship. Both parts of the church were functional. We add educational buildings, social rooms, and parking space because they are necessary in the program of the church.

Good church management demands the best in lay leadership. After an organization is established which provides for the use of many people in its program it seeks the best men and women to work the program. It goes along with the apostolic injunction to seek men of good report, full of the Holy Spirit and wisdom, who may become overseers in the church. The church of today with its many diversified tasks makes the selection of adequately qualified leadership a most important function. The task of financing a new church building requires a different temperament and training than that of teaching a class in church school. It requires conferences with bankers, organization of financial drives, interviews with prospective contributors, etc. Church tasks are numerous in many areas.

Good church management seeks not alone a man's money but the man himself. It has done a great deal to broaden the scope of stewardship. It has in part recovered the spirit of the days when great churches were built through the contributions of men's hands. It has found many tasks which help to promote the program of the church. In the chapters which follow you will find several suggestions for putting many types of individuals to work.

Nothing develops personal stewardship like exercise. The legend of Our Lady and the Juggler is often quoted to show that the offering of the poor juggler, scorned by the priests, was acceptable to the Virgin. Each worker in the church likes to feel that his offering is pleasing in the sight of God. Nothing builds confidence in a man as the thought that he is doing an important bit of work and that his life is counting in the up-building of the world.

I recall the shining face of the Negro driving the station-wagon which served as a limousine for a certain vacation spot I visited. The car was clean; it had been polished from front to rear. The engine was free from noisy knocking. I congratulated the driver on his craftsmanship.

"Yes," he replied. "I've got the glory. Mr. —— has placed the entire responsibility for this automobile in my hand. If it breaks down, it is my fault. I ain't going to let it break down."

Good church management believes that as a man gives, he grows. It qualifies the idea, however, by insisting that the man's growth is dependent upon his belief that the work he is doing is worth while. This is important in the entire philosophy of church administration. To illustrate it, take this instance. In giving the charge to the pastor in a certain installation service, the speaker gave this illustration.

> My father had his own way to deal with tramps. He always had a wood pile convenient. When a man came along begging a meal, he pointed out the wood pile.
>
> "Take this wood and re-pile it over here," he would say, pointing out the new location. "When that is completed, your meal will be awaiting you."
>
> When the wood had been moved the man got the meal. Perhaps the next day another tramp came, asking for a meal. Father then reversed the movement. He took the tramp to the wood pile, pointed to the earlier spot and said, "Move the wood over there and when it has been moved, your meal will be waiting for you."

> Looking directly to the pastor elect, the speaker then said:
> Young man, my father knew how to have a successful church.
> Always have a job to give people. When people work in the
> church they become good churchmen. Keep some wood piling
> tasks around.

Good church management would not follow this line. Participation makes good churchmen but not by wood-carrying tasks. The good leaders have a program so challenging that those who work in it are sure that they are doing the work of the church and through the church, the work of the Kingdom of God.

Good church management follows democratic procedures. In our day, that is a big challenge. The marginal people on our rolls are increasing. The demand on the time of our people is such that year after year we are faced with the fact that a large percentage of our membership is not attending the services of worship or participating in the program of the local church. The recovery of these people is a most important duty of the church. The recovery may be hastened by pastoral and lay visitations but the cure usually comes through some kind of plan for integrating the whole congregation into the church program. It requires at times the combined skill of the pastor and psychiatrist to find just what kind of work will interest some individuals but a place in the program should be found for them.

Even in this matter there are exceptions. Good church management recognizes that there is no pattern which can fit every situation. The inflexibility of denominations has often proven disastrous in this respect. Local churches must have the freedom of creating programs to fit their local needs. There are always some individuals who seek in the church an opportunity for worship. They like good music, good preaching, good liturgy. They resist activation. Church management sees no need to push them into the tasks of serving tables. We do not carry our philosophy so far as to believe that every man and woman must serve on a committee or head an organization.

Working with People

Good church management places the emphasis upon program and people in contrast to theology, liturgy, or parliamentary procedure. It seeks the methods of the executive rather than the parliamentarian. It tries to move men to action rather than to decisions. It is interested in meeting but it is also interested in what goes on between meetings.

Here is where the good church executive differs from the platform chairman. The chairman must know the adopted "Rules of Order." He must rule as to who has the right to speak, what motion has precedent, what committees to appoint.

The executive measures the work by periods of time. The chairman of the meeting appoints a committee for a certain purpose. The good executive sets the time clock for the committee to see that the task is accomplished step by step before the next meeting. Meetings are but stepping stones to accomplishment. Good church management seeks good executive leadership.

The tools of a theologian are the creeds of his church; the tools of the parliamentarian are the accepted books of rules and procedure; the tools of the executive are people. He must move them into position to meet the ends in view.

Such procedure will at times conflict with the rules of the past. The man who believes that the rules of the denominational discipline or constitution must be followed minutely may not have much sympathy with the executive procedures which put action ahead of precision. Often the executive leader feels that the old must not be disturbed; instead he adds to or supplements the historic authorities. This will be most apparent in record systems. Some denominations still require a bound record of church membership. The person who wishes to move into the field of church management will count heavily on direct mail publicity. He knows that the traditional records are almost totally inadequate for direct mail contacts. But he lets the authorized stand while he builds a system that works around it.

The same applies to the membership system in regard to the newer pastoral counseling techniques. The date of birth, date of baptism, date of joining the church, and date of marriage are pretty thin material for counseling so here again the wise minister leaves the old in place but moves around it with a more effective set of records.

The Place of the Minister in Church Administration

The traditional training for the ministry does little to qualify the minister for this executive work. Instead it exalts the ministry to the point where it makes it difficult for him to give leadership to others. He is the big "I" in the church. Executive procedure would prefer that he be one of the "We." A triumphant pulpit ministry is no evidence that a man is well qualified as an executive.

The minister, however, is the head of the local church. As such, he must assume the duties of leadership. As social and pastoral duties are forced upon him, he needs some knowledge of executive methods that he may secure the proper lay leadership to carry on the tasks. Otherwise, he will kill himself doing the work that others are able and willing to do.

If he feels that he is not qualified for this service, he should start to steep himself in the language of successful executives. He will learn from volumes on the psychology of leadership. The bibliography which follows this chapter will offer many suggestions. Some very valuable material may be found in *Influencing Men in Business* by Walter Dill Scott (long in print but still useful); the still good *How To Win Friends and Influence People* by Dale Carnegie (Simon & Schuster); and *How To Work With People* by Sumner Harwood (Cambridge Analytical Services).

The transfer from the philosophy of speech-making to action-leadership is difficult for many ministers. A veteran YMCA executive advises the author that he has found it difficult to use ministers in his organization for the reason they could not make the transfer. They still feel they should tell the committee how to do its work rather than lead the members in its accomplishment.

What is being said in this chapter is that good church management is a necessary and valid servant of the church for the contribution which it makes to program and individuals. The study and production of technical tasks which may at times seem to lead away from the traditional practices of piety make an important contribution to the purpose for which the church was instituted. The best administrative methods are dated to fit their times. They will change from age to age as business and professions find newer and better ways to produce greater results through leadership.

Executive Leadership

BARNARD, C. I., *The Functions of the Executive.* Harvard University, 1953.

———, *Organization and Management.* Harvard University, 1936.

BOWER, M., *The Development of Executive Leadership.* Harvard University, 1949.

BURSK, E. C., *How To Increase Executive Effectiveness.* Harvard University, 1953.

COYLE, G. L., *Group Experience and Democratic Values.* Women's, 1947.

LAIRD, D. A. and E. C., *The New Psychology of Leadership.* McGraw-Hill, 1957.

———, *Sizing Up People.* McGraw-Hill, 1951.

———, *The Technique of Handling People.* McGraw-Hill, 1954.

LEACH, W. H., *Putting It Across.* Cokesbury, 1925.

MCCORMICK, CHARLES P., *The Power of People.* Harper, 1949.

OSBORN, A. F., *Applied Imagination.* Scribners, 1957.

ROETHLISBERGER, F. J., *Management and Morale.* Harvard University, 1947.

TEAD, O., *The Art of Administration.* McGraw-Hill, 1951.

2 | DIVERSITIES OF OPERATIONS

IN A BOOK OF THIS NATURE, THE AUTHOR IS AWARE OF ONE
great source of resistance: the different methods of organization in the more than two hundred denominations to be found
in the United States. It is obvious that the book cannot provide
a complete analysis of the methods of every group nor of any
one group, but must seek to find the common denominator so
that a common language may be used.

Christianity, in its organization, has resisted regimentation.
When Saint Paul visited the various churches of his day, he
was interested to find this quality and pointed it out in his first
letter to the church at Corinth. Though the church had existed
less than a generation, the differences in theology and administration were evident.

> There are differences of administration but the same Lord,
> and there are diversities of operations but the same God which
> worketh all in all.

Each denomination sets up not only its form of organization,
but its vocabulary as well. One almost needs a denominational
dictionary to understand its history and procedures. The same
word means different things in the various groups. For instance
the term "elder" in the Methodist system describes the highest
rank of ordination; in the Presbyterian, it means a man taken
from the ranks of the laity of the local church and ordained
to rule over the local congregation; in the Disciples Fellowship,
the elders are selected laymen who direct the spiritual life of
the congregation and officiate at the weekly service of communion. The responsibility of this service in the Disciples lies
with a selected lay group. The term "deacon" in the Methodist

and Episcopal churches is a degree of ordination; in the Presbyterian system, the deacon is a layman selected for the distribution of alms and the direction of the charities of the local church; in the Baptist and Congregational churches, which have no elders, the board of deacons becomes the highest spiritual body in the church.

In the Episcopal church, the rector lives in the rectory; in the Presbyterian church, the minister lives in the manse; in the Methodist, Congregational, and Baptist churches, the pastor lives in the parsonage; and in many cities of the south, the Baptist pastors live in pastoriums.

The term "trustee" is a legal one and the prerogatives vary not alone with denominations but with local churches. Some adhere to a strict legal interpretation of the office; in others the office is broadened to include authority over the spiritual program of the church. This is discussed at length under the chapter dealing with church law. It is little wonder that people become confused as they go from church to church. Newspaper reporters caught in these confusions throw up their hands in distress.

Traditionally, each denomination felt the responsibility to justify its own plan of organization by finding scriptural authority for both the plan of operation and the terms used. The Christian church has been a receptive institution and has added from other cultures as it has lived through the ages. Necessity has, as always, been the mother of invention. New ideas and new methods have been added through experience and the modern local church can hardly be identified with the simplicities of those of apostolic days.

There have been attempts to break down the many denominations into three classifications. They are the Episcopal, the Reformed, and the Congregational. But under pressure from "the cares of this world, the deceitfulness of riches and the lusts of other things," forms have changed for greater efficiency and no one could place the various groups into these three molds.

The Episcopal form is that type of church organization which passes authority from the top down. The best and perhaps only complete example is the Roman Catholic Church. The Pope of Rome receives his authority from God. He then selects his cardinals, archbishops, and bishops. He calls ecumenical councils to advise him but he is always the head of the church and his word is law. Unquestionably the practice of democratic principles has been creeping into the local programs of the Catholic churches and it may be that more authority of independent action is being extended.

The Protestant Episcopal church which normally would be in this group is organically a democratic body with its two houses of the triennial convention, the House of Bishops and the House of Deputies which includes clergy and laymen. This is the supreme legislative body of the church dealing with organization and doctrine.

The Methodist church, which up to a very few years ago carried the name "Methodist Episcopal," in its beginnings borrowed Episcopal terminology and confessions but its bishops have always been administrative officers carrying out the enactments of the General Conference. This conference is a legislative body dealing with theology, administration, and church practices. Delegates are elected by annual conferences from both clergy and lay ranks. Recently, sectional conferences called jurisdictional conferences have been set up to localize the direction of the presiding bishop. These jurisdictional conferences now elect the bishops. So, the Episcopal form hardly exists.

The Reformed system is best exemplified by the Presbyterian and the Reformed denominations. It is a product of the reformation and the control of the local church is invested in laymen selected by the local congregation. In the Presbyterian churches, this group is known as "The Session," in the Reformed churches, it is known as "The Consistory." The genius of the Reformed system is in this order of ruling men at the center. They are ordained, not merely installed. They usually take the same vows

as the minister. They have control of all the church activities
of the local church and represent it in the high judicatories.
Here again, however, change is taking place. Through the
ascendancy of the trustees in some Reformed denominations,
much of the consistorial strength is being sapped. In the merger
of the Reformed and Evangelical churches, a concession has
been made to congregationalism in this respect and it seems that
the further merger with the Congregational church will produce further compromise.

The third general classification is the Congregation form.
This group includes the Congregational, Baptist, Disciples of
Christ, and others. The Lutheran churches in America have not
continued the European practice of having Bishops. Their present policy would seem to be a combination of Reformed and
Congregational. Its theology is colored by the concept of local
church autonomy and in origin its plan of organization was
completely democratic. Every business matter must be referred
to the congregation or to an authorized committee of the congregation. Members were originally received only by the vote
of the congregation. Congregational and other churches in this
classification recognize no higher judiciary than the local church.

But here again, time is taking its toll. A church of any size
finds it very inconvenient to consult the entire congregation
on every item. More and more authority is being taken by the
Board of Deacons and the Board of Trustees. The local congregations are being welded into denominations. Some of the most
autocratic denominational agencies are found in these so-called
democratic bodies.

The reader naturally senses that these three types of organization emerged from the historic periods in which they were
created. Perhaps he is also aware that each of these systems is
deficient in a quality which is very essential for today. If our
own period is characterized by one method more than any
other, it is that of executive procedure.

This is a period of great industrial prosperity and of great

engineering achievements. But back of these stand leaders who
know how to use the knowledge of other men. Regardless
of great engineering, no great industry can arise without executive skill.

The whole art of church management is based on the new
knowledge of executive procedure. The church is a community,
an organization which needs direction. Many, many programs
must be developed and projected and as much skill is required
to direct a program of youth as to write a curriculum. Moreover, an organization must be adapted for the promotion of its
program. None of the generalized forms above were created
for executive procedure and membership integration.

Organization For Executive Procedure

Up to comparatively modern times, the local church was a
single-celled institution. Its building was one unit erected for
public worship. Today's churches—at least in America—have
become many faceted organizations, not as a result of conscious
direction on the part of the churches themselves but of a growing society pressing in on the church. About one hundred years
ago, Sunday schools began to become important; today, the
church that does not have one is unusual.

Though apostolic churchmen met around a meal table, it has
been only in recent years that dining room facilities have had
a place in the program of the church. Young people, filled with
surplus energy, sought methods for organized fellowship. The
church seemed to be the proper place for such gatherings.

As churches appreciated the value of their physical property,
it seemed wise to elect trustees to act for the congregation in
the matter of legal property, claims, etc. State laws were
amended to permit the incorporation of religious bodies. Because the historic organization did not provide for these activities, church societies developed apart from the actual church.
They had their own organizations, collected their own money,
and used it in the way they desired.

Though national bodies soon recognized many of their activities in the formal organization of many churches, they are still considered as "apart" from the church. "Going to church" still refers to the service of worship. "Going to Sunday school" is quite a different affair. "I am not a member of the church but am a member of the Ladies' Society" is a common expression. In the historic forms of organization these societies circled around the orbit of the church yet never quite became a part of it. Conflicts between groups were inevitable.

Because of this situation, programs were arranged by the individual groups. There was little synchronization of intentions or worship. If we were to create new churches today, there is little question but that we would plan a simple but efficient method of organization for action. Local churches patterned after the historic organization fail to meet the executive challenge in a number of ways.

1. There is no clear line of authority. Years ago a salesman pointed out one limitation to me. When he called on a business house he was directed to a purchasing agent and in a few minutes he had a yes or no. When he went to the church he consulted first of all the minister. There he was told that the pastor had no authority to purchase and that he should see the president of the Board of Trustees. The president referred him to the chairman of the House Committee; the chairman of the House Committee told him that his particular item was usually provided by funds from the Ladies' Aid Society. The president of the Ladies' Aid took the matter under advisement. In the end the cost of selling was so great that he decided he would no longer seek sales from churches.

2. The church lacks the unity necessary for executing a good program. In the mind of its own members it is a group of organizations rather than one church.

3. The traditional church does not have one program but rather a number of small programs, often formulated without reference to others.

4. It is difficult to define the authority of the minister and other staff members. In the average church which has but one

minister he is in an impossible position. He may have very little authority in the church except for the pastoral obligations of sermons, worship, pastoral calls, and so on. Around him are self-created groups running their own programs. He is advised that the financial responsibility is with the trustees. Yet, the congregation seems to hold him responsible for every phase of the work.

Remedying the Situation

It is too much to expect that denominations will revise their entire constitutions to organize for executive procedure. It is not necessary that the program be as drastic as this. It is quite possible to build your program around the traditional form.

If, however, yours is a new church of the community or congregational type unhampered by historic forms, you would be wise to organize it for the activation and direction of its entire program. Do away with the various societies and label them as departments of church work. Try to get all people interested in the church to think of it as an organism rather than a preaching service together with a lot of miscellaneous activities.

As a new church it will probably have one minister. Most churches are in this class. If it is free from denominational tradition, it will probably be a community or congregational type. The congregation will be the controlling body and will elect the board. Make this a single board to avoid the confusion of one board for the spiritual work and a second one for the secular. The distinction is not clear in most instances.

Place the minister above the board as he should be over all activities. Drop the idea of various committees of the board and instead divide the work into departments. The Methodist Church has done well in recommending that the various activities of the local church be considered as "commissions." The 1956 Discipline requires that every local church shall have four commissions: Membership and Evangelism; Education; Missions; and Finance. It permits if the local church desires two more commissions: Worship and Social and Recreational Activities. The word "commission" is a stronger one than "committee"; "department" is still stronger.

Even with the six commissions recommended, the entire program of the average church is not covered. Others should be considered by any new church.

ADMINISTRATIVE.

Supervision of staff, public relations, internal and external publicity, etc.

MEMBERSHIP.

Records, enlistment, new members, church attendance, parish organization, fellowship programs, women's societies, men's clubs, etc.

WORSHIP.

Corporate worship, music, family and personal devotions, communion and baptism, drama, art, ushering.

EDUCATION.

Church school, extended sessions, communicant classes, weekday instruction, vacation schools, audio-vision instruction, scouting, camping, etc.

FINANCE AND STEWARDSHIP.

Stewardship education, budget-making, budget campaigns, special financial efforts with the exception of capital funds.

EVANGELISM.

Prospects, year-round evangelism, special meetings, etc.

WORLD OUTREACH.

Missionary education and giving, interdenominational projects, missionary projects.

PROPERTY.

Upkeep, custodian service, insurance, building projects.

SOCIAL OUTLOOK.

The community, the nation, the world, conferences and discussions on current affairs.

Even with this extended list you will find it difficult to place all of the activities such as the women's work. In this outline the Women's Society or Ladies' Aid would be under Membership, the Women's Missionary Societies under World Outreach. Men's Clubs would go under Membership, most youth work would be under Education, etc. Some churches may want to separate stewardship from finance to emphasize the larger purpose of stewardship. That might then be placed under Education.

Another suggestion introduces a department of Pastoring which recognizes the new counselling program so important in many churches. It also sets the Women's Work in a department of its own, a point appreciated by the leaders of the women.

DEPARTMENT OF WORSHIP.
Includes the service of worship, music, ushering, etc.

DEPARTMENT OF PROPERTY AND FINANCE.
Functions as the church trustees.

DEPARTMENT OF EDUCATION.
Includes the church school and youth work.

DEPARTMENT OF CHRISTIAN FELLOWSHIP.
Building the local church into a real fellowship through visitation, dinners, etc.

DEPARTMENT OF MISSIONS AND BENEVOLENCE.
Implements the expanded interests of the church.

DEPARTMENT OF SOCIAL ACTION.
Represents the social action program of the denomination and interests itself in neighborhood programs, community relief, political life, etc.

DEPARTMENT OF PASTORAL WORK.
Puts the entire church back of what is now considered the task of the minister alone.

CHURCH BOARDS AND THEIR COMMITTEES

I BOARD OF PROPERTY AND FINANCE (TRUSTEES)

Committees:
1. Financial Planning, Budgeting, Issuing of Periodic Statements
2. Banking, Investing, Insuring, Auditing
3. Financial Canvassing and Recording of Gifts and Pledges
4. Upkeep and Improvement of Property and Furnishings
5. Supervising Custodian, Regulating Use of Property

Related Officers:
Treasurer
Financial Secretary

Related Employees:
Custodian, Business Manager

II BOARD OF WORSHIP AND MEMBERSHIP (DEACONS, DEACONESSES)

Committees:
1. Services of Worship: Ushering, Attendance, Bulletins, Advertising
2. Flowers, Decorating
3. Preparations for Lord's Supper, Baptisms, Weddings, Funerals, etc.
4. Church Roll; Visitation of Needy, Sick, Inactive; Correspondence with Those Removed; Friendly Visitation
5. Visitation Evangelism; Preparation and Admission of New Members

Related Officer:
Clerk

Related Employees:
Director of Music, Organist, Church Visitor, Secretary

III BOARD OF EDUCATION AND FELLOWSHIP

Committees:
1. Church School Administration: Personnel, Equipment, Curriculum
2. Educational Aids: Library, Audio-Visual, Drama, Texts, Music, etc.
3. Leadership Education, Workers' Conferences
4. Social, Athletics, Recreation, Camping
5. Sponsoring and Regulating All Societies for Interest and Age Groups

Related Officers:
Church School Superintendent
Society Presidents

Related Employees:
Director of Education, Youth Worker, Hostess, Youth Choir Director, Athletic Coaches, etc.

IV BOARD OF BENEVOLENCE AND COUNSEL

Committees:
1. Cooperation with Denominational Projects and Missions
2. Cooperation with Non-denominational and Social Agencies; Homes
3. Vocational, Family, Psychological, Religious Counseling and Aid, Monetary Aid
4. Educational Counseling and Scholarship Aid
5. Social and Benevolence Promotion and Budgeting

Related Officers:
Benevolence Secretary and Treasurer
Church Delegates

Related Employees:
Pastoral Counselor, Church Visitor

The First Baptist Church of Fitchburg, Massachusetts, has set up a series of boards to simplify the problems of its administration.

DEPARTMENT OF WOMEN'S WORK.
Logically or not, segregates the women's work programs from
the work of the church at the local, denominational, and ecumenical levels.

Why Departments?

Why departments instead of societies or committees? There
are several reasons for presenting the church program as a unit.
This plan would not do away with the organizations but classify
them under proper headings. Successful administration must get
away from the idea that the church consist of many little orbs
circling in the universe called the church.

Departments convey the idea of a functioning body. The
heritage of the church has been worship, preaching, and prayer.
We need to create the impression that the church is a functioning organization in contrast to a debating society which follows
"Rules of Order." The Modern church must follow techniques
of movement.

In contrast to committees, departments convey the idea of
permanency. Committees emphasize one particular item, departments include many activities. Departments show at a
glance the entire program of the church, in both its strength
and weaknesses. About the time you departmentalize your
church, someone will point out an activity that was not included.
The official board will have the responsibility of either placing
it in one of the listed departments or creating a new department which will include this and parallel items.

Established Churches

When the local church belongs to an historic denomination,
it is not easy to reorganize. What can the older churches do for
better efficiency in organization? The local church can hardly
challenge the denominations, but some things can be done.

One of the first things is to replace the dual system which
provides for a legal incorporation and a religious or ecclesiasti-

cal body with a single administrative board. When religious congregations were not permitted to incorporate, the dual system may have been necessary but it certainly does not lend itself to good administration. Congregationalism, very old in American history, has found that the dual organization is a handicap and is recommending that the plan be abolished for one in which the congregation is the corporation and as such elects its own trustees or legal officers.

A second method which will help is the unification of the two boards necessary under the dual system. No corporation can serve two administrations. One board is definitely a unifying force. State laws do require the election of trustees but the tests made have shown that these can serve as a department of the church or a committee of the official board.

If for any reason legal, ecclesiastical, or emotional, the single board seems too difficult, unity can be approximated by the election of some men to each board. Failing that, the next best plan is to have the two boards meet at regular intervals where their mutual interests may be discussed. Some means must be found to stop the friction and misunderstanding behind the double incorporation and two boards if that is at all possible.

A third technique to accomplish unity is to create a church council or pastor's cabinet which can act as a planning board and consulting body on the program of the church. If this is not provided in the constitution of your denomination, it may be purely an advisory, non-official group, but it can be most valuable in unifying the work of the church.

It should consist of the members of the church board or boards, together with the heads of each organization in the church. Competing lines will soon be seen but the positive advantages will also be evident. The various members will see the work of others and, better than that, they will begin to see the work of the church as a whole and may develop a sympathetic understanding of the other organizations.

This council will be limited in its authority. It can advise and recommend but the power of action belongs to other groups. It is valuable in survey and planning, but the execution belongs to the departments below.

Finally, any local church regardless of its denominational affiliation could set up a paper departmental system to give the impression of a unified program without making any change in the regular organization. The various agencies and societies could be placed under their proper departments. They, at least, would see their relationship to the church as a whole and this unity is most important for good administration.

Diversities of Administration

BACH, M., *Report to Protestants*. Bobbs-Merrill, 1953.

BRADEN, C. S., *These Also Believe*. Macmillan, 1949.

BRAUER, J. C., *Protestantism in the United States*. Westminster, 1936.

CLARK, E. T., *Small Sects in America*. Abingdon, 1938.

FERGUSON, C. W., *The Confusion of Tongues*. Doubleday, 1936.

GARRISON, W. E., *The March of Faith*. Harper, 1933.

HARGRAVE, R. W. ed., *The Denominational Heritage*, Harper, 1930.

MEAD, F. S., *Handbook of Denominations*. Abingdon Press, 1956.

———, *See These Banners Go*. Bobbs-Merrill, 1936.

Religious Bodies. Census Bureau of the U. S. Department of Commerce, 1936.

STUBER, S., *How We Got Our Denominations*, Association, 1948.

SWEET, W. W., *The Story of Religion in America*. Harper, 1930.

3 | THE CHURCH AS A CORPORATION

ONE OF THE GREAT AMERICAN CONTRIBUTIONS TO HUMAN progress, the principle of separation of church and state, was not born in the minds of the founders of our land. They were church-minded and the early colonies were definitely religious communities. But very early in the history of our nation, shrewd leaders recognized the growing numbers of religious sects and saw the difficulties which would develop unless all religious groups enjoyed equal privileges.

The Virginia Act for Establishing Religious Freedom, adopted by the legislature of that republic in 1779, was written by Thomas Jefferson. It is one of the great landmarks of organized religion. The authorized religion in Virginia had been that of the Anglican faith; the officers of the church had the power to assess taxes for the support of their church. This legislation was a courageous act to which all America is indebted.

> Be it therefore enacted by the General Assembly, that no man shall be compelled to frequent or support any religious worship, place or ministry whatsoever, nor shall be enforced, restrained, molested, or burthened in his body or goods, nor shall otherwise suffer on account of his religious opinions or belief; but that all men shall be free to profess, and by argument to maintain their opinions in the matter of religion, and that the same should in nowise diminish, enlarge or affect their civil liberties.

One most interesting part of the paper reveals the basic thinking of Jefferson. He was conscious that a succeeding legislature might repeal this act and again impose a state church. So he concludes with these words:

We do declare that the rights hereby asserted are of the natural rights of mankind, and if any act shall be hereafter passed to repeal the present or to narrow its operation, such act will be an infringement of natural right.

This same principle, that there are basic rights which are not created by the state but are a natural inheritance, is enunciated in the Declaration of Independence. All has been given by the Creator.

Although most originally had establishments of religion, the same spirit was felt in other states of the new nation. By the time the Constitutional Convention was held in Philadelphia in 1787, New York, New Jersey, Virginia, North Carolina, and Georgia had discarded their state churches while Massachusetts, Connecticut, and New Hampshire retained their Congregational establishment and Maryland and South Carolina retained their Church of England establishment. One by one these latter states swung in favor of separation. Massachusetts was the last hold-out and it was not until 1833 that a popular vote disestablished the church in that state. Pennsylvania and Rhode Island never had a religious establishment.

Relics of Establishment

While the separation of church and state has become a national principle, there still remain relics of the days of establishment and the attempt to define the American concept is a hazardous one. We see this in the provisions for tax exemptions for churches and religious institutions and the exemption of ministers from jury and military service. The military exemption applies to divinity school students, pastors and ordained ministers functioning in official positions in any denomination. It does not apply to ordained men who function in other than recognized religious bodies. Many ordained ministers have refused to accept the idea of non-participation in war and have served in the various military services as chaplains, commissioned and noncommissioned officers. Many of them have volunteered as privates.

It is also obvious that the state must be very conscious of the existence of the church and the church is conscious of the existence of the state. There are areas where authority will conflict and there are areas where there must be joint action. An example of the first is the field of education; segments of the church feel that education is the responsibility of the church. Marriage is a good illustration of an area where cooperation is essential.

The clergyman and other employees of the church are also American citizens and are entitled to the protection of the laws of the land. They have the responsibilities of citizens and must pay taxes as citizens. They are subject to the courts in cases of crime and negligence. The churches themselves are institutions and though exempted of certain taxes must be subject to the laws of the community in which they live. As employers they must pay agreed wages and be subject to damage suits if others are injured by their property or building deficiencies. They are part of the state when they negotiate for the purchase of land, contract to build, hire artisans, and function in other ways.

While disestablishment gives freedom of worship which has been interpreted as separation of church and state, the church must function as a part of the state or nation in which it exists. Before disestablishment there was no need of incorporation. The officers of the church were the officers of the town, county, or state. When the church was released from the union it was necessary to recognize it as a corporate individual whether or not it had gone through the legal procedure of incorporation.

As the territorial church or parish church, it was a part of the political unit. When the church became separated from the state, it was necessary for it to have some form of organization by which it could legally move, contract, buy, sell, and act as an individual. It is here that incorporation comes into the picture.

Types of Incorporation

In order to function as a legal body the churches found it necessary to have officers competent to deal with the legal community. Most states in the union provide for incorporation of churches, but no state requires it and there are many churches in our nation which have never gone through the formality of incorporation. They elect trustees who usually have the responsibility of the care of the property, real and intangible. The limits of their responsibility are defined by the local church constitution and they are usually recognized as legal representatives of the church. All trustees, however, are subject to state laws in their care of the property. It is a fundamental law that trustees are intrusted with the care, management, and in many cases with the title of the church property. Traditionally the work of the trustees does not in any sense interfere with the functions of the ecclesiastical officers of the local church. They have nothing to do with the services of worship, the planning of the music or the sermons, the organization of the educational work, evangelism, or other functions of the church. On the other hand the ecclesiastical officers are not qualified by their office to function as trustees, to buy or sell, to appear before courts, or to enter into legal contracts.

While the earlier court decisions were very clear as to the limited field of the trustees, there was a broadening of their powers in later years. There has come into being the church with a unified official board where the trustees have a larger part in the administration of the parish. In several recent instances congregational churches have elevated the trustees to the supervision of all church activities including the spiritual programs. They do this while still maintaining their legal responsibilities. There have been, and still are, three types of incorporation: Corporation Sole; Trustee Corporation; and Membership Corporation.

Corporation Sole naturally rose because the churches were not ready for incorporation. Someone had to act legally for the church so the pastor stepped in and the courts recognized him as the corporation. A Massachusetts court in 1811 said:

> When a minister of a town or parish is seized of any lands in right of the town or parish, the minister for this purpose, is a sole corporation and holds the same to himself and his successors. (Brunswick *vs.* Dunning. 1811. 7 Mass. 445, 447.)

When the churches began to organize as Voluntary Religious Societies, this type of corporation did not seem sufficient and trustees as elected officers of the parish took over the property. Corporation Sole gradually passed from Protestantism. But not so in the Roman Catholic Church. It is a common practice to have the bishop of a diocese designated as Corporation Sole and all property to be under his control. In event of his death the fee passes to his successor.

Individual Protestant churches have available two forms of incorporation. These mentioned above are "Trustee Incorporation" and "Membership Incorporation." Trustee Incorporation is that type in which the board of trustees is incorporated and holds the property of the church as a legal body. This type may be a natural evolution from Corporation Sole. It has its virtues and its limitations. The congregation does elect the trustees and has that control over them, but in some instances the papers of incorporation have specified that they appoint their own successors and this has placed dangerous power in the hands of these boards. In at least one Trustee Incorporation the papers provided that the property descend to "their heirs" rather than to "their successors" and really provided trouble.

There are plenty of instances in which the incorporated trustees have transferred property without consulting the congregation and the courts have held that they have that power. Usually, however, the power does not extend to buying real estate for a new church building, placing a mortgage on the property, nor contracting for a new building without a vote of the congregation. We would not encourage any pastor whose church has a board of trustees to attempt to act as Corporation Sole

and enter into any contract for the church even when authorized by the congregation. The Massachusetts courts have held
that such a contract is invalid. (C. A. Dodge Company vs. Western Avenue Tabernacle Baptist Church. 1924. Mass. 330. 142,
N.E. 64.) Since they have control of the funds of the church
they have the power of veto in the call of a minister. Such trustees claimed the right and the courts agreed with them that all
contracts made by the church must be submitted to the trustee
board for approval.

Abuses such as these filled the courts and led to the third and
the increasingly popular method of Membership Incorporation.
In this plan the society itself is incorporated. The trustees are
elected by the society and are responsible to the society. Their
powers are definitely limited. Carl Zollman in *American Church
Law* (West, 1933) describes the change in these words:

> These evils led to an abrogation of this particular theory of
> religious corporations in a number of states, not by legislative
> action but by judicial legislation. The New York Court served
> as a pioneer. After struggling until 1850 under an ever in-
> creasing mass of intricate trust questions growing out of the
> relation of society and the corporation, the court at last over-
> threw the entire theory and eliminated all of its consequences by
> simply adopting another construction of the New York Reli-
> gious Incorporation Act. . . . The corporate franchise was
> therefore to all members of the society, and the trustees from
> exclusive incorporators were reduced to mere officers of the
> corporation. The distinction between the society and corpora-
> tion was abolished; so that churches henceforth presented only
> a twofold aspect (church and corporation) instead of a three-
> fold (church, society and corporation). It followed, since the
> trustees, though still called such, were in fact only officers. . . .
> The entire theory of a trust arising out of this relation was thus
> brought down in a crumbling mass by one blow.
>
> *(Used by permission of West Publishing Company.)*

Membership Incorporation

This type of incorporation of course changes the entire concept of church property administration. The society owns and

controls its property and elects trustees at regularly held meetings. The members are the incorporators. The trustees of the church act on authority given them by the congregation. The congregation or the denomination will provide the rules for their election and terms of office. Unquestionably this is a movement toward democracy in local church administration, but there are still many local churches which have trustee incorporation. In some denominations this better fits the historical traditions and there is a reluctance to change to the membership incorporation.

Responsibilities of the Trustees

The trustees must be elected at a duly called meeting with the advance notices being made so that the membership is informed of its purpose. The local church constitution may provide that the election is by majority vote or some other fraction of those present and voting. The meeting must not alone be properly announced but must be properly conducted. The trustees are elected by the society and not the church, except as it shall be afterward discussed in this paper. There are variations in the laws for church trustees but some of the universal features follow.

Meeting of the board must be regularly called and conducted. A quorum of the trustees must be present and voting. While a congregation is based on a majority of those present, the trustees are required to have a majority of the trustees.

Minutes of the meetings should be carefully kept.

The trustees have the control of the church property. The courts will usually protect them in that right even against the intrusion of ecclesiastical officers including the pastor.

Trustees have the power of contract, but in the membership corporation they have no right to set the minister's salary, or salaries of other employees if this has been done by congregational action. If the trustees exceed their authority in making contracts they and not the church society will be individually responsible.

To protect themselves the trustees should seek authority from the congregation for out-of-the-ordinary contracts such as land purchases, etc.

In signing notes trustees should protect themselves by using the name of the corporate church as the debtor and not merely themselves. Unless this is made clear there is individual liability.

The trustees are entitled to administer and control all revenues derived from church property. We do not understand that this includes control of money raised for services of public worship, education, missionary causes and other funds which are used in the ecclesiastical program of the church.

Powers of the Religious Corporation

It may continue in perpetual succession and fill vacancies which may occur even though the original incorporators pass away.

It may regulate its membership and decide who is qualified to vote.

It may provide for elections, fill vacancies, and remove from office.

It may sue, be sued, or compromise legal claims.

It may make contracts.

It may acquire and convey real property.

It may hold property in trust for other bodies.

It may establish branch preaching stations, missions, etc.

Further Steps Toward Unity

In this discussion we at one time saw a three-faceted church —church, society, and corporation. Then the society was incorporated and the trustee corporation eliminated. So we are left with a two-faceted church—church and society. At the present time a new tendency is appearing. The society is being eliminated and the church (the ecclesiastical church) is being incorporated. One annual meeting, not two, will elect the trustees as well as the spiritual officers. The trustees serve the church, the society no longer exists as a legal body. Many states are recognizing this kind of corporation and it serves a real purpose in unity. There is a peril seen in some instances where the trustees are elevated above the deacons, elders, or other spiritual officers of the church and this should be avoided.

Most administrators think a single controlling board for the church is desirable. For instance, in a Presbyterian church, the Session Board of Elders is the controlling board of the church and would have authority over the trustees. If the society and church are combined and incorporated into one body, the session can designate certain members to serve as trustees. This action would eliminate any friction between the two boards and the trustee committee would report its activities to the session as a matter of course.

The elevation of the "trustees" to the head of the ecclesiastical church as has been done in some recent instances so that the trustees are above the spiritual officers is doubtless legal but is an unfortunate use of a term which has been associated for many generations with the legal and business side of church administration.

Legal Liabilities of Churches

Even though in the United States we have no official establishment of religion, the religious bodies and local churches have very definite legal liabilities which are imposed by the state. Our churches thrive in a land dominated by the democratic spirit; church loyalty expressed through gifts to religious institutions reaches high levels in a land of democratic ideals. If not a part of the state we are at least existing within the boundaries of a state and as such must obey its laws, share its moral responsibilities, and pay taxes toward its support.

Church buildings as a rule are not subject to taxation. This may be because the churches have inherited an exemption from the early days of establishment as one of the relics of union of church and state. On the other hand it can be argued that the exemptions are given not because the church is a religious institution but rather because it has the same privilege which is given universities, libraries, orphanages, museums, etc.

There have been varying court decisions on this basic matter but there is no common agreement as to the reason for tax exemption. Carl Zollman in his most complete volume *American Church Law* (West, 1933) says that regardless of the motivation of such exemption it came about at the time of disestablishment because it had become customary for churches to enjoy it. He says:

> Such custom did not cease when the church was disestablished and full religious freedom was achieved. The practice of exempting church property was universally considered to be proper and was 'so entirely in accord with public sentiment that it universally prevailed.' (State *vs.* Collector of Jersey City, 1853, 24 N. J. Law, 4 Zab. 108, 120)
>
> *(Used by permission of West Publishing Company.)*

A Georgia court, however, placed the exemption on another basis. It said:

> The duties enjoyed by religious bodies and the enforcement by them of the obligations arising therefrom, though beyond the power and scope of the civil government, such as benevolence, charity, generosity, love of our fellow men, deference to rank, to age and sex, tenderness to the young, active sympathy to those in trouble or distress, beneficence to the destitute and poor, and all those comely virtues and amiable qualities which clothe the life in decent drapery and impart a charm to existence, constitute not only the 'cheap defense of nations,' but furnish a sure basis, on which the fabric of civil society can rest; without which it could not endure. (Trustees of the First Methodist Episcopal Church, South *vs.* City of Atlanta, 1886, 76 Ga. 181, 192)

It has been generally held, however, that the exemption of church property is not inherent in the constitutions of the various states and must be secured by special legislation. For this reason the states in the new republic enacted legislation to replace the tax exemptions which had been enjoyed during the years of establishment. As a result church edifices are to a greater or lesser degree exempted from taxes in every state in the union. The application is not so universal when applied to the real estate upon which the church rests nor upon extended land areas which may be the property of the church. Twenty-two states do give exemption to the real estate.

There are so many variations of statute laws in the states, and so many distinctions of interpretation that it would require a large volume or volumes to run down the many instances. In some instances the amount of property a church may hold is limited by its charter. A Massachusetts court held (1910) that the Evangelical Baptist Benevolent and Missionary Society, which was permitted by its chapter to hold property equal in value to three-hundred-fifty thousand dollars without taxation, must pay taxes on its property above that amount. A Maine court held (1912) that First Parish in Gorham which sold some of its tax-exempt property must pay taxes on the money received from the sale of the property. It has also been held that churches which have bought real estate and other property against which there are tax liens, must pay such liens before the title can be cleared.

Taxation of Real Estate

As we have indicated the general purpose of the law is to exempt the edifice of worship and the real estate upon which it stands. There is a difference of opinion among the courts as to how much land is required for a church building and how large an area the church may enjoy about the building. Churches of today are being built in a sprawling style of architecture which requires more space than our fathers used. We need space for automobile parking, open air activities, etc. Most states which do not exempt the real estate by statute do give it exemption in actual practice. For instance, an Ohio court gives a very satisfactory ruling where this matter is discussed. It says (Gerke vs. Purcell, 1874, 25 Ohio St. 229) that the Ohio statute which exempts houses of worship does not prevent the tax body from exempting the grounds attached to such buildings necessary for the proper occupancy, use, and enjoyment of the same. Such an exemption would fit very well the present day demands for larger building areas. A broad interpretation of this kind would be appreciated by many churches in the various states. However it is doubtful if it could be used as an argument for tax exemptions on large acreages held by churches for future development. One of the difficult points in a discussion of this kind is the taxation of this unused property.

The courts are clear on one point. Churches should not enjoy exemptions from taxation on land bought as a speculative investment. Indeed the courts frown on churches in any speculative business. As a rule also real property held as a future site of a church is taxable. Some courts have held that such lots must be definitely dedicated to religious purposes before they can secure such exemption. The word "dedicated" has a distinction quite apart from its liturgical usage in the church. It means that building, chapel, or some substantial material structure must be erected to show the intent of the purchase. In a case involving Trinity Church in New York City the justice very eloquently laid down this principle.

> A contemplated structure resting purely in imagination, no stone of which has ever been laid, or even extracted from its primitive quarry, is not such a building for public worship as an assessor is bound to see. When actually erected, it will be time enough for the officer of the law to notice it. (Trinity Church vs. New York, 1854. 10 How. Pr. N. Y. 138)

When the actual construction begins the church has the right to claim the tax exemption privilege. The building is evidence that the land is to be used for religious purposes and that seems to be the test for the desired exemption.

Three things would seem to be essential for the exemption of taxes on building and grounds. First the property must be owned by the religious society. Exemption is not available to the lessor if the church pays rent to the owner of the property. Next it must definitely be dedicated to religious worship. Third the acreage of land must be essential for the large program of the church. When a society qualifies on these three points, regardless of its religion or denomination, it may claim this real estate and building tax exemption.

The question often arises about the effect of renting or leasing part of the church building to other agencies or individuals. What about lectures and demonstrations which are held for profit, the proceeds going to church use? As a rule the assessors have been very lenient in these instances. If the proceeds go to the work of the church they have held that such activities do not violate the tax exemption theory. However, if a portion of the church is rented to an individual or agency which is using the space for personal profit, that portion of the church is technically subject to taxation. For instance, a day nursery conducted by the church as its own program would not subject the church to taxation for that part of the building used; but if the rooms should be rented to a private school which charged fees and sought to make a profit from the transaction, legally the church would be subject to tax.

Special Assessments

Churches, however, do not enjoy the privilege of exemption from special assessment taxes for street, sewerage, and other improvements made in the community. Because any tax exemption is a state subsidy to religion, every taxpayer, whether he attends church or not, pays for the support of religion. It would be pressing the matter too far to expect the church to have exemption from the financial and moral responsibilities incident to improvements or a free use of city-owned utilities such as water and electricity.

Exemption of Parsonages

The parsonage, rectory, manse, or whatever term we may call it is not primarily a religious institution nor is it a public institution. Only when the parsonage is joined to the church or is built on the same piece of real estate could it be tax exempt as religious property. However, the parsonage like any other residence can be exempted from taxation by the state legislature and this has been done in a great many states. While twenty states have passed legislation declaring the parsonage tax-exempt, few of the remaining twenty-eight actually assess the building. In some states the county is the taxing unit, not the state itself. County assessors are frequently lenient in taxing any church property on the ground that it is unconstitutional to so tax. Local officials are often similarly reluctant. Where the church owns no parsonage and rents one for the minister that property is exempted from taxes, if local convention decrees tax-free parsonages. The table on page 39 presents a good summary of the present tax situation with respect to the taxing of real estate owned by churches.

The exemption of the minister from the income tax for the rental value of the parsonage in which he lives is one of the most perplexing problems of our tax laws. He is not exempted on any other income. It probably is not based on religious use but rather on the same principle that applies to a teacher in a private school or the custodian of a building who must live at his place of employment to do his work. In the above instances the principals are also exempted from income taxes on their living quarters. Its application to date, however, has not taken into consideration our current practice of locating a parsonage miles away from the church. The solution of that problem will rest with the future.

Within the past few years the Supreme Court of Massachusetts (Worcester District Stewards of New England Conference vs. Assessors of Worcester, 73 N.E. 2cd. 898) held that the district parsonage of the Methodist church was not entitled to tax exemption on the ground that the law exempted only parsonages used by pastors—not administrators.

TABLE OF LAWS ON TAXATION OF CHURCH-OWNED REAL ESTATE

TE means tax exempt — T means taxed

	Buildings for Worship	Buildings Used for Sunday School	Parochial (Day School) Buildings	Parsonages	Undeveloped Real Estate Owned by Church	Income Producing Real Estate Owned by Church	Real Estate Owned by Clergymen
Alabama	TE	TE	TE	TE	T	T	T
Arizona	TE	TE	TE	TE	T	T	T
Arkansas	TE	TE	TE	T	T	T	T
California	TE	TE	T	T	T[1]	T	T
Colorado	TE	TE	TE	TE	TE	T	T
Connecticut	TE	TE	TE	TE	T	T	T
Delaware	TE	TE	TE	TE[12]	T	T	T
Dist. of Columbia	TE	TE	TE	TE	T	T	T
Florida	TE	TE	TE	TE	T	T	T
Georgia	TE	TE	TE	TE[2]	T	T	T
Idaho	TE	TE	TE	TE	TE	TE	T
Illinois	TE	TE	TE	TE	T	T	T
Indiana	TE	TE	TE	TE	T	T	T
Iowa	TE	TE	TE	TE	T	T	T
Kansas	TE	TE	TE	TE	T	T	T
Kentucky	TE	TE	TE	TE	TE	TE	T
Louisiana	TE	TE	TE	TE	T	T	T
Maine	TE	TE	TE	TE	T[1]	T	T
Maryland	TE	TE	TE	TE	T[1]	T	T
Massachusetts	TE	TE	TE	TE[4]	T	T	T
Michigan	TE	TE	TE	TE	T	T	T
Minnesota	TE	TE	TE	TE	T	T	T
Mississippi	TE	TE	TE	TE	T[1]	T	T
Missouri	TE	TE	TE	TE	T	T	T
Montana	TE	TE	TE	TE	TE	T	T
Nebraska	TE	TE	TE	TE	TE	T	T
Nevada	TE	TE	TE	TE	TE[3]	T	T
New Hampshire	TE	TE	TE	TE[4]	T	T	T
New Jersey	TE	TE	TE	TE	TE	T	T
New Mexico	TE	TE	TE	TE	TE	T	T
New York	TE	TE	TE	TE[5]	T[1]	T[9]	TE[6]
North Carolina	TE	TE	TE	TE	T	T	T
North Dakota	TE	TE	TE	TE	T	T	T
Ohio	TE	TE	TE	T	TE[7]	TE[7]	T[8]
Oklahoma	TE	TE	TE	T	T	T	T
Oregon	TE	TE	TE	TE	TE	T	T
Pennsylvania	TE	TE	TE	TE	TE	T	T
Rhode Island	TE	TE	TE	TE	T	T	T
South Carolina	TE	TE	TE	TE	T[1]	T	T
South Dakota	TE	TE	TE	TE	TE	T	T
Tennessee	TE	TE	TE	TE	TE	T[9]	T
Texas	TE	TE	TE	TE	T	T	T
Utah	TE	TE	TE	TE	T	T	T
Vermont	TE	TE	TE	TE	T	T	T
Virginia	TE	TE	TE	TE	TE	T	T
Washington	TE[10]	TE[10]	TE[10]	TE	T[1]	T[11]	T
West Virginia	TE	TE	TE	TE	T	T	T
Wisconsin	TE	TE	TE	TE	T	T	T
Wyoming	TE	TE	TE	TE	T	T	T

1. Land held for the convenience of the church, but undeveloped, such as offers parking facilities or necessary for the future growth of the church is not taxed.

2. Exempted in practice but not by law.

3. The tax exemption of undeveloped real estate is dependent upon decisions of the courts.

4. The first $5000 of valuation is exempt from taxation.

5. The first $3000 of valuation is exempt from taxation.

6. Property of a clergyman engaged in active work or retired by age or disability is exempt on the first $1500 of valuation. The widow of a retired minister has the same exemption.

7. Such property is exempted up to a valuation of $2500.

8. The clergyman is allowed tax exemption on his library and office equipment used in his profession.

9. All property used in a business which competes with a secular business which pays taxes will be taxed. If a part of the property is used for such competitive business that portion will be taxed.

10. To secure exemption churches and schools must be open to all on equal terms.

11. The property is given exemption if used for church purposes. In case part is used for church purposes and part for secular that portion used for secular purposes is taxed.

12. Parsonages are taxed in the city of Wilmington, except where they contain a chapel or confessional. They are not taxed elsewhere in the state.

Other Taxes

Income from church endowment funds whether invested in bonds, stocks, mortgages, or lands are taxable unless exempted by a specific statute in the state laws. The church must pay an inheritance tax on money which is bequeathed to it. The reasoning is that it is a tax on the giver and not on the receiver. This tax too may be exempted by specific legislation. A New York State court has said:

> The spirit of philanthropy and charity will not be fostered or strengthened, nor the state enriched, by a system of laws which permits an opulent sectarian church to gather into its coffers, tax free, the legacies of its donors, while the great humanitarian and practical charities of the age must first yield tribute to the state, before they can take that which is given them to do their good works. (Matter of Watson Estate, 1902. 171 N. Y., 246, 262, 63 N. E. 1109)

Some churches still maintain their cemeteries. They are usually exempt from taxation as non-profit institutions. However, the introduction of the profit-making cemetery has somewhat complicated the situation and the assessor has the obligation to find out whether the church cemetery is entitled to the exemption.

Churches and the Sales Tax

States, hungry for more money, have found the sales tax very productive. It is a comparatively small tax paid by the purchaser on the items he buys. It is usually 2- or 3 per cent of the cost of the purchase. New York state does not levy a sales tax but permits counties and municipalities to do so; several have taken advantage of the opportunity.

The churches are affected both as purchasers and vendors. Although more than half of the states impose the sales tax, many exempt churches and other non-profit organizations. Other states insist that the churches pay the tax. Among these are Alabama, Arizona, Arkansas, Georgia, Iowa, Kansas (food for resale only), Louisiana, Maryland, New Mexico, North Dakota, South Carolina, and Washington.

As a vendor the church has the responsibility to collect a tax from those who buy its merchandise. Such "merchandise" consists most frequently of prepared food. Many churches serve meals to which a paying public is invited. Unless specifically exempted, by law a church may have to collect sales tax from those who eat and pay for the meals. Lawmakers distinguish between service of "occasional" meals to the public and the serving of dinners as a business enterprise. Ohio law permits a church to serve four meals per year free of vendor status. Colorado is more generous—the church need not collect sales tax so long as it serves an average of less than one meal per week to the public. In Connecticut, service of more than two meals per year classifies the church as a vendor. Oklahoma permits a church exemption from the tax collection unless the serving of meals actually competes with commercial restaurants.

It should be pointed out that the church which goes into business, using its building in the operation, may find its real estate taxable. In California the local church is permitted to serve meals to the public but must pay a real estate tax on that portion of the building which is used for such enterprise.

Some Areas of State Control

The concept of separation of church and state does not mean that the religious organizations do not have to obey laws of the land. In many areas they are subject to the laws of the state and must conform with such. Religious beliefs which conflict with accepted standards of morality and necessity are not to be tolerated nor can a local church disregard its obligations to society. There are several areas in which this has been clearly enunciated by state and federal laws.

ZONING LAWS. It has been held in several recent decisions that church building, as is the case with residential and business building, is subject to local zoning ordinances. It is also apparent today that many residential neighborhoods do not desire the presence of a church, particularly if the activities of such a church include a school for children and social functions. The courts of Maryland upheld a zoning law which barred an Evangelical-United Brethren Church from the Ten Hills Community of Baltimore. In Michigan the Circuit Court similarly held that a United Presbyterian Church was barred by the zoning laws from building in a residential area. The judge said:

> A church is obviously not a nuisance but it still may not force its way in an area restricted to residential use.

In a California case, the District Court commented on the criticism that this violated the freedom of religious worship. He said:

> We find no merit in the contention that the . . . ordinance . . . results in unwarranted restriction of religious worship. The petitioner is not a congregation [The distinction between a congregation and corporation is discussed earlier in this chapter.] but builds his property as a corporation . . . the existence of which depends upon the laws of the state. Having such right from the state, the enjoyment of the property is subject to reasonable regulations. The denial of the permit did not prohibit anyone from religious worship and there is nothing . . . to indicate that the church building could not be erected located in an area zoned for that purpose. (Corporation of the Presiding Bishop of Jesus Christ of Latter Day Saints *vs.* City of Porterville, California. 203, Pac. 2d. 823)

A New York court, drawing a fine distinction, declared a village ordinance void which prohibited the erection of a church in a zone which did permit the building of municipal buildings, railroad stations, schools, etc. The judge in this case pointed out that the California case mentioned above and which had been quoted by the defendants did not permit such buildings in the zoned area but limited it to residences.

The church corporation must observe all of the regulations

of the state and community building codes as does any other public agency. These codes in many communities go very much in detail. They concern the building area, window space, entrances and exits, lighting, and toilet facilities and many other considerations. A church must secure a building permit from the local municipality or other authority before it can build; then it is subject to regulations of the code which refer to churches. Freedom of assembly for worship does not give freedom from restrictions made for public safety.

Contrary to Public Policy

In two instances the state has interfered in religious practices where such religious practices seemed contrary to public policy. One religious practice of the Chinese is to remove the bodies of their dead to their native land. The courts upheld a statute stating that this practice is illegal except under a license of the Board of Health and insisted that it did not violate the religious rights of the Chinese. Several decisions have sustained the right of the state to resist polygamy though the practice may be in harmony with the religious faith of the practitioners.

In one decision on this subject the court phrased a very interesting distinction between marriage "for time" and marriages "for eternity." The law does not interfere with marriages for eternity.

A marriage for eternity is a thing for which the law takes no cognizance, and by which no party is legally bound. It amounts to a mere abstract belief in a form of polygamy with which the civil powers have no concern. Constitutions and statutes care nothing about what men believe with reference to a future existence. . . . It follows that a believer in the Mormon religion can, so far as the government is concerned, by 'celestial' marriage or marriages for 'eternity' create a harem for himself in the other world, provided he is able to avoid more than one terrestrial marriage at any one time. (Carl Zollman, *American Church Law*. West, 1933.)

(Used by permission of West Publishing Company.)

Churches are subject to the same laws regarding public nuisances as individuals. While most states have laws which protect a worshipping church from unnecessary noise, rowdiness, and unwelcome guests, at the same time it holds churches responsible for orderly services. While the courts have held that vendors of religious tracts and books do not need a license, it has acted differently in regard to street parades and carnivals held under the auspices of the churches. Unless especially exempted under state legislation, churches must obey anti-gambling laws. In some states churches and charitable organizations do enjoy exemptions.

Church Liability

The church society of course is liable for contracts made in its name and for damages caused to others by intent or unintentional carelessness. This is not an inherent right but one which rests upon statute laws by the various states. This entire area is in a period of evolution. The responsibility of a church to its employees needs restating in law because before our present generation a church had few employees; many of them had but one full time employee, the pastor. As legislation has been passed protecting employees, churches have had many exemptions. It has been difficult to include clergymen in the workmen's compensation act because the minister is so much a master of his own time.

In a Pennsylvania case a minister, called to arrange for a funeral, did not go directly to the place of assignment but drove to another community on an errand of his own before making the call. An accident occurred on this by-trip. The courts held that he was not an employee of the church at the time of the accident because he was on an errand for himself. Had an accident occurred injuring the sexton or some other employee of the church while on duty in the building such employee would doubtless be awarded damages by the court. More and more states are making it possible for churches to participate in the workmen's compensation acts which protect employees in this way.

Laws have also been lenient so far as the churches are concerned where worshippers, volunteer workers, or visitors suffer injury while in a church building. In recent years since churches have maintained full time programs there has been more pressure upon churches to observe all liability laws. Building codes now generally include churches. Dark hallways, litter-strewn passages, and varying floor levels are the cause of damages and for these churches have been assessed damages in cases of injury. A Wisconsin court has held that the failure of a church to properly light a stairway and its permitting a floor to become oily, greasy, or slippery constituted a violation of a state statute because of its omission to maintain the building in a safe condition.

An Appellate division of the Supreme Court in New York State ruled that a church society owed to those who entered its doors "a duty of reasonable care." Its failure to keep stairs and hallway lighted was a neglect of this duty, so the visitor injured by such neglect was entitled to compensation.

Regulations Which Protect Churches

Most states have aided organized religion by protecting the worshipping congregation from nuisances and annoyance. Laws for Sunday observance still remain in some states. There is a growing liberalization which permits in many communities games, races, and entertainments prohibited in earlier legislation. But business houses are usually closed on the Christian Sabbath and churches are protected from noisy gatherings which might interfere with worship. Zoning laws usually protect churches from saloons, taverns, places of entertainment, and sports which might interfere with worship.

While the state is very reluctant to enter into a religious quarrel, its courts will arbitrate disputes where a matter of fact or law is involved. In a New Jersey case a Baptist church denied members delinquent in their dues the right to vote at a church meeting. The unhappy delinquents appealed to the court which ruled that they had a right which could not be taken away because of such delinquency. Had the constitution of the church specifically provided for such denial, the decision of the court might have been different.

In an Ohio case the Court of Common Pleas upheld the Methodist Conference which appointed a minister whom the majority of the local church did not wish. The decision of the court was based on the practice of the Methodist Church which gives the conference the right to appoint ministers to the local churches.

In a California case involving the dismissal of a minister the court held that the civil courts had the right to inquire into the regularity of the procedure. Here again a Baptist church was involved and the court reasoned that inasmuch as there was no higher judiciary to which the aggrieved members could appeal, the court had a moral obligation in the matter. (Providence Baptist Church of San Francisco vs. Superior Court of San Francisco, 251 Pac. 2d. 10.)

In a Missouri decision the court laid down the principles of court interference with local church action. In Trott vs. Lambeth, Mo. App., 195 S.W. 2d 524, the court said:

> If the problem was whether the pastor was preaching a theology contrary to the denominational doctrine or conducting religious services in a manner out of harmony with the ritual of the church, it would clearly not be within the province of a court to interfere, and the controversy would have to be settled by the church tribunals. But where, as here, the question presented is whether the property and funds of the church are being handled in accordance with the by-laws and rules of the church corporation or such by-laws and rules are being properly observed by the governing body of the church, those aggrieved may seek redress through court action.

The Federal Government and Church Taxation

To date the only area in which the Federal Government comes into the church picture is in the District of Columbia and in the Social Security laws. Church employees pay income tax as citizens of the state, not as servants of the church. For some time churches have had an option of giving their lay employees the protection of the Federal Old Age Insurance plan. Under this plan churches share with the employees in payments into the fund.

There has been a reluctance on the part of the government to include clergymen in this system. Recently, however, the way has been opened so that they may take advantage of the plan on a voluntary basis. In this plan the church does not share in the payments, the entire responsibility devolves to the minister of the church.

Church and the State

BRAND, N. F. and V. M. INGRAM, *The Pastor's Legal Adviser*. Abingdon, 1942.

BROWN, W. A., *Church and State in Contemporary America*. Scribner's, 1936.

BURNSTEIN, A., *Laws Concerning Religion in the United States*. Oceana, 1950.

DAWSON, C., *Religion and the Modern State*. Sheed & Ward, 1936.

EBERSOLE, L., *Church Lobbying in the Nation's Capital*. Macmillan, 1951.

JOHNSON, A. W. and F. H. YOST, *Separation of Church and State in the United States*. University of Minnesota, 1948.

LINCOLN, C. Z., *Civil Law and the Church*. Abingdon, 1916.

TOUPEY, W. G., *Judicial Doctrines of Religious Rights in America*. University of North Carolina, 1948.

VAN DUSEN, H. P. and others, *Church and State in the Modern World*. Harper, 1937.

WEBER, J. C., *Church and State in Massachusetts*. Western Reserve University, 1938.

ZOLLMAN, C., *American Church Law*, West, 1933.

4 | LOCATING & ESTABLISHING NEW CHURCHES

A COMBINATION OF FACTORS IN THE UNITED STATES AND Canada has brought one of the greatest eras of church building in our history. I can think of only one other period in which more churches may have been erected than have been constructed since the second world war, the quarter century from 1875 to 1900. During that period Methodist Bishop Charles C. McCabe wired the great infidel Robert Ingersoll that the Methodists were building one church for each day and that they proposed to make it two. He was speaking factually.

One important cause is population growth resulting from a very high birth rate. Another is the great wealth of America which makes money available for churches and other philanthropies. The infusion into the church field of ably staffed firms engaged in fund raising is a phenomenon in itself. These two considerations are enough to cause an expansion of church building. But we are just starting the story.

The new industrialization is changing the face of the continent. Where today finds quiet streams, tomorrow will find thriving communities. A new community requires public utilities, schools, and churches. The techniques of industry in its placement of laboratories, factories, and offices are bewildering to a layman and the speed of creation is amazing. The results are new churches, new schools, new shopping centers—indeed, often new cities.

Churches change in a decade as their community changes. The churches in an older section may be fighting for their lives while new churches in the residential suburbs find it difficult to build fast enough to keep up with the families seeking church relationships. So the old passes away and the new arises.

There are still other considerations in the confusing situation. New ideas of construction are compelling and church programs are changing. It is difficult to fit new concepts of worship and education to the older buildings. Parents whose children go to the new and beautiful functional schools hesitate to send their children to old buildings built for the days of verse-by-verse instruction in the Bible.

Add that our day is probably less denominationally minded than any other period of church history and you can appreciate the demands upon the churches. Denominations have raised special funds to aid in the placement of new churches. These funds have totaled many millions of dollars but they have been but a small percentage of the requirements of communities and churches which see wonderful opportunities for new churches in days ahead.

The last quarter of the nineteenth century when churches were being built so rapidly was one of intense denominational rivalry. The nation was beginning to get its industrial legs and revivalism was the practice. In this period the modern Sunday school had its birth. People were reading the Bible and discussing theology.

The churches of the various denominations crowded the village square—if there was a square. Most of the communities had no method of public transportation and the business center was within walking distance for most people. It was natural that the churches would be located in that particular area and no recognized church would go to the outskirts. Those which did were usually the small nonconformist sects which had but slight appeal.

Today the entire situation has changed. Growing cities have influenced the growth of suburban areas. Schools are located near the children; shopping centers are developing at the rims of the cities; less and less are the families finding it necessary to go "downtown."

Some cities have grown up with the churches crowded together in the downtown area. These churches with great buildings, unsuited for modern functional purposes, form civic points of congestion. Reluctantly, for churchmen are usually conservatives, they are reaching the conclusion that they should seek new sites for future work. They know very well the disadvantages of crowding all the churches in one area. As a result there has come a consciousness of the need of careful church planning.

Before we get too far into the techniques of locating new churches, it is well to take a look at the city itself. In the beginning the city was a small settlement. Then as a village it consisted of a community which had at its center business houses, stores, schools, and churches. This was the natural center and here the various churches congregated. As the city grew in size, the single-cell pattern developed into a multiple cell organization. Each of these cells consisted of a community in itself with its own shopping center, schools, and churches. The traditional denominations located new churches in these areas.

Around these cells were barriers. The barrier might be an industrial unit, a lake or river, a railroad, a cemetery. A railway track was such a barrier and created a social distinction in which "the people across the tracks" bore a typed handicap. A nationalistic community is such a barrier. Through these barriers the size of the particular cell was determined that in turn determined the number of housing units and the number of church members.

A community up to five thousand population may continue as a one-cell community. After that mark is passed, new cells will probably develop. The public schools are very alert to changing population and the superintendent of schools will probably be the first who sees the new developments requiring additional schools. Business will be next. The churches, however, will be close behind.

Any minister looking toward a change of location for his church should pay special attention to his members in the new community. If the community continues to grow, new churches will come into the new cell and the families may decide to cast their lot with those organizing a new church.

The evolution at this point begins to follow a pattern. The family by tradition and choice is tied to the old church while the children are placed in the schools of the new community. Distance makes it difficult for the child to participate in the weekday activities of the old church. Gradually they begin to attend youth service in one of the local churches. The parents see the change taking place and must decide between their own children or the older church.

Usually, as it should be, the children win and the family decides to join a local church. As the cells multiply and the membership of the old church is divided and congregations grow smaller, the church decides to survey the situation to see if it should move its work to a new location. It may realize that other churches have been going through similar experiences. It finds that some of the cell areas which have a goodly proportion of its members already are "churched" and it must seek further for a new location.

This quest for a new location may be undertaken by the single church, by the denomination, or by a cooperative effort under the direction of a local church federation or a ministerial association. No matter which technique is used, the following principles and procedures apply.

First no church should decide to move to a new site until it has made an effort to find out what the other churches in the community are doing. There should be some method for an interchange of information and plans. The one great motive for the location of a church is to preach the gospel of Jesus Christ. To do this effectively, a site must be chosen which has a sufficient number or will soon have a sufficient number of unchurched people to justify the organization of the new church. Any church will be limited by the population of its geographical cell; usually a church should see a minimum of five hundred members within a five-year period before it decides to move to any particular site.

It has often been stated that every community is entitled to the services of a church but at the same time, every community is entitled to the protection from over-churching with its resultant poor churches and excessive and unhealthy competition.

When a church has learned the plans of its neighboring churches, it is in a position to look for sites which might be appropriate for its own work. It will recognize the moral claims of other churches and denominations. This may be accomplished by taking a committee through the various parts of the area, noting the residential sections and the presence or absence of churches. This does not mean that a community should be passed by because it has one or two churches. If it is going to grow into a community of ten or fifteen thousand people or more, there will be room for several churches.

If one community seems outstanding in its opportunities for a new church, the next step might be to make a more accurate survey. This can include a sampling of the residential areas to learn the affiliations of the families, their preferences, and their income brackets. If the church is satisfied by the survey, it is time to look for a proper site.

Preferably the site should be in the social and business center of the cell. It should be large enough for the erection of a modern building. Three acres should be the minimum for a church planned for five hundred members. Larger space is even more desirable. It should be erected near a street which carries much traffic but not necessarily on such a street. An ample site a block away providing it is a site from which the church may be seen from the well travelled boulevard will be more desirable. The church needs to be seen but the noise and hazard of traffic is not particularly desirable.

Frederick A. Shippey in his book *Church Work in the City* (Abingdon) gives six principles to keep in mind in planning a location for a new church.

1. A concentration of people
2. Freedom from barriers
3. Freedom from competition

4. A conspicuous, accessible site
5. An adequate plant
6. An effective ministry

Many of the facts needed can be secured from local agencies making a house-to-house canvass of the community unnecessary. From the city building inspector you can secure information regarding any new housing units planned. From the school superintendent you can secure information on the birth rate and the population movements. The public utilities often will share their information. They are usually thinking ahead for promotion. The Chamber of Commerce can advise on the location of new industries. It is well to use all of these sources. Statistics on religious affiliations are a different matter and well within the sphere of the church itself.

If the new church is to be a relocation, the proper technique is to call together those members who live in the new area and suggest that they organize either as a mission of the old church or form a new congregation of the same denomination. In anticipation of an eventual move of the entire church to the new site, resources will be available to help in the establishment and the building so that the heavy burden will not fall on the infant church. Fortunately the real estate prices in the business sections of a city usually are higher than land areas in the new cells so that the sale of the property gives a good lift to the new project.

Cooperative Action

Very few of the new projects of today are independent. The denominations have been planning their work on a city-wide basis and the location of a single church is an interest which all of the churches share. Most denominations have qualified personnel for surveying areas and advising the local churches. Often some denominational resources are available which will help churches during the struggling years.

The denominations of today view the city-wide work plan as a city-wide ministry, which means churches for differing types of service. They have their "town" work, their neighborhood churches which vary with economic classes, and their mission fields which serve the underprivileged. Any denominationally affiliated church will seek the guidance and leadership of the proper officials to make the relocation of a church a denominational project.

Working Through Church Federations

But just as the local church should seek help from neighboring churches, so the denominations need to consult with sister denominations in planning their new church projects. Alert to the needs of this kind of cooperation church federations across the country are setting up well-staffed departments of research and location which act as clearing houses for this purpose.

The progress in interdenominational activities has been slow—much slower than most of us wish and much slower than is good for the cause. These departments have not yet developed to their full influence, mostly because few denominations offer full cooperation. The slogan "A church for every community and a community for every church" is not realized because the most careful planning cannot protect any new church from encroachments by religious bodies which do not recognize the principles of cooperation.

In the choice of location, churches have much freedom. There are restrictions in zoning laws which we shall soon discuss, but every individual in the country is free to organize a church and erect a building even though it competes with one across the street. Every denomination has the right to build a new church in an already crowded community. There is not much that can be done about it once the work has been started.

Slow as the progress is, most of us are still for the American way. We accept the Jeffersonian idea that there would be more danger in a state religion than in a multiplicity of religious sects, so we depend on surveys, interdenominational cooperation and zoning pressures to bring about a state of reason. The word comity often used in this connection simply means "courtesy," i.e., that in seeking a location for a church we have the courtesy to consult with others about it. It is a gesture which is very effective in this sensitive area.

Independent Churches

While it is still possible for individuals to found churches, it is a very difficult task. Some outstanding evangelists have done it successfully. They have erected their tabernacles without reference to any other religious organization and apparently prosper, but it is hardly an area for the average man to enter. While the federations will recognize an independent church in case of a contest of ideas, a denominational church will usually receive preference. The Department of Church Development and Enonomy of the Church Federation of Greater Chicago studied the pros and cons of this matter and came up with the following conclusion.

Conclusion: On the whole we are satisfied that, judged solely from the contribution which a denominational church could make, as compared with a non-denominational one, the interests of the Kingdom are more truly advanced by having a church which is organically related to one of the established Protestant groups.

The sub-committee believes that at the present time, the denominations provide the best available foundation for the building of the local church and that no matter what may be the ultimate form of the religious organization which we call the church, that now as it enters new communities the best interests of the future will be served by continuing the principle of denominational affiliation.

Accordingly we recommend that the Comity Commission continue to hold its position in favor of the denominational church in new communities in all cases where the public sentiment will effectively endorse this principle, with the understanding that the denominational church shall seek to minister to the needs of the entire Protestant constituency, and not aim to glorify one denomination nor one special set of doctrines.

In cases where in the view of a local group the situation is difficult of unification, and where there is a definite objection to a denominational church, then we should cheerfully consent to such modification as may be necessary, thus respecting the convictions of a worthy group of truly Christian people who may wish to build a church in a different way. In such cases, we shall feel it our duty to foster the Christian welfare of such a church with its community—

(a) By relating it to the spirit and program of other churches;

(b) By urging upon it a definite religious program;

(c) By helping it to a world program and thus prevent it from the self-destruction of living only for its own self;

(d) By helping it to noble, positive, and enlarging programs of Christian thought and endeavor.

The Chicago Church Federation under the leadership of the Reverend John W. Harms has developed a very effective strategy for the placement of churches. In the Detroit, Michigan area, the Detroit Council of Churches under the Reverend Raleigh E. Sain, is doing outstanding work. We are reproducing the paragraphs from the brochures of each of these as they deal with policies.

The term "Temporary assignment" as used below means the initial decision made by the Department permitting a denomination to start new work in a given community. The term "permanent assignment" means that the denomination has established the work satisfactorily and the "temporary assignment" has been changed to a "permanent assignment" and removed from the "Review of Temporary Assignments" list as provided for in Paragraph (d) of the following section.

Chicago Church Federation

POLICY AND PROCEDURE AS IT RELATES TO COMITY

(a) Comity procedure shall apply to the starting or relocation of local churches, Sunday schools, services of worship, missions, chapels, and institutional churches; to the purchasing of prop-

erty for such work, and the renting of meeting places except temporarily in such emergencies as fire; to special work in mission areas; and/or to any other form of religious work which affects relations with other denominations.

(b) Any communion, local church, local group or individual, wishing a temporary assignment to start a new work or relocate an established work as defined in Paragraph (a) shall present to the Department a request in writing, with supporting data, before taking action. The request shall be referred, without debate, to the proper Area Planning Committee for recommendation, and with a date set for report.

(c) Decisions of the Department on assignments for work in new fields or relocation of churches shall be conclusive and not subject to review by any other body. No such recommendation made by an Area Planning Committee shall be final until it has been reviewed and approved by the Department. When such a recommendation does not receive a two-thirds vote, final consideration shall be postponed until the next regular meeting of the Department upon request of any voting member.

When such postponement occurs, the chairman shall appoint a committee of three to confer with the communions concerned and endeavor to secure a meeting of minds. If the committee is not successful in this, the communions shall prepare written statements which shall be mailed to members of the Department not less than a week before the next meeting. At this meeting, discussion shall be limited, parliamentary procedure shall govern, and a majority vote shall be conclusive.

In case it is impossible to carry out this procedure before the next regular meeting of the Department, consideration may be deferred for a second month, but in no case shall it be deferred longer.

No decisions so reached shall be reconsidered until after a period of six months has elapsed after action was taken.

When a temporary assignment has been approved as outlined above, it shall be listed by the secretary of the department on the list of "Annual Review of Temporary Assignments," where it shall remain until it has been declared to be a permanent assignment by the Department. Temporary assignments shall be reviewed at least annually, in January if possible, until (a) t

church has been organized, (b) adequate ministerial leadership secured, and (c) an adequate building erected.

As the work of the department develops, statements of policy and/or procedure covering particular subjects, may be adopted by the department and added to these By-laws as supplements to be numbered serially in the number of their adoption. Each such statement shall be considered as a part of the By-laws and shall be subject to the provisions of Section XII as to amendment.

The Detroit Council of Churches is a second very active body in this field. Its policy differs somewhat from that of Chicago.

SECTION IV. POLICY

1. Churches, adequate in both number and quality, should be provided, area by area, in Metropolitan Detroit; and adequate opportunities for all churches within these communities should be assured, with due regard to spacing and available supporting constituency.

2. Territorial fields shall be allocated to cooperating denominations through comity processes by the Department for establishing adequate churches within a reasonable time.

3. In allotting fields and approving new churches, the interests of existing religious groups should be carefully considered, and thorough investigation and consultation should precede final action.

4. A church receiving an allocation should feel responsible to undertake its ministries in an inclusive spirit, without violation of the principles of the denomination.

5. Each proposed allocation should be judged on the basis of all interrelated factors, rather than dependence upon any single criterion. These varied factors will include:

a. Number, density and characteristics of the population.

b. Genuine prospects of population growth or change.

c. The structure of the city or area including natural or artificial barriers—industry, business, resorts and other land use.

d. Number, location and character of existing churches.

e. Adequacy of plans, leadership and financial resources available for the proposed projects.

f. Preponderant faiths and denominational preferences of the people of the neighborhood.

g. Attitude of the community with respect to the proposed project.

h. Consultation with the local ministerial group or council to secure their judgment and cooperation in regard to the adequate churching of their community.

6. An urban or suburban area shall be considered adequately churched when it has or will have one church for each 2,500 population within a given area.

7. In considering distances between churches, the following ought to apply:

a. Churches of the same denomination should be at least two miles apart.

b. Density of population, actual or reasonably in prospect, should be considered the primary factor in determining the distance between churches of different denominations. It would appear advisable that churches should not be less than one-half mile distant from each other.

c. In areas where the population is sparse churches of different denominations should not be less than one mile apart.

8. The responsibility of the Department shall be to maintain a continuous program of research, church planning and denominational consultation in order to provide for the adequate churching of the community.

Is there any rule as to the proper distance from another church for a new placement? Many suggestions have been offered but no uniform rule adopted. Dr. Shippey says that the distance between churches of the same denomination should be at least one and three-quarter miles; the Detroit Council says two miles; the Chicago Federation says one-half mile. A better method would deal with the density of population. Each church needs a minimum of five hundred members for its work; that probably means a potential available population for each church of 2500 souls.

Subnormal Communities

In every community there are areas where low income families reside which are unable to build and maintain their churches. The establishment of self-supporting churches would be hazardous, yet these communities definitely need the services of the church. Neither the denominations nor the federations can escape the responsibility for churching such communities. This surely is the place where the "haves" have the responsibility for aiding the "have-nots." The help must be given in such a way that it will stimulate self-help and a joy of service in the local church. Every community, no matter how poor economically, needs the services of the church.

As a matter of principle, the two most difficult fields for the Protestant churches are those of the very rich and those of the very poor. The responsibility for serving these groups must not be neglected.

Zoning Laws As They Affect Churches

In the past it was axiomatic that a church was a desirable asset to any community. Today the residents of a community sometimes feel that a church is undesirable and they ask for zoning laws to keep churches away from their particular neighborhood.

Some of the cases discussed in the earlier chapter indicate that a zoning ordinance which bars churches from a community is valid. Where other institutions such as railroad stations, libraries, and business places are permitted, the church will have a good chance to win an appeal from the zoning board.

In an instance where a Jewish synagogue was denied a permit by a pro-Gentile board, the court held that the board could not refuse a building permit. A Protestant church can certainly qualify for one if a Roman Catholic church has previously been given permission. In a case in Florida, Jehovah's Witnesses were denied a permit on the ground that they failed to qualify with adequate parking space (Florida Supreme Court. October 6, 1950. State *vs.* City of Tampa, 48 So. 2cd. 78.). The law requires 100 square feet for each three persons. The court decided that the church had sufficient space for persons as the actual maximum attendance was only 182. While this was the basis for the decision that the zoning board must issue the license, the judge delivered quite a speech on the rights of a church to enter any community.

He pointed out that the city streets were not crowded on Sundays and that church attendance offered few hazards compared with other institutions, including the home. He emphasized that the churches were an essential part of a civilized democracy and had the right to ask for some preferences in the community. We could enthusiastically endorse this statement.

> A people unschooled about the sovereignty of God, the Ten Commandments and the ethics of Jesus, could never have evolved the Bill of Rights, the Declaration of Independence and the Constitution. There is not one solitary fundamental principle of our democratic policy that did not stem directly from the basic moral concepts as embodied in the Decalog and the ethics of Jesus.

We doubt, however, if this jurist, sympathetic to the churches as he evidently is, would reverse the court decision in this case unless he found that the church actually did have sufficient space to park the cars of the worshippers.

There is a moral question involved in the attitude of the church. If barred from a community should it go to law to protect its rights? Should it plead that because it is a church and has enjoyed special privileges, it is entitled to receive special consideration? Inevitably the churches and church leaders will decide the kind of regulations which concern the zoning of churches. The kind and the amount of public regulation will depend upon the voluntary action taken by the churches themselves.

Frederick H. Bair, Jr., Executive Director of the Florida

Planning and Zoning Association, writing in *City Church* (297 4th Avenue, New York 10) makes some suggestions regarding the locating of churches in harmony with modern zoning practices. He points out that the streets of a city are planned for varying types of traffic. If the church contemplates a large number of people, it should locate to take advantage of streets with pavements heavy enough for such traffic. The church should provide for traffic which has peak loads in a short period of time. The elimination of on-street parking is important as a safety measure. With large numbers of people filtering across the street between parked cars, the hazard is great.

Churches do generate noise varying from gentle congregation murmurs to shattering broadcasts from the tower. Mr. Bair makes a keen observation in pointing out that the electronic carillons have placed small churches on the level with the large ones in this respect. He suggests that there must be a regulation of these noise makers as to hours and the quantity and quality of the program offered.

> If it becomes necessary to use public controls to regulate the placement, design and operation of the church plant, there is a wide range available. Churches might be permitted in districts in which they are desirable under certain carefully-stated conditions set forth in the zoning ordinance. These would amount to performance standards.
>
> Falling back a step, there is the possibility that in certain areas, churches might be permissible as special exceptions through action of the board of adjustment after recommendations from the safeguards appropriate to the individual circumstances.
>
> In the process of subdivision regulation and plan review, there are ample opportunities to suggest the advantages of providing suitable church sites. As a private measure, developers may wish to attach deed restrictions to land used for church purposes.
>
> The courts are already becoming aware of the need for some public control of location, planning and operation of churches. If church created conflicts with the public interest are not reduced voluntarily, there is little doubt that the judiciary will uphold increasing legal restrictions.

It is hardly possible that the churches will keep ahead of the law in respect to location and land areas. We have too much accumulation in building. Many churches and trustees will resent instructions from the city council. They will ask for special concessions regarding the size of parking space, open area around churches, multiplicity of entrances, fireproof construction.

There is definitely a moral obligation on the part of churches, exempted from taxation, to deal fairly with codes which have been made for public safety and good health. Churches crowded for building area sometimes try to get special concessions to build close to the sidewalk or to the next lot residence. Even if aesthetics did not require this, simple courtesy should encourage a church to deal agreeably with these restrictions.

We have noticed a tendency on the part of some churches to "talk through both sides of the mouth." Certain states have laws prohibiting the location of a classroom below ground level. Churches have learned that by simply indicating basement space as "assembly" rooms, they can secure acceptance of their plans to put the church school class in the basement. So while they are publicizing to their members the splendid quality of their church school, they make application for a building permit which will be accepted because they list the school space as "assembly room space."

The transitions necessary from the old to the new bring many perplexing problems. They have to be taken one by one and settled morally. Out of the confusions there are arising some very definite principles both of policy and procedures. No area in church administration is more sensitive than that of new site choice and placement.

The most difficult areas for churches are those of the sub-normal economic class and the super-rich class. Slums and exclusive suburbs are difficult for church work, but both of these areas must be considered in a city-wide program. Every community is entitled to a church; every community is entitled to protection from too many churches. These points are basic in church growth.

Church & Community

DOUGLAS, H. P. and E. D. BRUNNER, *The Protestant Church as a Social Institution.* Harper, 1935.

KINCHELOE, S. C., *The American City and Its Church.* Friendship, 1938.

KLEMME, H. F., *Your Church and Your Community.* Christian Education, 1957.

LEIFFER, M. H., *The Effective City Church.* Abingdon, 1949.

MILLER, K. D., *Man and God in the City.* Friendship, 1954.

SANDERSON, R. W., *The Church Serves the Changing City.* Harper, 1955.

SHIPPEY, F. A., *Church Work in the City.* Abingdon, 1951.

SMITH, R. C., *The Church in Our Town.* Abingdon, 1945.

———, *Rural Church Administration.* Abingdon, 1953.

The City Church. National Council of the Churches of Christ, 297 Fourth Ave., New York 10 (bi-monthly).

VAN VLECK, J., *Our Changing Churches.* Association, 1937.

WARREN, R. L., *Studying Your Community.* Russell Sage, 1955.

5 | INTEGRATING THE CONGREGATION

A LOCAL CHURCH WHICH CONSISTS OF A BODY OF BELIEVERS is quite a different thing from a "preaching station." In the very best sense it is a Christian fellowship. Techniques are used to weld the individual believers into such a body so that they not alone will attend the services of worship but actively participate in the various programs which promote Christian growth.

In the small parish the minister accomplishes this by personal contact. With one hundred families this is not so difficult, but as churches and communities grow larger the minister finds it increasingly difficult to keep his finger on the live pulse of each family enrolled in the church. Mechanical means must be evolved to correct the situation.

The minister should know his people; he should have the information necessary to contact each one when the occasion to do so arises; he should understand their history, present problems, joyous experiences, and their various abilities to work in the church program.

The place to start, of course, is with the membership records. Many churches still use very primitive record systems that supply the information needed for denominational statistics, but little more. They give the place for the date of birth, baptism, joining the church, marriage, death—what we call vital statistics. Some denominations still require that church records be kept in these primitive forms. The local church should of course comply, but also when necessary be ready to create supplementary forms for keeping the information needed about each member.

The simplest forms have the name, address, and telephone number. Adding the business, profession or employment of the husband and the places of employment of the children will be

Family Name _____

Husband's Christian Name
1. _____

Wife's Christian Name
2. _____

Residence
1. _____
2. _____
3. _____

Telephone _____

Occupation _____

Business Address _____

Church Paper _____

Names	Relation	Born	Baptised	How and When Received	Removal*	Building Fund Pledge	Paid	Annual Pledge	Activities (See Code)	Interests and Talents (See Code)	Personality Traits
1.											
2.											
3.											
4.											
5.											
6.											
7.											
8.											

RECORD OF CALLS

Year	Jan.	Feb.	March	April	May	June	July	Aug.	Sept.	Oct.	Nov.	Dec.

ACTIVITIES AND INTERESTS

1 Elder		18 Church School	
2 Official Board		(a) Administrator	
3 Trustee		(b) Teacher	
4 Steward		(c) Student	
5 Vestryman		19 Youth Groups	
6 Warden		20 Young Adults	
7 Deacon		21 Men's Association	
8 Deaconess		22 Women's Association	
9 Usher		23 Kitchen	
10 Choir		24 Public Speaking	
11 Soloist		25 Publicity	
12 Pianist		26 Drama	
13 Organist		27 Secretary	
14 Flowers		28 _____	
15 Canvasser		29 _____	
16 Visitor		30 _____	
17 _____		31 _____	

*Enter here details regarding removal or dismissal.

A membership record printed inside a filing folder provides pertinent data. The folder retains information on the family, confidential counseling material, and other useful data.

helpful. A check of their church activity and interests is valuable, but the best of church records need even more information than these offer. A social, marital, and clinical history of the family is required.

Some of the better record forms are now being supplied by commercial houses. The minister as both a pastor and an executive needs to know more than bare statistics about each individual in his church. He surely needs to know as much about his members as an employer needs to know about an employee.

Once the record system has been established a plan must be made to keep it effective. Addresses and telephone numbers must be up-to-date and this is quite a job in a good-sized church. Professions and callings change. Members die or move away. Some go to jail. Automobile accidents happen. Children enter college. Pastoral attention requires all of this information. The uninitiated may feel that all that is necessary is to ask the church members to report any changes. The experienced know that at best very few will do this. Other methods must be provided.

Using the Mail

The United States Post Office, if you distribute a weekly or monthly publication, provides a method of getting corrections. First class letters are not effective in this respect because they are delivered to the forwarding address given to the postman before any change is made. The publications, however, would normally be mailed either second or third class and such mail is not automatically forwarded. Neither will it be returned to the sender unless definite instructions are given.

Of the two methods of doing this, one is simply to have imprinted on the mailing envelope or wrapper the words "Return Postage Guaranteed." This will bring the mailing piece back if the member has changed his address. Returned mail may be followed up with a first class letter. The probabilities are that a return letter will give the information desired. Failure to respond is pretty fair evidence that the individual to whom the letter was

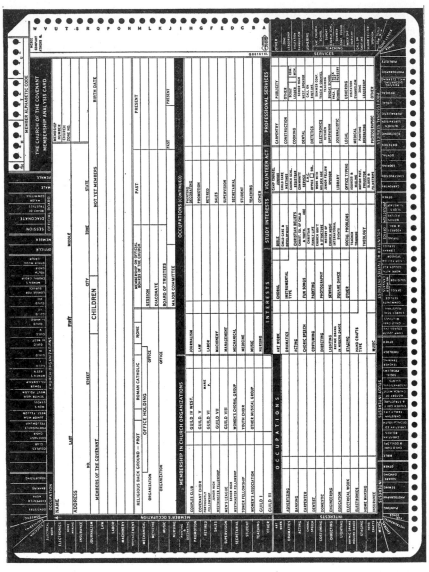

Membership form used by Church of the Covenant, Cleveland, Ohio.

addressed has little interest in the church and should be removed to the inactive list.

There is still another way to secure the information you wish. This is by imprinting the slogan

Form 3547 Requested.

conspicuously in the lower left corner of the envelope or wrapper. By this notice the postmaster is requested to send you information for correcting the address in your records. A charge of four cents each is made for this type of service. It is an inexpensive aid to the church which does wish to keep its addresses correct.

A warning, however. Don't expect this service to be one hundred per cent efficient. No government service is—nor is any personal service, for that matter. Some postmasters will neglect to follow the instructions of the notices, but most will be helpful in keeping addresses up-to-date. Pew cards will bring some help also, but their efficiency will be less than that of the Post Office. You can request in your publication that those who move write or phone their new addresses. Some will, more will not.

An occasional visitation or survey of the parish is still necessary to make the study complete.

Most churches make the annual every-member canvass discussed in another chapter. It is usually a very thorough procedure in which the home of every member and every contributor is contacted. The solicitors will find that some addresses are wrong. If the chairman is wise he will insist that the solicitors try to learn from neighbors or others the new address. When this information is received by the every-member canvass committee it should also be turned over to the individual keeping the membership record.

Some churches, in addition to the financial canvass, have an occasional visitation Sunday when the entire parish is visited for purposes of fellowship. The checking of changes of address can be one of the main values of this visitation. At this point the correction of addresses blends into the larger program of securing information regarding the individual families which may go into

First Congregational Church – Wilmette, Ill.

Surname	Given Name	Middle Name
DOE	FLORENCE	JAMES

Father's Name

Married (date): to whom John R. born 7/14/—

Children: girl Susan, born 3/5/40 – SB

boy William, born 4/17/38 – SP

Other members of family:

	Activities in Church (See Code below)								
	1941	1942	1943	1944	1945	1946	1947	1948	1949
					C5				
	1950	1951	1952	1953	1954	1955	1956	1957	1958
	1950								

Birth (Date) 12/16/—

Baptized (Date)

Joined Church

By Confession of Faith

By Letter from

Serial No.

High School — Year Grad.

College — Year Grad.

Graduate Degree — College — Year

Moved from Wilmette (Date)

Letter Trans. (Date) to Church (Name & City)

Dropped (Date)

CODES

Boards
Trustees ....T
Deacons ....)......D
Deaconesses)
Religious Educat.,REE

Committees
Music...........Mu
Chris. Service...CHS
Cabinet..........CAB
Radio............RAD
Representation...REP

Church School
Cradle Roll.......CR
Nursery..........N
Kindergarten -4...K4
Kindergarten -5...K5
Primary thru Jr..1-8
Senior Hi........S

Contributor (Ann. Budget) – Con,
Contributor (Bldg. Fund) – BF

Social Orgs.
Circle (No.)....Cl
Kappa...........K
Men's Fell.......MF
Cpls.Club – Fri.CCF
Cpls.Club – Sat.CCS
Univ. Club......UC

Residence Address: 123 CENTRAL ST.

Res. Tel. No.: Wil. 123

Surname	Given Name	Middle Name
DOE	FLORENCE	J.(Mrs. J.R.)

Membership record used by the First Presbyterian Church, Wilmette, Illinois.

70

the church records. Efficient records are but one item in this program.

Registering Guests

One way of securing prospects for church membership is through the registration of guests who attend the services of worship. Ushers may prompt guests to write their names and addresses in a guest book placed in the foyer. If they are from out of town a note can be sent in appreciation of their visit. If they are located in the community the names definitely should go into the prospect list and either the minister or a caller should visit the family.

Pew cards are also effective for this information. Recently cards have been used for what is called the "Ritual of Friendship." These are cards which all in attendance are asked to sign to show that they have attended the service. The act is recognized as all present, regular attendants and guests, sign their names. Each indicates his church affiliation.

The minister then has a record of both members and non-members who have attended. The non-members will go onto the prospect list. The reason for having all sign is to relieve guests from any embarrassment of signing. In the First Presbyterian Church of Dallas, Texas, this method has been carried still further. Pads are made up which will hold the names of six worshippers. The pad is placed in an attractive leather cover and passed through the pews. A sufficient number of the booklets are available so that the registration really requires but a few moments. After all have signed the book goes into the pew rack.

Organizing the Parish for Administration

Even if every member is correctly listed on the records and the church office has the telephone number of each member this is not sufficient for the proper administration of the church program. Out of the congregation must come leaders, workers, and participants. How is the minister to know whom to select for the various tasks?

Certainly a public invitation for volunteers to teach the school classes or sing in the choir is a poor way to make selections. Fortunately churches are not born big; they usually start from small beginnings. The screening at the time the church is organized is informal but usually very effective. The new membership usually includes people who have had experience in church work. As the church grows the minister and his board recognize individual talent as it comes to the organization and there is a ready place for those who wish to work.

It is when the church begins to achieve a large membership that the first method begins to fall down. More and more burdens are assumed by the old leaders. New members with both unusual gifts and the desire to work are not known. The task of securing leadership becomes a difficult one.

The first step may be to analyze the possibilities of each member as he is received into the society. Many churches require a brief period of instruction before an individual is received into the membership. This is a splendid time to have a personal interview to find out just what his experience has been and determine just how his talents can be woven into the work of the society.

In churches where the pre-membership discussions are informal or are held in the homes in connection with pastoral visits, there is a splendid opportunity to discuss the interests of the prospective member. A few minutes of serious conversation will develop more information concerning the abilities and interests of the individual than can be secured by any formal mass collection of material.

A good procedure is to record the information received and place it in an "Application for Church Membership." The familiar pew cards may offer an invitation to become a member and provide a simple confession.

> Believing in the leadership of Jesus Christ, Son of God, and desiring to work in his church, I would like to become a member of the First Christian Church of Doeville.

I hereby make application for membership in the Evangelical and Reformed Church.

Name ....
    (Last name)   (First name)   (Middle name)

Residence .... City .... Phone ....

Business Address .... Phone ....

I believe Christ to be the Son of God, and the Savior of the world. I promise to follow Him as my Lord and Master. I am resolved, with God's help, to serve Him, to keep His commandments, to become a maturing, useful member of His Church, to attend its services, to give generously of my material possessions for the furthering of its program at home and abroad, to take, as far as is possible, an active part in its work, to be faithful in my attendance upon the Lord's Supper; and unselfishly to seek to make His will effective in my community and in the world.

Date .... Signature ....

Have you been baptized? (yes or no) ....

Are you uniting: (a) On confession of faith? ....

    (b) By reaffirmation of faith? ....

    (c) By letter of transfer? ....

If you are uniting by (b) or (c), please give the name and address of the church with which you were connected.

Name ....

Address ....

Shall we write for your letter? (yes or no) ....

Please specify any church offices previously held.

....

In order that we may know the organization to which you would automatically belong, please place a check mark beside one of the following:

YOUTH GROUPS

☐ Junior: 9-11 years
☐ Junior High: 12-14 years
☐ Senior High: 15-17 years
☐ College: 18-23 years

ADULT GROUPS

Single
☐ 24-40 years
☐ 40-50 years
☐ over 50 years

Married
☐ under 30 years
☐ 30-40 years
☐ 40-50 years
☐ over 50 years

If you are now attending one of our church organizations, please state which. ....

The following are members of my family:

Name .... Member Yes ☐ No ☐ Age ....

Name .... Member Yes ☐ No ☐ Age ....

Name .... Member Yes ☐ No ☐ Age ....

Name .... Member Yes ☐ No ☐ Age ....

Name .... Member Yes ☐ No ☐ Age ....

The following are acquaintances who do not have an active relationship with a Christian Church:

Name .... Address ....

Name .... Address ....

Name .... Address ....

Application for church membership recommended to the churches of the Evangelical and Reformed Church.

The church needs much more information before receiving a member. A four-page form used by the churches of the Evangelical and Reformed Church asks much more. Not only does it ask affirmation of the creed but seeks also to uncover the talents of the individual members that they may be woven into the active fabric of the parish. With this record on file, together with the information secured in the pre-membership consultation, the minister and officers of the church have a much better idea of the qualities of leadership offered by new members.

The minister or anyone else doing the interview must be careful not to promise too much. It is easy to make the mistake that is often made with the popular ballot method. Do not promise the new member a Sunday school class unless you are sure that one is available. Do not be too hasty to send the choir director another soprano when he already has more than he can use. The placing of volunteer workers can be a very sensitive thing.

Geographical Organization of the Parish

The best way to secure information and to keep up with the changing parish is through some plan of geographical division of the parish with a qualified layman over each individual group. This plan has taken various names and forms but generically they are the same. It may be called the Centurion plan when the congregation is divided into tens, then hundreds, or the Shepherd plan where shepherds are assigned to various sectors, or any other name. The techniques vary but the purpose is the same— to provide some plan of dividing the parish leadership in such a way that no family is lost in the parish administration or pastoral oversight.

An interesting thing about the parish organizational plans is that both the pastoral and administrative program are served by the same plan. Efficiency in one area strengthens the other.

Typical Plan

While the techniques of parish division may vary with local situations the following analysis of one of the widely publicized plans will help one to visualize the possibilities. *The Under-shepherd Plan* was evolved by the Reverend Elam G. Wiest when he was serving as pastor of the Trinity Evangelical and Reformed Church, Cleveland, Ohio. It is primarily an evangelistic program but suits splendidly the demands of executive procedure. It has been widely used in his own denomination and in others.

NAME. The plan takes its name from the concept that Christ is the Good Shepherd. The pastor of the local churches and the volunteers who work in this program are called the undershepherds. The scriptural basis is the Gospel of John 21:15-17 in which Peter gets his instructions from Jesus to "Feed my lambs."

DIVISION OF PARISH. Locate on a map every family in the parish. Then divide the entire parish into districts with not more than six families in each district.

ENLISTMENT OF WORKERS. Select two undershepherds for each district. Often these are husband and wife; in other instances they may be two men or two women. They need not reside in the district to which they are assigned.

ORGANIZATION OF UNDERSHEPHERDS. The pastor calls a meeting of all the undershepherds to explain the plan and make the assignments. During the operation of the plan he will call other meetings as he feels they are necessary. Personal experiences will be shared in these meetings.

UNDERSHEPHERD LISTS. It is the responsibility of the church office to provide each team of undershepherds with a complete list of their families. Then the calls will be made. They seek a one hundred per cent cooperation from each family visited.

CHURCH ATTENDANCE. The undershepherds will check the attendance of the families in their area, greet them and introduce them to other people. They will tactfully call on the absentees to urge them to greater interest. They will report cases of distress and illness which should be brought to the pastor's attention.

UNDERSHEPHERDS OPEN-HOUSE. The families in their areas will be invited for social evenings. Hosts will try to extend the missionary spirit to members of the group, urging them also to become undershepherds.

VAN SPOTTERS. The entire group should organize into van spotters who watch for new people moving to the community. They should call on these people and invite them to the services of the church.

CHURCH GREETERS. The undershepherds furnish the nucleus for an effective group of church greeters. They will in particular see that those in their group are introduced to other worshippers.

NEW CHURCH MEMBERS. When a new member from any area joins the church the undershepherds will work with him to see that his abilities are recognized and that he is given every opportunity to serve in the church.

Mr. Wiest gave the following purposes of the undershepherd plan.

1. To promote acquaintance, friendship and love among the members.

2. To work with the pastor in showing a loving concern for the people in the spirit of the Master.

3. To encourage regular church attendance, to discover pupils for the Sunday Church School and to widen the base of participation in the program and organization of the church.

4. To discover new people moving into a given area and, if they are non-Christian and unchurched, to invite them to become Christians and church members. Names may also be given to the evangelism committee. Usually, however, the experience of inviting one's fellow members gives confidence and courage to visit and win new recruits for Christ.

5. To report illness and special need, lack of interest, change of address and other information to the pastor. He can then give these people immediate attention and because of the quick check-up of the entire congregation he can be more effective in his pastoral ministry. The more work the laymen can do, the more the pastor will do. One does not substitute for the other; each supplements and strengthens the other. Faithful laymen and a faithful pastor mean a vital and fruitful church.

Other group plans are being used, but all have the basic geographical assignment. Bernard Clausen years ago perfected in his church at Syracuse, New York, what he called the Centurion plan. He used the decimal organization but the program paralleled the Undershepherd System. Many churches are now so organized that they can use the benefits of this plan without changing or adding to their present organization.

In several denominations it is a good system for the work of the deacons. Properly organized it makes any group in the church not only a listening class but a dynamic part of the program for the benefit of the church, the newcomer and the visitor.

The Talent Ballot

The talent ballot is often recommended as a means of getting workers to fill the vacancies in church leadership. Effective when used with caution, the talent ballot simply presents a list of the lay activities of the church. These ballots are placed in the hands of church members who are asked to indicate the work which will interest them. Unquestionably some names and candidates for service will result, but the selection of leadership without considerable knowledge of the individual may not develop the best leadership, especially when applied to the choir and the church school. If the names are used only as a basis for further consultation and study much of the danger can be eliminated. But then the minister runs into the possibility of offending someone because that person's offer of service has not been accepted.

Integration of New Members into Church

Churches are learning that growth does not come from simply taking in new members. These members must in addition be integrated into the activities of the church. Several methods have proven effective for this.

When a new family or a single member is received into the church, an older experienced member or family is assigned as the "buddy" of the novice. Sometimes this starts with a reception on the day of joining the church. At this reception the new members get acquainted with each other and are introduced to their

NAME. . . . . .DATE. . . . .

RESIDENT ADDRESS . . . . .TEL. . . . .

BUSINESS ADDRESS . . . . TEL. . . . .

OCCUPATION—PROFESSION . . . .

Please check below if you have engaged in or are willing to engage in the following opportunities of Christian service:

A talent ballot.

Have Done		Will Do		Have Done		Will Do
SUNDAY SCHOOL				**CHURCH OFFICERS AND COMMITTEES**		
___General Superintendent		___		___Church Clerk		___
___General Associate		___		___Church Treasurer		___
___Department Superintendent		___		___Church Librarian		___
___Department Associate		___		___Usher		___
___Teacher—What age?___				___Greeter		___
___Gen. or Dept. Secretary		___		___Trustee		___
___Cradle Roll Visitor		___		___Deacon		___
___Extension Visitor		___		___Junior Deacon		___
___Vacation Bible School		___		___Baptism Committee		___
___Class Officer		___		___Building Committee		___
___Mission Sunday School		___		___Contact Committee		___
___Nursery Worker		___		___Evangelism Committee		___
				___Finance Committee		
TRAINING UNION				___Flower Committee		___
				___Hospitality Committee		___
___General Director		___		___House and Grounds Committee		___
___General Associate		___		___Library Committee		___
___Department Director		___		___Lord's Supper Committee		___
___Department Associate		___		___Church Ministries Committee		___
___Counselor		___		___Missions Committee		
___Leader		___		___Music Committee		___
___Sponsor		___		___New Member Committee		___
___Union Officer		___		___Nominating Committee		___
___Mission Training Union		___		___Nursery Committee		___
___Nursery Worker		___		___Publicity Committee		___
				___Scouting Committee		___
W. M. U.				___Youth Committee		___
___President		___		**MUSIC**		
___Young People's Director		___				
___First Vice-President		___		___Solo Work		___
___Second Vice-President		___		___Choral Work		___
___Recording Secretary		___		___Directing		___
___Corresponding Secretary		___		___Play Piano		___
___Treasurer		___		___Play Organ		___
___Committee Chairman		___		___Play _____		___
___B.W.C. Adviser		___				
___Circle Chairman		___		**SPECIAL SERVICES**		
___Y.W.C. Counselor		___		___Typing		___
___G.A. Counselor		___		___Telephoning		___
___R.A. Counselor		___		___Transportation		
___Sunbeam Band Leader		___		___Operate Motion Picture Projector		___
___Sunbeam Baby Visitor		___		___Woodwork and Handcraft		___
___Mission W.M.U.		___		___Coach Sports		___
				___Direct Games		___
PERSONAL				___Plan Socials		___
				___Give Reading		___
My Hobby or Hobbies: _____				___Storytelling		___
				___Soul Winning		___
_____				___Make Posters		___
				___Aid in the Kitchen		___
What I Would Like to Do Most in My				___Operate Mimeograph		___
				___Interior Decorating		___
Church: _____				___Painting		___
				___Direct Plays and Pageants		___
_____				___Act in Plays and Pageants		___
				___Make-Up Artist		___
_____				___Set Designer (Stage)		___
				___Electrical Knowledge		___
My Second Choice: _____				___Operate Public Address System		___
				___Playing Service Tape Recordings to Shut-ins		___

"buddies." One church we know goes farther than this. When an applicant has been approved for church membership, he is assigned to a sponsor who walks to the altar with him and then for a period of time introduces him to the various organizations.

The duty of the buddy is to introduce the member to the various activities of the church, to help him make a selection of the various areas which will interest him, and to give him information regarding the denomination and local church practices. The term of the buddy may be a minimum of three months or it can be extended to a longer period of time if that seems desirable.

A second and very effective method is to have material on the local church and work in the membership instruction. Time is at a premium here but a few helpful rules of personal development can be included. Many lonely people join churches in search of Christian companionship. If they can be given assurance that others will like them, it will help their adjustment.

A personnel file started for each member when he joins the church and continued from that time on will be invaluable to the pastor in keeping in touch with the members. If the church requires an extended member application, it can be filed in the personnel folder.

The greatest asset in integration is the spirit of friendliness which characterizes a truly Christian church. We do not mean the facile hand-clasp, but a spirit of welcome which newcomers will recognize. One new member, finding after he joined the church that he was left on his own, suggested that the church could do its work by simply investing in an electric hand-shaking machine into which the newcomer could put a quarter and get a mechanical welcome.

A local church is a Christian fellowship in the best sense of the word. The purpose of the leadership is to weave the membership into a harmonious whole. There is an old adage which is worth keeping in mind in these days of growing churches: *"When a church becomes too big to be a fellowship, it is too big to be a church."*

Integrating the Church

BEAVEN, A. W., *The Local Church: Its Purpose and Program.* Abingdon, 1947.

――――, *Putting the Church on a Full Time Basis.* Harper, 1950.

BROOKS, A. T., *The Practical and Profitable in Church Administration.* Judson, 1930.

CASHMAN, R., *The Business Administration of the Church.* Willet Clark, 1937.

CONRAD, P. N., *This Way to a Thriving Church.* Abingdon, 1947.

CROSSLAND. W., *Better Leaders for Your Church.* Abingdon, 1955.

DOBBINS, G. S., *Building Better Churches.* Broadman, 1947.

DOLLOFF, E. D., *The Efficient Church Officer.* Fleming, 1949.

FENN, D. F., *Parish Administration.* Morehouse, 1938.

LEACH, W. H., *Toward a More Efficient Church.* Revell, 1948.

LEMMON, C. E., *The Art of Church Management.* Bethany, 1933.

MITCHELL, W. S., *A Seven Day Church at Work.* Funk, 1929.

PLEUTHNER, W. A., *More Power to Your Church.* Farrar, 1952.

6 | THE CHURCH WITH A MULTIPLE MINISTRY

AN OLD STORY OFTEN TOLD BUT STILL TO THE POINT RELATES that a certain clergyman who had been serving as a professor in a college decided to try the pastorate. It was his first experience and he was amazed at the multiplicity of tasks which were entrusted to him. At the end of a year he resigned his job to go back to teaching.

"In the college," he told a friend, "I occupied a chair. In the pastorate, I found that I had to spread across an entire davenport."

The work of the minister has become a very complex and often confusing task. The minister no longer lives the quiet life pictured in the fiction of the Victorian period. The traditional tasks of the pulpit and pastoral tasks remain but to these have been added administrative and public relations tasks which challenge the ingenuity and strength. At the same time churches have maintained their individual characteristics and by far the majority of churches have but one regular employee, the minister. He must be preacher, priest, director of education, pastor, administrator, typist, and operator of the duplicator. He is indeed a minister with many portfolios.

During the past few years, there has been a decided growth of churches with a multiple ministry. This has been caused by the increasing size of the membership of churches, and liberalized budgets. Associate ministers are becoming quite common, churches with three clergymen on the staff number into the hundreds, and larger staffs are not infrequent. At the same time there has been an increase in the size of non-professional staffs of secretaries, typists, custodians, etc. The addition of business managers to the church administration has reached some propor-

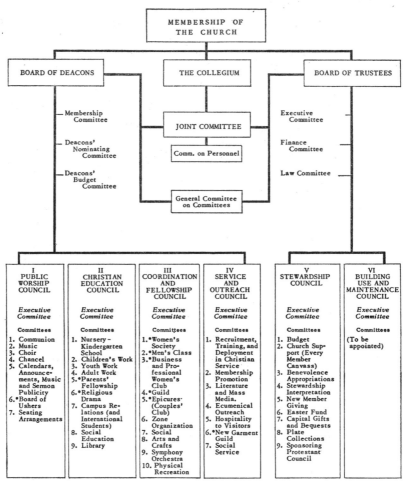

		MEMBERSHIP OF THE CHURCH			

BOARD OF DEACONS	THE COLLEGIUM	BOARD OF TRUSTEES
Membership Committee	JOINT COMMITTEE	Executive Committee
Deacons' Nominating Committee	Comm. on Personnel	Finance Committee
Deacons' Budget Committee		Law Committee
	General Committee on Committees	

I PUBLIC WORSHIP COUNCIL	II CHRISTIAN EDUCATION COUNCIL	III COORDINATION AND FELLOWSHIP COUNCIL	IV SERVICE AND OUTREACH COUNCIL	V STEWARDSHIP COUNCIL	VI BUILDING USE AND MAINTENANCE COUNCIL
Executive Committee	*Executive Committee*	*Executive Committee*	*Executive Committee*	*Executive Committee*	*Executive Committee*
Committees	Committees	Committees	Committees	Committees	Committees
1. Communion 2. Music 3. Choir 4. Chancel 5. Calendars, Announcements, Music and Sermon Publicity 6. *Board of Ushers 7. Seating Arrangements	1. Nursery - Kindergarten School 2. Children's Work 3. Youth Work 4. Adult Work 5. *Parents' Fellowship 6. *Religious Drama 7. Campus Relations (and International Students) 8. Social Education 9. Library	1. *Women's Society 2. *Men's Class 3. *Business and Professional Women's Club 4. *Guild 5. *Epicures (Couples' Club) 6. Zone Organization 7. Social 8. Arts and Crafts 9. Symphony Orchestra 10. Physical Recreation	1. Recruitment, Training, and Deployment in Christian Service 2. Membership Promotion 3. Literature and Mass Media. 4. Ecumenical Outreach 5. Hospitality to Visitors 6. *New Garment Guild 7. Social Service	1. Budget 2. Church Support (Every Member Canvass) 3. Benevolence Appropriations 4. Stewardship Interpretation 5. New Member Giving 6. Easter Fund 7. Capital Gifts and Bequests 8. Plate Collections 9. Sponsoring Protestant Council	(To be appointed)

Groups other than Committees

Division of responsibility in Riverside Church. Each of the four ministers has leadership responsibility for one° of the first four councils. The collegium (ministers) selects one of its number who becomes the chief administrative officer of the church.

82

tions and marks a new step in church organization. For the first time there is a growing recognition that there is a place in the local church for a qualified business executive who is not ordained. It has seemed wise to divide this chapter under two main heads—the division of tasks for the clergy and the division of tasks among the lay members of the staff.

Division of Work of the Clergy

In theory it is easy to divide the tasks of the clergy, but in practice it is very difficult. For instance when a church adds a second minister the senior may take the church services and the pastoral duties incident to the church, while the second minister may become the director of Christian education. When a third minister is added to the staff, the pastoral duties may be stripped from both and the third minister assigned to all pastoral tasks. A fourth minister could take over the administrative and public relations duties. In reality it does not work out this way.

One reason is that the responsibility of the church rests upon the pastor. He must be the directing head regardless of the number of the clergy. He must be responsible for decisions and staff meetings. The technique may be a very democratic procedure but the work of the church must be organized. Another very practical reason is that simply calling the senior minister the Pulpit Minister is not going to keep from him the necessity of taking on a good share of the pastoral work. Weddings and funerals will usually be shared by the clergy as requested by the principals. Consultation is increasingly important in the work of the modern church and this function is usually shared by the clergy. There is no clearcut division of the tasks.

The Collegiate Reformed Church of New York City was originally a church with a multiple ministry. As its work expanded the various ministers were assigned different churches where they assumed the duties of the local pastor although they were part of the one church. The Riverside Church in the city of New York calls its staff "The Collegium." They are supposed to supervise all of the work of the church with the minister of preaching acting as chairman. The policy in the division of tasks in this church is given in the excerpt from a survey of the church program recently made.

> Members of the Collegium must be our leaders in the conduct of the program of the church. The theory of the Collegium is equality among its members with the preaching minister acting as its chairman. Responsibility is divided in accordance with each minister's special skills and experience. Each member of the Collegium should have executive authority over the portion of the program within his jurisdiction and should also supervise and evaluate the services of the related ministers of his staff. . . . Every reasonable effort should be made to minimize the administrative routine, time-consuming duties of members of the Collegium, and especially their attendance at meetings, so as to afford them the maximum time and energy for the performance of their essential ministerial functions. (*The Riverside Church Survey Report*, 1956.)

A study of the organizational chart on another page will help the reader to interpret this passage. The departmental organization of a church helps in the division of the duties of the staff. It gives a breakdown which suggests a division of ministerial duties.

Most churches today may be operating under traditionally separate ecclesiastical and civil organizations. One board directs the religious program and a second directs the legal or civil activities. Where there are but two ministers one can be assigned to the religious program and one to the trustees. The senior minister would naturally be the one for the religious or spiritual program.

North Methodist Church, Indianapolis, Indiana, a church of 3000 members, has a clergy staff of three. They are known as the Minister, the Minister of the Parish, and the Minister of Education. The division of the ministerial duties in this church was analyzed in minute detail. A study of the survey which follows will reveal that each of the three ministers have sufficient tasks to tax several average men.

The Heart of the Matter*

The heart of a multiple ministry is the happy, helpful relationship of the ministers who work together in serving their people under the leadership of Christ, and the complete understanding of a team ministry by a devoted congregation. We lean here on the counsel of Paul to 'encourage one another and build one another up.'

This outline of ministerial responsibilities is itself an illustration, for though authored by the minister, it grew out of the cooperative effort of many individual North Church leaders, a number of committees and commissions, the Official Board, and the staff. These many persons drew in turn from the *Discipline of the Methodist Church*, from various plans that are in use across America, and from their own experience in our growing, developing church. Nor is it a fixed, finished thing. It will change and develop as new insights evolve.

Such cooperative team spirit is essential. Lines of communication, responsibility, and authority must be kept open between the members of the staff, appreciated by the people, and used in harmony with the will of God. Together we seek to emulate the disciples, of whom Luke said: 'All these with one accord devoted themselves to prayer.'

Each minister has both specific and general responsibilities contributing to the total ministry of the church. Each is called of God, trained professionally, ordained by a bishop, and entrusted with the gospel. Each one invests himself completely in his own area of work, and also helps his colleagues in their work, so that together the ministerial team sets forward the work of Christ in the lives of our people.

The Minister

The minister is the spiritual and executive leader of the church. He is the servant of the people, and is responsible to the bishop, the annual Conference, and the congregation for the total life and program of the church. His functions are:

* The analyses which follow were made by Dr. Hiram C. Weld, minister of the North Methodist Church, Indianapolis, Indiana. They are used by courtesy of *Church Management*.

1. Nourish the spiritual growth of people and staff in a reciprocal ministry that is worthy of our beloved fellowship in Christ.

2. Coordinate the many functions of the church as chairman of the Official Board, the Policy Committee, and the Committee on Nominations, and as consultant to the Committee on Pastoral Relations.

3. Preach and plan the worship program, that is, coordinate the Commission on Worship with its committees of altar, communion stewards, communion ushers, music, ushering and welcome; and administer Holy Communion, baptize infants and adults, perform the marriage ceremony, conduct funerals, and receive new members into the fellowship of the church.

4. Perform pastoral visitation and, through the minister of the parish and various committees, carry out the goal of seeing to it that every member of the parish is called upon during the year; counsel with those in need.

5. Teach throughout the church school where possible, and through the minister of education, carry out the goal of a strong Christ-centered educational program.

6. Counsel with the Woman's Society of Christian Service, and the Wesleyan Service Guilds and integrate their programs into the total life of the church.

7. Provide ministerial leadership for the Commission on Finance and its several committees of audit, Christian stewardship, budget, finance campaign, pledges, and tellers, and work with the treasurers.

8. Preside at staff meetings and coordinate the work of the entire staff so that the program of the church is carried forward and so that each member of the staff grows in competence and Christian grace.

9. Coordinate policy on all property matters which undergird the program through the Board of Trustees, and Committee on Memorials, Wills and Legacies, and Legal Advice.

10. Administer the provisions of the *Discipline* and see that the ordinances and regulations of the church are duly observed.

11. Provide ministerial leadership for public relations and information through the *North Churchman*, bulletin, sermons, *Official Family*, and other publications; and represent North Church at outside church and community events that will extend the reach of the parish in its larger ministry for Christ.

Conclusions for the Minister

The minister seeks to provide leadership for his staff and people so that the multiple ministry for Christ is effective. He seeks to be responsive to the will of God, and the needs of his people so that the church lives on the growing edge of the gospel in meeting the challenges and opportunities of a changing parish and world. Through a total ministry the gospel is preached, the sacraments administered, the will of God made known, the Holy Spirit given a home and the redemptive fellowship in Christ so nearly achieved that hearts are strangely warmed and the New Testament days are lived anew in our modern time.

The Minister of the Parish

The minister of the parish is a part of the total ministry. He is a fully ordained minister and colleague who works as associate to the minister with responsibility for the parish program of the church. Hence, he is the administrator and coordinator of the parish work as it undergirds the total ministry. That is the minister of the parish views the program of the church as a whole and seeks ways for the parish ministry to enrich it. His specific responsibilities are:

1. Provide the ministerial leadership for the Commission on Membership and Evangelism. This means to work with the committees on membership rolls and records, prospects, visitation, evangelism, the parish organization, deepening the spiritual life, visiting the sick, and visiting the shut-ins.

2. Provide the ministerial leadership for the Commission on Missions. This means to extend our work through the committees on missions and church extension, hospitals and homes, interdenominational cooperation, short-term mission projects, and the city council.

3. Provide the ministerial leadership for the house committee, 'grounds committee and committee on church use, as that part of the Commission on Administration pertaining to our building, grounds, and equipment.

4. Provide the ministerial leadership for lay activities, that is, Methodist Men, Fall Fellowship Dinners, and Lenten Fellowship Dinners.

5. Help recruit and train leaders in developing the parts of the program for which he is responsible, and also suggest persons as possible leaders in other areas of the church program.

6. Provide pertinent articles regarding parish activities for the bulletin and the *North Churchman.*

Insofar as the minister of the parish shares in the total ministry of North Church, as well as leading the parish department, he (1) reports on his area of work at weekly staff meetings and attends the Committee on Policy, the Official Board, and the Quarterly Conference; (2) assists in the regular Sunday morning worship services, preaches and administers Holy Communion as assigned by the minister; baptizes, officiates at weddings and funerals, speaks to classes of the church school and the Angelus Fellowship as requested, and is available to any member of the church who may wish to consult him or avail himself of his service; (3) participates in outside church and community events, insofar as such participation is helpful to the North Church program and the larger outreach of Christ. The minister of the parish's plan to serve beyond the boundary of North Church are made in harmony with his total schedule of responsibilities and subject to approval by the minister.

Relationship to Others in North Church

1. The minister of the parish's relationship *to the minister.* The minister is the pastor in charge, responsible to the bishop, the Annual Conference, and the congregation for the total program. The minister of the parish therefore works as colleague and associate to the pastor in planning with him the church's parish program.

2. The minister of the parish's relationship *to the staff*. The minister of the parish maintains a cooperative and helpful relationship with the minister of education, the director of counseling, and the director of music. He reports to staff meetings regarding his own work for consideration and approval, and he shares in the discussion and approval of the work of other members of the staff, so that the total church program is mutually undergirded by a total ministry. It is a procedure in North Church that all plans and proposals, before being put into effect shall be presented to the staff as a whole for consideration and final approval. Thus, when the minister of the parish presents a staff-approved idea or plan to a group, he is speaking on behalf of all the ministers.

3. The minister of the parish's relationship to *groups for which he is responsible*. The Commission on Membership and Evangelism, the Commission on Missions, the Commission on Lay Activities, and the House, Grounds, and Church Use Committees of the Commission on Administration: These groups look to the minister of the parish for creative thinking and planning. Yet, he is consultative rather than directive, for in these various meetings some ideas originate with the minister, some with the minister of education, some with himself, some with the director of music, some with the commission members, some with the commissions and organizations. These ideas are presented for consideration by the entire group and may be modified by the discussion.

4. The minister of the parish's relationship to *lay workers*. The minister of the parish's relationship to lay workers is that of a counselor and friend. He spends much of his time planning with workers and coaching them in ways of carrying out their particular duties. His responsibility as a leader is to help the lay workers carry out the many ministries of the church rather than trying to do the whole job himself. Everyone grows in such a cooperative process.

Conclusions for the Minister of the Parish

In summary, the minister of the parish leads the parish program that undergirds and strengthens our total church life; wins new members who are committing their lives to Christ and who are seeking to participate in the total life of the church; helps win and train persons to take places of leadership throughout the church; and helps develop understanding among the people of the congregation of the specific work of the several ministers and of the total multiple ministry in action.

The Minister of Education

The minister of education is a part of the total ministry. He is a fully ordained minister and colleague who works as associate to the minister with responsibility for the educational program of the church; hence, is the administrator and coordinator of the educational ministry, as it is a part of and undergirds the total ministry. The minister of education views the program of the church as a whole, and seeks ways for the educational ministry to enrich it. His specific responsibilities are:

1. Work with the Commission on Education, lead the entire program of Christian education, the General Officers of the church school, and the teachers and officers of the children, youth, and adult divisions of the church school.

2. Recruit teachers, develop a program for teacher training, and have substitute teachers on call. Have an active recruitment committee. This committee should be helpful also in recruiting leaders for the total program of the church.

3. Supervise church school records.

4. Call in the homes of members of the church school and those of the officers and teachers as much as possible, so that by knowing the people, he can render a greater service to the church.

5. Win new members for the church school.

6. Be responsible for Church-Time Infants' Group and develop a second session.

7. Develop a church library and promote its use.

8. Supervise the use of audio-visual materials.

9. Arrange special worship services of the various departments, and the combined worship services of the entire church school.

10. Develop new programs on all levels, such as a Golden Age club (55 years of age or over), a rounded dramatic program, and new study groups or seminars.

11. Work with the Girl Scout committees, Boy Scouts, Brownies, Cubs, etc.

12. Publicize church school and youth activities in the bulletin, *North Churchman*, and the press through the proper channels.

13. See that information concerning Methodist schools and colleges is provided to the youth of the church.

14. See that special studies such as vocational opportunities in the church, marriage and home building, Christian citizenship, etc., are provided when the need arises.

15. Supervise the Angelus, the young adults, college students from Butler, and other youth groups in study, recreation and activities.

16. Organize the youth membership class and the preparatory membership class.

17. Share in the total church program insofar as such participation develops and promotes the church school and the total educational program of North Church, for example, lead a Lenten service, or fall school of religion.

18. Promote attendance at regular Sunday morning worship services in the youth and adult divisions of the church school so that North Church as a great church family is a worshiping church.

Insofar as the minister of education shares in the total ministry of North Church, as well as leading the education department, he (1) reports on his area of work at weekly staff meetings and attends meetings of the Committee on Policy, the Official Board, and the Quarterly Conference; (2) assists in the regular Sunday morning worship services; preaches and administers Holy Communion as assigned by the minister; calls on sick or shut-in persons who are related to the educational program; counsels with, baptizes, officiates at weddings or funerals of members as requested; and is available to any member of the church who may wish to consult him or avail himself of his service;

(3) participates in outside church and community events insofar as such participation is helpful to the North Church educational program and the larger outreach of Christ. The minister of education's plans to serve beyond the boundary of North Church are made in harmony with his total schedule of responsibilities and subject to approval by the minister.

Staff Problems

That there will be staff problems in a church with the multiple ministry may be taken for granted. Clergymen are as a rule rugged individualists and take pride in the role of prophet. It is difficult for them to adapt themselves to democratic procedures which challenge their wisdom on matters of church organization and procedures.

The distinction between an assistant minister and an associate minister is very important here. An associate usually is one who has been called by the church and possibly installed as a pastor of the congregation. He is entitled to the full rights of the pastor. An assistant, on the other hand, is selected and hired to be an assistant to the minister.

Where the staff is made up of associates, it is very necessary that the tasks of the church be divided and each man have authority in his own particular area. Where the staff is made up of pastor and his assistants, the additional ordained members of the staff are there to work under the direction of the pastor.

The First Methodist Church, Schenectady, New York, practices democracy in the fullest sense. It has three ministers known as ministers, not as associates nor assistants. The church carries this to the point of furnishing four identical automobiles—one for each of the ministers and one for the director of Christian education. Yet one man is definitely the head of the staff and assumes the authority to preside at meetings which assign work. Funerals and weddings are assigned by rotation. In the Riverside Church, New York, the administrative work of the church is divided among the several clergymen but chairmanship of the

Collegium (ministerial staff) is given to the preaching minister. Just how strictly division of tasks can be maintained is an open question. The minister who is selected for the preaching task and that only is sure to find it necessary to conduct some funeral services and to take some weddings. Almost every ordained minister wants an occasional chance to preach and no director of Christian education is willing to turn over all of his charges to the pastoral minister. Any program which is set up must be given wide tolerance in interpretation.

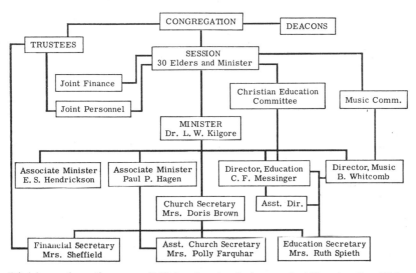

Division of staff responsibilities in the Lakewood (Cleveland), Ohio, Presbyterian Church.

The Lay Staff

In the small church the lay staff may consist only of a part-time custodian. He is under the direct charge of the minister or a house committee which supervises his employment. The traditional poverty of churches made it necessary for them to rely on part-time and often unqualified persons for this task. But his contribution is a very important part of church administration. The cleaning, heating, lighting, ventilation is in his charge. A separate chapter in this book deals exclusively with building maintenance, evidence in itself of the importance of the task.

The second lay employee will be the ministerial or church secretary. If this is a part-time job, usually a married woman who can get away from her household duties gives some days to the church. She takes care of the pastor's correspondence, keeps the church records up-to-date, handles the telephone conversations, and so on.

The church which has a full time secretary can add financial duties to her tasks. She can keep both financial and membership records. As she is in the office full time, she can take over some of the internal publicity such as preparing the local church publication and worship program, assisting the minister in his miscellaneous typing, possibly including the typing of sermons.

As a church grows in size and the staff is increased, the use of paid employees grows and the task of administration becomes greater. There must be direction for these workers and their duties should be clearly defined. Again we are indebted to Dr. Hiram C. Weld of the North Methodist Church, Indianapolis, Indiana, for the following analysis of the lay employee program in that church.

Secretary to the Minister

(Used by courtesy of *Church Management*)

The secretary is to help the minister in all secretarial matters pertaining to his leadership of the church. Her specific responsibilities are:

1. Supervise and coordinate the secretarial staff in office procedures, work load, and secretarial matters.

2. Keep record of minister's schedule; study hours, pastoral calls, counseling appointments, meetings, speaking engagements.

3. Receive all incoming telephone calls for the minister, transferring the call to him, or in his absence take message and com-

plete procedure. Place outgoing calls for the minister as directed.

4. Keep a file for baptisms, marriages, and funerals that the minister performs; keep minister's files of committees, correspondence, and general work; and supervise filing system for all office procedure.

5. Check all details for worship services and use of the sanctuary; regular worship, Holy Communion, Christmas Eve, Good Friday, weddings, etc.—such as kneeling pads, candles, material in pew pockets, flowers, lights, orders of worship, etc.; clear with ushers, musicians, acolytes, custodians, etc.

6. Handle all correspondence for the minister. Receive all mail for the minister. Open and prepare for reading. Prepare his outgoing mail, including transcribing of his dictation. Prepare special letters such as: (a) Weddings: Letters following weddings that are held in the church. Also, letters on first anniversary and letters to those celebrating their silver and golden wedding anniversaries. (b) Memorial Letters: also, acknowledge the memorial fund gifts, a card going to the family of the person being signed by the minister. (c) New Born Infants: When an infant is born, letter to the parents from the minister on behalf of the church. Record sent to records secretary. (d) Letters to bereaved persons one year hence. Also, send flowers at the time of death.

7. Prepare for printing the work of the minister that is to be published in any form, such as sermons and articles for the *North Churchman* and *Bulletin.*

8. Send newspaper publicity to *Times, News, Star,* neighborhood paper, *Hoosier Methodist,* and other journals as directed. Regular press ads to be handled by the office secretary.

9. Attend church functions as directed by the minister.

10. Order office supplies in consultation with the properly designated persons and the financial secretary.

11. Recruit volunteer help, planning in advance for special mailings such as Easter, Christmas, campaigns, and church activities.

12. Prepare and display materials for inside bulletin boards and literature tables.

Office Secretary

The office secretary, responsible to the secretary to the minister, has the following duties:

1. Serve as receptionist, greeting all who come into the office.

2. Receive all telephone calls and direct them to the proper persons. Also, keep record of dinner reservations for various church-wide functions.

3. Receive and distribute all incoming mail.

4. Keep a schedule of events in the office date book and on the wall calendar, clearing with the head custodian to see that all rooms and the building in general is set up for the various meetings, events and programs. All organizations other than church affiliated groups should be first referred to the Church Use Committee for approval.

5. Prepare regular press ads to be sent to each of the three daily newspapers on Monday, also to the *North Side Topics*.

6. Gather all articles for the *North Churchman* and formulate others that are necessary. Present to the minister for approval, take to printer, proofread copy, return for printing, and mail out.

7. Collect and prepare material for the weekly bulletin. Have it approved by the minister, take to printer, check proof copy, and return for printing.

8. Mail out notices for standing meetings, such as Official Board, Commission on Education, Commission on Finance, etc.

9. Prepare correspondence, work on mailings ahead of schedule, type, mimeograph, or stamp correspondence, when requested.

10. Handle lost and found articles.

11. Send bulletins to shut-ins, and welcome letters to visitors and new residents.

12. Handle appointments for director of counseling.

13. Be a part of the secretarial pool for taking care of undesignated work.

Bookkeeper

Under the authority of the minister and in compliance with policies, rules, regulations, and orders of the Committee on Personnel and the Commission on Finance and its several committees, as ratified by the Official Board, the bookkeeper shall perform the following duties:

1. She shall be responsible for the records of the church pertaining to the financial transactions with the exception of those transactions dealing with the building and captital account funds which are handled by the building fund treasurer, and in general she shall perform all the duties usually assigned to and normally expected of a general bookkeeper.

2. Acting with the treasurers of the church, receive and disburse funds in behalf of the church.

3. She shall be responsible for all cash receipts. Loose plate collections and Christmas and Easter offerings shall be first processed by the official tellers of the church. She shall count and deposit such receipts promptly; and maintain detailed records of all such receipts. She shall post and balance the individual pledge accounts; prepare and mail quarterly statements; maintain accurate pledge records showing all additions and deletions on a current basis; and answer any and all inquiries pertaining to these accounts promptly.

4. She shall audit all incoming invoices; secure proper approval for payment; and see they are paid promptly in order to take advantage of all cash discounts and to protect the financial credit of the church. She shall be responsible for all cash disbursements; processing all checks including countersigning; presenting all checks to the church treasurer for signature; and seeing they are mailed promptly.

5. She shall prepare financial statements, exhibits, and schedules reflecting the financial transactions of the church, prepare financial reports required of the minister by the district and Indiana Annual Conference, and material available for the *Bulletin* and *North Churchman*.

6. She shall maintain detailed and accurate records of all financial transactions by entering such transactions in books of original entry; posting all budget and general ledger accounts; and keeping same in balance in accordance with double entry methods.

7. She shall maintain adequate detailed records regarding employees' salaries, showing hours worked, wage rates, deductions, etc. and she shall prepare all government reports, both federal and state, such as withholding tax reports, social security reports, gross income tax reports, etc.

8. She shall process all correspondence pertaining to the financial matters of the church, mail the boxes of offering envelopes, and assist in the preparation of materials for the budget and finance campaign. She shall be responsible for the proper filing of all documents, vouchers, invoices, checks, correspondence, etc., pertaining to the financial transactions of the church and she shall be responsible for the protection of all ledgers, journals, cancelled checks, bank statements, and other items of major value by seeing that such items are properly housed in the fireproof safe provided for the purpose.

9. Render such assistance as the Official Board, committees, boards, groups, and organizations of the church may request in bookkeeping, accounting, auditing and reporting with respect to funds received and disbursed by those committees, boards, groups and organizations.

10. To notify from time to time the chairmen of committees and boards which supervise budgetary expenditures, of the states of their budgets and expenditures charged thereto.

11. She shall be responsible in general for the over-all efficiency, operation, and protection of the financial department as will insure a sound business operation of the church.

Records Secretary

The records secretary, responsible to the secretary to the minister, has the following duties:

1. Keep all church membership records. Prepare and keep card index membership file accurate and up to date. Record infor-

mation regarding new members joining the church, members transferring to other churches, and handle the necessary correspondence. Prepare materials for membership instruction. Keep office copies of membership books up to date.

2. Keep the church school records.

3. Work with the associate ministers in handling their correspondence as well as in other aspects of their work.

4. Operate mimeograph.

5. Keep addressing machine plates up to date, including church membership, personnel of various commissions and committees, and church school.

6. Receive telephone calls and direct them to the several offices in the absence of the office secretary.

7. Work on mailings: typing, mimeographing or stamping correspondence as needed.

8. Prepare the year book for printer.

9. Be a part of the secretarial pool for taking care of undesignated work.

Conclusions for Secretaries

This outline of responsibilities is, of necessity, brief, but it does indicate the specific things which each secretary—secretary to the minister, office secretary, bookkeeper, and records secretary—is expected to do. Each one should feel a definite responsibility for her own job and for the total work and life of the church. A gracious, cooperative office spirit is helpful to every member of the staff and a great satisfaction to our people, who appreciate good work procedures and jobs well done.

Custodian Job Analysis

Under the authority of the minister and directed by his delegate (at the present time the minister of the parish), in compliance with policies, rules, and regulations of the Personnel Committee, and the Property and Church Use committees, as ratified by the Official Board, the head custodian shall be responsible for the following duties:

1. Receiving instructions through the office, he is to work with and direct the assistant custodians in housekeeping, maintaining and improving the property; assign specific duties, keep a balanced work load and schedule for all, and constantly inspect assistant custodians' work to be sure a high standard of housekeeping is maintained.

2. Keep the church property looking respectable and in readiness for all functions, dusting and cleaning offices each day, keeping floors properly cleaned. Clean steps at entrance of buildings each Sunday morning. Keep windows washed, except where inaccessible. Keep grounds and walks clean. Keep walls and floors clean, painting when necessary, and on a rotation system of rooms so that painting is kept up. Dispose of refuse. Do minor electrical, plumbing, furniture repairs and carpentry.

3. Have the sanctuary in order for every worship service, that is, Sunday morning, Holy Communion, Baptism, Angelus Hour, weddings (give the organist signals during wedding ceremony), and keep sanctuary in order for individual prayer and meditation at all times.

4. Arrange for use of rooms upon instruction from the church office, and make necessary set-ups of chairs and tables for dinners and meetings in fellowship hall, or where else designated. Set up and adjust public address system in fellowship hall when necessary for meetings or dinners.

5. Keep all of the kitchens clean. Give assistance to groups cooking in kitchen only when some lifting is required, or some item of maintenance needs attention.

6. Look after the heating and ventilating system and see that building is properly heated, and dispose of ashes and refuse when necessary.

7. Look after the lighting system, replacing bulbs and globes when necessary and keep clean. See that all lights are turned off when not in use.

8. Police buildings, grounds, and parking lots.

9. See that building and offices are properly closed and locked every night.

10. Keep a stock of necessary supplies on hand for economical maintenance such as soap, wax, cleaners, tools, light bulbs, paints, etc.

11. Be available for duty in case of emergencies, and handle all special details for once-a-year events such as Christmas and Easter as they occur.

12. Assist where needed so that together with the ministers, staff, and people, the work of the church is spiritually effective.

Director of Food Services Analysis

Under the authority of the minister and directed by his delegate (at present the minister of education in lieu of an administrative assistant) and in compliance with policies, rules and regulations of the Personnel Committee, the director of food services shall:

1. Work in cooperation with the Woman's Society of Christian Service, church dinner committees, Wesleyan Service Guilds, Sunday school classes, Boy Scouts, Methodist Youth Fellowship, Methodist Men, and any other groups in the church using our kitchen and dining room facilities; and cooperate with groups helping outside organizations such as serving dinners for district meetings, conference meetings, Church Federation, etc.

2. Supervise the three kitchens, having general responsibility for the kitchen equipment.

3. Keep an inventory of all equipment through the inventory manager of the Woman's Society and make recommendations for additions or replacements of equipment.

4. In cooperation with the custodians, see that the rooms of the kitchens are kept clean and in good order.

5. Plan meals in accordance with good dietetic procedure. Order food and materials for preparation of meals and supervise their preparation.

6. Hire suitable part-time cooks, dishwashers, or other help as needed and authorized by the organizations paying for same.

7. Keep in mind that all church meals have as their goal the promotion of Christian fellowship for those who are dining and those who are serving. The church is not a restaurant business.

8. Exemplify a gracious, cooperative spirit with the people and members of the staff so that everyone participating in our kitchen and dining room activities will be spiritually enriched and grow in Christian grace.

The Business Manager

Some of the larger churches are now adding business managers to the lay staff. If churches continue to grow this profession will become increasingly important. The clergyman usually lacks training in the details of business administration, and time taken from his pastoral tasks for this specialized work is costly. Our new church buildings are institutions and require skill and understanding in maintenance. Staffs number dozens (in some churches at present, paid staffs are nearing one hundred persons) and this requires special skill in administration. At the time this is written there are more than two hundred church business managers in the churches of the United States and other churches are seeking this kind of help.

The business manager is usually a layman. Men in the profession feel that it is better that they remain so and no special training to date has been provided by the denominations. The managers have come from public school service, Y.M.C.A. experience, and business houses. Some of the most efficient are women who have entered the profession from a business background.

Their duties vary from church to church. Procedures are crystallizing as the profession matures and in most instances the following would be included.

1. The manager has charge of building control including direction of the employees, purchasing, etc.

2. He manages the finances of the church including the every-member canvass, bookkeeping systems, collections, etc. Usually, however, he does not supervise capital fund campaigns; for these the churches employ a professional fund raising agency.

3. He hires the paid employees and has charge of the payroll and discipline. Exceptions are made for the ministerial staff. He does of course consult with the ministers in the employment of their own secretaries.

4. Both internal and external publicity are his responsibility. By internal publicity we would mean the preparation of local publications such as the church weekly and monthly papers, letters, etc; by external, we mean newspaper, radio, and television publicity.

5. He supervises the dining room and kitchen including the hiring of the hostess, kitchen help, etc.

6. He possesses a large degree of independence in these areas but remains, of course, responsible to the board of the church.

Employee Staff Meetings

In churches employing up to a dozen persons, one general staff meeting is the rule. As the number of lay employees increases, staff meetings may come under the direction of the business managers. Clergy will of course attend as ex-officio members.

Traditional ecclesiastical offices have been inefficient and often times this inefficiency is excused on the grounds of good will. The addition of a church business manager with experience in directing the work of the employees can increase the daily output of each worker. Most employees welcome the direction of these men and women, as their own responsibilities are clarified.

The multiple ministry is with us to stay. In the present controversy as to how large a local church should be, some wise men are questioning the building of congregations with thousands of members. While they continue to exist, and they probably will be with us a long time, there is need for adequate administration. For some of these the business manager may be the answer.

Duties of the Church Manager

According to Mr. Bob Stotts, administrative assistant of the Oaklawn Methodist Church, Dallas, Texas, the obligations and duties of the church business manager are as below.

Basic Function

The Business Administrator shall be responsible directly to the Pastor and indirectly to the Official Board and Pastoral Relations Committee for the efficient administration of the business matters of the church and the maintenance of church property, the direction of the church staff and as purchasing agent as shown in this organization chart.

Conditions of Employment

1. The normal hours of employment shall be observed—6 days per week. However, it is recognized that this is a dedicated service and the incumbent will find it necessary to spend many hours in attendance at various meetings and in visitations outside the normal hours. Compensatory time off for hours beyond reasonable expectations may be arranged by mutual agreement with the pastor.

2. Annual paid vacation shall apply in accordance with the policy of other staff members.

3. Incumbent shall be expected to be a member of that church and be regular in attendance at worship and to support the church with his gifts and services as any other layman.

4. The incumbent shall be bonded by the church.

5. The salary for this position shall not be changed, except by mutual agreement, thirty days in advance of the new budget year.

6. Thirty days notice shall be given incumbent before severance and incumbent agrees to give the church like notice.

Duties and Responsibilities

1. Maintain the church financial records in good order according to established accounting practices.

2. Make periodic financial reports to Official Board.

3. Periodically review the status of pledges to church funds and inform members of their accounts. Recommend action to Financial Committee on delinquents.

4. Review all expenditures of church funds and approximate disbursement of authorized funds within the limits of the church budget.

5. Give administrative direction and detailed assistance to all fund-raising campaigns authorized by Official Board.

6. At the Pastor's direction, correlate the efforts of any group, or groups within the church to coincide with the desires of the Pastor and the Official Board.

7. The incumbent is a member ex-officio of the Official Board and must have the qualifications required of any member of the Official Board.

Membership Records

1. Be responsible for maintaining the church membership records in good order to the end that church membership is accurately known, new members are recorded, transfers, withdrawals, births and deaths are recorded, changes of address are obtained and recorded.

2. Recommended changes, additions, or deletions of church membership records to the pastor.

3. Using such information services as are available (including Sunday School rolls) make every effort to record new Methodist families in the area served by the church.

4. Make periodic lists of new families for the Pastor and Committee on Membership and Evangelism for the purpose of visitation.

5. Record the results of Pastoral and Committee visitation and recommend further action to the pastor.

Church Property and Equipment

1. Maintain all church property in good condition authorizing necessary repairs to be done in the most economical manner and within the limitations of the church budget.

2. Report to the Pastor and Board of Trustees any extraordinary maintenance required and make recommendations for action to be taken.

3. Direct the church custodians to see that the church buildings and grounds are maintained to standards of cleanliness and appearance that befits the status of this church in the community.

4. Schedule the use of church facilities to groups or organizations that are approved by the Official Board. Recommend procedures and rules for the use of church property and see that all groups conform to the rules. In cases of conflict, the administrative assistant's decisions are final and subject to change only by the pastor.

5. Establish and maintain an accurate inventory of all church equipment (furniture, fixtures, athletic equipment, etc.), maintain adequate supplies of expendable items. Recommend new capital investments.

Personnel

1. Supervise the activities of the church staff as shown in the Organization Chart.

2. Handle all personnel matters of the church staff, such as scheduling vacations, setting hours of work, making recommendations to the pastor for promotions or discipline or granting of extraordinary privileges, etc.

3. See that the church staff is adequately covered by unemployment insurance, social security benefits or other benefits to which they are entitled.

4. Make recommendations to the pastor for general changes, additions or deletions to the staff.

5. Assist pastor by having knowledge of capable persons available to substitute for or replace Religious Educational Director, Choir Director, organist, etc.

6. Handle all routine requests for small financial assistance and consult with pastor on unusual cases.

7 | ORGANIZATION FOR A NEW BUILDING

ANY PROGRAM FOR A NEW CHURCH BUILDING SHOULD NOT BE entered into lightly. The average church will not build more than one church building a generation and that building should include the best ideas for a church structure tailored to the local situation. General concepts of architecture and church facilities may be found in books and periodicals, but the local congregation has the responsibility of appraising its own needs. That can hardly be delegated to architect or builder.

This chapter is concerned with the organization of the local church for realizing the structure that will best fit its needs and ideals. Three main functions are involved. First, the building must be visualized very thoroughly in terms of the site, size of real estate, style of building, activities to be housed, estimated number to attend church services, estimated attendance for the various grades in the church school, number of people to be fed in the dining rooms, etc. Next, the funds must be pledged or raised to pay for the real estate and the building; and third, the building must be erected.

Because these three objectives must be realized, the best beginning is an organization which will direct a survey of all the departments of church work to study the desires of those who direct the activities. Secondly, there must be a committee or organization which will organize the church for a financial effort to secure the pledges or gifts. Thirdly, there is need for a committee or organization to oversee the actual construction of the building.

Just how shall these three groups be created? The proper academic procedure would be to appoint a general committee from the church which could be known as a building committee.

This general committee might be large, representing all departments of church work. From the larger committee an executive committee of no more than ten and preferably five members can be created with the authority to act between meetings of the general committee.

The first job of the executive committee is to appoint the three subcommittees described above. One may be called the survey committee as its task is to survey the needs of the local church. On this committee should be placed those who are especially interested in the program of the church and who realize that the church building should be created to aid the program of the church. Sometimes a church is unfortunate enough to have to work the other way around. It feels it must create a program to keep its building busy.

A good technique for this survey committee is (1) to study various books and magazine articles on modern church building; (2) to visit new churches in nearby areas to see just what their buildings offer; and (3) to approach each department of the church—education, women's work, men's work, youth work, choir, Boy Scouts, etc.—to learn what each expects in the new church building.

The findings of this committee with its recommendations should be reported to the general committee. In the end they will furnish the data for the architects who will plan the structure. For instance, the committee might make a report on the worship unit in words like these.

Our church should plan for a sanctuary which will seat five hundred in two Sunday morning services. We prefer that it be a rectangular church with a deep chancel. The chancel should be open with a pulpit on one side, a lectern on the other. We prefer a communion table to an altar. The choir shall be seated on either side of the chancel, in pews which are placed parallel to the walls. If the committee finds one chancel it thinks particularly appropriate, it may give the architect a picture of this.

CHECK SHEET ON PHYSICAL PROPERTY
The Worship Unit

The Nave.
( ) Are its proportions good for worship?
( ) Is the seating capacity sufficient?
( ) Does it have a center aisle?
( ) Are all aisles wide enough?
( ) Is there sufficient foyer space?
( ) What are the congestion areas?
( ) What about exits and entrances?

The Chancel.
( ) Center pulpit style?
( ) Open chancel with lectern and pulpit?
( ) Altar?
( ) Communion table? Which?

The Choir.
( ) Is the organ satisfactory?
( ) Space for choir adequate?
( ) Seating arrangements for choir satisfactory?
( ) Are practice, assembling and robing rooms available?

The Educational Unit

( ) Does the present unit provide for all groups at the recommended floor space?
( ) Nursery .... 25 to 30 square feet per child?
( ) Kindergarten ...25 to 30 square feet per child?
( ) Beginners ..... 25 to 30 square feet per child?
( ) Primary .... 18 to 25 square feet per child?
( ) Junior .... 18 to 25 square feet per child?
( ) Junior High ...15 to 18 square feet per child?
( ) Senior High ... 8 to 15 square feet per pupil?
( ) Youth ... . 8 to 15 square feet per pupil?
( ) Adult .... 10 square feet per pupil?
( ) Are the classrooms of departments together within departmental walls or closely united?
( ) Are assembly rooms provided for Primary, Junior, and Junior High departments?
( ) Are the departments arranged in an age sequence with the youngest children nearest the worship unit?
( ) Are provisions made for social events and recreation?
( ) Is there a stage for dramatic work?
( ) Are toilet facilities available to each department?

Building for Fellowship

( ) Kitchen adequate?
( ) Does church have any general social room besides the dining room? Dining room adequate?
( ) What recreational facilities are provided? List those provided and those desired.

At Present   *Would Like*

Use of the Out-of-Doors

( ) Is off street parking available?
    For how many cars? ....
( ) Are any other accommodations available for out-of-door meetings, parties, public worship?
    Others? ------------------------------------

This recommendation gives certain instructions to the architect. He will be saved much labor by knowing in advance the wishes of the church. A similar recommendation could be made regarding the kindergarten room.

> The kindergarten shall be placed on the floor level of the sanctuary, near to one of the entrances of the church. It should provide space for twenty-five children at the rate of thirty-five square feet per child.

Definite recommendations of this kind made for all of the various departments immediately supply to the architect a concept of the church. He then has no excuse for designing the church for too few or too great a number of people. Remember that the architect is to adapt his design to the program of the church; he is not to create a program. In actual practice many times, perhaps in a majority of instances, the survey work is done by a special group before the decision to build a church is made. Whether these three functions are processed by three self-contained committees or by a part of the general committee is unimportant. The main considerations are that each part of the program be carefully projected and no one phase neglected.

The survey work is the one which usually gets the least attention. People attend church all their lives and are not aware that some patterns of church building are much more desirable than others. They are apt to call a church a church and let it go at that.

Sometimes a committee that has never thought of the church building as being a tailor-made suit of clothes for a local congregation, finds it helpful to sit down with scissors and cardboard and cut out floor plans by units—one layout for education, one for fellowship, one for worship—and then try to place them together in a complete building. By trying their own hands at this, first outlining the departments and drawing the sections by scale, then assembling them into the complete church, the committee members soon learn something about arrangement in the church building.

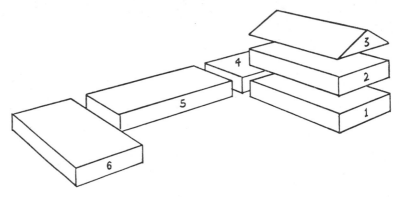

Estimating the cost of a Church Building. Each separate block represents a building unit 50′ x 100′ x 10′, a total of 5000 cubic feet. Ten-foot ceilings are sufficiently high for educational rooms and smaller assembly rooms. The church proper requires higher ceilings. By taking the average cost of school buildings per cubic foot one can easily estimate the cost of the building needed to fit the needs of the local church.

Who Shall Decide the Site?

Many churches have the problem of a new site. It brings a problem they have never faced and that is really outside the province of any of these three committees. If the recommendation of the survey committee is for a building which cannot be erected on the small present site, or if it seems desirable for other reasons that a new location be secured, the work might better be placed with a separate committee. This committee, however, can best do its work if it has the recommendations of the survey committee to guide it.

The Finance Committee

Formerly one committee, called the church building committee, directed both the financial campaigns and the construction. We have learned that it is better to have two committees for this task. There is enough work in either area for a strong committee. The building program naturally separates itself into these three functions—survey, finance, and construction.

The finance committee has the responsibility of planning a long range financial program to pay for the proposed new building. Appraising the resources of the congregation, it may decide that the gifts are of such proportions that it can direct the campaign with local leadership. On the other hand, it may feel that it is necessary to bring in a fund raising agency.

There is probably no way to estimate in advance just what a congregation can give under the inspiration of a building campaign. Comparison with other churches which have gone through a campaign is of course helpful. Doubtless minimum goals can be safely set, but the only way to find out just how much a congregation can give is to organize a campaign to raise the pledges.

If the committee decides that it needs outside help, it will so report to the executive committee and ask for authority to employ a fund raising agency. It will make the contract and the committee will then serve with the local workers in the financial campaign which will follow.

The organization of the financial campaign will be discussed in a later chapter. It should be explained here, however, that the authority of the committee extends beyond simply directing a campaign. It will have the responsibility for all financial arrangements, negotiating any necessary bank mortgage or bond issue, and setting up the procedures for the collection of pledges.

The best practice is to segregate the building fund from other monies of the church and to have the account handled by its own treasurer. Since the fund during the period that pledges are being paid will probably be greater than the normal budget of the church, the task of proper accounting is a heavy one.

The finance committee will of course report periodically to the executive committee which in turn will pass on the report to the official board. In actual practice the church building fund report is often presented directly to the board.

The Construction Committee

The work of this committee is to take the recommendations of the congregation for the facilities desired, the record of the financial campaigns and other financial assets, and initiate the actual plans for construction. It will have authority for the selection of the architect and the supervision of the structure. The reader will notice that in the organization of a three-way program each of the three committees has a professional counterpart. The committee on survey may, if it wishes, employ a church building consultant who can help it appraise its own needs in the light of the experiences of other churches. This service is comparatively inexpensive, the church paying the consultant a *per diem* rate. The financial committee can select from a dozen or more good fund raising agencies in the church field. The charges are based upon the type of services rendered. The committee on construction will of course seek the services of a good architect. Many of the states require the employment of an architect for all public buildings, so this is not optional.

Leaving aside all legal requirements, any church would be foolish to try to erect a building without the services of an architect. You place in his hands the various needs of your own church and he brings to you a wealth of knowledge and skill in weaving your requirements into a useful and beautiful building.

The architect selected should be a man skilled in his profession. It is desirable that he have experience in designing both church buildings and church schools. The church building of today is more than a worship center; it is a school as well. It is wise to commission an architect who is a good churchgoer. His instinctive knowledge will be helpful.

There is an increasing use of specializing architects though the term "specialist" may be anathema to the American Institute of Architects. While professional architects work as individuals, many churches employ a church architect of reputation from another city and he in turn employs local architects to supervise the construction.

The construction committee is the authority above the architect. As laymen, its members watch the construction. They must pass on the quality of the work.

The three-way method of dividing the responsibilities of the building program has proven very satisfactory. If your church has already done its survey work, you will need just two committees, the financial and the construction. If the money for the new structure is available, there is need for only the construction committee.

The three functions are a necessary part of a good church building, regardless of how the work is organized. The order is also correct: first, survey and appraisal; second, finance; and third, construction.

The Financial Campaign

In another chapter the organization for an effective annual budget campaign, usually termed the every-member canvass is discussed. The general principles listed there will apply to a capital-funds effort, but because the amount sought is so much greater and the necessity for sacrificial giving more urgent, more thorough planning and competent leadership will be required. One of the phenomena of religious life in our era is the rise of numerous fund raising agencies which offer professional services to local churches. They have introduced skills and techniques which are most helpful. The local church can conduct its own church building campaign, but the methods used by a church for an every-member canvass are not sufficient for this larger effort.

Traditionally the every-member canvass is conducted on a geographical basis with visitors going from home to home in a given area. The capital funds requires a much deeper study of personal incomes and the approach to the congregation will probably be through income groups or social-contact groups. The twenty-five-thousand-dollar solicitors will call on the twenty-five-thousand-dollar men; the five-thousand-dollar men will call on the five-thousand men and so on. Men who belong to a social club may be solicited by a fellow member; lawyers may be solicited by a lawyer, etc. There is already an established common ground for understanding and their incomes are probably in the same area.

A second distinction is that in an every-member canvass a period is set for the campaign and all homes are visited simultaneously, while in a well directed financial campaign a good share of the solicitation may be made before the open canvass begins. Each step in the organization is a move toward securing pledges and the chairman selected should be the individual who will make the largest pledge. Once he has agreed to serve and made his pledge the organization moves to the next man on the committee; he has had an example of stewardship in the pledge of the chairman. A good rule to follow is that each person selected for the committee will have made his pledge before his name is announced. In this way the pacemaking pledges are in hand before the public solicitation.

The importance of the preliminary effort cannot be overestimated. When the week arrives for the general solicitation the committee will know very well whether the effort will be a success or a failure.

A third distinction between the campaign for the annual budget and one for capital funds is that very few churches expect to raise the capital funds within a period of one year. The pledges must be made for a longer period. At present, two years, thirty months, or three years are the average terms for paying pledges. The scheduling of pledges depends on a number of considerations. Of course the church wants the money as soon as it can get it. Ideally the total amount should be raised for payment within a month, but in most instances the requirements are so great that pledges must be spread over a longer period. The time must not be so extended that pledges are lost by removal or death. To permit members to pay from their incomes, pledges will vary with the incomes of the families in the congregations. Too short a payment period will reduce the total pledge; too long a term risks nonpayment through death or removal.

The committee will need a much more accurate picture of

the incomes of the church families than is required in the every-member canvass. Public libraries and local Chamber of Commerce organizations have available reports compiled for business which give the average family incomes of the shopping area or county. This data can be used to show what a small percentage of the income of families is being asked for the new building. For instance a congregation of two hundred families in a community with an average family income of five thousand dollars should have a total gross income of one million dollars. A tithe of this is one-hundred thousand dollars. If this is the amount sought in the campaign, a tithe for one year will make the full amount. Every leader knows that it is not realistic to expect this amount to be paid in one year. Spread over three years, the requested payments amount to only one-third of the tithe and look much simpler. As the average family income in the United States is more than five thousand dollars per year, our example is very modest.

Every church planning a capital funds campaign will face a choice between employing a fund raising agency or having it directed by local leaders. The decision will have to be made by each church. In the average situation, a reliable fund raising agency will take a burden from the shoulders of the minister and local leaders—a burden which is a heavy one to those uninitiated in the mysteries of fund raising. If the church decides to conduct its own effort, it can learn much from the professional fund raisers.

1. The amount of money any church can raise in a building fund campaign does not depend so much on the wealth of the church as on its giving habits. Ministers and church leaders have a tendency to resist a campaign, saying, "We do not have any wealthy members." They search for an angel to pay half the cost of the new building. The professionals look over the church reports to see what the giving habits of the church really are and base their estimates for the campaign on past performance.

The results of any fund raising effort are based upon the sacrificial giving of the members. A church with a high rate of giving will give more than a church with the same number of families of equal or greater wealth but a lower rate of giving. This is contrary to the belief of some that because a church has been giving above average for years it may be difficult to ask for more money. The consecration of money and personality to a righteous cause is so satisfying that the high-budget church is the one which will have success in its effort.

The theory of some churches that because their members have not previously given generously they will be in a better position to make generous pledges does not work out. The generous givers will be those who have experienced, through giving, the compensations of stewardship.

2. There is a strong motivation in the philosophy and vocabulary traditionally used in religious appeals. The professional fund raisers believe in spiritually motivated campaigns. Sometimes their words put ministers to shame as they talk of the privilege of giving to God. There are many fields of philanthropy in the world, but the church is the only such institution with a program based on spiritual revelation.

Some fund raisers carry their philosophy of stewardship to the length of insisting that the purpose of the financial effort is not to raise money for church building but to give the individual the privilege of spiritual growth. In this rationalization the giving of money promotes an evangelistic message. As one man expressed it, "You need to give to save your own soul."

This is the basis for the proposal that the campaign be conducted before plans for the building are completed. The same philosophy dominates the new technique of prebudget canvassing for the annual budget of the church. Stewardship, sacrificial giving, sharing, and similar terms have a larger part in the terminology of the professional fund raiser than they usually do in a self-conducted campaign.

3. Large gifts stimulate large gifts. The criticism made of the professional fund raisers that they put too much emphasis on large gifts and givers of large gifts does not take this idea into account. An effort is made to find men of financial re-

sources to head the committees and these men are urged to make their own pledges early and generous. The amounts will probably be publicized early in the program, men and women with financial resources are moved to larger giving by the gift of a business associate who contributes a substantial amount from his plenty.

In this category falls the technique of having solicitors confine their efforts to prospects in their own economic class. This is a principle not to be followed consistently for there are exceptions, but the concept that large giving is followed by large giving proves true in practice.

4. Spade work is very important in the success of the program. This follows very closely the point regarding large gifts just mentioned. Much of the spade work in the financial effort consists in the study of the church membership and the appraisal of the amount which should be expected from the members. Fund raising campaigns are usually won or lost during the first few days after the arrival of the director. During this period the cards must be analyzed, chairmen and subchairmen selected, large gifts received, publicity set up, and the techniques for dinners, canvasses, and other activities planned.

Of course back of this intensive spade work is the preparatory work which has been done by the local church for years preceding. All of the instruction on the virtues of giving bears fruit when a capital-funds campaign is conducted. This of course denies the theory often expressed that there is some trick by which a clever campaign director can secure large giving from a church which is traditionally a poor stewardship body.

5. Workers need careful training for their tasks. The everymember canvass has been losing its appeal because so many workers think they know all there is to know about the technique. Because of this egoism they neglect the instruction periods and assume that their task is merely to ring doorbells and to accept the pledges which are held out. That means small pledges and little interest.

The building of attendance for these training sessions is a

difficult task in most churches. First, there are the absentees who know so much they do not feel the need to attend; next there are those with conflicting business and social engagements. It stands to reason that a capital-funds campaign requires much more effort and organization than the budget canvass, so it is most important that every solicitor have the vital information needed to properly present the matter to each family.

This means new techniques to get both attendance and interest. One method is to have classes by groups. If a solicitor misses one session he can catch up by attending with a different group. Some directors go so far as to call in for individual instruction solicitors who miss the group meetings.

6. Pledges should be made in the home with the entire family present. The canvass dinners are for information and publicity, not for the solicitation of additional pledges. Announcements may be made at the kick-off dinner of certain pace-setting pledges, but no new pledges are accepted. They are to be made during the visit of the trained solicitor. More and more in the visits the solicitors are insisting that the amount of the pledge be a matter of prayer by the whole family. Solicitors themselves must make their pledges before they go out to seek pledges from others.

Perhaps the best explanation of the method of securing pledges would be to call it a nudging process. It starts when the director of the campaign comes to the community. He gets together the minister and the few leaders and places the responsibility upon them. He nudges them toward the goal. When they are sold, they in turn nudge others and the process continues. The leaders will be the minister, the chairman of the campaign, the chairman of the canvass, the divisional heads, and so on down the line. The congregation as a whole may see only the every-member solicitor and not be aware of the intensive over-all work so necessary for a successful effort.

7. Solicitation and stewardship training should not stop with completion of the canvass. The fund raiser helps the church

plan its collection system so that results may be secured. At the same time he will recommend a continuing campaign. This may mean that each new family joining the church is given the privilege of sharing in the effort. This is presented by a competent individual or committee. A second though not quite so complete method is a repeat canvass held at intervals of three or six months to secure gifts from new members and other prospects who were not reached in the original canvass.

Of course, a competent system of bookkeeping and a method of collecting delinquent pledges are an essential part of the procedure. Whether or not the fund raiser sets up the collection system, the church definitely needs one with individuals who will work it.

8. Some features of the campaign are not flexible. There are certain "musts" for any financial effort. The professional fund raiser has a great advantage over the local leader because he is protected by a contract. The church has agreed to use the methods of the professional and refusal to follow any part means a breach of the contract. The local leader does not have this protection. He may set up the most perfect effort plan only to find that under pressure it must be compromised.

For example one church insisted that the congregational dinner was never desirable nor necessary in its community. The fund raiser read from the contract that the church had voted to follow his leadership in each detail. The dinner was held and attendance was splendid. The presentation and announcement of pace-setting gifts were well presented and the campaign was most successful. Under local leadership pressure would have eliminated that part of the program.

In another instance the local leadership committee refused to go along with the idea that no one should be permitted to solicit until he had made his own pledge. The result was that the usual canvass with solicitors not consecrated to the task produced too many small and indifferent pledges. The fund raiser must be a catalyst injected in the local situation which changes the finan-

cial and spiritual atmosphere of the church. Having done his
work he goes to another field. The local leader is not in so fortunate a position as this. The ability of the professional to force
the acceptance of each feature of the campaign may be one of
the strongest arguments for his work.

Of all the suggestions in this chapter, this is the most difficult
for the local leader to accomplish. Every congregation has its
negative thinkers who know that the money cannot be raised
or doubt that a new building is either desirable or necessary.
Local leaders seldom have the stamina to stand against the resistance of those who wish to simplify every operation.

Again the local leader finds it difficult to deal objectively
with individual appraisals. Perhaps the worst offender in this
respect is the local financial secretary who feels he is an authority on the prospective gift of every contributor. Lots of
money may be found where the church secretary insists there
is none. Fortunately the fund raiser can more easily resist this
information than can a local leader. There are other limitations
in the local effort of course. But in situations where it seems
wise to use local leadership instead of importing a specialist,
some of the suggestions of this chapter may prove helpful.

Getting Mortgage Money

Very few churches are able to dedicate a new building without debt. One of the first places to look for additional needed
money is the church building department of the denomination.
At present most church groups have many more applications
for aid than they can possibly grant. Nevertheless, the wisest
procedure is to investigate the possibilities of a denominational
loan and at least to find out what the conditions are. A self-
supporting church will probably soon be looking for other
sources.

Some churches have been fortunate enough to find individuals of wealth in the congregation who will lend the money
at a modest rate of interest. Security for the loan will probably

be a mortgage which pledges the real estate and building as security. In some instances, however, the lender prefers a note signed by the trustees of the church.

The next effort may be directed to a local bank. Church loans are not popular with some banks. Others who might like to lend the money are limited in their resources and cannot carry the obligation. The majority will, however, look with favor upon a church mortgage if they are satisfied with the financial reputation of the church. The term of years, the mortgage, and the rate of interest are included in the note and the terms of payment made plain. The rate of interest usually follows the money market at the time the mortgage is issued.

There is a very good reason why most banks prefer a trustee's note to a church mortgage. The traditional church building is not easily converted into residential or business buildings. If the congregation should desert it the bank will surely take a loss. A note endorsed by the trustees as individuals makes each trustee liable for payment. The bank in this case has some protection.

The next attempt would be to contact a lending agency and there are several in the church field. Some do not lend their own money but distribute the total amount up in mortgage bonds which are offered for sale to the public. The overhead charge on this type of financing because of the required publicity and the sometimes necessary clearance with the state agency is such that only mortgages of one-hundred thousand dollars or more would seem to be economically wise.

By another technique the church distributes the indebtedness by placing the notes or bonds with its own members. This is becoming a very popular method. It is well to point out the legal difference between selling bonds to your own members and selling them to the public. Most states require that bonds sold to the public be first cleared by the state securities commission. If the sale is only to its own members the church may be freed from this restriction.

Execution of this plan is usually left to local leadership and deserves a thorough study. The organization is similar to that of the every-member canvass. The teams are set up for solicitation, but they are not sent out to ask for money; they go to the membership to ask them to buy bonds which will pay good interest. The members help their own church and make profit on the transaction. The technique of payments and credit is as follows. (Used by courtesy of *Church Management*)

In this church program, the church has agreed that it would set aside out of its revenues two dollars per week for each one thousand dollars of the money it needed to borrow. This has been done by depositing that sum in its local depository bank. Against this assignment of revenue the church issues its bonds, payable at the bank out of the proceeds of such deposit. The bank is authorized as the agent of the church to pay the bonds as they mature without any further authorization from the church, so the bondholder has no further dealings with the church insofar as the bond is concerned after he purchases it, but present it to the bank on its due date. Some of the bonds mature each six months during the thirteen and one-half year period. The bonds all bear interest at the rate of five per cent per annum, the interest being payable semi-annually. The required deposit (two dollars per week per one thousand dollars) is calculated mathematically to be sufficient to retire the bonds and to pay the interest as the same comes due.

As stated before the Broadway Plan places the emphasis on the revenues of the church rather than upon the real property, as the security for the church obligation. This, it is thought, is the soundest approach to the problem of church indebtedness. Actually the revenues of the church are extremely constant, there being as little variation in them as in city or county tax revenues, or even public utility revenues. Consequently, if a church does not overextend itself in obligating its revenues, the constant flow of income affords the best security possible for a church indebtedness.

The bonds are sold principally to people who have a direct or an indirect interest in the church. As a matter of fact, a program cannot ordinarily be successful unless at least one-half of the bonds are absorbed within the membership itself. This oftentimes involves considerable sacrifice, but experience has shown that the church is actually strengthened by its endeavor in this respect.

8 | THE ERECTION OF NEW BUILDINGS

A GENERATION AGO THE ERECTION OF A NEW CHURCH IN the average American community was an event widely publicized. Today the number of new structures has reached such proportions that they are taken for granted. Many good churchmen are not conscious of the transformation in the concept of church building which has been taking place.

The Protestant churches have built thousands of new churches and the total expenditure runs to many millions of dollars. The movement started shortly after World War II and has continued without interruption through the present time and will probably continue for years ahead. This chapter is an attempt to show the trends in church architecture which have been taking place in this period and to help the church to plan not only the building but the procedures necessary for the successful church building effort. A part of this effort will of course be the financing of the new church building, discussed at length in chapter 7.

During World War II many churches received gifts and bequests for new church buildings. Their local budgets were relatively high and they started planning for the new buildings which had been needed for years. For a generation churches had been placing the emphasis on religious education yet the number of local churches which had erected buildings adequate for this program were very few indeed. Conceptions of educational needs were not very clearly defined. There had been little synchronization between the literature on church school organization and the building which had been erected. Most church schools had been departmentalized on paper but inadequate space separated classes and grades in the same departments. Logical administration of the work was difficult.

Architects employed by churches for the proposed post-war buildings were handicapped by the traditions of the past. Congregations wanted traditional churches. They wanted them to look like Gothic churches and any church which had a steep pitched roof and tower was considered Gothic. Church school rooms in these new structures were not placed for good administration or instruction and most classroom space was too small. Architects with creative ability were handcuffed by denominational officials who protested the liberties taken with the tradition.

Fortunately a scarcity of materials challenged many of these architectural plans. Prices went up—and up. Soon churches learned the sad news that the church they thought could be built for one-hundred thousand dollars would cost fifty thousand more. That architects were asked to change their plans to meet the financial situation was one of the best things that ever happened to church buildings. It gave churches a pause in which to think things over. Out of this delay came the idea that the churches should be built to fit the programs which churches had recently adopted rather than the needs of their fathers before them.

This brought into the picture the new American church building which is different from the church buildings of any other period or era. The buildings are different because the programs of the modern church are quite different from that of the old church. Our fathers built for worship. If a building cost one-hundred thousand dollars, seventy-five thousand went into the worship unit. The balance went into Sunday school classrooms, social rooms, boiler or furnace space, and miscellaneous uses. A few of the older churches provided an office or study for the minister, but most of the church offices were improvised in the pre-war period. Few had been designed for either study or administration. So-called ladies' parlors were as a rule barren rooms with stiff and uncomfortable furniture. This waiting period gave churches and architects an opportunity to sit down and rethink the type of building necessary for the program which the modern church had developed. In today's church at least one half of the cost goes into educational and social rooms. Many more feet of floor space go into these rooms than into the worship unit.

Out of this thinking period has evolved the new American church. Some would classify these new structures as either traditional or contemporary, but such distinctions are quite arbitrary. Most traditional churches now have some contemporary features and most contemporary buildings have enough of the traditional to make them recognizable as churches. Perhaps it would be better to describe all church architecture which incorporates the new features as "pragmatic" architecture, or "useful" architecture, or even "family" style for the churches of today are building for the entire family.

The Five Point Church

The church of today is a five-fold church. It builds (1) for worship, (2) for education, (3) for Christian fellowship, (4) for administration, and (5) for the parking of automobiles. In each of the first four areas there must be provision for storage space. The planning of a church resembles closely the planning of a home by a modern parent. A living room and dining room are necessary for the whole family, but so are other rooms as well. The children must have their rooms for sleep and play. If money is available, the adults may have additional space. There is an out-of-doors space for pleasure and gracious living and there must be space for the parking of automobiles. The criteria for judging each feature of the new American church are whether it adds to the program of the church and has an integral part in the life of the church family.

The selection of the site is important for the church building should be so located that it may easily be reached by most of the congregation. Accessibility and visibility from a busy highway are advantages, but the building itself should be located so that the noise and confusion of heavy traffic do not interfere. Avoid locations on dangerous highways and consider placing a traffic light near the church as a safety factor for children will learn easily to cross only with the green light.

Select a lot that is large enough for both the building to be erected and the anticipated outdoor activities, which will of course include the parking of cars. Churches of three hundred or more members should consider not less than two acres, five are better, and larger churches may well invest in ten or more acres of land for new building. Parking is not the only reason for the larger lot; the new buildings require more floor space than the old and churches are now recognizing the possibilities of using out-of-door space for social activities. A secluded corner for youth picnics is appreciated and other areas for open-air classes and committee meetings will prove valuable. Except in congested cities where real estate prices are prohibitive, churches should buy large areas of land for new buildings—three acres, five acres, ten acres, or more.

Some Basic Plans for Building

A look at some of the newer buildings will reveal some basic concepts regardless of the style of architecture. First, churches are no longer being built in several stories. The older churches started with the basement, which probably doubled as dining room and church school, and were "piled-up" in higher stories. The modern church is built close to the ground and occupies a much larger area of land. Today's churches are "spread-out" and probably a majority are built without a basement—or per-haps with a small basement which will house the heating plant of the church. Classrooms are definitely above ground. Wor-ship units have been pulled down to ground level and one or two steps at the most take one directly into the church. The tendency in churches is similar to that in ranch-style homes and the motive may be somewhat the same.

Among the contributing factors in this new architecture are

state and city building codes that more and more require all class and assembly rooms to be above ground. New public school buildings in every community seem to be stripped for educational purposes with classrooms close to the ground and brick, steel, and glass used to bring simplicity and utility to the building. Religious education buildings should follow this precedent.

The assumption that church and church school architecture are identical has caused confusion in church building and headaches for architects who are asked to design new educational buildings as additions to existing churches. As the purpose of the educational building differs from that of the worship building, so the concepts of design must differ accordingly. The shape, height of ceiling, windows, seats, chancel, organ, and color of the worship unit of the church should inspire communion with God. The purpose of the educational rooms is to provide adequate space and equipment for religious education and their design should follow the lines of the public schools. Classrooms need adequate floor space, good light, electrical outlets, and toilet facilities, but the construction may be very simple and the materials used need not be expensive. Many churches are getting good schools through the use of concrete or cinder blocks.

In planning a new church any committee needs to appreciate that they are really building two distinct units—one for worship and one for education—very different in concept. This may be the main reason for separating the educational building from the worship unit. But even if they are combined under one roof, they should be so constructed that the layman will appreciate which is the church and which is the school.

Building for Worship

One of the most commendable trends of the modern church is the new emphasis on worship—both in the increase of the practice of individual devotions and in the quality of public worship. The passage from one era to another is never marked by a definite line, but rather we pass through a shaded area. This is very evident as our Sunday services have been evolved from the "preaching service" to services of worship. The clergyman's technique has improved as has the vocabulary of the people. More and more we find that laymen are going to a service to worship rather than to listen to a sermon.

The great difference between listening to a sermon and worshipping God is reflected in both the policy of the minister and the people. The preacher becomes the priest of God and through music, liturgy, prayer, and the spoken word, tries to lead his people into an experience with God. The pastor plans his work so that he not only preaches a sermon, but conducts a service of worship. This does not give less emphasis to the sermon, but it does give larger meaning to the "conduct of worship."

This trend, so obvious in our churches, is definitely shown in the new architecture for worship. The new American church is seeking through architecture to build into its worship units those features which are conducive to prayer, meditation, and devotion.

Traditionally the worship unit of the church consisted of the nave where the worshippers were seated or stood, the chancel which accommodated the minister and the choir, and the transepts which were aisles crossing the church between the nave and the chancel. We are somewhat impoverished in our nomenclature for all parts of our new building. The "Church Building" is no longer a single unit. We easily designate "social rooms," but get confused in discussing the worship unit.

The nonconformist churches referred to the room where public services were held as "The Auditorium," but that term no longer describes the purpose of the place of assembly. Some years ago, we started to use the term "Sanctuary" to indicate the worship unit. In doing that, we ignored the historic "Sanctuary" of the church which was the holy of holies in the chancel. "Worship Unit" is probably the most definite term, but at the same time lacks the softness and imagination which is desirable. On the whole the term nave is best for that portion of the building where the people are seated for worship. This usage is supported by tradition, ecclesiastical favor, and exactness in meaning. The following features will be found in the nave and chancel design of most churches being constructed today.

1. The unit is placed near the ground level with but one or two steps into the narthex which in turn leads into the nave.

2. The worship unit of today is usually rectangular in shape. The old auditorium style with a central pulpit is rapidly passing from the scene; the Akron plan is no longer respected.

3. The entrance to the nave preferably is at the end opposite the chancel. Also it should open directly into the middle aisle at the back of the nave. This is very important.

4. There are several very good reasons for having an aisle running the length of the nave. Traditionally and usually it is a center aisle but very recently architects are designing churches with the main aisle off center. The purpose is to unite the choir on one side of the chancel. The worshipper coming through the door will have a vista down the long aisle to the symbols of worship in the chancel. Even before he passes through the door he will be conscious that he is in a house of worship. Protestants do not worship symbols but even the most austere of churches will include some. These would include the open Bible, the altar or communion table, cross and candlesticks with lighted candles, the pulpit and lectern, and letter symbols such as the Alpha and Omega.

The first inducements to worship when one enters the nave should be these symbols of God and His church. It is for this reason that the nave should have an aisle from foyer to altar and that churches should be rectangular in shape. There are others. The long aisle is suitable for liturgical processions, necessary for an orderly wedding march, and helpful for the church funeral. If the church is to be built for oratory and sermons alone, these arguments have little point. But when we build for worship, we see the need of center aisle.

5. When the "Pulpit Platform" becomes a chancel, it does

more than give standing room for the preacher. This feature in the church, however, does raise a controversy. More and more churches are introducing what is known as the "open chancel" or "divided chancel" but there are still many defenders of the central pulpit. The altar at the back of the chancel seems to be preferred to the communion table so common in the non-liturgical churches. But here again, there are some energetic supporters of the communion table. The proper location and seating arrangement for the choir is another dividing issue.

Arguments for the open chancel with the altar, lectern, and pulpit are many. The unbroken line leads the eye from the entrance to the nave to the altar and its symbols. The center pulpit, we are told, breaks that line and exalts the minister rather than his God. The usual arrangement of the choir in the open chancel is to continue the aisle through the choir so that its members sit facing one another.

Those who prefer the center pulpit insist that it puts the open Bible in the focal center. "The prophet back of the open Bible" is the greatest symbol of Protestantism they say. They also will present the argument that the pulpit-centered chancel makes possible the united choir preferable for choral singing.

Similarly there is plenty of discussion on whether churches should have communion tables or altars. This is not a matter of architecture alone, but involves theology as well. The communion table symbolizes Christian fellowship and has its origin in the Last Supper of Jesus with His disciples. The liberal churches which cannot accept the communion service as an ordinance may still keep the service of the Lord's Supper as a remembrance or a service of Christian fellowship. In the church, the communion table is usually so placed that it becomes a meeting place for the priest and the worshipper.

The altar is more ancient in its origin, but probably takes its physical proportions from the tombs of the Roman catacombs. Traditionally the place of sacrifice, the altar is retained by the historic churches where liturgy commemorates the death of Christ. In practice, the clergyman in such a church prays facing the altar with his back to the congregation. As a distributor of the body and blood of Christ, he stands between the altar and the congregation. In churches with communion tables, the clergyman administers the sacrament from behind the table facing the congregation.

In one chancel design, the table is placed at the back of the chancel, but spaced far enough from the wall so that the minister can face the congregation. More prevalent in Presbyterian churches than in some others, this arrangement combines the aesthetics of the altar church with the theological implications of the communion table.

There has been some reaction developing against the altar in both Roman Catholic and Protestant Episcopal churches. We are beginning to see a change in the position of the altar as the result of a new tolerance which recognizes that no one particular type or location alone has historical sanction. The tendency of the Roman and Episcopal churches to move the altar from the wall to a place where it brings the communicants closer to the priest is discussed by Walter Lowrie, an Episcopal clergyman in a book entitled *Action in Liturgy* (Philosophical Library).

> Although the Roman Catholics encounter some special difficulties in restoring the altar to its proper place, it is easier for them than it is for us. For we must remember that what we ill-advisedly call the Roman Church is the Church of Rome, or rather to use the New Testament expression, the Church in Rome. That church cannot regard it as an innovation to insist that the altar be in the midst, for so it is in every basilica where the Bishop of Rome or his vicar celebrates, and so it is also, in every church, big or little, which was built before a late period in the middle ages.

The congregation building a new church needs to be very wary of any recommendation for the choir as being the "approved" location. There are several variations in practice, any of which may be considered legitimate. In the location traditional with the evangelical churches the choir sits in the chancel behind the platform occupied by the clergy, the singers facing the congregation. Many churches still use this plan.

Another design which has become popular during the past generation was introduced by the Protestant Episcopal Church. The choir is seated on either side of the chancel in two sections facing each other across the altar aisle. This form is splendid for processionals, but offers some difficulty to directors who seem to prefer to have their choir in one unit.

To meet the objection of choir leaders some churches which have altars have placed the choir together back of the altar. A grille or screen is dropped to separate the choir from the rest of the chancel. The singers are somewhat dimmed so they are not on exhibition as with the usual centered choir. St. Paul's Episcopal Church of Cleveland Heights, Ohio and the First Presbyterian Church of Muncie, Indiana are good examples of this practice.

Other churches have sought to meet the difficulty by placing the choir in one side of the chancel and placing the organ console, organist, and director, concealed by a screen, on the opposite side. Effective so far as the music is concerned, this arrangement worries some sensitive individuals because the chancel lacks balance. To overcome this some architects are eliminating the center aisle in favor of an "off-center" aisle. The aisle leads to the altar so that the altar is similarly off-center. The larger side of the chancel seats the choir, the smaller the organ, organist, and choir director. Christ Episcopal Church in Cincinnati has placed its choir on one side of the chancel, but the organ console, organist, and director are in a side balcony from which the director may see his choir.

Another tendency is to remove the choir from the front of the church and place it in the rear balcony. This is fine for music but it is a poor position from which to lead the congregation in song. The director has his choir together with no sense of exhibition. Some discipline is required to keep the members interested in the service because of the temptation in their seclusion to read or sleep.

Another plan raises a real issue. Is the choir part of the ministry of the church or is it part of the congregation? In some Lutheran churches the choir is placed in the transept of the church at the congregational level or one step above it where it may definitely lead the congregation. The organ console, organist, and choir leader are placed across the church in the corresponding transept or in many instances with the choir. One church has moved its choir to the front pews of the nave with the members facing the altar. Here is a fine place from which to lead the congregation.

While there are differences of opinion regarding the place of the choir, there is general agreement on a point concerning the director. He should direct unseen by the congregation. All groups agree on this. A choir leader with his back toward the congregation and a baton waving before his choir is no longer welcome in the churches. The present popularity of several choirs in the church must also be taken into consideration. Is the added capacity for a massing of all of the choirs wise when such occurs only a few Sundays in the year? The answer here seems to indicate that the secondary choirs should find space in the transepts. A further discussion of the choir situation will be found in the chapter on "Music in the Church."

In planning a new church the space required for an organ must be estimated and put into the plans. If the church is to have a pipe organ considerable space is necessary, but no rule of thumb can determine exactly how much. While the director wants his choir in one unit, divided chambers are preferred for the larger organ. The best position probably is the front of the church— but not crowded into one corner or side. Any echo organ could then be placed in the rear. The organ console can be placed in any effective position for the organist, choir, or directory.

One pipe organ maker has given the following figures which can supply a somewhat limited rule for placement. In building a pipe organ, a minimum allowance should be one pipe for each seat in the church. Double and triple the allowance is more satisfactory.

SPACE REQUIREMENTS

Seating Capacity		Minimum Space
200 seats		4' 6" x 8' x 10'
250 seats		5' 6" x 8' x 10'
300 seats		7' 0" x 9' x 10'
400 seats	one chamber	8' 0" x 10' x 10'
	divided chambers	6' 0" x 10' x 10'
		5' 0" x 10' x 10'
500 seats	one chamber	9' 0" x 10' x 10'
	divided chambers	6' 0" x 10' x 10'
		6' 0" x 10' x 10'
600 seats	one chamber	9' 6" x 10' x 10'
	divided chambers	6' 6" x 10' x 10'
		6' 6" x 10' x 10'
700 seats	one chamber	10' 0" x 10' x 10'
	divided chambers	6' 6" x 10' x 10'
		6' 6" x 10' x 10'
900 seats	one chamber	13' 0" x 13' x 18'
	divided chambers	9' 6" x 11' x 18'
		8' 6" x 11' x 18'

Other features in the worship unit include proper seating for the congregation, windows, lighting, and ventilation. Pews are still the accepted seating for the nave of the church, but some feel that they are the most uncomfortable type of seating ever devised. They do, however, offer the rigidity and straight lines which seem so necessary. The only competition at the present time is offered by theater chairs fastened tightly in rows with pew ends at the aisles. This seating arrangement is now being manufactured in a way that gives it the same rigidity as pews have.

Windows and lighting can be considered together. Though each has a literature of its own, both have a common purpose—the creation of the atmosphere of worship. Each contributes to the proper lighting of the church and traditionally and correctly a house of worship should not be too brilliantly lighted. Stained glass windows not only assure a soft light but they bring a symbolism to worship which is helpful. Electric lighting in the nave and chancel also serves and may be supplied from lantern fixtures or some other kind. This gives sufficient light for general purposes, but some directed light must fall on the pews to enable the worshippers to follow the hymns and litanies.

Church lighting must also serve as an adornment. Concealed barrels projected through holes in the ceiling may deliver the necessary light for worship and reading, but leave nevertheless the room barren and weak. A combination of visual fixtures and concealed light is usually desirable.

The style of the windows will be largely determined by the style of the church. Good stained glass windows will fit most any style of architecture, but are most essential in the traditional neo-Gothic or high ceilinged church. The education building should have translucent or transparent windows providing much natural light.

Rooms for Choir

The church choirs are rightly demanding adequate space in the building. The minimum would be sufficient room for the storing of vestments and the filing of music. Many feel that they have need also of practice rooms. This is a problem for the architect as the number of choirs in each church is multiplying. Then there is need of soundproof rooms for Sunday morning rehearsals. Here is one place where basement facilities can be adapted to the purpose and several churches have found their solution in this way.

Others prefer to have choir rooms above ground. The problem of soundproofing can be solved by thick masonry walls and ceiling. The problem of room for massed choirs is also reflected in the changing of the church worship unit. One recent tendency is to add choir space in one or both of the transepts.

Other Areas in the New Building

Of the social and recreational rooms, the dining room has long had a distinctive place in the church building. Congregational dining rooms and large kitchens are still needed. Like other rooms where people gather, they should be above ground level. The present tendency is to combine the dining room space with other fellowship activities. A common practice is to have a kitchen at one end and a stage for dramatics at the other. Under the stage there is space for storing the chairs and tables when rooms are used for basketball or other physical activities.

The church parlor has also become a must in the modern church. Some may call it the Ladies' Parlor but its use is larger than that. It is the luxury room with heavy carpets and well-upholstered chairs and can be used for receptions, mid-week lectures, group parties, and as a classroom on Sunday. A kitchenette for the preparation of lunches is almost an essential.

Many churches now feel the need of small worship chapels in addition to the large worship unit. This need not be large, but it must be located near the street so individuals passing who feel the need may enter easily for prayer and meditation. Worth all the affection lavished upon it, this small chapel for many will be the holy of holies and will be sought for small weddings, funerals, worship services for small groups, and prayer cells.

Finally the need for club rooms for both boys and girls is inherent in our present educational architecture. Most rooms are planned for double service and clubs meet in rooms intended for the corresponding age groups in the church school. Boy Scouts, Camp Fire Girls, and other specialized activities require spaces of greater utility than the classrooms offer. Wood-working shops offer splendid opportunities for adult hobbies. While it is preferable that even these rooms be above ground, if a church does have a basement they can be assigned to this less desirable space.

Air Conditioning

More and more, air conditioning and cooling become a necessity for the church building. Most churches in the south have some kind of cooling system. The churches in the north have been more reluctant because of the few warm days and the high cost of installation.

The simplest form of air conditioning of course is found in the single-package window coolers and these have been developed to a size sufficient to cool large sanctuaries. A more complete central system reaches all parts of the building through ducts installed in the walls and the floors and a church with hot air heating already has this first unit for air cooling and screening available. Very recently there has been a new interest in cooling a church by pumping cold water through the pipes of a warm water heating system. The earlier objections of condensation seem to have been overcome through the use of fans blowing through the radiators. If this plan proves acceptable, there unquestionably will be a new impetus for air conditioning in churches which have resisted it because of the cost of installation.

Where air conditioning does not seem practical, churches can do a much better job than at present by installing fans for air circulation. In many instances the real problem is not temperature but circulation.

Bells and Carillons

Our grandfathers installed bells in their churches and our fathers thought them unnecessary, but today bells of one kind or another are coming back to the church. We are using the term *bells* in a very broad sense for many of the installations are synthetic. The best way to explain the situation is to start with the most modest installation.

Some churches—but not many—are installing single bells for the call to worship. Other are using record-playing systems which ring out the bells through loudspeakers located in the towers of the church. Good records are available and if the record player is efficient, the results can be pleasing. Similarly, organ chimes played from the keyboard are amplified from the tower electronic system.

Various kinds of magnetized wires and tubes are used to reproduce the sound of bells from keyboard or records. The argument for such a system is reliability of tone since true bells are difficult to tune and are affected by weather conditions. A very popular system of a generation ago used "tubular" bells played from the organ console or by an automatic device. All automatic systems can be connected with timeclocks to strike the hour of the day or to give sacred concerts when desired.

Some carillons of real bells are being installed, though not many. The distinction between chimes and a carillon seems to lie in the number of bells. A set of twenty-three or more cast bells are called a carillon. For fewer than twenty-three, the term chimes is correct. There were an estimated ninety-eight true bell carillons in the United States and Canada in 1956. Installations are expensive—the replacement cost of the carillon in Riverside Church, New York City, would approximate one million dollars.

Just what constitutes a bell has been a matter of debate and litigation for many years. Even the Federal Trade Commission has entered the discussion. Has a "bell" a definite pear shape? Will any hollow tube which produces tones when struck by a hammer or instrument be a "bell"? Does the definition include the magnetized metal rod which gives out bell-quality tones? Much more tolerance in defining a bell is used today than earlier and possibly each of these and various other forms of tone creation will be included in the definition. It is pretty well conceded today that an electronic instrument is an organ and that an electronic system of creating bell tones is a carillon.

Using the Out-of-Doors

The term *out-of-doors* naturally includes parking space, but there are other uses. Communities are now demanding and rightly so that there be a good clear area around a church building. City codes specify the number of feet back from the curb, the number of feet between the church and adjoining buildings, etc. Parking space is usually based on the seating capacity of the church. Commercial lots usually allow two hundred square feet per car, but for church lots three hundred square feet should be the minimum. The parking lot will of course need supervision. During the hours of services, the direction should be under the ushers. If the church has a good parking area available, the entrance from the lot will be almost a main entrance; the building should be erected with this in mind.

The out-of-doors space can mean other activities. If space is available a shady place can be provided for open-air meetings of classes and committees and for young people to have their wiener roasts. A rose garden is always attractive and will provide a space for summer weddings. The old-timers were more sensible in using the out-of-doors than are modern congregations. They not only found places for their horses but also for picnic tables and the games for the young which were very much in evidence in many parts of the country two generations ago.

Good Educational Rooms

The tremendous amount of church building during the past decade has established some very definite principles as to what makes a good church building. The departures from the past may seem extreme to many, but the spirit of exploration is to be commended. If God speaks through creative minds He can be successfully worshipped in temples of various concepts and design. Whether the building is traditional or contemporary, modern practice decrees that it should have certain basic features. A building placed close to ground level on a large area of land with stairs unnecessary for entrance and an altar or communion table fixed as the focal center of worship at the end of a center aisle can easily be incorporated in any period design. Similarly, failure to recognize valid trends in school design may make a new educational building obsolete before it is built.

An educational building, even though the entire church be under one roof, requires a different type of architecture than that part which houses the worshippers. Note the floor plans displayed here. One does not have to be an artist or designer to see that the educational wing is built from a different pattern. The room for worship, commonly called the nave, may be high, but the educational rooms have low ceilings. The worship unit may have stained glass; the educational wing has clear windows. The contrast of the interior is still greater. The educational and social rooms are well-lighted, have warm floors, attractive walls, blackboards, coat racks, and toilet facilities.

The best pattern for the church school building is a recently constructed public school. Some are one or two stories in height, but higher buildings are out. Inside the school building informality has replaced the old rigidity. These are good patterns for the church school rooms.

School Organized by Departments

At one place the church educational building departs from the public school pattern. While public education is administered on the basis of grades, the church school is organized by departments. Some will recall efforts of a generation ago when leaders sought to have the church schools organized on a grade basis. They did not last very long, perhaps because too many churches had very small grades. Out of that system has grown the departmental church school.

It is most important to remember this when planning a church school building. The first essential of organization is that the departments should meet in their own room, surrounded by four solid walls. Many churches of a generation ago offered separate, wall-enclosed rooms for each grade. This system of departmentalization goes at it in a different way. Each department should have its own area, enclosed by solid walls (not curtains), preferably divided into class rooms where classes meet by grades. The opening worship is by departments, the study and discussion classes by grades. If individual class rooms are not available, dividers may be used. But, if possible, keep the department together.

Of just what does the department consist? It varies with denominations and local churches. Here is a traditional arrangement.

PRE-SCHOOL GROUPS
Toddlers (Nursery Roll) ages 1½-2
Nursery age 3
Kindergarten ages 4, 5

PRIMARY DEPARTMENT
Grades 1, 2, 3 ages 6, 7, 8

JUNIOR DEPARTMENT
Grades 4, 5, 6 ages 9, 10, 11

JUNIOR HIGH DEPARTMENT
Grades 7, 8, 9 ages 12, 13, 14

SENIOR HIGH DEPARTMENT
Grades 10, 11, 12 ages 15-20

YOUNG PEOPLE'S DEPARTMENT
Beyond school age

ADULT DEPARTMENT
Ages 22 and up

Some leaders have been questioning during the past few years whether this is the best form of departmental organization. At least one denomination (The Disciples of Christ) is adapting its lesson material to two grade levels per department. When this is done the school ages would be organized as below.

DEPARTMENT 1 Grades 1 & 2	DEPARTMENT 4 Grades 7 & 8
DEPARTMENT 2 Grades 3 & 4	JUNIOR HIGH DEPARTMENT Grades 9 & 10
DEPARTMENT 3 Grades 5 & 6	SENIOR HIGH DEPARTMENT Grades 11 & 12

This kind of department organization seems to fit the needs of the middle-sized church school. Very small schools probably fit well into the three-grade department, while large schools require a completely graded arrangement. The two-grade department certainly fills the needs of the average school and simplifies the architecture.

Each department must have a place to assemble for study and today we are trying to supply this need within the department walls, getting double use of each room every Sunday. Further multiple use may be secured by holding all the social activities of the department meet within its walls. The simplicity of the two-class assembly is illustrated in Exhibit I. The two grades meet for their worship service. When they go into class sessions a flexible partition is pulled across the room and two good-sized classrooms are available. The portable partitions are not noiseproof but inasmuch as the department is enclosed in solid walls, no one outside the department will be disturbed. With the three-grade department plan the same double use is available as shown in the plan in Exhibit II, but it is not quite as convenient.

The total utility of this kind of department room has not been fully appreciated. The addition of a Pullman kitchen in one of these rooms equips it for social purposes. Several age groups can meet at the same time without disturbing one another. This development seems so logical that it doubtless will find increasing favor in the newer churches.

Economizing on Assembly Rooms

Not every church can be sold on this new economic arrangement of departmental rooms. Some will insist on separate assembly rooms for the worship session. A separate assembly space for each department at present day costs is an expensive luxury used only about fifteen or twenty minutes each Sunday. If the church feels it must have such rooms, the assembly periods may be staggered. For instance, the primary department and the junior department can use the same room if one department opens its work with the assembly while the second holds its worship serv-

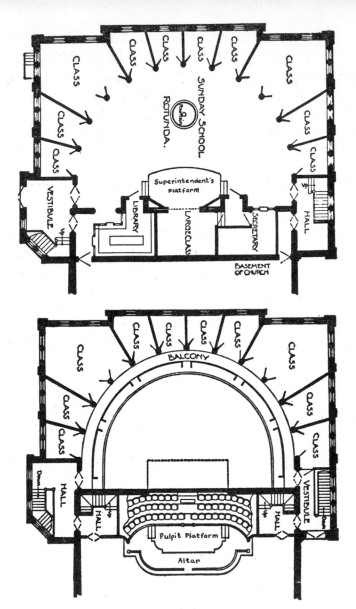

The much-maligned Akron Plan, while not suited to to-day's needs, performed a functional role in its day. Conceived to meet the needs of the International Lessons, it permitted the single-assembly for opening exercises, and rapid division into the respective classes. Main floor is at top; balcony, below. (Illustrations from *Housing the Church School*, by Marian Lawrence, Westminster Press, 1911.)

ices at the close of the session. If by chance the church has two school sessions, four usages can be made of each double purpose room each Sunday. That begins to make sense.

There is a tendency today for the larger schools to by-pass the departmental system entirely and to organize by grades. The worship session and the instruction session are held in the one classroom. With this has come the trend to larger classes. In the junior and senior groups classes of twenty-five to thirty certainly are acceptable. When a school reaches a size where there are several classes to each grade, each class may have separate rooms. Or, if desired, the three classes may meet in the same room. Separators are not necessary and may really create confusion.

Orderly Arrangement of Space

The first principle stated above is that each department shall have its own space. The second principle is close to the first. Department rooms must be so arranged that administration is easy. The little children should have the areas nearest to the nave. If a tower joins the educational unit with the worship unit, the nursery and kindergarten should be located so that parents may conveniently place their children in the proper rooms before going to the service. After the little children have been placed, arrange the other departments in order by age groups. Let the primary follow the kindergarten, the junior follow the primary, etc. The younger children should be on the ground floor; the older age departments may be located on the second floor.

These two principles are seriously violated in many present day churches. We find the classes in the same department meeting in different parts of the building. It is not unusual to find two grades of the junior department meeting in the dining room while the third grade is meeting in the choir loft. For a generation our educational leaders have been discussing and perfecting the departmental school, yet the arrangement of the building has limited the administration of the school. This limitation must be removed in the new buildings of today.

The third requisite for a good educational building is that each department shall have adequate floor space and equipment for the best work. After having housed little children of kindergarten age in a ten by ten feet room in the basement, some churchmen experience a shock when they learn that educational authorities feel that these children need thirty-five square feet each. Primary children get along with slightly reduced space, juniors still less, high school students are reduced still more. Adults' class rooms, they tell us, need ten square feet per person.

Thus the modern authorities would reverse the old reasoning of churches. For generations the adults were given the largest space, next the youths, the little children got least of all. But this larger floor area is entirely unnecessary unless the leaders of children plan to use it. New educational directors who use these figures for the kindergarten, yet seat the children around two tables at one end of the room, have gained space but are not qualified to use it. Program must go with space.

Equipment

Equipment varies with the age groups. Toilet facilities and furnishings should be based on the group ages. If the nursery accepts babies under fifteen to eighteen months, there will be need of cribs, mattresses, linens, pads, bottle warmers, play pens, a rocking chair for the leader, and a place for caring for wraps. All children's departments should have warm, clean floors. Carpets are desirable if the church has the resources for their necessary cleaning. If carpets are not available a good rubber or plastic tile is recommended.

In the toddler's department (from fifteen to eighteen months up to three years) there should be a place to hang their clothes. Toys are needed in both of these children's departments: for the little ones, washable dolls and animals; for the toddlers, sand boxes, slides, trains, climbers, rocking horses, educational blocks.

In the kindergarten the use of tables will begin, but here no children are expected to spend the entire session in chairs. Play-work and handwork have their place. Blackboards and book

shelves will first be seen in the primary department. Chairs will
be graded for the age group. The seating height of chairs for first
and second grade should be eleven or twelve inches; tables,
twenty-two inches; for the third grade select chairs of fourteen
inches and tables of twenty-four inches. The junior department
should be equipped with sixteen-inch chairs. A worship center
may be placed in the primary; it is essential in the junior and
higher departments.

Every department needs easy access to toilet facilities and the
children from each department should have exit directly into a
corridor making it unnecessary to pass through other departments. Each age group in the church should feel that it has its
own area. These department rooms can be used not only for
classes but also for the social activities of the groups. Multiple use
is the keynote in the modern educational building.

When we reach the high school age a different room arrangement may be desirable. The youth lounge which combines classroom with social room fits well into the youth program. When
equipped with a kitchenette the lounge can house most of the
youth activities.

In addition to the youth lounge a church parlor is needed in
most churches. I prefer to call this a church parlor rather than a
ladies' parlor as it should not be the property of any one group.
It can well be the room for the meetings of the ladies' groups,
for small wedding receptions, and it should be made available to
other groups requiring a touch of comfort in their meetings. This
may be the luxury room of the church and must be equipped for
preparing lunches and snacks.

None of these smaller lounges can take the place of the main
dining room and kitchen, essentials in most churches. Keeping
the multiple use idea, the dining room can double as a social room
for larger parties and receptions. With a stage at one end it is
suitable for dramas and entertainments. This use puts the kitchen
and dining room in the area of education as well as Christian
fellowship.

Architecture & Church Building

ATKINSON, C. H., *Building and Equipment for Christian Education*. National Council, 1956.

CONOVER, E. M., *Building for Worship*. National Council, 1945.

———, *The Church Building Guide*. National Council, 1946.

HARRELL, W. A., *Planning Better Church Buildings*. Convention, 1957.

LEACH, W. H., *Protestant Church Building*. Abingdon, 1948.

McCLINTON, K. M., *The Changing Church*. Morehouse-Gorham, 1957.

MILLS, E. D., *The Modern Church*. Praeger, 1956.

SCOTFORD, J. R., *The Church Beautiful*. Pilgrim, 1945.

———, *When You Build Your Church*. Doniger & Raughley, 1956.

SHEAR, J. K., ed., *Religious Buildings Today*. Dodge, 1957.

SHORT, E., *A History of Religious Architecture*. Norton, 1951.

WATKIN, W. W., *Planning and Building the Modern Church*. Dodge, 1951.

9 | CARE OF THE CHURCH BUILDING

IN MOST CHURCHES THE CARE OF THE CHURCH BUILDINGS rests with the house or buildings and grounds committee. The actual work is done largely by the custodian and his assistants. The following check lists show the responsibility of the committee and the custodians for the various parts of the buildings and grounds. While the paid caretaker must be eternally vigilant in watching for defects in the building as indicated in the list, he is not usually responsible for making important repairs or alterations. For example, if he finds that a gutter is leaking and reports it to the house committee, the job will be passed on to a roofer. If a wall needs painting, the custodian will pass on this information to the committee. While it is his obligation to see that faucets are functioning and that the kitchen drain is open, he has no responsibility to do more than minor plumbing jobs to restore the equipment to working order.

Church Maintenance Check List

OUT OF DOORS

Sidewalks. Sweep in summer, shovel snow in winter; watch for breaks in cement, etc.

Drives. Clean as necessary, watch breaks in cement; if slag drive, keep weeded, etc.

Lawn. Keep fertilized, watered, mowed, and trimmed; rake leaves in fall.

Trees and shrubbery. Trim as necessary, keep clear of litter; water and fertilize.

Curbs. Watch for weeds and grass between lawn and curb; keep cleaned.

Parking Area. Keep directional signs in place; if cement, watch for breaks; if slag, clear out weeds.

BUILDING CUSTODIAN DAILY WORK SCHEDULES

DATE _____

WORK AREA

Column headers (tasks):
- EMPTY WASTEBASKETS — ASHTRAYS
- DUST WW — (FURN.)
- CLEAN TOILETS — URINALS
- CLEAN BASINS
- TOILET PAPER
- TOWEL BOXES
- SOAP
- CLEAN DRINKING FOUNTAINS
- DUST RADIATORS
- SWEEP
- VACUUM (BARE FLOOR)
- VACUUM (CARPET)
- DAMP MOP
- MACHINE BUFF (BRUSH)
- MACHINE BUFF (STEELWOOL)
- MACHINE SCRUB
- VACUUM (WET PICKUP)
- SPOT WAX
- MACHINE STRIP — REWAX
- HOSE DOWN
- VACUUM (FIXTURES — WALLS)
- CLEAN BLINDS
- CLEAN LIGHT FIXTURES
- REPLACE BULBS
- POLISH METAL TRIM
- WASH WINDOWS (INSIDE)

EMPLOYEE

AREA:

JOB COMPLETED

AREA:

JOB COMPLETED

AREA:

JOB COMPLETED

AREA:

JOB COMPLETED

SPECIAL ASSIGNMENTS: _____

FV-CGF(76.360)H

152

Roofs. Need almost constant attention, especially the gutters and downspouts; remove leaves and debris, flush out sewer connections when needed.

Walls. Need frequent inspection (water is the enemy of all exterior walls); check tuck pointing of brick and stone, paint on wooden walls.

Windows. Need care from within and without; should be opened for fresh air periodically, but should be kept closed during storms.

Outdoor Sign. Watch for falling letters, breaks in glass, condition of paint; clean periodically.

Outdoor Lighting. Watch for burnt out bulbs.

Painted Walls. Watch for breaks and spots; wash as needed.

Ceilings. Watch for leaks.

Lighting. Watch for burned out bulbs; clean fixtures.

Windows. Watch for missing glass, case of opening and closing; wash as needed.

Doors. Insure opening and closing without noise or friction; check knobs and locks, oil hinges and locks.

Pews. Dust before each service (full instructions for dusting will be found on another page); thoroughly clean once a year.

Floors. Light cleaning every week, thorough cleaning twice a year (see instructions on another page for various types of flooring).

Chancel Furniture. Dust before each service; thorough cleaning once a year.

Organ. Dust Console before each service; close keyboard after each playing so that dust will not fall between keys.

Brasses and Altarware. Dusted before each service unless done usually by church altar guild.

Pew Cushions. Use vacuum cleaner once a month; watch for evidence of pests.

Baptismal Font. Dust exterior before each service; clean and polish metal container before each use.

Baptistry. Clean and Drain after each use; use warm water and soap to remove scum from walls.

Heating Units. See that they are functioning noiselessly.

Air Conditioning Unit. See that it is working noiselessly.

THE EDUCATIONAL UNIT

Walls and Ceilings. Check for breaks and leaks; dust frequently, wash as necessary (may offer some problems because of pictures and maps).

Windows. Wash as needed, check cords and weights.

Floors. Dust each week, clean thoroughly twice a year; use vacuum cleaner once a week on rugs.

Chairs and Tables. Dust before each use, clean thoroughly once a year. (Unless social meetings are held between classes, keep chairs in order during week.)

Pianos. Have tuned; dust before each use, keep keyboard covered, clean keys with damp cloth.

Assembly Rooms. Dust every week; thoroughly clean and wash twice a year. (If not used between assemblies, keep chairs in order.)

Nursery and Kindergarten. Dust but do not disturb various items placed in position by teachers.

FELLOWSHIP UNITS

Kitchen. Occasional thorough cleaning; see that all water faucets and drains function properly.

Dining Rooms. Walls, floors, and tables all need attention; store chairs and tables. (Floor is important and needs much care; walls need dusting and cleaning.)

Windows. Usual attention, including washing; make sure that sash cords and weights are in good condition.

Church Parlors. Use vacuum cleaner weekly; dust furniture and paneling.

Hallways. Keep clear of chairs, desks, and other obstructions; keep floors clean and carpets free from tears; reset loose linoleum or tiles; keep lights bright and working.

WASHROOMS AND TOILETS

Walls. Keep clean.

Coat Hooks and Racks. Install if lacking.

Towels. Make clean towels, paper or cloth, available.

Toilet Paper. Insure adequate supply.

Lights. Keep bright and working.

Mirrors. Clean as needed.

Toilets and Basins. Insure sufficient water pressure so that toilets flush properly; check for leaks.

OFFICE AND STUDY

Books. Dust shelves and books; allow minister to arrange.

Desks. Dust once a week, polish periodically.

Windows. Wash and insure easy opening.

Other Furniture. Dust weekly.

Sacristy. Dust room and walls weekly. (The cleaning of worship items is usually left to other hands.)

Choir Room. Dust and clean weekly. (The care of the vestments belongs to the choir.)

Heating and Air Conditioning

There is no uniform method of heating the church, nor is there any single approved method of air conditioning. Many times the cooling system uses the same pipes for circulation as does the heating system. Skilled help is needed to keep the mechanics of the process in good condition, but some very definite instructions should be given to the custodian.

Fuel. Provide some plan for warning in advance when supply is low.

Ashes. Remove promptly to out-of-doors, have fireproof area for their deposit. (A mechanical lift will help custodian raise ashes to surface for collection.)

Chimneys and Flues. Check for leaks.

Planning. Chart engagements for week and proper temperatures for each part of building.

Fire Doors. Keep closed at all times except when used for passage.

Boilers. Have annual cleaning by qualified tradesman who will report defects.

There are in use three general methods of air conditioning: the packaged conditioners which come intact and are placed on the floor in various locations; the general refrigeration method used in public buildings and business; the smaller refrigerating system which does not operate at all times but can be started several hours or days in advance of need.

Packaged System. Turn on at a time sufficient to reduce temperature in room.

General Refrigeration. Keep motors or thermostat on at all times.

Smaller Refrigeration Unit. Estimate number of hours of refrigeration necessary to reduce temperature to degree desired.

Most of the larger installations today have valves which make it possible to direct heat selectively into building units. The custodian will need instruction in the proper use of these valves.

WIRING AND LIGHTS

Bulbs. Keep supply of the varying sizes; replace burned out bulbs.

Wall Switches. Keep supply on hand for replacement purposes.

Loose Wires. Avoid if possible, otherwise place to minimize danger of tripping.

Extension Ladder or Bulb Remover. Necessary to replace bulbs in ceilings.

Capacity of Wiring. Check current load; re-wire if necessary to avoid overheating.

The Parsonage

The instructions here are for the minister rather than the church custodian. Usually the minister cares for the house in which he lives and makes requests for repairs or new facilities as the need may arise. However, the trustees should keep in mind that the parsonage, manse, or rectory, as one may prefer to call it, is the property of the church and the church is responsible for its upkeep. Here are some items which need to be checked periodically.

Heating Systems.

Chimney and Flues.

Electric Wiring.

Roof.

Walls (especially those of masonry).

Floors.

Interior Walls (need for new paint or new paper).

Bills for Heating (to see if furnace is efficient).

Plumbing.

Church Building Insurance

One of the best ways to assure that your building is in good physical condition is to have periodic inspections by a reliable insurance appraiser. Fires take a heavy toll of churches and may be the first consideration, but there are other considerations and other types of insurance which are desirable.

Destruction by fire is mostly caused by overheating. The custodian or some other person forces the stove or furnace beyond its capacity and the result is that fire starts in partitions.

Defective wiring comes second as a cause of fires. Many custodians are not aware that there is a limited capacity to wire as there is to pipe. The wiring may have been sufficient when the church was first erected but the increasing use of the building has put a strain on the wiring which it cannot stand and so overheats, causing fires to start. Each year a limited number of church fires are started by natural lightning. The high spires and towers make churches good targets, but properly installed lightning protectors will reduce the hazard.

Lighted candles used in worship ceremonials also take their toll and must be used with caution. Do not permit children to march with candles in their hands. There are now available electric candles which may be safely used and these should be substituted for the wax or tallow ones.

Human carelessness is another cause of many church fires. Waste paper and other inflammable materials are permitted to accumulate in wastebaskets, corners, or stairways where a carelessly thrown match or cigarette may start a conflagration. Of course there is always danger of fire from arson. Some people are so depraved that they will set a flame to a church.

To be adequately protected against fire is a must for every church. The Standing Committee on Insurance of the United Church of Canada has sent to its churches the following recommendations on fire prevention.

Recommendations

1. At regular intervals secure from competent appraisers information as to the actual value of the church buildings and contents and make necessary adjustments in the amount of insurance carried.

2. Compile and keep up to date inventory of contents of all church buildings.

3. Arrange for regular inspection of heating equipment by competent persons. Also inspect condition of chimneys at regular intervals.

4. Arrange for regular inspection of electrical wiring by competent persons, with particular attention to capacity of fuses. (A reduction in rate may be allowed if certificate of approval is secured from the local electrical authorities.)

5. See that a metal-lined cabinet or metal box is provided for the storage of mops, brooms, cleaning cloths, etc., except if such equipment is kept in a fireproof boiler room. (Reduction in rate may be allowed if this precaution is taken.)

6. Particular attention should be given to cleanliness about church premises. Papers, trash, etc., should not be allowed to accumulate. If coal is used for heating, ashes should be deposited only in metal containers before removing them from the premises. No accumulation of dust should be permitted, with special care in organ lofts. This area should be kept clean by those experts servicing the organ.

7. Determine the advisability of installing the requisite number of fire extinguishers suitable to your particular church building. (Reduction in rate may be secured for this precaution.)

8. It is very important that in the portions of buildings used for Sunday school purposes or for the accommodation of younger persons, exits be clearly indicated by prominent signs.

9. Regardless of the number of agents placing insurance on the church's property, it is recommended that one agent be appointed to supervise, so that proper and uniform coverage is arranged.

10. It has been found advantageous by many congregations to so arrange an insurance schedule, that approximately the same amount in premiums is payable each year. This assists those responsible for making up the annual budget.

11. If more than one fire policy is in force on any one risk, care should be taken that all such policies are concurrent (i.e. —similar in range, form, and wording).

In these days of rising construction costs, the church should have periodical examinations to make sure that it is carrying full insurance on the building. Full insurance means the replacement cost, at present day prices, less depreciation. Co-insurance, in which the church agrees to keep the building insured at eighty or ninety per cent of the replacement value, is available to churches at a reduction in rate. Here are two examples which show that the church which does not carry all of the available insurance becomes a self-insurer in case of a loss.

EXAMPLE A

Church property with actual cash value (replacement cost less depreciation) at time of loss $100,000

Insurance to comply with 80% co-insurance of at least 80,000

Insurance carried for full compliance 80,000

Amount of loss 16,000

Collectible loss $\frac{80,000 \text{ (amt. of ins.)}}{80,000 \text{ (80\% of val.)}} \times 16,000 =$ 16,000

Insurance pays 16,000

EXAMPLE B

Church property with actual cash value (replacement cost less depreciation at time of loss	$100,000
Insurance to comply with 80% co-insurance of at least	80,000
Insurance carried ($\frac{5}{8}$ of compliance)	50,000
Amount of loss	16,000
Collectible loss $\dfrac{50,000 \text{ (amt. of ins.)}}{80,000 \text{ (80\% of val.)}} \times 16,000 =$	10,000
Insurance pays	10,000
Uncollectible loss $\frac{3}{8}$ or	6,000

In insurance terminology the word "building" includes storm doors and windows, door and window screens, shutters, fences and all permanent fixtures, including bells, pews, altars, fonts, but excluding movable property such as organs, organ blowers, chairs, desks, etc.

Other Building Insurance

While fire insurance is a "must" for churches there are other types of insurance which also give valuable protection. These would include public liability and property damage, contingent liability insurance, plate glass and stained glass window insurance, communion set and altarware insurance, and insurance on equipment such as projectors, typewriters, and business machines.

Care of Floors

The proper care of floors is so important that we go into it in detail. A good wood floor will last for several generations if it has proper care. When a new floor is laid the treatment consists of four separate operations. The first is sanding to make the surface smooth. Next is cleaning. Neither soap nor water is used in this process. There are cleaners available which do a good job. Next, a filler is applied. This sinks into the grain of the wood and destroys any porosity. Then comes the waxing. This is usually the final process though some prefer to add a fifth process and apply a dressing.

In caring for an old floor this process will be in part duplicated. It will need periodic cleaning. Do not use water or soap. Do not use grease nor oil. Use one of the several dust-laying preparations and then sweep it up with a cotton sweeping brush.

Some churches allow their floors to become so dirty that when cleaned it is necessary to sand. Where this is true, the floor must be again cleaned, sealed, and waxed after the sanding. If it is watched carefully, the sanding may be avoided by sealing and waxing every six months to a year.

Other Floors

Many other types of flooring are used in the churches of to-day. Given the care they deserve, most types will serve for years. Probably asphalt tile is the most commonly used next to wood. The first step in the care of asphalt tile is to know what not to use. Grease or oils act as solvents and eventually tear down the floor. The steps to be followed are these.

1. Clean the flooring with any one of the neutral cleaners now on the market. Apply with a clean mop, then squeeze off or wipe dry. Soaps and powders are poor cleansing agents because they cannot be rinsed.

2. After cleaning, seal the floor with one of the new synthetic liquid sealers. The seal protects against moisture, dirt, and grease.

3. Apply a good emulsion wax.

Next to asphalt tile, linoleum and rubber are popular. The general rules for cleaning these are identical with the suggestions for asphalt tile. Alkaline solvents if used for any period of time will destroy the tiles. The damage will show up much quicker in the case of asphalt or linoleum. Rubber resists misuse and then, finally, goes to pieces all at once. Many churches blame the quality of the rubber when the responsibility really belongs with the caretaker and the materials with which he has been supplied. Vinyl floor tile, a comparatively new product, will give many years of service.

Terrazzo and cement are also used in churches. Terrazzo is a cement floor in which marble chips have been imbedded. It can be a very beautiful floor. Cement is probably never a beautiful floor but it can give long service if properly treated. For these floors:

Avoid acids, abrasive powder cleaners, and alkaline soaps.

Avoid spirit wax sealers.

Avoid varnish sealers.

Follow these instructions:

Clean with a safe chemical cleaner.

Seal with a penetrating (not a surface) filler or seal.

Maintain with a non-greasy dressing.

The sealing is very important with the terrazzo and cement floors. A proper seal will prevent discoloring or chipping and the white powder which so often appears on cement floors. After sealing, the application of a good dressing will keep such floors in good condition for many years.

Fire Safety Check Sheet

HEATING SYSTEM

( ) Is the furnace enclosed in a separate room with fire resistive partitions and ceiling?

( ) Is a self-closing, fire resistant door provided at the opening into the furnace room?

( ) Are metal containers provided for the storage of ashes?

( ) If oil burner, gas fire, or mechanical stoker is provided, are fully automatic controls installed?

( ) Is all equipment including chimney flues, smokepipes, and hot air ducts:

(a) in good serviceable condition and well maintained?
(b) properly insulated and separated from all combustible material by a safe distance?
(c) regularly serviced by a qualified inspector at least once a year?

EXITS

( ) Are exit doors marked with signs and lights?

( ) Do the exit doors of rooms of fifty or more capacity open in the direction of exit traffic?

( ) Are all doors at required exits provided with panic bolts or kept unlocked during occupancy?

KITCHEN

( ) Is the range safely installed away from combustible material and nearby floor protected?

( ) Is there a hood above the range and is it vented to the outside?

( ) Is the vent pipe insulated or separated from combustible material by a safe distance?

( ) Is a fire extinguisher provided and is it in good order?

( ) Has the electric refrigerator been serviced during the current year?

FIRE EXTINGUISHERS

( ) Are fire extinguishers provided on each floor not more than one hundred feet distant from each exit?

( ) Does each extinguisher carry a tag showing the date of last charge?

LIGHTNING

( ) Is the building, particularly the steeple, spires, and towers, properly equipped with a system of lightning rod protection and does it carry the Master Label of Underwriters' Laboratories, Inc.?

( ) Are all fuses on lighting and small appliance circuits of not more than 15 ampere capacity?

SPRINKLERS

( ) Where automatic sprinklers or standpipe and hose are installed, have these been thoroughly inspected within the past year?

ELECTRICAL INSTALLATIONS

( ) Are all alterations of electrical installations made by qualified electricians?

RUBBISH

( ) Are decorations of combustible nature provided in any room used for assembly purposes, and if so, have they been fireproofed?

( ) Is the collection and disposal of trash safely handled in a manner avoiding hazardous accumulations at any point?

( ) Are spaces beneath the stairs free from accumulations or storage of any combustible material?

Care of Church Building

McCLINTON, K. M., and I. W. SQUIER, *Good Housekeeping in the Church.* Morehouse-Gorham, 1952.

VINCENT, R. F., *The Industrial Bookkeeping Manual.* National Foremen's Institute, 1945.

WHITMAN, R. C., *Church Maintenance Manual.* Doubleday, 1945.

10 | THE MINISTER
AS AN EXECUTIVE

THE PASTOR OF THE CHURCH SHOULD BE THE HEAD OF THE organized work. He should lead the church in the making and execution of its program. There will be protests to this from two points of view. First there will be the protest that neither the constitution nor tradition of the local church gives the minister such authority. Second will be the protest from those who believe that the pastor should keep to his preaching and let the laymen take care of the organizational work.

There is logic in both of these attitudes, but the fact remains that any good organization must have a leader who is able to visualize the program the local church needs and has the ability to organize the program and direct the workers. The same people who insist that the minister should keep to his preaching and let the layman handle the financial affairs will be the first to place the blame for falling resources upon the minister.

There are many ministers who have no desire for leadership and would prefer that it be handled in some other way. They plead that they are not required to give this kind of leadership and legally they are right. But churches must have leadership and the minister usually is the only person available who has been exposed to the whole religious program sufficiently to see the possibilities of the local parish and in many churches is the only person available required to give full time service to the local churches. He is the natural interlocutor between the denomination and the local community; he is the logical person to make contacts with the other communions.

Of course the technique of administering a small church where the minister is the entire staff is quite a different proposition than in a large church with associates. But whether by constitutional authority or by personality, the minister is the chief executive of his local church.

The traditional training for the ministry is hardly ideal for an executive. It is scholastic and marks him as a student and is so specialized that it sets him apart from his fellow men. He is to proclaim the truth and preach the gospel. The organized church must do these things but its program is not merely the pulpit voice but the creation of the Christian community.

It has been said that the three qualifications for the minister executive are these: (1) He must like people; (2) he must be able to put them to work; (3) he must be able to put them to work at something they consider worth while.

To some it will seem strange that there could be a clergyman who does not like people, yet there have been many such ministers. They dislike all human contacts and prefer to proclaim the scholastic theological message. This type of man may force others to work in his program but he is not a good executive. The good pastor, however, has the first qualification for a good executive. He likes people and likes to work with them. He is always looking for new recruits for his program not only because the program is in itself worth while but also because of the effect it will have on the individuals who become interested in the program.

The third point is becoming increasingly important simply because of the abundance of good community programs which compete with the church. The average useful person is crowded with committee work, club work, lodge work, and church work. Just what can the church offer to secure his time? The chief attraction may be the quality of the program in which he is to engage. A person may not react favorably to petty tasks given just to test his loyalty.

One minister sought to enlist the services of a contractor as chairman of the "property" committee. He gladly accepted and took the job seriously. To familiarize himself with the church property, he sent some of his own men out to check the foundations, walls, roofs, etc., so that he could give a good report to the board on the physical property. When his report was presented he was rebuked by the chairman.

> You have evidently misunderstood the task given to you. Your committee is the property committee; your task is to see that the hymn books are picked up and put in the racks, and that the custodian takes care of his tasks and things of that nature.

Naturally the new chairman felt that his professional services were not needed in the church and resigned his chairmanship. There is a prevailing superstition that administrative procedures in church are contemporary in origin. As good a historian as John Knox disputes this.

> We are likely to suppose that the administrative work required in a first-century church was much more simple than in a modern congregation of the same size. But this supposition is probably mistaken. When a first century Jew or pagan decided to become a Christian, he became dependent upon a new community for supplying all his needs in a way in which the modern Christian, at any rate within the West, can scarcely imagine. The church had to assume almost total responsibility for the whole person of its members and for every aspect of their relations, with one another. In even the smallest congregation in even the earliest period every one of the concerns we have mentioned (and obviously we have not begun to exhaust the possibilities) would arise; and as congregations grew larger, as they rapidly did, the "business" of the church would become correspondingly more difficult and complex. When we remember that congregational meetings had to be planned, called and conducted, and that their actions must be recorded, communicated to those concerned, and actually implemented and carried out, we shall hardly wonder either that there should have been from the very beginning, and in great variety, "helps" and "governments" as the King James version translates the terms in I Cor. 12:28 or that of the offices of "bishop," and "deacon" became so important in the church of somewhat a later period. (From Chapter 1 of *The Ministry in Historical Perspectives*, Niebuhr and Williams, editors. Harper, 1956. By permission of the publishers.)

In the same volume we are told by George H. Williams in a chapter on the "Minister in the Later Patristic Period" of the detailed organization of the church which required seven degrees of ordination with special responsibilities for each degree: (1) Grave digger; (2) doorkeeper; (3) lector; (4) subdeacon; (5) deacon; (6) presbyter and (7) Bishop. Simplicity of administration was evidently not the rule in the churches of that period.

One problem is to realize that the work of the minister is to lead the Christian community into the moral and theological concepts of the Christian life. It is not merely one of prophetic ministry. During the evangelistic period in American history so much emphasis was placed on the preaching ministry that we lost the concept of "building the Christian community." Church buildings were constructed for preaching and that alone. Now we are conscious that the local church is more than a preaching station. The American period of evangelistic meetings did not rightly interpret the historic traditions of the church. Out of that period came confusion over the pastor-people relationship. In a debate years ago over the comparative virtues of the long and short pastorate, the minister speaking for short-term pastorates put his argument very understandingly. He said: "I have never lived in a community for a year without finding people I am glad to move away from."

The man with this idea could never be a good executive either in business or in the church. The executive must like people and be willing to work with them regardless of their personal limitations. In the small church, trustees and lay officers have tried to handle all the organizational details and the results have not always been pleasing. Some reason that the church is a voluntary society and that it is better to endure inefficiency than to be overly anxious for perfection. An alternative is to have some responsible person at the head of the organization who can give constant supervision.

As churches grow in size and the staff increases, the supervision may be distributed, but the pastor still retains the position of chief leader directing the staff in their activities. Even in those churches which have employed business managers with definite duties, the pastor is still the head of the church. In another chapter we discuss the division of tasks under the multiple ministry, including the instances in which there is a business manager.

The executive minister will, in the end, be judged not by the effectiveness of his pulpit ministry or the charm of his own personality but by the quality of the program which he is projecting. This may seem like a hardship to some but it is really one of the most effective protections that the minister can have. No clergyman can shine forever without personality conflicts but a good program will grow better and better. If trouble arises between the minister and his board he is in a much better position if he can keep the debate on the quality of the program rather than on his own personality.

The Tools for Program Making

The tools for a successful local church program are not found entirely in methods, books, or pronouncements of the denomination. The tools of progress are men and women, boys and girls. The minister who knows how to lead people into ways of action can have a continually growing church. More important than charts on the wall are the personalities of those who work in the program.

In discussing his own minister, a lay officer of a church said: "He is the best preacher by far we have had in our church. If we just had some way to lock him up Sunday night and keep him on ice until the next Sunday morning, we would have a great church. The trouble is that he gets around during the week. He is one of these men who has an individual point of view. If you suggest that the house across the street is white, he will try to convince you that it is black." This is a somewhat extreme example of a minister who can never be an executive.

Fifty years ago, when American business began to expand, there was increasing need for skilled engineers, chemists; for men of trained mind and hand. Since that time there has developed the professional executive, who may have come from "the ranks" because of an ability to lead and direct employees that enhanced his familiarity with technological abilities. The rise of the executive minister has followed, somewhat belatedly, the pattern of the industrial executive. The executive minister is not only the man who knows what shall be done, he also knows how it shall be accomplished and through whom. He needs to know the names of his people and the motives which will move them to action.

While it would be nice to assume that every member of a church is moved only by the highest ideals, a realistic observation will not substantiate the idea. The forces which move men to church participation are many. The wise administrator will know how to use these to secure men and women to work in the various church activities. The forces which follow are at least honorable, but of course they vary in nobility. They are placed in an ascending scale.

SELF-INTEREST. Here belongs the person who can profit socially, intellectually, and sometimes financially by becoming active in the church program.

DESIRE FOR RECOGNITION. The quest for leadership can be rewarded by the church program.

LOVE OF CEREMONY AND LITURGY. Many people like to participate in parades whether or not they know the reason for them.

PRESTIGE AND IMITATION. A neighbor, socially prominent, is a good church member. It seems to be the way to become known and to associate with the right people.

COMPETITION. Most people like to excel in something. Church leadership may give the opportunity.

FORCE OF PUBLIC OPINION. The anti-communist philosophy has led many people to ally themselves with churches to demonstrate that they are not "atheistic communists."

LOVE OF FAIR PLAY. "The spirit of fair play in its deepest origin, is a kind of religion" (Henry Van Dyke). The Church has a strong voice in pleading the cause of individual freedom and fair play.

THE DESIRE TO BE OF SERVICE. We are getting close to the top of the list here. This is the motive which leads men and women to give themselves as teachers in the church school and youth organizations.

THE LOVE OF CHRIST CONSTRAINETH US. Here we reach the peak of spiritual appeal.

Of course, not many individuals have ever been moved alone by this last appeal. Each life rather is a combination of various appeals. Apparent humility may be based on personal avarice. The motive for self-sacrifice may be partially the love of Christ, but may have in it the appeal of recognition as well. Personal ambition has had its part on the elevation of many ministers to higher offices where there they rationalize that they have a greater area for service.

The Minister and His Official Board

There is no place where the minister's ability to lead is more important than in his relationship with his official board. Official boards are set up for a purpose. Formally or informally the pastor is the leader of the board, but his leadership should be based on democratic principles. Sometimes ministers despair of getting action from the board and turn to personal dictation to accomplish the end sought. This compares with the frequently uttered statement that the best committee is a two-man committee with one man absent. This is not true of a committee or a church board. The best board consists of men and women specially and intelligently selected for their tasks and given the proper leadership.

"I inherited my board," said one minister. "There is not a single person on it who is qualified." Too often there is some truth in a statement of this kind. The solution is to start the selection of leadership before the church elections are held. The wise minister will constantly be looking for good officer material. He will have the opportunity to suggest to the nominating committee the names of those he thinks are qualified. In this way though he inherits an official board, there will be a continuing change of personalities on the board.

Most churches at the present time elect their officials on a rotating basis. This implies that after a man has served a full term, he must retire at least for one year before he can be re-elected. If a church does not have this rotary system it would be well for it to consider changing to one. As a rule perpetual service is not desirable; if the board is self-perpetuating the situation is basically wrong.

It is true that there are some men who are so well qualified for official positions that the church would profit by their continuous service for life. Because they have retentive minds their service gives a continuity to the program of the church. Fortunately these men usually have the wisdom to understand that their particular ability notwithstanding the church profits by occasional change of church officers and the building of new leadership.

Once having set up the board desired the minister has the task of leading it into action. Some of the steps toward this end are artificial but necessary. The parliamentarian thinks of a single meeting as an end in itself, the minister-executive thinks of it as a means to the end. He is as much interested in what happens between meetings as in the gatherings themselves. The committees are appointed in the meetings but their program is accomplished between meetings.

Each board should have its own time for meeting at least once a month. The day and the hour should be set and the date observed. Publish it in the Sunday calendar, then send out postcard notices so there will be no possibility of the member not knowing when he is required to attend. After a board has responded to meetings, perhaps the postcard announcements can be discontinued. If that is done, be sure to start again when a new board takes over.

The most effective way to announce any official board meeting, regular or special, is by mail. The mail notification is superior to the publication in the calendar and is better than a phone call. The phone call may come when the individual is away from home and the person receiving the notice may forget to pass on the information. The mail system is not perfect but is more effective than other methods.

Perhaps the ideal way is a notice by mail followed by a phone call the day before or the day of the meeting confirming the officer's presence. Know the situation well enough to decide what address for the notice and phone call will get the best results. In one instance both should be sent to the residence. In others the business address will be preferred. If the individual is a top-level employee with a full time secretary, the office probably is preferable; if he is employed on a lower level, there may be objection to his receiving personal mail at the office. It will depend much on the attitude of the man's wife and family. Some wives are very careful to see that all messages reach the individual for whom they are intended, others have little interest in the church and will neglect to pass on church communications.

A successful board meeting needs not only good attendance but a good agenda. This usually is the responsibility of the pastor. The quality of men desired for an official board brings a challenge to make the time spent in official board conferences worth while. The best way is to put down on paper the various items to be considered, then have the program duplicated so that each individual may have a copy in his hands.

With meetings once a month a busy man may find it difficult to keep the details of any proposition in mind. The minister can be of much help here if he will have a filing folder for each member of the board. In this will be placed a copy of the outline of the agenda and material on the various items to be considered. At the close of the meeting, collect these folders of items for further consideration, then file them until the next meeting. It is much safer to have these folders filed in the church office than to let the officials carry them away to their homes or offices. Follow the same technique at each meeting.

Another technique which speeds consideration is to telephone the committee chairman a few days before each meeting to find if he has a report ready for presentation. Too many chairmen simply report "progress" which usually means that nothing much has been done. It is amazing how much committee work can be done in three days if the minister puts pressure on the chairman before the monthly meeting.

In some churches, the minister is not permitted to chair the official board; in still other instances the board meets without him. He can, however, still control the action. Certain personalities can get better results from the floor than by presiding at a meeting. As chairman, one may be inhibited from presenting his point of view, fearing that he is taking advantage of his official position. If he speaks from the floor he is not handicapped by this inhibition.

The pastor of a Congregational church who was not included in trustee groups found that he could still direct their work by a very simple procedure. A few days before the trustees' meeting he would pay a visit to the chairman of the board. In conversation with him he would in an informal way suggest some items which he thought should be considered at the meeting. The chairman who was very jealous of his own authority would absorb these ideas and sponsor them. In the days of the second world war, he felt that the church should have a very definite program to encourage the servicemen. He had found his board rather indifferent to such a program. Here is the story as he told it.

> I made my regular monthly visit to the chairman of the board. I suggested that I thought it would be nice if a modest flag mast could be placed over the main entrance of the church and a flag be purchased and hung there every day of the year. Next I mentioned that it would be fine if every young man

and young woman in the church who joined the armed forces should go away with a copy of a Bible presented by the church. My third suggestion was that a monthly letter be sent to each man and woman in the service keeping them up to date on home affairs.

His only reaction was a grunt showing that he had at least heard what I said. Imagine my surprise when I learned that he had proposed that the church secure not a small mast for the entrance but erect a sixty foot flag pole in the church yard, that the Bibles be given by the church to every young man and young woman in the community when they joined the forces and that the church publish a monthly paper carrying the news of the home town and, also, a letter exchange in which the various enlisted personnel could tell others of their experiences.

Each of these was presented as his own program without any reference to me. I was completely satisfied and felt sure that I had secured this program more easily by this method than if I had attended the meeting personally.

The minister-executive should have as his objective the accomplishment of a definite program which will be helpful to his church. Whether he or some one else gets the credit for the ideas is of little concern. If the chairman of the board helps to put across the desirable program, that is sufficient. The program should be placed above personality, and it is wise to share sponsorship with others.

Some Techniques

Here are some of the techniques which a minister can use to get the desired action through the proper board.

Never suggest a cold proposition. Any program that is worth while is worth warming before it is formally presented. If a man has sufficient strength, he might put through a new program unheard before the meeting. But it would not be fair to the program itself.

When you have a program to suggest, mention it long before the time it is introduced. To be specific, suppose you wish an educational addition or building. Don't just come before the board and make a proposition. Prepare in advance. Run items in the church calendar which tell of the work which would be done in such a building. Build up the idea in conversation. Tell the various organizations about it. Prepare a chart or statement of costs. When the background has been prepared, you will be in a position to introduce the subject. I know one successful minister who makes it a point to talk informally with officials before the vacation season about the program items he will present in the autumn.

Get the sponsors for it before it is introduced. Let someone else introduce the subject. If no one is sufficiently interested to sponsor the matter, probably it should not be introduced anyway. A minister loses prestige by always being the person to introduce a subject. Let someone else do the talking. If the discussion is close, the chairman or someone else is sure to ask the minister's opinion. This is his chance. His words at such a time can control the vote. He should save himself for such a moment.

Don't ask for passage as a personal favor. If you do, you may get it. A board of honest men and women should never be asked to vote except to express their own convictions. The minister who makes the personal loyalty appeal is unfair to the proposition he proposes. If it is reasonable and he used the right technique, he can almost surely get support. The personal favor appeal is too elementary.

Don't ask for a decision on any important matter until you know how it shall be put into effect. To pass a resolution or an important motion without having a program to accomplish its purpose is like proposing to a girl without any conception of what marriage means. If the board votes to start erection of the educational building mentioned above, the minister should know just what committees should be appointed to get the work started.

Remember that there is a distinction between a parliamentary meeting and executive procedure. The parliamentary meeting deals with motions and votes. The executive procedure deals with programs. Know the steps to be taken to get the matter consummated.

Professor Richard W. Miller of the Garrett Biblical Institute, Evanston, Illinois, suggests that the best method of enabling the minister to see his task is by a constant use of check sheets dealing with his own ability and the officers who will direct the work of his church. In a communication to the author he gave samples of this art of self-analysis. His insistence that most of the failures of leadership rest on the minister rather than his laymen is worth considering but let his letter present the point of view.

The Minister As An Executive

The word executive comes from two Latin words: *Ex*, meaning out; and *Sequi*, meaning to follow up to the end; *Exsequi* is the participle of *Executus*, from which we derive the word.

The minister as an executive is the one who, in matters pertaining to the success of his organization, "follows up to the end." Such a minister attempts to conclude constructively all activities related to his professional responsibilities. To execute is to bring about an end result. The minister-executive is responsible for bringing about an end result through education, personal action, delegation of responsibility and follow up. To be a strong executive in the ministry a man must develop certain abilities and see the value of action.

Following is a check sheet which a minister might study for the sake of personal evaluation. Not all items are of equal significance, but all are important.

Am I well acquainted with the basic organizational plan of the denomination in which I work?

Have I studied anything within the past six months which assisted me in seeing more clearly the philosophy back of the organizational plan of my denomination? List such specific reading.

Am I capable of relating the recommended organizational procedures of my denomination to my people? (This assumes a thorough knowledge of both the organizational plan and the local organization.)

Do I attempt to warp my people into the organizational plan?

Have I made a thorough study of my local and denominational organization and discovered clear relationships to local needs and Christian principles?

Am I the kind of man who must be the recognized leader in all activities or I feel insecure?

Can I delegate responsibility and do I do so with the realization that the person so delegated needs such responsibility for personal, spiritual development? Do I think out the delegation of authority carefully or am I simply trying to get someone to take a bothersome task off my shoulders?

Am I so enthused about the work of the Kingdom of God that I approach all executive and administrative tasks as important action closely related to Christian teaching?

Am I able to find a strengthening fellowship in conferences with my denominational superiors?

Have I ever considered these men who occupy the 'higher seats' as men like myself, who have heavy responsibilities and need me as I need them?

Do I see myself as a mere cog in a vast denominational machine? Do I see myself as a significant individual free to work within my denomination and free to express myself in matters important to the Christian emphasis of my day?

Do I get along well with most people? Have I ever spent time attempting to see the types of people with whom I seem to violently disagree? Have I ever tried to see myself in the light of those whom I like and those whom I don't like?

Have I ever written out my basic theological concepts and attempted to evaluate them as to consistency? Can I state such ideas in simple, clear fashion so that people with average vocabularies can understand?

Have I ever evaluated an executive failure in terms of my own inability to clearly state the problem, the procedure, and the goal?

Why do I work? What do I really want in terms of professional achievement?

If I have not achieved what I want, whom or what do I blame? Too often ministers resent being classified as executives. Such an attitude is perplexing to community and church lay leaders who are, almost without exception, working in some sort of executive capacity. To belittle executive ability is to misunderstand the value of personal development achieved as the individual participates in the procedure leading to final worthy accomplishment.

The minister of a church is an executive. It is his responsibility to see that the organization functions with purpose and efficiency. To facilitate such work the minister may find certain tools of great assistance. These tools or instruments can be of his own making and should be improved year by year.

One such tool or instrument, called a check sheet or job analysis sheet, relates to specific executive duties and assists in ordering and completing any particular task. Such an instrument need not result in rigid, cold efficiency but will assist the already overworked memory of a busy pastor. Check sheets should be corrected *after* each use, that unimportant items be deleted, important items added, and that a proper sequence of action be established.

A logical order of procedure can result from such a well thought out device. Such instruments may well be developed by a small committee and the pastor. Such a committee, made up of mature, thoughtful people, can through group effort, do much in correcting and ordering the instrument. The wide experience found in a group is not to be discounted in the developing of a job analysis. The alert pastor will use a carefully selected group and profit by their total wisdom.

Group procedure in this work may result in the members gaining a new and more complete understanding of the multitudinous executive tasks confronting their pastor. Such understanding will result in a more wholesome regard for the importance of his task.

If the pastor does not desire group participation in the building of these check lists he can develop them independently. Careful consideration of any one task and a careful listing of items in proper sequence is basic. Usually the items are worded as questions. Care should be exercised in closing such an analysis that the final items actually conclude the activity in a positive way.

Following is a specimen instrument to be studied. Perhaps it will stimulate the reader to experiment in the development of other useful and time saving orders of procedure.

Chairman:—Board of Trustees

The statement of responsibility of the Board of Trustees is:

[*The statement which is to follow should be carefully worded to apply to the local situation. Pastor and trustees can formulate the role from past experience and make additions as they arise. The following analysis of the chairman's work would vary greatly with the definition of the responsibility of the Board of Trustees. However, some of the following items would appear in almost every case.*]

Are all the members of the Board informed as to the purpose of the Board, its responsibilities and its limits?

Is this statement of responsibility posted where all church members may study it? Are the names of Board members listed on the statement?

Are regular meeting dates agreed upon and properly announced? Are regular meeting dates set in relation to congregational meetings and official Board meetings, that the most efficient use of time may be accomplished?

Are members asked to hand in agenda items prior to the meeting date, that the chairman may organize the meeting?

In relation to the statement of Board purpose, are responsibilities delegated to proper persons and a time set in each case for a report?

Is the individual or committee properly informed as to what their responsibility is before they accept the committment?

Is assent to accept responsibility always gained from individual or committee before responsibility is delegated?

Are these clearcut, specific responsibilities accepted by individual or committee properly recorded in the secretary's minutes?

In subsequent meetings of the Board are the above mentioned responsibilities read just prior to the report from individual or committee?

Executive leadership is the most sought quality in the business and political world today. The technical specialist is necessary in any industry but more valuable and higher paid is the man who knows how to direct the work of the specialist. With the increasing size of the churches, the ability to direct the activities of men becomes increasingly more important. As important as it is to know the way to win friends, it is much more valuable to know how to get them to work in the program to be projected.

A Program for the Official Board

INSURANCE:

( ) When were the properties last appraised?

( ) Is enough insurance being carried to cover all risks? Is it the right kind?

( ) Have the premiums been paid for at least a three-year period? Are the dates of the policies arranged so that a proportionate amount of the premiums come due each year? Are the policies kept in a safe place?

CARE:

( ) Are the buildings and equipment clean?

( ) And in good repair?

( ) Are the entrances and halls attractive and well lighted?

( ) Have the organ, pianos, chimes, and other musical instruments been inspected, tuned, and adjusted regularly as needed?

( ) Are the carpets and other floor coverings in good condition? Have they been cleaned?

( ) Have the boilers, heating system, plumbing, electric wiring, etc., been gone over at regular periods by experts?

( ) Is the ventilation adequate, and is it supervised during meetings?

( ) Is there cracked or broken glass in any of the windows? If there are leaded or art-glass windows. have they been inspected by experts for possible needed repairs?

( ) Are there "squeaks" in any of the machinery, hinges, etc., that should be oiled?

( ) Are there any leaks in the roof? Gutters? Water spouts? Any broken tiles or slates, or loose shingles?

( ) Has the catch-basin been cleaned, as needed?

( ) Have the roof-beams and braces been inspected?

( ) Have brick and stone work been painted?

( ) Broken rails, steps, and sidewalks restored? (An institution is liable to an individual if personal harm comes from collective carelessness or neglect).

( ) Does the sexton have adequate tools and supplies? (It has been proven long since that time costs more than materials. Often we carry good workmen on our payrolls but do not provide them with needed equipment for their work, i.e., garden tools, water hose and sprinklers, cleaning fluids, brooms, brushes, carpenter tools, ash containers, shovels, etc.)

( ) Are properties being used to full capacity? America has an investment of $4,000,000,000 in her church properties. Business men might become more interested if they felt that worthy dividends were being returned.

DECORATING:

( ) Is any of the plaster cracked or loose?

( ) Is the interior color scheme harmonious and restful, an inspiration to the services of worship?

( ) Have floors been kept stained, painted, waxed, or varnished, as needed?

( ) Has the outside woodwork been kept painted (one coat every two years or two coats every four years) and does the color scheme represent the dignity of the church?

TREES, SHRUBS, FLOWERS, LAWNS:

( ) Are there too many trees (too much shade)? Or just the right number? Or not enough? Are they properly trimmed each year? (If more trees are needed, they may be secured easily as memorial gifts, with proper services of recognition.)

( ) Have bushes been put against the foundation to soften the effect of barrenness? Have they been pruned, as needed? Is there a variety of flowering shrubs to make the grounds attractive, as the seasons pass?

( ) Is there a place for a flower bed, which might become a "project" for the children? A definite part in the beautification of the church properties would become a helpful influence in interesting some department of the Sunday School.

( ) Are the lawns in good condition? Level? Fertilized? Watered? Cut? Green and fresh? Free of weeds? (Another good "project" for the Boy Scouts or the Men's Club).

PARSONAGE:

( ) Is it insured against all risks?

( ) Has it been repaired and decorated on the same basis as the church?

( ) Does it have a garage for the minister's car?

( ) Are the furnace, gas-stove, electric wiring, (with convenient wall plugs) and plumbing in good condition?

( ) Is there an electric refrigerator?

( ) Are the yards attractive?

( ) Have we made the parsonage a place in which the minister and his family may be proud and happy to live?

POSSIBLE IMPROVEMENTS:

( ) Is there a hand-rail at each flight of steps? Especially on the outside of the buildings?

( ) Has provision been made for coats, hats and baggage? Are the hooks for children's wraps at a height where they may be reached?

( ) Are there enough drinking fountains? Conveniently placed? Especially in the children's departments?

( ) Are there adequate wash rooms, with mirrors, soap and towels?

Are they clean? Arranged for children, as well as for adults?

( ) Is there a table, shelf, or wall rack near the entrance for booklets and literature? Is there a visitors' registration book?

( ) Have robing rooms been provided for the minister and his choir?

( ) Is there complete and suitable equipment for Baptisms? The Holy Communion? The Offering? Weddings? Funerals? Is there adequate storage provision for such equipment, when not in use?

( ) Has the possibility been considered of electric fans or air-conditioning, for summer comfort?

( ) Could better signs and bulletin boards be installed?

( ) Does the church possess flags and banners for special occasions?

( ) Has the church considered the economy, as well as the satisfactions of a small chapel, suitable for the mid-week meetings, weddings, funerals, and special services other than those of the Sunday morning program?

FINANCES AND ACCOUNTING:

( ) Is the budget adequate for the program that ought to be carried out?

( ) If you have a church debt, are you making definite plans to liquidate it?

( ) Is the salary of your minister satisfactory? Does it compare favorably with that of others with similar ability, training, and experience? Do you furnish an automobile for your minister? If not, do you make him an allowance for the expense of using his own car?

( ) Are salaries paid custodian, office

helper and other employees adequate for the work required?

( ) Are employees, including minister, protected under any plan of insurance or social security? The church should try to be as generous as business in giving such protection.

( ) Should every church have a "Unified" budget, where all departments clear their budgets through a general treasury?

( ) Are the financial records audited at least annually by a certified public accountant?

( ) Are the books and other records being kept in accordance with the policies and the supplies of your denomination?

( ) Are all persons bonded who have custody of church money?

( ) Do you vary your program for raising the annual budget? For example, by an every-member-canvass, telephone solicitation, letter-campaign, presentation at a public service, annual roll-call, the Joash chest, etc?

( ) Are you seeking bequests for an endowment? Or memorials for the beautification of the church (stained glass windows, altar, chimes, pulpit, reading desk, chancel chairs, Bible, etc.)

( ) Would it be well to pay the treasurer a nominal salary?

( ) Is stewardship being emphasized in the church?

MEMBERSHIP AND ORGANIZATION:

( ) Have the rolls been revised so that the lists of members, givers, and prospects may be considered accurate?

( ) Have you set goals or quotas for future growth?

( ) Are you following-up the absentees?

( ) Is the membership divided into

colonies or other groups (as the Women's Circles) for more intimate fellowship and closer supervision of activities?

( ) Is there an Advisory Council or cabinet, which includes the heads of all departments of the work of the church?

( ) Are junior organizations being formed, as Junior Ushers, House Committee, Canvassers, etc?

( ) Is any member holding more than one major responsibility? (Better to spread it, and give others the joy of achievement.)

( ) Is some definite forward step being taken on every anniversary of the church?

( ) Does your church have a Board of Religious Education? A Men's Brotherhood? A Children's Church? A High School Church? A Mothers' Council? A Sunday Evening Club (or Forum)? A College of Life (for adult education)? A Religious Drama Department?

( ) Are the ushers appointed and organized a year in advance?

( ) Do you have an official historian?

ADVERTISING AND PUBLICITY:

( ) Has your church a publicity committee? Does it furnish items of news to the local press, and to the denominational papers?

( ) Is the weekly bulletin worthy of the church?

( ) Do you issue a Year Book, including historical data, program, budget, organization and membership directory?

( ) Is your church utilizing its opportunities of promotional letter-writing, issuing souvenirs such as blotters, paper weights, photographs, picture postal cards, badges and buttons?

( ) Are minutes being kept of all official meetings, and are copies sent to absentees to maintain their interest in the program of the church? Could your services be broadcast by radio?

LIGHTING:

( ) Is the church lighting adequate and well-distributed? With no glare in the eyes of the congregation?

( ) Are there fixtures, as needed, for the pulpit and the choir? (At slight additional expense, dimmers controlling different sets of lamps may be installed—also color effects—which greatly enhance the value of dramatic effects for certain types of services).

( ) Are the lighting fixtures appropriate for programs of worship? Suitable church fixtures and lighting cost no more than those designed for commercial purposes.

SPIRITUAL OFFICERS:

( ) Are the elders, deacons, or other spiritual officers standing close by the minister in all the spiritual problems of the church? Securing of new members? Dignifying membership? Caring for the poor, the sick, the sorrowing, and the needy? Are they welcoming the strangers? Providing pulpit supplies in the absence of the pastor? Cooperating with his family? Encouraging them?

THE CHOIR:

( ) Have rooms and instruments been provided for rehearsals? Wardrobes and lockers for garments?

( ) Are there good files for music? (vertical, four-drawer steel files are recommended rather than the old-style wooden cupboards, library boxes and ordinary shelves.)

( ) Is the lighting suitable?

( ) Does the financial budget of the church provide adequately for gown repairs and replacements? Cleaning and laundry? Rental or purchase of new music?

WOMEN'S SOCIETY:

( ) Has the church provided a suitable parlor with equipment for the educational, social and workshop needs of this important group?

( ) Are there convenient facilities for serving refreshments?

( ) Are there closets, cupboards and shelves for the storing of materials when not in use? For wraps?

( ) Is the kitchen equipment adequate (stoves, sinks, tables, shelves, cupboards, refrigeration, etc.) for the social needs of the church?

( ) Does the present financial program (especially the money-raising activities) have a tendency to materialism, thereby detracting from the spiritual emphasis of the church? Is there a better way?

LIBRARY:

( ) Are you building a good working library, with helps for all church officials, teachers in the church school, and leaders of special groups? Current volumes on religion, missions, philosophy, and international friendship may prove also of great help.

SUMMER PROGRAM:

( ) Have you made it possible for your minister to travel, perhaps to Europe or the Holy Land, during his vacation? If not, to a summer school? Or a convention?

( ) Have delegates been chosen from the young people of the church for attendance at youth conferences and assemblies? Scout Camps, etc?

( ) Has a Sunday School picnic been planned in some attractive place?

( ) Had you thought of a "Retreat" for the official board, where Christian fellowship and planning for the new year might go hand in hand for an inspired church program?

( ) Have you suggested the appreciation of the board if those who are to be away for the summer would pay their pledges in advance?

( ) Are you planning a Daily Vacation Bible School for the children who have leisure?

Robert Cashman

Check List for Making the Year's Program

WORSHIP

( ) 1. Occasional worship service in charge of a church-school class.

( ) 2. Period of silent meditation and prayer on entering the church.

( ) 3. Planned entrance periods for late-comers.

( ) 4. Conduct a Junior church—an extended church-school period.

( ) 5. A children's sermon.

( ) 6. A Junior choir—choir gowns.

( ) 7. An adult choir—choir gowns.

( ) 8. An occasional musical service with stories of great hymns.

( ) 9. Illustrated hymns with stereopticon slides.

( ) 10. Hymnals for youth.

( ) 11. Regular administration of the Sacrament.

( ) 12. Printed or mimeographed Sunday bulletins, supplied by missionary agencies.

( ) 13. Provide flowers for church services.

( ) 14. Dramatize Bible stories.

( ) 15. Observe special days.

( ) 16. . . . .

( ) 17. . . . .

EVANGELISM

( ) 18. Conduct a class for visitation-evangelism teams.

( ) 19. A house-to-house canvass by the minister and laymen to secure new members.

( ) 20. Get high school enrollment list of the unchurched.

( ) 21. Declaration Day in the church school.

( ) 22. Conduct a round table discussion with young people's groups on their personal religious problems.

( ) 23. Mid-week evening meetings in homes in different sections of the parish.

( ) 24. A religious census of the community to locate prospective members.

( ) 25. Classes in preparatory church membership.

( ) 26. Special evangelistic services preceding Easter.

( ) 27. Regular religious news service in daily or weekly newspapers.

( ) 28. . . . .

( ) 29. . . . .

RELIGIOUS EDUCATION

( ) 30. Conduct a Vacation Church School.

( ) 31. Week-day Religious Education in co-operation with the public schools.

( ) 32. An institute in church school methods.

( ) 33. A parent's class in the teaching of religion in the home.

( ) 34. A standard leadership training class.

( ) 35. A normal class for training new teachers.

( ) 36. Hold a conference quarterly for workers in the church school.

( ) 37. Start a library for church workers with books on recreation, story-telling, stewardship, missions, handwork, dramatization, evangelism, etc.

( ) 38. A children's story-telling and dramatization hour.

( ) 39. Send the pastor and some laymen to a summer training institute.

( ) 40. Put one or more young people on each of the church boards.

( ) 41. Provide transportation for church-school pupils from outlying districts.

( ) 42. Regular graded missionary instruction.

( ) 43. A weekly or monthly forum on community problems.

( ) 44. Graded lessons in the church school, including training in giving and budget building.

( ) 45. . . . .

( ) 46. . . . .

SOCIAL AND RECREATIONAL LIFE

( ) 47. A social and dramatic club for young people.

( ) 48. Special-day celebrations.

( ) 49. Monthly church-school class socials.

( ) 50. A New-comers' social.

( ) 51. Monthly community socials.

( ) 52. Nature hikes and educational trips.

( ) 53. A training class in recreational leadership.

( ) 54. Supervised athletics—basketball, baseball, volleyball teams.

( ) 55. Father-son and Mother-daughter banquets.

( ) 56. Girl Scouts or Campfire girls.

( ) 57. Boy Scouts.

( ) 58. 4-H Clubs.

( ) 59. Conduct an annual musical festival.

( ) 60. A lyceum course.

( ) 61. . . . .

( ) 62. . . . .

FINANCES

( ) 63. Conduct a class in stewardship.

( ) 64. Distribute stewardship literature.

( ) 65. Arrange for two treasurers, one for current expenses and one for World Service.

( ) 66. Prepare and print an annual budget.

( ) 67. The every-member canvass.

( ) 68. Promote the duplex plan of giving, in the church and also in the church school.

( ) 69. Designate missionary gifts for the different church organizations.

( ) 70. Monthly remittance of missionary obligations.

( ) 71. Issue individual financial reports to givers, quarterly.

( ) 72. . . . .

( ) 73. . . . .

CHURCH BUILDING AND EQUIPMENT

( ) 74. Provide appropriate pictures for classrooms.

( ) 75. Purchase Biblical maps and charts.

( ) 76. Procure a stereopticon.

( ) 77. Provide suitable coverings for church-school classroom floors.

( ) 78. A room with movable chairs, for church socials.

( ) 79. Curtains or screens to separate classes.

( ) 80. Small tables and chairs, a sand table and handwork— for beginners and primary department.

( ) 81. Blackboards.

( ) 82. Suitable musical instruments.

( ) 83. A separate room for each department in the church school.

( ) 84. Staging facilities for plays and pageants.

( ) 85. Toilet facilities.

( ) 86. Remove unsightly horse-sheds.

( ) 87. Provide adequate parking space.

( ) 88. Beautify the church grounds, plant shrubbery trees, flowers, vines and lawn according to landscape plans.

( ) 89. Keep the lawn mowed.

( ) 90. Provide an electrically-lighted bulletin board near the street in front of the church.

( ) 91. Redecorate the interior of the church.

( ) 92. Repaint the church.

( ) 93. Volleyball and net, basketball, indoor baseball equipment.

( ) 94. Remove glaring lights near the pulpit.

( ) 95. Get adequate fire insurance on church and parsonage.

( ) 96. Repair the church.

( ) 97. Build a sidewalk and drive.

( ) 98. An equipped kitchen in the church.

( ) 99. Build a parish house.

( ) 100. Provide furniture for the parsonage.

( ) 101. Labor saving devices for the parsonage.

( ) 102. Install an adequate heating system in the church and in the parsonage.

( ) 103. . . . .

( ) 104. . . . .

MISSIONS

( ) 105. Use missionary hymn-slides in evening services monthly.

( ) 106. Stereopticon lectures on mission work.

( ) 107. Mission study classes, foreign and home.

( ) 108. A missionary play or pageant annually.

( ) 109. Church-night programs with missionary topics.

( ) 110. Talks by missionaries on furlough or by foreign students.

( ) 111. A judicious distribution of a limited amount of missionary literature.

( ) 112. Send delegates to missionary institutes.

( ) 113. Monthly Church Day with morning and afternoon sessions devoted to missionary topics.

( ) 114. Use of special-day programs.

( ) 115. Organize women's missionary societies.

( ) 116. Sermons from the pulpit on missionary themes, at least bi-monthly.

( ) 117. World-Friendship socials for young people.

( ) 118. Establish a missionary museum or exhibit.

( ) 119. Include missions in the every-member canvass.

( ) 120. A fixed goal or a definite missionary budget.

( ) 121. Increase missionary interest by adopting a special missionary or field project.

( ) 122. . . . .

( ) 123. . . . .

FAMILY WELFARE

( ) 124. A discussion class or lectures on the creative use of the Sabbath.

( ) 125. Talks on marriage and home life for young people's groups.

( ) 126. A class of clinic in Child Guidance for parents of pre-school children.

( ) 127. Baby health clinics at the church in cooperation with the county nurse.

( ) 128. Arrange a deputation team of young people to visit the county home, the children's home or a hospital.

( ) 129. Cooperate with the judge of the children's court, the county children's agent and the county probation officer in finding homes for dependent children.

( ) 130. Thanksgiving and Christmas baskets for needy children.

( ) 131. Regular visit to sick and shut-ins—take fruit and flowers, also send greeting cards.

( ) 132. A class or occasional lecture in sex hygiene.

( ) 133. Arrange a series of talks for vocational guidance.

( ) 134. Cooperate with the home demonstration agent in promoting homemaking projects —giving free use of the church.

( ) 135. A nursery for small children during church sessions.

( ) 136. Observe "Family Day" with special home topics, annually.

( )137. . . . .
( )138. . . . .

CIVIC IMPROVEMENT

( )139. Plan a campaign for building a school playground, with play equipment, swings, slides, seesaws, jungle-gym.

( )140. Plan a campaign to remove unsightly places, including billboards.

( )141. Conduct a class in home nursing with the county nurse as instructor.

( )142. Arrange a citizenship committee to deal with law enforcement, commercial dance halls, motion pictures, news stands, clean politics.

( )143. Plan a campaign to secure electric lights, water system or fire department.

( )144. A village or community park with tennis courts and baseball field.

( )145. Conduct a campaign for beautifying all public buildings, including school, church, grange, town hall and railway station.

( )146. Secure lectures on local and county government subjects.

( )147. Conduct a forum or discussion class on civic or community problems.

( )148. . . . .
( )149. . . . .

COOPERATION WITH OTHER AGENCIES

( )150. Secure social workers as speakers, county nurse, home demonstration agent, agricultural agent, judge of the children's court, 4-H club agent, etc.

( )151. Cooperate with social service agencies, community chest, hospital, county nurse, etc., in public meetings, financial support and specific family service.

( )152. Cooperate with the county council of religious education, Y.M.C.A., and Y.W.C.A.

( )153. Cooperate with the grange in an annual joint program.

( )154. Give the church building for free use of social welfare agencies.

( )155. Cooperate with the county executives of the scouts or 4-H clubs in the conducting of local groups in the church.

( )156. Make provision in the church for a depository of the county library.

( )157. Support the state council of churches.

( )158. Arrange pulpit exchange annually with churches of the other denominations in the community.

( )159. Arrange joint meetings quarterly of young people's organizations of all nearby denominations.

( )160. Hold union church-school picnic annually.

( )161. Appoint a small committee to meet with the other churches in the community to arrange for a united church or a Cooperative Larger Parish.

( )162. Arrange to cooperate with the other churches in the community in as many of the above projects as possible.

( )163. . . . .
( )164. . . . .

[This list of projects or activities was originally prepared by the class in Social Research and Field Surveys, Drew University, Madison, N. J.]

11 | THE ADMINISTRATIVE CENTER

THE CHURCH, AS AN ORGANISM, REQUIRES AN ADMINISTRA-tive center. Back of the administrative center is the administrator who is of course the minister. Some will protest that the work of the minister should be separate from administrative duties. Whether or not the law of the denomination or the constitution of the local churches provides that the minister may keep to his pulpit and pastoral ministry, in actual practice he is the head of the church. Even a church which will insist that its pastor be freed from all administrative duties will place the responsibility upon his shoulders if the congregation dwindles or the budget shrinks.

While the minister's study should be quite apart from the church office, it seems desirable to discuss the study in connection with the church administrative program. The modern preacher is a many-faceted individual and his administrative side is receiving considerable emphasis. His skill may enable him to chart the program of the church and the building in which it is executed and still leave him sufficient time for his sermonic and pastoral needs. If he can do that, he has achieved the greatest administrative success available to the pastor of today.

The purpose of the minister's study is quite different from the office of the church. At the head of the church is a man of many duties but who first of all must bring a vision of God to the people of his parish. To keep in condition for this and to keep one step ahead of his congregation requires not only special training but special facilities. While the general church offices should be in the most accessible part of the church building, the study of the minister should be somewhat isolated so

that he is not too easily disturbed. Fortunate is the minister who
has sufficient secretarial help so that he can have his regular
hours for study, meditation, and prayer each day. The old rule
was that the minister should have the morning for his study,
the afternoon for his calls, the evening for his public engagements and his family. That program has never been improved
upon but changing situations have taken more and more of both
the morning and afternoon for executive tasks.

The pastor of the church must still have some protected time
for study, but it is difficult to decide what hours these shall be
or how many. Can he refuse telephone calls during certain periods of the day? The average man resists any idea of exclu-
siveness yet he must draw the line some place. It is a brutal and
un-Christian thing to refuse to accept a call which comes because of human distress. On the other hand, a refusal to

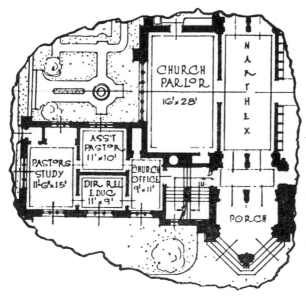

Office Plans, The Trinity Methodist Church, Albany, New York. The
plans show a good arrangement for the church with a professional staff.
The first entrance is to the office, and the pastor's study is given further
protection by the offices of his associates.

listen to an extended bit of parish gossip during the study hours might be a Christian act.

In the last generation there has been a transition of the location of the study from the parsonage or manse to the church. Many churches, however, have not been wise in their location of this all-important room. Many ministers prefer a quiet room in the parsonage for their hours of study. Even if the church provides such a space, a secondary space in the manse will be desirable. If guests are to be received in the home, the room must be so located that they can be received and dismissed without passing through rooms in use by the family. The pastoral consultations need the privacy accorded to the doctor and the lawyer. The confessional in the historic church gives the seeker a confidential approach to the ear of the priest. When a clergyman holds his consultations in the parsonage, rectory or manse, it is difficult to assure the privacy needed for successful healing.

Study Equipment

Once the location of the study is decided we come to the equipment. In a small church the one room may serve as both office and study. This is regrettable for the simple reason that the functions are widely separated. A minister will find a room uncluttered with files and office machinery much more conducive to spiritual meditation. If one room must serve for both, it would be well to put a partial partition across it so that the office machines and mailing devices are not visible from his desk.

There are two exceptions to this. Many ministers think with their fingers on the typewriter and one should always be close at hand. The other is the telephone. In the one-man office, it should be close by; in the office with secretarial help, an extension phone may be on the desk for only necessary calls need be referred to the minister.

The minister does need a good and large flat-top desk. In the drawers he will keep his pencils, paper, and other items. One of the drawers should be large enough for the filing of letters, or if such a drawer is not available, a filing cabinet should be close to the desk for constant reference. If he has no secretary, he will soon learn the technique of using file folders by which each category is placed in its own folder filed alphabetically.

The desk is a work bench, not a storage shelf. The temptation to pile book after book upon it leads to disorderly thinking. The typewriter should be of standard office size, not a light portable. If money is not available to buy a new standard machine, buy a good used or rebuilt machine. It will be more serviceable than a lightweight portable.

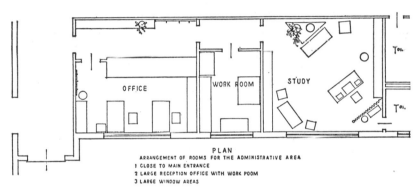

PLAN
ARRANGEMENT OF ROOMS FOR THE ADMINISTRATIVE AREA
1 CLOSE TO MAIN ENTRANCE
2 LARGE RECEPTION OFFICE WITH WORK ROOM
3 LARGE WINDOW AREAS

A modern office-study arrangement.

The minister will also learn to make carbon copies of everything he produces on the typewriter. No letters should go out without a carbon copy for his file. No copy should be sent to the printer without keeping a carbon. These copies will help out many times in establishing responsibility for statements and typing errors.

Care of Books

The study should provide a liberal amount of book shelving. No minister will probably ever reach the place where he does not have to call on the public library but he needs his own reference books and those new, precious volumes which bring him his moments of inspiration. When the books accumulate to several hundred in number, he will need some system so he may find the book he needs without too much effort.

Everybody knows something about the Dewey decimal system of classifying books for ready reference. This is a system devised two generations ago by Melville Dewey, librarian of Columbia College and later director of the New York State library.

In brief, it divides the world of books into ten basic subject areas. To each of these is assigned a number which in turn has sub-topics of given classification under the general subject. In classifying books, the various numbers are used to list the books, which are placed and numbered alphabetically by author. Of course there cannot be a number for each book, so the decimal point comes into use.

The following table shows the divisions of books by subjects and sub-topics.

Dewey Decimal System of Library Classification

000 GENERAL WORKS
010 Bibliography
020 Library Economy
030 General Encyclopedias
040 General Collected Essays
050 General Periodicals
060 General Societies, Museums
070 Journalism, Newspapers
080 Polygraphy, Special Libraries
090 Book Rarities

100 PHILOSOPHY
110 Metaphysics
120 Special Metaphysical Topics
130 Mind and Body
140 Philosophic Systems
150 Psychology
160 Logic Dialectics
170 Ethics
180 Ancient Philosophers
190 Modern Philosophers

200 RELIGION
210 Natural Theology
220 Bible

230 Doctrinal, Dogmatics, Theology
240 Devotional, Practical
250 Homiletics, Pastoral, Parochial
260 Church: Institution Work
270 General Church History
280 Christian Churches and Sects
290 Nonchristian Religions

300 SOCIOLOGY, SOCIAL SCIENCES
310 Statistics
320 Political Science
330 Economics
340 Law
350 Administration
360 Associations and Institutions
370 Education
380 Commerce, Communications
390 Customs, Costumes, Folklore

400 PHILOLOGY
410 Comparative
420 English, Anglo-Saxon
430 German and Other Teutonic
440 French, Provençal
450 Italian, Rumanian

460 Spanish, Portuguese
470 Latin and Other Italic
480 Greek and Other Hellenic
490 Other Languages

500 PURE SCIENCE
510 Mathematics
520 Astronomy
530 Physics
540 Chemistry
550 Geology
560 Paleontology
570 Biology, Anthropology
580 Botany
590 Zoology

600 USEFUL ARTS, APPLIED SCIENCE
610 Medicine
620 Engineering
630 Agriculture
640 Home Economics
650 Communication, Business
660 Chemic Technology
670 Manufactures
680 Mechanic Trades
690 Building

700 FINE ARTS, RECREATION
710 Landscape gardening
720 Architecture
730 Sculpture

740 Drawing, Decoration, Design
750 Painting
760 Engraving
770 Photography
780 Music
790 Amusements

800 LITERATURE
810 American
820 English, Anglo-Saxon
830 Germanic and Other Teutonic
840 French, Provençal
850 Italian, Rumanian
860 Spanish, Portuguese
870 Latin and Other Italic
880 Greek and Other Hellenic
890 Other Literature

900 HISTORY, BIOGRAPHY
910 Geography and Travels
920 Biography
930 Ancient History
940 Modern Europe
950 Modern Asia
960 Modern Africa
970 Modern North America (including Central America)
980 Modern South America
990 Modern Oceania and Polar Regions

Here are the classifications of four books as they sit side by side in the religious book section of the Cleveland Public Library. They give a good illustration of an adaptation of the Dewey Decimal system.

Hiltner
The Counselor in Counselling
250
3754

Holman
The Cure of Souls
250
377

Hiltner
Pastoral Counselling
250
3755

Holman
Getting Down to Cases
250
3773

From these few listings you will see that the books are first of all classified alphabetically by author. Next comes the titles, alphabetically under authors. Then the numbers. By looking at the chart above you will see that they fall under the general classification of religion. Under this they have further classification of Homiletics, Pastoral, and Parochial.

Information for the classification of religious books is found in a phamplet of 337 pages entitled *Library of Congress Classification Schedule, Class B. Part II, BL–BX, Religion.* This is not a free phamplet, but costs several dollars so make inquiry before you request it. Even the largest ministerial library is small compared with public libraries and narrow compared with the area of books in a general library. There is some question of the need for the minister having an elaborate indexing system.

In my own library, I have found a very effective classification is to set up the subjects into general classification, running alphabetically and then placing the various books, by authors, under the classification. My shelves cover one side of the room. At the upper left hand are placed the books which have the earliest alphabetical classification. In my case they happen to be the books dealing with administration. That "Administration" in my library means "Church Administration" is assumed in making up the shelves. At the lower right are the volumes listed under the subject "Youth." In between these are the various classifications such as "Bible," "Biography," "Catholic," "History," "Hymns," etc.

There are some sixty books under the head "Administration." On the back of each book there is a little label bearing the notation "Adm" to which has been added a number. The original numbers placed on the books were the odd numerals 1–3–5–7 etc. Only the odd numerals were used so that there would be a place for new books. These, as they are secured would carry the even numerals. In each classification the books are arranged alphabetically by authors.

For instance the first two books in the section "Administration" are indexed as follows:

Interchurch Government
Clarence R. Athearn
Adm 1

Putting the Church on a Full Time Basis
Albert W. Beaven
Adm 3

The last book in this particular classification is:

A Pastor's Cabinet
By a Business Man
Adm 109

Suppose I wish to locate a book. Let us take a chance title, *Knowing and Helping People* by Horatio W. Dresser. I would assume that this title would be found in the section labelled "Psychology." The eye would run down the shelves until it came naturally to that section. There the book would be instantly located.

Card Index

The second part of this system consists of a card index in which the cards are classified by authors' names. All of the authors whose names begin with "A" will be found under that heading, etc. If one can't remember the title of the book but knows the name of the author he can easily get the title and the classification. For instance you want to get a book by Arthur John Gossip. Turning to the card index you find a card with a legend like this.

Gossip, Arthur John
The Hero in Thy Soul
Scribner's.
Ser. 153

The book evidently will be found under the classification of "Sermons." The numeral position is 153. That is all there is to it. The price and publisher are included simply because of many inquiries regarding proposed book purchases. In actual practice the card index is used but little. The preparation of it does give the minister a chance to appraise his library. Once the books are placed in the proper position on the shelves his eye will do the rest. The system is simple, direct, and effective. It is not cumber-some to build and it is most automatic in its effectiveness.

Study Records

Membership and financial records are stored elsewhere, but some records need to be available for the minister in his study. The minister needs immediate access to mailing addresses and telephone numbers. He needs to have at hand constantly a list of prospective members who are to be solicited for membership or to be brought into training classes for members. He needs to have at hand also a secondary list for current pastoral attention. This may be based on the official records but is preferably a pocket record which he carries with him and which helps him in his parish visitation. He needs a desk calendar or appointment book where his future appointments will be available constantly. He should have a note book in which he can make notes after the call of any visitor. Much of this may not be of permanent value but it impresses on the mind of the minister what his observations were.

In-Church Consultations

Few churches provide separate rooms for ministerial consultations. The study will usually double for this purpose. That means that the furniture and pictures should help to create the proper atmosphere for this important side of the minister's work.

We have long since passed the stage where it was thought necessary to have a door half open between the study and the secretarial room when the minister was having a consultation with one who came to him for help. Privacy is necessary to avoid self-consciousness. This does not mean, however, that the minister will not have constant contact with someone on the staff should trouble arise. Perhaps a pushbutton under the desk could be used if the minister were in danger of physical violence.

The client who comes for confidential counseling should be assured of privacy both in coming to the study and in leaving it. Modern pastoral counseling is not the Roman confessional but it is entitled to the confidential courtesy of the confessional.

Equipping the Office

Apart from the study or studies, will be the office. Here will be found the files, the machines, the efficiency of a modern business. In administration the children of this world are wiser than the "children of light" and church offices need the same labor saving devices which business has found to be so valuable.

First would be the selection of the desks. A good desk is an office in itself. Select desks for their purposes and be sure they are large enough. Give plenty of room around them. Crowded desks mean lessened efficiency. The old concept that a crowded office indicated prosperity has been exploded. The only thing it indicates is the lack of administrative knowledge.

The top of the desk is a working space to be used during the working hours. It should not be considered as filing space. Before the day's work is completed the material should be filed in its proper place, books put back on the shelves and the desk top left clean.

The employee should try to analyze his paper work and arrange it to fit his desk. Every drawer should be classified according to its contents. This relieves the mind of the details and if the desk user is methodical he will find that he has few lost items. In business it is automatic that the best executive always has a clean desk top.

The telephone gives constant access to the church leaders, the community, the press, and others. It is a labor saving device which is essential for leadership.

Next comes the typewriter. The minister who cannot operate a typewriter is a helpless individual. Even though his method is the pick-peck one, he will want to persevere until he can think with his hands upon the keys. Because he has a typewriter, he will need a filing cabinet. These two helps go together. If the desk has one file drawer, a filing cabinet will not be necessary in the one-man office.

As mentioned previously the minister would do well to buy a standard typewriter from a recognized manufacturer. The work of the minister subjects any typewriter to hard service and a portable machine does not possess the weight nor the strength for this work. Any good typewriter will last for a generation; a portable, at best, will give service for only a few years.

A further investment of a few dollars on a machine with a wide carriage will enable the minister to cut stencils for the duplicating machine which reproduces the Sunday bulletin, letters, and other material to be mailed out of the office. The minister would do well to insist that this typewriter be bought and owned by the church. If he wishes a second machine for his homework that is his responsibility, but the equipment in the church office should belong to the church. In the one-man church, the same typewriter will probably be used for correspondence, sermons, cutting stencils, and other church work.

The minister will have a great deal of correspondence. For this he will need the proper envelopes and letterheads. The letterhead should give the name of the church, the address to which mail should be sent, and the telephone number at which the minister may be reached.

The filing cabinet is necessary because the minister will need to keep carbon copies of all of his letters and other work which goes out of the office properly filed for reference. You will need to have but one or two embarrassing experiences to appreciate the need of this.

In buying a filing cabinet the small church has a choice between a cabinet which offers a combination of filing drawers— some for letters, some for cards, or one made to fit either the letter size or legal size sheet. It is better to get the letter size cabinet which takes the standard eight and one-half by eleven sheet than the legal which is several inches larger.

To complete the cabinet equipment, buy some indexed folders so that the correspondence may be filed alphabetically as it is taken care of. Suppose you are replying to a letter from John

Smith. Write your letter in reply, making a carbon copy at the same time. Attach this carbon copy to Mr. Smith's letter and place it in the "S" folder. As other letters are filed, place them in front of this letter so that the correspondence for the year will run from the back to the front of the folder.

If the sermons are typed on the standard sheets, one drawer in the cabinet may be set aside for filing them. These may be filed by dates, by subjects, or by Bible references. If the sermon file develops to any size, it would be well to prepare a cross-reference listing on a card the classification of the filing folders where both the subject and Bible references are given for ready reference.

These items are about the minimum for the one-man church office which can, if necessary, double as the pastor's study. As a church grows in size the office must grow with it. That will mean larger space, increased staff and specialization of work. The one typewriter will multiply into several and the selection may be more specialized. If the typing program is heavy an electric machine should be considered for one desk. It is faster than a hand machine, makes a uniform impression, and is much easier on the typist. In some churches there may be a place for a battery of automatic typewriters which duplicate original letters at high speed. The letters are definitely typed and they have the individuality so much desired in personal correspondence.

Duplicating Machines

The next machine to be considered by a church is some kind of duplicator. The duplicator is any device which can reproduce original written or typed copy into several or thousands of copies for mass distribution. When the minister desires to send a message to the entire congregation, the personal letter must be reproduced many times. There are many varieties of duplicators available for the office today; they range from the simple hectograph to the great printing and offset presses which give us daily papers and periodic magazines.

In 1880 Alexander Shapiro, a German, invented the simple

gelatin or hectograph process. A gelatin substance is poured
into a tray and allowed to jell. A letter is penned with ink
which has been impregnated with a powerful aniline dye. The
letter is then placed face down on the gelatin and allowed to
remain a few seconds. After it is removed other sheets are
placed on the gelatin and each receives an exact copy of the
original letter. In the early years twelve to fifteen good copies
might be secured by this process. Typewriter ribbons which
have been treated with hectograph ink are available so that
typed copy is now reproduced and up to one hundred copies
can be obtained by this method.

One step higher we have what is called the "fluid duplicator."
The original invention of this antedates the hectograph, but
practical application came later. James Watt, the Englishman
who was responsible for the steam engine, is credited with creating the idea in 1780. He used a glutinous ink with which he
wrote a message on a sheet of paper. This ink did not dry rapidly and he found that by placing a sheet of paper on his original copy a duplicate was imprinted. As these were negative
copies, he used very thin sheets of paper. Then the sheets were
placed on a windowpane and he read through the paper. Business was very reluctant to accept this invention as it was feared
that it might make forgery easy.

The fluid duplicator follows the idea of Watt. Instead of
glutinous ink, it uses hectographic ink. While Watt's copies
had to be read through transparent paper, the modern process
places the print in readable form on the upper surface of the
paper. Both methods require the moistening of the impression
paper. Watt used water, the modern manufacturer uses a fast
drying spirit. How is the copy converted from negative to positive in the reproduction? The carbon sheet containing hectographic ink is simply placed underneath the copy sheet with
the carbon reversed so that the message is written on the back
of the master sheet. The moistened impression sheets are pressed
against this and the positive letter results. Modern fluid dupli-

cators will produce several hundred copies of three or four colors in an hour.

Up one more step in cost and efficiency are the stencil duplicators. Historically this method goes back many, many years. In our own country two names are associated with the process: the great inventor Thomas A. Edison and a middle western lumberman named A. B. Dick. The stencil as it is used today is a thin sheet of fibrous material covered with a plastic chemical coating. This sheet may be placed directly in the typewriter and typed as one would type a letter. The keys spread the chemical coating so that the letters are visible on the resulting porous background. When the stencil is placed in the machine and inked, the ink passes through the porous material and when the rotating drum presses against the paper the letter is printed.

The ordinary stencil is capable of making as many as five thousand positive impressions. The mechanics of impression have been improved through the years and it is possible to make runs of color as well as black. By means of a stylus, illustrations may be drawn on the stencil. Line cuts often can be pressed into the stencil to give a good impression and a method of transferring half-tone cuts to the stencil is available. The larger machines are motor driven, so a good duplicator is to all purposes a small printing press made especially for office use.

We have used the term "duplicator" in a generic sense. Many call all stencil duplicators "mimeographs." This, however, is the trademark of but one manufacturer—the A. B. Dick Company. The word "mimeograph" we are told was coined from two Greek words, *mime* and *graph*, with the letter "o" placed between for euphony.

Up another step in efficiency we come to offset printing in the general classification of lithography. Lithography was first conceived by a Munich actor-playwright named Alois Senefelder in or about 1796. Printing costs were so high that he decided to learn the engraving and printing trade so he could publish his plays. He started to learn the art of the engraver and found the most difficult task was to place the copy in reverse upon the copper plates. One day he wrote directly upon a laundry stone. Curious to see what the result would be, he placed a sheet of paper over the stone and, having pulled the sheet off, discovered that a most satisfactory impression resulted. Lithography was on its way.

Stone lithography has given way to metal and even paper master plates, but this idea is still basic. There are a number of offset machines available to churches at a price which compares favorably with the best stencil duplicators. They are cylinder machines where a master sheet, usually metal but sometimes paper, contains the original copy. This is transferred to a rubber roller, which in turn "offsets" the copy to the impression sheet.

Offset duplicating has the advantage of reproducing illustrative matter. Halftone pictures clipped from magazines may be reproduced effectively. Photographs are given splendid reproduction. Another advantage which some churches appreciate is that offset duplicating is classed as lithography and magazines printed by this process are eligible for second-class entry in the post office. During the year a large church would save a considerable amount of money by this method of printing.

In just which kind the church should invest if it invests in any depends on the local situation and program. The stencil duplicator is a good all around work horse for any church. The quality has been improved with passing years and the investment is nominal. The offset machine may be secured at a little higher cost, but the highest priced stencil duplicator will probably cost more than the lowest priced offset printer. The offset machine requires more skill and its use is somewhat limited by location. Few churches will have facilities for preparing the metal plates required by many offset machines—it is thus necessary to have access to a shop which does this work. More skill, too, is required to do a good offset job than is required for simpler duplication methods. A church recently visited had installed an expensive offset machine, but no one on the staff felt competent to operate it. As a result it was necessary to secure from outside sources a trained operator for one-half day each week to do the work. A typewriter and stencils are about all an office needs with a stencil duplicator.

One of the interesting phenomena of recent years has been the growth of the so-called "letter shops." These houses are specialists in the field of duplication and have good machines which are carefully serviced. Churches located in communities with such shops should look around to see what is offered. It is possible that duplication from the local letter shop will cost less than if it were done in the church office. The work of the letter shops includes so many items such as duplicating, addressing, folding, mailing, etc., that such a shop becomes a valuable assistant. A wise church will investigate this possibility before investing in any additional machinery.

The Addressing Machine

With the duplicator it is a simple matter to reproduce letters, announcements, programs, and other things useful in the church. There is still the necessity of getting these into the hands of the people who should read them. The quickest and most efficient way is through the use of the United States mail. This means addressing envelopes for the congregation or heads of families and if the church membership runs into hundreds it is a tedious task. So the next labor saving machine the church should consider is an addressing machine.

Here again the machines offered are many, as were the duplicators, and run in price from a few dollars to hundreds of dollars. There are simple hand machines which use the fluid duplicator idea and sell for as little as ten dollars. These address from a paper tape and are suitable for lists which do not run much more than one hundred. But for the longer lists the church will have to choose between two basic types—the machines which use the wax stencil address plate and the kind which use the embossed metal plate. The distinction here is the same that is found between the duplicator which uses the wax stencil and the multigraph which prints through a ribbon. The Elliott system made for various sized groups uses the wax stencil address plate; the Addressograph system uses the embossed metal plate which prints through an inked ribbon. There are virtues and limitations to both systems.

Hand driven models of either type may be purchased for less than one hundred dollars; the power driven models which are necessary for the larger churches will run into the hundreds and even into the thousands, depending on the features of the individual machine.

The addressing machines which use stencils offer more than simple addressing. They give a complete double check on your lists. Both types may be equipped with selectors which make it possible to pick out and address any particular group in the church. Suppose, for instance, you want to mail only to heads of families. The selectors will permit the machine to skip all stencils except those which indicate by a symbol on the plate that they are heads of families. You can mail to Sunday school attendants, contributors, marginal members, or others as you may wish. Any church of five hundred members needs a power driven machine with the selector.

The stencil plates which are used in the Elliott system may be cut on your own typewriter by yourself or someone in your office. The metal name plates must be embossed by an expensive machine which may cost as much as the addressing machine alone. If you do not have this machine you must send the list to the nearest Addressograph office to have the work done for you.

If you want a filled-in letter you can probably match the inking of your letter much better with an Addressograph than with the Elliott.

Folding Machines

It has been customary in our churches to call in a group of women to fold and enclose the letters which are going out to members. It is slow work and the folding committee usually finds itself short-handed. The recent introduction of folding machines at a modest price will interest all churches. For under two hundred dollars such machines are available. They are motor driven devices which will fold your letters, bulletins, and other publicity in a fraction of the time taken by the hand method.

In addition to these office machines which are almost essentials in the church office, there are others which should be considered. If the church accounting is done in the office, an adding machine is a necessity and a coin counter very desirable. And there is always use for hand stapling machines at any desk which deals with correspondence or other papers. The person who cuts the stencils for the church bulletin may wish a mimeoscope or some similar device for tracing illustrations. A pencil sharpener will be appreciated by every worker.

Stampers and Sealers

There are various gadgets to help the office secretary with the sealing of envelopes and the stamping of the envelopes. Some of these imprint a postage stamp and seal at the same time. A pre-deposit of money at the post office is required to offset postage cost. Sealing machines are available in both hand powered and motor powered machines.

Relationship of Study and Offices

As the size of the church membership increases and more staff personnel are available, the study-office relationship is simplified rather than complicated. The minister's time can be better protected. Guests must pass a reception desk before reaching his office. He must not be a recluse and the arrangement of space must not entirely bar him from those who seek him, but there will be an increasing insistence on the need for appointments.

While he prefers to be located away from the confusion of the business office, the pastor remains the head of the executive program of the church and he must know what is going on in the business office. In this effort he is more or less dependent upon those to whom he has assigned the details of the work.

12 | FINANCING THE LOCAL CHURCH

THE EARLY SETTLERS IN THE AMERICAN COLONIES brought their churches and religious practices with them. As churches were established Old World methods based on government subsidy and taxation were used to finance them. This was true in most of the New England states, in New Amsterdam, Virginia, and the Carolinas. The birth of new denominations soon made this a rather embarrassing situation for the colonies. Virginia, through the influence of Thomas Jefferson and James Madison, very early legislated for separation of church and state and thus put the responsibility for financing the local church on the members themselves.

There are still some relics of the state church in America. Churches enjoy exemptions from various types of taxation and the clergy are usually free from jury and military duty. But the cost of building church edifices and the responsibility of paying the expenses of salaries and incidentals in the maintenance of church services rest upon the denominational bodies and the individual churches. The effect of this has stimulated religious activities and is to a great degree responsible for the strength of religious institutions in the United States.

The local church is a unit in the denomination. It has the responsibility not alone of maintaining its own services but of giving its share of support for the world-wide work of the denomination. The system of raising pledges and support which we have today did not spring full grown into being. Early churches depended very heavily on the families of wealth and later on pew sales, pew rentals, chicken suppers, pound parties, the annual subscription pledge, sales schemes and bazaars, the weekly collection, the mite box, and other forms of financing, some of which remain with us in one form or another. From these devices evolved our present conception of Christian stewardship, fairly modern in its meaning and practice.

Christian stewardship has as its basic concept that every Christian, whether rich or poor, has received his life and his possessions from God. As a Christian steward he dedicates himself and his wealth to the work of God. As an act of worship he gives a portion of his income to the support of the church and other worthy social causes.

As the best method of doing this the church asks its members to pledge the amount of money in weekly installments each will give to the church for a calendar year. To make accounting easy, printing presses have been perfected which number and date envelopes for the entire year. Such envelopes become an automatic accounting system.

As a scriptural basis for this method of supporting the church, the churches have used the words of Saint Paul.

> Now concerning the collection for the saints, as I have given order to the churches of Galatia, even so do ye. Upon the first day of the week, let every one of you lay by him in store, as God hath prospered him, that there be no gatherings when I come.   I Corinthians 16:1,2

The proportion of money to be given to the church and its work is left to the individual. There are many teachers of stewardship who feel that the tithe, defined as one-tenth of the individual's income, should be the minimum. "Tithers" are often the bulwarks of the local church, but only in very few instances do they represent a considerable segment of any church membership. Studies indicate that the percentage of an average member's income given to the church is less than three per cent—usually between two per cent and three per cent.

There are perhaps four principles of stewardship which are basic to the program today.

1. God is the owner of all.
2. He has entrusted to us our lives and our wealth; we are stewards of that wealth.

3. As recognition of this stewardship each of us will return to God, in a systematic way, a portion of our income.

4. The giving of money and other resources strengthens the church but, also, enriches the giver.

There is apparently a basic spiritual law that one who shares of his wealth with others does receive a spiritual satisfaction. There are many testimonies of those whose lives have been helped through the practice of sharing.

The church method of today does go somewhat beyond the injunction of the Apostle. We feel that in the successful financial effort a pledge to pay is necessary. "A pledge is more than a gift." Without a definite pledge the church officers would hesitate to contract for salaries, to plan for missionary apportionments and building upkeep, or to accept other obligations. With pledges to guarantee the proposed budget these leaders are assured that they can go ahead with their plans.

The Mechanics of Fund Raising

While stewardship is a much larger subject than the raising of money for the church, the highly developed systems we have for fund raising would not be effective if a congregation had not been instructed in the principles of stewardship. On the other hand, stewardship principles must be supplemented with effective techniques if the local church is to prosper financially. There are three areas in local church finance: budgeting, canvassing, and accounting. There is another area of church finance which is very active today—the raising of pledges and funds for new church building. This subject will be considered in a special section of this study.

Making the Budget

An important part of a financial program of any church is the projection of the budget for the year to come. Even the small church with a budget of a few hundred dollars finds this important and as the church grows in financial resources, it becomes a necessity. The basic operation is very simple but in the larger congregations it becomes extended and complex.

Churches may at one time have depended entirely on voluntary offers to balance income with the outgo. Churches which respect their commercial credit cannot be satisfied with that procedure. They like to know the giving habits and resources of the congregation and they feel it wise to project a program which may require sacrifice but still well within the realm of reality.

Ideally we could appraise the annual income of the congregation, multiply it by ten per cent to find the tithe of the families' income, and agree that the tithe will pay the expenses. If any church ever received a tithe of the incomes of its congregation, it would have a wealth undreamed of to use in its program. Realism in finances requires more than estimation of the tithe. In its simplest form, the budget-making process consists of listing the expenditures of the current year and projecting the work for the next year based on current income. Salary increases and increased costs so common in this era must be taken into consideration.

The first step in making a budget is to find what the church is spending during the current year. Probably the financial reports are available. Divide the expenses into various categories and list them. At one side of the current expenses leave space for listing the amount for that particular item for the year ahead.

It is customary to list the benevolence monies separately from the local church budget. There is both a mathematical and a moral reason for this. Many feel that the ideal is for a church to give as much to others as it keeps for itself. Very few churches reach this goal. On the other hand there are church boards which would prefer to keep everything for themselves. So a separate listing shows the actual division and is a constant reminder that the church is not overly generous with its giving to missionary and relief work.

The small-church budget, then, would look something like this:

Local Church Budget

	SPENT IN 1957	PROPOSED BUDGET FOR 1958
Minister's Salary	$4,000.00	$4,200.00
Organist	250.00	250.00
Custodian	250.00	250.00
Fuel & Light	200.00	250.00
Building Up-keep	500.00	450.00
Sunday School Literature	150.00	275.00
	5,350.00	5.675.00

BENEVOLENCE		
Home Missions	200.00	250.00
Foreign Missions	200.00	250.00
Indian Missions	25.00	25.00
Per Capita Tax	150.00	155.00
	575.00	680.00

The process of appraising the present resources of the church and looking ahead to the next year is what constitutes "making the budget." The committee considers each item: the minister needed a raise and probably the organist and custodian would have liked one too. The benevolent budget was increased because the membership had grown somewhat missionary-minded. The Sunday school literature allowance was raised to meet the increased cost of this item. The actual making of the budget rests with a committee of the official board. It considers every item of expenditure, breaking it down into smaller units, to see if employees are being treated fairly and if the church is being overcharged for any item in its budget.

The chairman of the committee should be, if possible, one who has had experience in this kind of work. He should have the privilege of selecting his committee members. Members having earlier experience in one particular church can provide a good general picture of the financial progress or recession.

As the church grows the system becomes more complicated and time consuming. The second example is a church with a local budget of fifteen thousand dollars. The committee insists on a breakdown of several of the items. They ask the treasurer what is meant by miscellaneous. Why should the parsonage expense be so high? Could paper and ink really cost nearly four hundred dollars per year?

Although the treasurer is required to submit a breakdown of all items, we are including only three of the classifications. Major repairs on the parsonage are not likely to recur the following year. Seventy-five dollars, the amount involved in the call of the new pastor, can be dropped from miscellaneous items, but it is hard to see how the cost of office supplies can be reduced. So the reasoning goes as the budget for the new year expands.

Annual Expenditures of $15,000 Budget

CURRENT EXPENSE DISBURSEMENTS ITEMIZED

Salaries	$4,325.05
Church Maintenance	1,285.98
Parish House Maintenance	116.40
Parsonage Maintenance	1,228.35
Supply Pastors	595.00
Water	69.03
Telephone	188.15
Electric	224.50
Gas	635.46
Taxes	150.62
Insurance	528.26
General Church Supplies	459.51
General Office Supplies & Expense	381.64
General Equipment Expense	413.65
Pension Fund	239.17
Bible School	158.39
Miscellaneous	785.57
TOTAL	$11,784.73

BENEVOLENCE DISBURSEMENTS ITEMIZED

American Lutheran Church	$2,775.00
District Dues	190.00
Lutheran Welfare League	310.00
TOTAL	$3,275.00

BREAKDOWN OF SEVERAL CATEGORIES OF THE MAINTENANCE BUDGET

Bathroom Repair	$131.71
Screen Repair	10.35
Papering	368.52
Floor Sanding & Finishing	175.00
Antenna	103.85
Carpet, Rods, Cleaner	123.79
Lumber & Screen	6.98
Plumbing	34.95
Molding, Wall Covering, Cement	42.13
Toilet Seat	5.85
Screws, Nails, Tacks, Screens	9.43
Plumbing Repair	4.00
Electrical Repair	9.61
Insulating	145.00
Papering Breakfast Nook	57.18
TOTAL	$1,228.35

MISCELLANEOUS DISBURSEMENTS ITEMIZED

Christmas Decorations	$29.22
Music	27.63
Flowers	33.09
Expense of Call	75.20
Choir Robe Material	25.61
Moving Expense	344.93
Seed & Fertilizer	12.69
Picnic Supplies	33.96
Prints	2.68
Safe Deposit Rent	2.20
Conference Expense	8.00
Planning Committee Expense	25.00
A.L.C. Christmas Fund	74.73
Gifts	60.00
Freight on Clothing	30.58
TOTAL	$785.57

GENERAL OFFICE SUPPLIES & EXPENSE ITEMIZED

Paper	$31.34
Postage	16.40
Checks	5.32
Printing & Envelopes	97.75
Plates, Ink, Stencils	119.50
Forms & Journals	36.33
Miscellaneous	75.00
TOTAL	$381.64

The work sheet (on page 216) for a budget committee is much more thorough than in most churches. Note actual figures for the past two years, estimates for the present year, and the adjusted budget for the balance of the year. Later in discussing budget control accounting we will show the budget for the year that followed which was based on this study.

Insofar as possible, the committee should try to present a complete budget of all church activities through some may be self-financing. An over-all budget should be compiled so that the congregation can know just what the total operating cost of the church may be. The womens' organizations may resist inclusion on the grounds that they finance their own work and should report separately. Some church schools still finance themselves. The present tendency definitely is to combine all income in one report, whether or not the expenditures are made from different treasuries.

Publicizing the Budget

The budget in its mathematical form may be presented to a board of the congregation. There are some people, however, who can't read figures and need an imaginative, graphic presentation. One common practice is to break down the figures into various departments and describe, in brief, just how the money is spent.

Another method is to reduce the budget into percentages. The budget just presented, when broken down shows the di-

	1954 Adjusted Budget	8 Months 1954 Actual	Estimated 4 months	Total 1954 (estimated)	Actual 1953	Actual 1952	First Suggested Budget
WORSHIP SERVICE							
Minister	$ 6,000.00	$ 4,000.00	$ 2,000.00	$ 6,000.00	$ 5,500.00	$ 5,000.00	$ 6,000.00
Pulpit Supply	60.00	25.00		25.00	50.00		75.00
Sacred Music							
Choir Director	675.00	375.00	300.00	675.00	550.00	450.00	675.00
Organist	600.00	400.00	200.00	600.00	440.00	360.00	600.00
Choir Services & Supplies	100.00	57.60	75.00	132.60	111.99	109.88	125.00
Calendars	900.00	530.50	350.00	880.50	793.40	781.51	900.00
Worship Supplies	50.00	75.09	25.00	100.09	42.32	43.42	100.00
	8,385.00	5,463.19	2,950.00	8,413.19	7,487.71	6,744.81	8,475.00
PROMOTION AND EDUCATION							
Minister of Christian Education	3,875.00	2,735.00	1,140.00	3,875.00	4,083.32	3,600.00	3,420.00
Min. Christian Ed.—manse rent	325.00	130.00	260.00	390.00			780.00
Fanfare (monthly newsletter)	400.00	203.64	100.00	303.64			350.00
Boy Scouts	50.00		20.00	20.00	9.25		50.00
Youth Budget	475.00	250.00	225.00	475.00	475.00	400.00	475.00
Min. Christian Ed.—travel expense	280.00	186.91	93.09	280.00	214.60		
Library	50.00	32.50	17.50	50.00			
	5,455.00	3,538.05	1,855.59	5,393.64	4,782.17	4,000.00	5,075.00
STAFF BENEFITS							
Minister's Retirement	615.00	414.00	207.00	621.00	585.09	517.50	621.00
Min. Christian Ed.—retirement	400.00	224.00	61.50	285.50	319.91		300.00
Social Security (OAB)	92.00	58.62	25.00	83.62	60.58		95.00
Industrial Accident Insurance	50.00	16.94	8.52	25.46	35.76	13.91	40.00
	1,157.00	713.56	302.02	1,015.58	1,001.34	531.41	1,056.00
ORGANIZATION EXPENSE							
Congregational Fellowship Dues	90.00	84.30		84.30	86.40	70.50	90.00
Presbyterian Assessments	563.00	562.38		562.38	534.00	422.22	590.00
	653.00	646.68		646.68	620.40	492.42	
ADMINISTRATION							
Treasurer's Expense	40.00	33.40	6.60	40.00			20.00
Financial Secretary's Expense	130.00	80.00	40.00	120.00	120.00	66.67	150.00
Canvassing & Pledging	100.00	45.61	40.00	85.61	58.98	56.36	100.00
Church Secretary	2,700.00	1,800.00	900.00	2,700.00	2,400.00	2,000.00	2,700.00
Contingencies	810.00				63.70		900.00
Travel Expense—Minister	320.00	220.62	99.38	320.00	320.00		400.00
Office Expense	550.00	419.87	120.00	539.87	947.53	897.20	600.00
Annual Meetings	20.00	20.00		20.00			40.00
Interest	186.17	128.78	57.39	186.17	226.86	263.44	143.62
	4,856.17	2,748.28	1,263.37	4,011.65	4,137.07	3,283.67	
BUILDING OPERATION & MAINTENANCE							
Custodian	2,000.00	1,416.69	666.64	2,083.33	2,000.00	1,813.35	2,085.00
Hostess	300.00	400.00	200.00	600.00	300.00	253.61	600.00*
Fuel	1,500.00	1,247.48	300.00	1,547.48	1,327.31	1,231.51	1,400.00
Telephone	250.00	166.88	80.00	246.88	246.76	185.74	250.00
Church Maintenance	2,500.00	541.51	3,500.00	4,041.51	817.53	1,411.74	4,000.00
Manse Taxes	135.00		130.00	130.00	121.20	117.05	130.00
Insurance	650.00	557.48		557.48	616.29	435.70	500.00
Manse Maintenance	550.00	511.01	40.00	551.01	201.89	104.25	150.00
Utilities	550.00	443.18	160.00	603.18	573.98	446.73	600.00
	8,435.00	5,284.23	5,076.64	10,360.87	6,204.87	5,999.58	
CAPITAL							
Principal—manse	833.83	551.22	282.54	833.76	793.14	756.56	876.30
SPECIAL PROJECTS							
Centennial Celebration (net)		50.00		50.00	245.65		
Moving Expenses—Min. Christian Ed.					300.00		
		50.00		50.00	545.65		
OLD ACCOUNTS DROPPED OR NEW ONES ADDED							
Promotion & Education—Supplies (new)							150.00
Elders & Deacons Fund (old)					136.70	197.25	
					136.70	197.25	
Total Budgeted Expenditures	$29,775.00	$18,995.21	$11,730.16	$30,725.37	$25,709.14	$22,006.10	$30,141.00

* We pay $600 already. $300 is contributed by the Woman's Association. This amount merely reports as factual the $600.
PROPOSED PROJECTS: Repair chimney and dormer window Ed. Hall $300; new desk and chair for minister's study $300; new typewriter for church office $150; remodel nursery room Ed. Hall $1500; new adding machine for church office $200.

Working sheet for the budget committee. The above is a reproduction of the actual presentation made to the budget committee of the Federated Churches, Corvallis, Oregon. Note that the committee is given information of the previous budgets together with the proposed changes for the new year. Later in this chapter we will show how during the year of operation of this budget the treasurer made a report of expenditures "to date."

The Proposed Budget For 1957 Is $117,637.05
How Will It Be Spent?

MINISTRY OF THE WORD AND SACRAMENTS $17,982.90

> To provide salaries for Dr. Hughes and Mr. Cockcroft, guest preachers in the summer, flowers not provided as memorials, and tracts for the narthex racks.

MINISTRY OF RELIGIOUS EDUCATION 12,075.00

> Salary for Mr. Knight, student assistant, training and equipment for nearly 100 volunteer members of the Church School Staff; purchasing materials for nearly 900 participating in the Church School program; providing adequate visual aids for all ages; curriculum books and magazines; summer conference scholarships for young people; reference materials for the Church School Library; supervision of baby-sitting.

MINISTRY OF MUSIC 10,500.00

> Salaries of Mr. Hart and members of the Quartet who provide competent professional training and direction for 250 volunteers in our Primary, two Junior, St. Cecelia, Senior High Carolers, and Chancel Choirs; summer organists and soloists; sheet music and hymnals for all Choirs; laundering, cleaning, and replacement of Choir Robes; awards for Choir Sunday. (A modest increase has been granted the professional musicians for their extra work at the early Service.)

MISSIONARY ENTERPRISES OF OUR CHURCH 20,855.60

> Partial support of our Missionaries: Dr. Homer V. Bradshaw, Dr. John Elder, Rev. Rafael Guerera, Dr. John P. McConnell; general benevolences in Ridgewood, the State of New Jersey, and across the country; assistance to two Presbyterian homes for the aged in our Synod of New Jersey; contributions to the Presbyterian Board of Pensions to assist aged and needy ministers of our denomination who lack adequate financial resources.

CHURCH AND OFFICE ADMINISTRATION 19,250.00

> Salaries of the Office Secretary, Assistant Secretary, Minister's Secretary, Assistant Treasurer, and additional stenographic help (in addition to 40 hours per week of volunteer help); postage for all church mailings; stationery; printing and publicity; telephone; supplies for the Church Office.

PROPERTY AND MAINTENANCE 24,550.00

> Salaries of two Sextons and some part-time help in the upkeep of two buildings and grounds; public utilities, fuel, insurance on all church property; replacement of worn-out equipment, piano and organ tuning; janitorial supplies and paper goods; disposal; repairs and general property maintenance.

SUNDRY BUDGET ITEMS 12,423.55

> Per capita tax for the support of the General Assembly of the Presbyterian Church, U. S. A., the Presbytery of Jersey City; social committee; membership committee; auto replacement allowance and auto maintenance for the ministers; social security tax on the Church payroll; property reserve for unexpected emergency large-scale repairs; rental allowances for ministers; repayment on account of Demarest legacy loan borrowed for extraordinary repairs in 1955.

A departmental budget break-down.

vision of a dollar into seven classifications. The amount which goes to each division is shown below.

1. Ministry of Word and Sacrament . . . . . . 16 cents
2. Religious Education . . . . 10 cents
3. Ministry of Music . . . . 9 cents
4. Missionary Enterprises . . . . 18 cents
5. Church Administration . . . . 17 cents
6. Property and Maintenance . . . . 21 cents
7. Sundry Budget Items . . . . 9 cents

This could be still further visualized by using a circle to illustrate the dollar and letting the various segments represent the part of the dollar applied to each department of work.

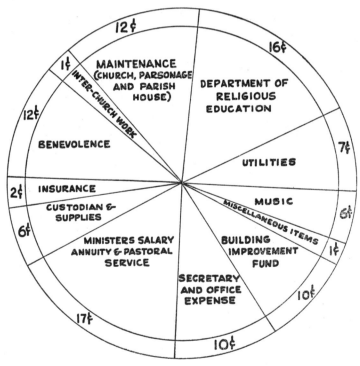

This is a very effective method of publicizing the budget of the local church. Illustration from the every member canvass material of the First Congregational Church, Waterloo, Iowa.

A Plan for the Every Member Canvass

The plan that follows is a general presentation. Some churches may prefer a more elaborate organization. Some may think that this is too complex for them. The basic formula from which one may select and adapt to a local program has the virtue of flexibility. Following this presentation, some substitutes for the canvass are suggested. It may be wise to skip the every member canvass some years and use one of the other methods to take advantage of change. But, year after year, no method is so rewarding as a good every member canvass and with some continuity in the leadership efficiency increases with repeated use.

The campaign committee to be appointed by the proper body should consist of the following: a General Chairman; a Chairman for Advance Gifts; a Chairman for General Solicitation; a Listings and Evaluation Chairman; a Publicity Chairman; a Meetings Chairman; a Dinners' Chairman; a Secretary; and the Minister *ex officio*.

THE GENERAL CHAIRMAN. An individual of good reputation in the community who is generous in his giving to the church.

ADVANCE GIFTS CHAIRMAN. He will have charge of the solicitation of the larger gifts giving attention particularly to those members who have not been giving according to their ability. This is a community fund technique transferred to the church field.

GENERAL SOLICITATIONS CHAIRMAN. He will direct the general campaign, cover all prospects except those taken care of by the Advance Gifts Chairman.

A LISTINGS AND EVALUATION CHAIRMAN. His committee will go through the records of the past year. Where possible the income of contributors should be secured and their giving habits indicated. Where larger giving might be possible this is indicated on the card.

PUBLICITY CHAIRMAN. His obligation is to plan the program of publicizing the canvass to the members of the church and the community. Every possible area for publicity should be probed.

THE MEETINGS CHAIRMAN. He will have charge of all meetings, provide for speakers, singers, and entertainment. He will see that arrangements are made for the rooms to be used, that they are heated and lighted. He also will serve as program manager for the dinners. This chairmanship may be combined with the dinners chairman if desirable.

THE DINNERS' CHAIRMAN. He makes the arrangements for all meals and lunches held in connection with the campaign. The work of this chairman may, if it seems desirable, be combined with that of meetings chairman.

When the chairmen have been selected and they have accepted the responsibility, the next step is to select the workers for their committees. When the selections have been made, the individuals should be contacted by phone or mail (preferably by phone) and asked to attend a meeting of the committee for instructions. All meetings may be held the same night if separate rooms are available or they may be staggered over a week. There may have to be some adjusting of personnel to meet the difficulty of stated engagements of the individual. If one cannot attend the meeting of the committee to which he has been selected, assign him to a different committee.

At the meeting each detail of the campaign should be presented so each person knows the purpose of his committee and the entire program. The general chairman must check each subchairman to see that work is progressing as it should.

Components of the Plan

The general plan of organization just described has been set up for a definite purpose. Organization, meetings, publicity, dinners, and a very thorough canvass are necessary for a successful campaign.

1. A list of all members and all potential non-member contributors.

2. A systematic evaluation of all pledges of the past year to see which members can lift their level of giving.

3. A briefing conference for all canvassers in which they will be instructed in the techniques of the plan with especial emphasis upon the amount of gift suggested by the evaluations committee.

4. Two dinner meetings: the first to bring the church membership together, the second a "kick-off" dinner for the canvassers.

5. A canvass which will extend over a number of days; all signed pledges to be turned over on the last Sunday of the effort, which may be known as Victory Sunday.

6. An advance solicitation of the larger givers who may need special briefing on the higher budget; and a three-day mop-up committee to bring in any pledges not in hand by Sunday.

Organization of the Solicitors

Nothing is of more importance in the campaign than the selection of the workers. The solicitors can be briefed on the techniques of the campaign but they should be men or women who have the interests of the church at heart and have an honest concept of Christian stewardship.

The campaign calls for two joint efforts. The first is that in which the larger givers are solicited by men in their own income brackets. The chairman of the advance solicitations committee should have first choice of the solicitors.

In both the advance solicitation and the general campaign the solicitors should be divided first into divisions and then into teams. A team consists of a captain and five men. For instance, if in a general campaign you have twenty solicitors, divide the twenty into two divisions of ten men each; each division will then be divided into two teams of five men each. Each division will have a chairman and each team a captain.

The more workers you have, the better. For every one hundred prospects, you will need twenty-five workers. If more volunteer, use them though this cuts down the number of calls the teams will make. Fewer cards given each team means more thorough solicitation.

All workers will be canvassed before the general solicitation. The Advance Gifts Chairman will solicit the gifts of each of his division heads. These men in turn will solicit the captains, and they will solicit the men on their teams. This same rule will apply in the general solicitation. In this process about one-quarter of the pledges will be made before the canvass is underway.

Shall the solicitation be individual or in pairs? The usual practice is to call in two's, the second man giving moral support to the spokesman. Others hold that many men work better alone than in pairs. This would be especially true in the advance gifts efforts. In assigning these few cards, it is well not only to assign the solicitor to a man in his own age bracket but, if possible, to assign him to those with whom he has personal influence.

In the general solicitation some churches will prefer to have individual workers, others will prefer teamwork. If two are to work together, the committee may assign the men to work together or the first man may be permitted to select his travelling companion.

The subchairman in charge of solicitations usually selects the division chairmen; the division chairman should select his own captains; the captains should have the right to select their solicitors. One method of doing this is to have the names of all prospective solicitors on index cards. As these names are read, the captains may indicate the ones they wish.

When the team for solicitation has been set up the next step is to assign the prospects. This is done in the small group which has charge of advance solicitations; it is more of a task in the general solicitation. A very effective way is to have a duplicate set of cards of all prospects. One set of these can be displayed alphabetically in a rack. Divide the number of prospects by the number of solicitors, or by the number of calling teams if the callers are going out in pairs. Then each caller or team of callers may select their own prospects.

Publicity Helps

THE BROCHURE. Possibly the most important publicity item

of the every-member canvass effort will be the brochure. It should present in an attractive, readable form the church budget, with an explanation of the various items. It can be either duplicated or printed. The latter is preferable as it will make a more attractive piece of publicity, which is important. The average church is justified in using a good two-color job, with appropriate pictures, for this purpose.

LISTING-CARDS. Every prospect should have a card. These cards should have an end or corner perforated so it may be torn off by the canvasser. The evaluations committee will write on this section the amount of gift which should be asked. It should be torn from the card so that the prospect will not see the amount suggested.

SUITABLE PLEDGE CARDS. Pledge cards adapted to the needs of the local church are necessary.

REPORT ENVELOPE. This envelope should be about six by nine or eight by ten inches. On the front there should be spaces for donors names and amounts of pledges received and any cash or checks which were accepted. When the report on the front is completed, the pledges, currency, and checks may be enclosed in the envelope and turned over to the team captain, who then passes it on to the division chairman.

The Dinners

The every-member canvass calls for two dinners. One called the Loyalty Dinner is really an announcement of the campaign and the entire congregation is invited. No charge is made to the members, the cost of the meal being placed in the church budget or in the expense-accounting of the campaign. The officers will explain the budget at this meeting. If the amount asked has been increased, they will tell why. At each place will be a copy of the brochure which will be referred to during the discussions.

The details of procedure will be explained and the members requested to think seriously of the project and be ready to welcome the solicitors when they call at their homes. No pledges will be taken at the dinner. The advance solicitations committee will, however, start its work immediately following the meal. A Wednesday or Thursday evening is a good time for this meal and the Kick-Off Dinner, the second dinner, can follow on Monday or Tuesday of the following week. The advance solicitations committee should have its work completed by the time of the Kick-Off Dinner.

Sunday following the Loyalty Dinner will be observed as Stewardship Sunday. The sermon will be devoted to the claims of Christian stewardship in relation to the local church. The congregation will be informed of the campaign to take place during the next few days and told that all pledges for the year which is to follow will be consecrated on the following Sunday. An invitation can be given for any who can work on the solicitations committee to hand in their names to the church office or chairman of the solicitations committee.

The Kick-Off Dinner to be held on Monday or Tuesday is for the solicitors. They will receive their briefing on the campaign and be given minute instructions for their work. They can start their activities immediately after the dinner and will be expected to have all pledges from their prospects in the hands of the committee chairman before Sunday. Seldom is a financial campaign completely successful in the first effort. There will be need for a follow-up effort on prospects who have been missed. Solicitors should be pressed to complete this work. When cards are turned in which show "no call," those cards should be given to a "clean-up" committee. Such a committee may be made up of the captains, who will make the final effort themselves.

Instructions to Solicitors

(As used in the Lakewood Congregational Church, Lakewood, Ohio.)

1. UNDERSTAND THE REASON FOR THIS CAMPAIGN. Many weeks of preparation have gone into the effort. The personal solicitation is the climax. Every home to be reached has received before your call two letters, copy of the large brochure, the fact card distributed on Easter, notices in *The Columns*, announcements

in the Sunday bulletins. Each family should be well informed and anticipate your purpose.

The best preparation you can have is to read and digest the literature mentioned above so that you can answer any questions which may be raised. Copy of each publicity item is being placed in your kit for that purpose. We are sure that your questions will be answered by the enclosures.

2. THE MASTER CARD AND THE PLEDGE CARD. The Master Cards which you have been given give your assignment. They contain very valuable, additional information. Each has a record of the family's giving habits and, also, a figure which our Evaluation Committee feels would be a fair gift from this prospect. *This information is confidential. The contributor is not to see this card.* This is the only complete list available and is vitally necessary in the work of the Church. Return these cards with your pledge cards to the Church Office, so they may get back into the proper files.

The Pledge Card is to be filled out and signed by the contributor. It provides for a pledge to be paid over a period of two years starting September 1955. The pledge may be paid weekly, monthly, quarterly, or by other method selected by the contributor. You may accept cash or checks toward the payment of the pledge; these should be indicated in your report to be turned in to the Church Office.

3. YOUR CALL SHOULD BE MADE ON THE FAMILY. The entire family circle is interested in the Church. Always check the family groups to see if there are not young people, now wage earners, who wish to make individual pledges. You will carry additional pledge cards for that purpose.

4. THE MEMORIAL FUND. As you know, many Memorial Gifts are now being made to the Church. These are for specific items. A brochure listing possible Memorial Gifts will be found in your kit. Your first effort in this campaign is to secure pledges and gifts for the general building fund. If in the conversation you find that the family is interested in a Memorial, advise them that you will give their names to the Memorial Gifts Committee which will call upon them. The Memorial Gifts Committee will follow up this information.

5. FRIENDS OF THE CHURCH. Some of your calls may be on families which are not members of the Church. Through their participa-

tion in our activities we have learned to call them "Friends of the Church." You may have no evaluation amount for these families. Some may give generously; others may not be ready to share in our effort.

Remember in calling on these families that your task is evangelistic as well as financial. Tell them that we are happy that they are interested in our Church and hope that they will continue their interest.

If in these or any other calls you run into situations which suggest the need of pastoral services, it would be helpful if you would indicate that on the back of the pledge card.

6. SALES TECHNIQUE. Tell the story the best you can. You can't make anyone write a pledge but you can give him the information which will lead to a decision to pledge. That is the best salesmanship.

Don't beg. The Church is not a mendicant. You are offering people who believe in the program the opportunity to share in a great work. Express your own faith in our program and your own confidence that our effort will succeed.

When you receive the pledge, be sure to fill out the receipt form attached to the card and leave it with the pledger. Advise that the Church will also make acknowledgment of gift.

Stay long enough for fellowship, but do not overdo the matter. Remember there are other calls to make.

7. DATES FOR THE SOLICITATION. A service of consecration and worship dedicated to the success of this effort has been planned for Sunday morning, May 1. A special section of the Church has been reserved for the canvassers. Plan to be there.

Solicitors will provide for their noon-day meal elsewhere and start their work at the earliest possible moment. Experience has shown that the earlier the start the more the pledges. Do not embarrass families who are in preparation for a meal, but advise them that you will call back.

We hope that you can complete your calls on Sunday, May 1. If you cannot, be sure to fill out a report of the calls made and return it, together with pledges, cash, checks, and master cards to the Church Office. The Office will be open afternoon and evening for that purpose.

Then continue your solicitation during the following days. All cards should be covered by May 8. If you are unable to locate the prospects on the first call, try again. If the address on the master card is incorrect, call the Church Office; perhaps the change of address has come in. Keep trying until the assignment is completed.

8. PRAYER. Above all, keep in mind that in this task you are a steward for God; ask him to give you the wisdom and the strength to serve well. Equipped with information and Christian faith, you will do a great work.

There still remains Victory Sunday. This is not a day for solicitation but for the consecration of pledges. This service can be most impressive. After a sermon of thankgiving for what God has done for the church, all of the people who have worked on the canvass are asked to come to the front of the church. This includes all from the general chairman, subchairman down to the solicitors. The pledges are heaped upon the altar or communion table. The congregation is asked to stand and a prayer of consecration for each pledge and each pledger is made by the pastor.

A few days of the campaign remain for the "clean-up" committee but Victory Sunday is the climax. If the procedures here outlined are carefully followed, the every-member canvass will have been concluded with honor and glory.

Variations and Substitutes

Some churches have found an occasional Loyalty Sunday effort in place of the complete canvass is helpful. This is a special Sunday set apart to receive pledges. They are made a part of the church service and the pledges consecrated by public prayer.

A considerable amount of advance planning is necessary for a successful Loyalty Sunday. Usually a succession of letters are used to tell of the campaign and to urge attendance. A division of the members into groups with an individual over each group can make last-minute calls on Saturday to get assurance that the family will be present Sunday. Of course, the entire Sunday service is given to the subject of "Christian Stewardship."

The committee men assigned as overseers will be responsible to secure gifts from any of their families who are not present at the morning service. Some churches have been able to raise a large percentage of their budgets through direct mail efforts.

Another variation is the pre-budget campaign in which the making of the budget is withheld until after the campaign. Churches testify that people respond well to this effort and the pledges make it possible to increase the budget of the church.

A good example of a pre-budget canvass has been practiced in the First Methodist Church, Shreveport, Louisiana. The officers detected a resistance to earlier pressure methods and planned a special Sunday in which the pledges could be brought to the altar at either the morning or evening service. The emphasis was on proportionate giving. While tithing was emphasized, the standard of giving was stressed as a spiritual matter rather than a mathematical one. The church was kept open all day Sunday, with organ music, and lighted candles on the altar so that those who could not attend the services could bring in their pledges and consecrate them with prayer at the altar. The slogan of the effort was, "Those Whose Hearts Are Willing." The response was so good that this church with an annual budget of two-hundred forty thousand dollars feels that this method is sufficiently productive to be continued into other years.

Accounting

Church accounting may be a very simple thing. Many churches have found that a system for recording weekly contributions, a bank deposit book, a duplicate deposit sheet, and a check book are sufficient. But for a church which budgets its income, it is rather necessary to have a budget control system so that the official board may know, at any time, just where the church stands financially.

1. RECEIVING. Most churches secure the larger part of their income from envelopes placed in the offering plates each Sunday.

YEAR ....

ACCOUNT NO. ....

Name ....

Address ....

PLEDGES

	Local	Benevolence	Building—Special
Indicate Which			
Weekly	$	$	$
Monthly	$	$	$
Quarterly	$	$	$
Annually	$	$	$

Instructions—Account may be indexed either by family name or account number. In listing name, let family name be placed first. Account should be balanced and statements sent subscribers quarterly.

BUILDING OR SPECIAL FUND

	1st Sunday	2nd Sunday	3rd Sunday	4th Sunday	5th Sunday	Total
January						
February						
March						
April						
May						
June						
July						
August						
September						
October						
November						
December						

Total for Year

FIRST QUARTER

Local	Benev.
DUE FROM LAST QUARTER	
PLEDGE FOR THIS QUARTER	
TOTAL DUE	
DATE	

| TOTAL PAID | |
| STILL DUE | |

SECOND QUARTER

Local	Benev.
DUE FROM LAST QUARTER	
PLEDGE FOR THIS QUARTER	
TOTAL DUE	
DATE	

| TOTAL PAID | |
| STILL DUE | |

THIRD QUARTER

Local	Benev.
DUE FROM LAST QUARTER	
PLEDGE FOR THIS QUARTER	
TOTAL DUE	
DATE	

| TOTAL PAID | |
| STILL DUE | |

FOURTH QUARTER

Local	Benev.
DUE FROM LAST QUARTER	
PLEDGE FOR THIS QUARTER	
TOTAL DUE	
DATE	

| TOTAL PAID | |
| STILL DUE | |

A record form for listing weekly contributions.

229

These are weekly payments on pledges made in the every-member canvass. To these receipts may be added contributions from individuals who have not pledged, income from investments, and the contribution of various organizations in the church.

In a church of some size the proper listing of the weekly contributions is a time-consuming task. There must be a method of crediting each pledge as payments are made. As most pledges are made on a weekly basis the forms provided by various houses give an opportunity to enter the payments of each week. Usually the payments are totaled at the end of each quarter and a statement is sent to the member showing his pledge for the quarter and crediting the amount which has been paid during that period.

Various methods are used to count the Sunday offerings. In some instances the finance committee gives some time Sunday to opening the envelopes, removing the money, and listing accurately the amount taken from each envelope on the face of the envelope. The currency is then deposited in the bank while the marked envelopes are given to the financial secretary for his records.

Other committees prefer to do the counting during the week. Occasionally we learn of a committee which meets in a bank room to do the counting. More and more churches, however, are giving this task to the church secretary or someone on the staff of the church. The financial secretary keeps the books on the weekly contributions so she is in a position to issue quarterly reports; the treasurer is given the duplicate deposit slip for his records.

Budget Control

Where the treasurer works on a budget control method, his accounting is based on the budget which the church has adopted. That the reader may follow this plan of accounting clearly, we are taking one actual budget and following it through the various procedures. This is a budget of the Federated Churches, Corvallis, Oregon. The federation consists of a Presbyterian and Congregational Church.

Annual General Budget

WORSHIP SERVICE

Minister	$ 6,000.00
Pulpit supply	60.00
Sacred music	
Choir director	675.00
Organist	600.00
Choir services & supplies	100.00
Calendars	900.00
Worship supplies	50.00
	8,385.00

PROMOTION AND EDUCATION

Minister of Christian	
Education	4,200.00
Fanfare	400.00
Boy Scouts	50.00
Youth Budget	475.00
Travel Exp.—Minister of	
Christian Education	280.00
Library	50.00
	5,455.00

STAFF BENEFITS

Minister's Retirement	615.00
Min. of Christian Ed. Ret.	400.00
Social Security	92.00
Industrial Accident Insur-	
ance	50.00
	1,157.00

ORGANIZATION EXPENSE

Congregational Fellowship	
Dues	90.00

Presbytery Per Capita	
Assessments	563.00
	653.00

ADMINISTRATION

Treasurer's expense	150.00
Financial secretary expense	....
Canvassing and pledging ..	100.00
Church secretary	2,700.00
Contingencies	900.00
Travel expense—Minister .	320.00
Office expense	550.00
Annual meetings	....
Interest	....
	4,720.00

BUILDING OPERATION AND MAINTENANCE

Custodian	2,000.00
Hostess	300.00
Fuel	1,500.00
Telephone	250.00
Utilities	550.00
Church maintenance	2,500.00
Manse taxes	135.00
Insurance	650.00
Manse maintenance	550.00
	8,435.00

CAPITAL EXPENDITURES

Principal	1,020.00

BUDGET TOTALS $29,825.00

Note, first of all, that the budget of this church is divided into seven classifications. There is nothing fixed in such a division, but this is the one selected by this particular church. Next notice that each division is divided into smaller divisions. For instance under Worship Service, there are eight sub-divisions of the budget.

2. DISTRIBUTING. The treasurer, first of all, must have a receipts

journal in which the contributions are all listed. Such entries must give the source and distribution of pledged monies. Note in the illustration below that the receipts side of the ledger balances with the distribution side. All funds that are not pledged are credited to "General Funds."

3. DISBURSING. A disbursement journal is the next need. When we speak of the various journals necessary in this system, we do not have in mind separate books. The accounting of the average church is not so great that it is necessary to have separate binders for each journal mentioned. Instead they can very well be accommodated within one large loose-leaf binder.

The disbursement journal needs to show the date when each check is issued, to whom, and for what purpose. It will show also to which division of the budget the expenditure will be charged. You will need a page with many columns for this. It may be necessary in the larger churches to use several pages to give listing to all of the divisions of the budget.

The Functional Sheets

4. CONTROLLING. We now come to a very interesting feature of budget-control accounting. This is known as the functional sheets by which the treasurer knows at any time just what the situation is in every part of the adopted budget. The functional sheets need but three columns the use of which is shown in the illustrations. First is the functional sheet for the general classification of Worship Service. Note that the amount approved in the budget has been placed in the upper right column. The expenditures for the month are placed in the middle column, one line lower. The expenditure for the month is subtracted from the budget figure and the amount unspent is given below. The left hand column is used for the accumulated expenditures to date. Then for each month, you will have an instant figure on the amount of the budget spent to date and the amount that is left for the balance of the year.

The same process is followed for each subtitle. Note that the last figure in the left hand column is always equal to the total of

THE FEDERATED CHURCHES
GENERAL FUND BUDGET REPORT

	(1) Expected to spend	(2) Adjusted our ideas	(3) Adjusted budget	(4) Exp. to last rep.	(5) Expended this mo.	(6) Expended to date	(7) Budget balance
WORSHIP SERVICE							
Minister................	$ 6,000.00	$	$ 6,000.00	$ 2,000.00	$ 500.00	$ 2,500.00	$ 3,500.00
Pulpit supply...........	60.00	....	60.00	....	.	....	60.00
Sacred music							
Choir director..........	675.00	. . .	675.00	300.00	75.00	375.00	300.00
Organist...............	600.00	....	600.00	200.00	50.00	250.00	350.00
Choir services & supplies	100.00	....	100.00	50.33	.	50.33	49.67
Calendars........	900.00	....	900.00	288.00	64.00	352.00	548.00
Worship supplies.	50.00	...	50.00	60.97	11.24	72.21	-22.21-
	8,385.00	....	8,385.00	2,899.30	700.24	3,599.54	4,785.46
PROMOTION AND EDUCATION							
Minister of Christian Education...........	4,200.00	....	4,200.00	1,400.00	350.00	1,750.00	2,450.00
Fanfare................	400.00	....	400.00	129.43	26 83	156.26	243 74
Boy Scouts.............	50.00	....	50.00	....	....	....	50.00
Youth Budget..........	475.00	....	175.00	250.00	.... .	250.00	225.00
Travel Exp.—Minister of Christian Education....	280.00	....	280.00	99.34	23.05	122.39	157.61
Library................	50.00	....	50.00	7.78	1.50	9.28	40.72
	5,455.00	..	5,455.00	1,886.55	101.38	2,287.93	3,167.07
STAFF BENEFITS							
Minister's Retirement	615.00	....	615.00	207.00	51.75	258.75	356.25
Min. of Christian Ed. Ret.	400.00	....	400.00	112.00	28.00	140.00	260.00
Social Security...........	92.00	....	92.00	29.62	8.00	37.62	54.38
Industrial Accident Insurance	50.00	....	50.00	8.46	2.13	10.59	39.41
	1,157.00	...	1,157.00	357.08	89 88	446.96	710 04
ORGANIZATION EXPENSE							
Congregational Fellowship Dues...............	90.00	....	90.00	84.30	....	84.30	5.70
Presbytery Per Capita Assessments..........	563.00	....	563.00	562.38	...	562.38	.62
	653.00	....	653.00	646.68	....	646.68	6.32
ADMINISTRATION							
Treasurer's expense.......	150.00	-110.00-	40.00	17.50	15.90	33.40	6.60
Financial secretary expense	....	130.00	130.00	40.00	10.00	50.00	80.00
Canvassing and pledging..	100.00	....	100.00	45.61	..	45.61	54.39
Church secretary.........	2,700.00	....	2,700.00	900.00	225.00	1,125.00	1,575.00
Contingencies............	900.00	-90.00-	810.00	....	....	....	810.00
Travel expense—Minister.	320.00	....	320.00	97.82	40.61	138.43	181.57
Office expense............	550.00	....	550.00	249.71	61.26	310.97	239.03
Annual meetings.........	....	20.00	20.00	20.00	.. .	20.00	....
Interest.................	....	186.17	186.17	66.67	15.96	82.63	103.54
	4,720.00	136.17	4,856.17	1,437.31	368.73	1,806.04	3,050.13
BUILDING OPERATION AND MAINTENANCE							
Custodian...............	2,000.00	....	2,000.00	666.68	166.67	833.35	1,166.65
Hostess.................	300.00	....	300.00	200.00	50.00	250.00	50.00
Fuel....................	1,500.00	....	1,500.00	886.28	137.89	1,024.17	475.83
Telephone...............	250.00	....	250.00	73.35	34.52	107.87	142.13
Utilities.................	550.00	....	550.00	257.05	52.49	309.54	240.46
Church maintenance......	2,500.00	....	2,500.00	297.13	108.75	405.88	2,094.12
Manse taxes.............	135.00	....	135.00	....	....	....	135.00
Insurance...............	650.00	....	650.00	55.00	25.00	80.00	570.00
Manse maintenance......	550.00	....	550.00	....	....	....	550.00
	8,435.00	....	8,435.00	2,435.49	575.32	3,010.81	5,424.19
CAPITAL EXPENDITURES							
Principal................	1,020.00	-186.17-	833.83	273.33	69.04	342.37	491.46
BUDGET TOTALS.......	**$29,825.00**	**$ -50.00-**	**$29,775.00**	**$ 9,935.74**	**$ 2,204.59**	**$12,140.33**	**$17,634.67**

entries in the middle column. The sum of the last figures in the
left and right columns is always equal to the top figure in the
right column which has been given as the total budget for the
year.

WORSHIP SERVICE

1954	(1) CUMULATIVE	(2) EXPENDITURES	(3) BUDGET BALANCE
January 1 (Total Budget)	......	......	8385.00
January 31	......	704.48	7680.52
February	1433.94	729.46	6951.06
March	2167.92	733.98	6217.08
April	2899.30	731.38	5485.70
May	3599.54	700.24	4785.46

*A sample functional classification sheet. Worship Service is one of
the seven main classifications. Under each of these are several specific
accounts. This method gives absolute control of the expenditures.
The last figure in column 1 is always equal to the total of column 2.
The addition of the last figure in columns 1 and 3 always equals the
total budget balance on January 1. Thus the financial secretary can
see at a glance that at the end of six months he has spent $3599.54 of
his budget of $8385.00, and has a balance of $4785.46 left.*

WORSHIP SUPPLIES

1954	(1) CUMULATIVE	(2) EXPENDITURES	(3) BUDGET BALANCE
January 1 (Total Budget)	......	......	50.00
January 31	......	2.28	47.72
February	10.84	8.56	39.16
March	38.59	27.75	11.41
April	60.97	22.38	10.97*
May	72.21	11.24	22.21*

*(red inked to indicate budget deficit)

*A sample functional account sheet. Worship Supplies is one of the
specific accounts under the main classification of Worship Service.
When the expenditures have exceeded the budget allowance, the
Budget Balance figure in column 3 is shown in red to indicate a
deficit.*

Now see how this kind of accounting can produce in a few minutes a report for the month, quarter, or year which gives the official board a complete picture of the financial situation.

5. REPORTING. An annual report made from the functional sheets would appear very much as the monthly reports made to the official board and may cover several years instead of months. For an unusual job, try to project a balance sheet of the assets of the church. We are indebted to Mr. Harvey Sherer, treasurer of the Federated Churches, Corvallis, Oregon for the several forms developed by him which appear in this chapter.

While this offers a magnificent goal at which to aim, we suspect that most churches will prefer a brief statement of how much received, how much spent, and how much on hand. The financial soundness of a church is judged by the amount of money that is left over after the expenses have been paid and for these churches we suggest the simple and compact form which follows.

Some Operating Principles

1. Similar funds should be grouped together.
2. Reports should be made monthly.
3. Documentary evidence should be kept for every expenditure.
4. Report expenditures by functions.
5. Keep books on a cash received basis.
6. Send out statements to contributors quarterly.
7. Reconcile all books of account monthly.
8. In reporting use the figures of the books of account.
9. Salaries and wages are liens on general funds.
10. The treasurer should be instructed to pay without further order certain basic obligations. Included would be salaries, withholding taxes, inspection fees (organ, boiler, etc.), industrial accident premiums, taxes, utilities, retirement annuities, travel expenses, and automobile allowances.

Wills and Endowments

Mention of invested monies should be made in this chapter,

BALANCE SHEET

GENERAL FUNDS

We Have		We Owe or Are Accountable For		
Cash in Bank	$ 3,344.46	Accounts Payable		None
Petty Cash on Hand	50.00	Collections from Employees Payable to:		
Prepaid Expenses:		US Government:		
Preaching Mission	10.00	Income Taxes	$62.50	
		SS Taxes	5.62	$ 68.12
		State/Oregon:		
		Income Taxes	40.80	
		Ind. Ac. Com.	.56	41.36
				109.48
		1954 Pledges paid in advance		1,716.00
		Balance (Exhibit B)		1,578.98
	$ 3,404.46			$ 3,404.46

RESTRICTED FUNDS

We Have			We Owe or Are Accountable For	
Cash in Bank		$ 23.07	Balances: (Exhibit C)	
Accounts Receivable:			Woman's Association	300.00
Men's Club	.50		Pond Memorial	28.00
Bal. Minister's Robe	15.43	15.93	Chamberlin Memorial	10.00
Bonds—E Bonds due 2/1/56		300.00	*Presbyterian Life*	1.00
		$ 339.00		$ 339.00

REPAIR AND REMODELLING FUNDS

Cash	4.95	Balance (Exhibit A)	1,200.69
Overdraft in Worship Center Remodelling Fund (to be raised in near future) (Statement D-2)	1,195.74		
	$ 1,200.69		$ 1,200.69

PHYSICAL PLANT

Manse (est. ins. value)	14,000.00	Contract Payable—Manse	4,104.08
Church Building including Education Hall (est. ins. value)	200,000.00	Advance from Board of National Missions (a permanent advance—Board protected by fire ins.)	10,000.00
Equipment (inventory)	18,980.90	Net investment in plant	218,876.82
	$232,980.90		$232,980.90

NOTE: The Benevolence Fund has no assets, no liabilities, and no balance. Such funds are forwarded every month to the proper agencies. A certain proportion of prepaid pledges belongs to the Benevolences, but this amount is not ascertainable until the Budgets for the coming year are approved by the congregation in January.

STATEMENT OF GENERAL FUNDS BALANCE

Balance as reported a year ago		$ 405.38
Less transfer to Repair and Remodelling Funds (Ball Memorial)		300.00
Adjusted balance		105.38
Add: Receipts from payments on Current pledges	$29,791.04	
Prior years pledges	1,353.97	
Plate collections	3,056.10	
Federated Women	325.00	
Rent	316.00	
Initial envelopes	17.95	
Miscellaneous	8.28	
	$34,868.34	
Less portion applicable to Benevolences	7,685.62	
		27,182.72
Available resources		27,288.10
Less: Expenditures per General Fund Budget Report (Statement B-1)		25,709.12
Balance December 31, 1953		$1,578.98

DISBURSEMENTS JOURNAL

MAY, 1957	DAY	CK. NO.	CR. CASH	WORSHIP SERVICES						PROMOTION & EDUCATION				STAFF BENEFITS		
				MINIS-TER	CHOIR DIR.	ORGAN-IST	CHOIR SUPPS.	CALEN-DARS	WORSHIP SUPPS.	MIN. ED.	FAN-FARE	TRAVEL	LIBR'Y	MINIS. RET.	RETIRE-MENT	O.A.B.
Board of Pensions	1	5-3	69 00											69 00		
Corvallis Water Dept.	1	5-4	4 05						4 05							
Blanch Hill	2	5-5	48 40			48 40										
Hill Printing	4	5-6	24 50					24 50								

even though it may be to many churches a purely academic question. As a rule the local church will find its mission better accomplished if it can live on an income from living donors. In many instances, however, the perpetuation of a local church in a changing community depends on other resources. This might be true in a church in a downtown area where it seems wise to maintain services of worship though the active congregation is diminishing.

For this purpose, some churches seek inheritances from members and friends. Such money is not usually secured through public solicitation. Rather, it is the product of careful study by a small committee. Some churches plan to bring the lawyers in the congregation together to discuss the encouragement of bequests. The ethics of the suggestion may be questioned as the lawyer is usually responsible for preparing a will which carries out the intentions of his client. But if the opportunity opens, he can testify as to the needs of the church in the future.

Care should be taken in the drawing of the will to see that instructions for the use of the income are not too specific. For instance a gift to the church with the condition that the investment should be returned to the natural heirs of the donor if the church ever moves from its present site would be unfortunate. Yet, many wills of this kind have been made. Others have stated that the money is to be returned if the church ever breaks its affiliation with a particular denomination. This is a day of mergers and heirs can contest the gift in the event of a merger which changes the name of the denomination.

There have been many wills which leave money to the "trustees of Blank Church and their successors." Some of these churches have passed out of existence but the board of trustees still controls the invested funds. In one instance the will read "to the trustees of the church and their heirs." After a struggle, the court permitted the church to have the money on the ground that the donor probably meant "trustees and their successors." If the person who wishes to leave money to the church really has confidence in the society the will should be made in such a way that it can apply to changing situations with the passing years. It could be given to support the cause of foreign missions, to maintain a high quality of music, to the support of the clergy, to the education of youth for the Christian ministry, or other generalized purposes. But to name the specific society, the name of the minister, or the seminary the youth shall attend will make administration difficult.

A select committee may be given the task of talking with prospects regarding their wills. It is a delicate task and needs men and women who are highly respected. Often the minister will be asked to advise his parish on the question. Society recognizes that the local church and the denomination of which it is a part are worthy enterprises and are entitled to financial support. No one, layman, lawyer or minister, need hesitate to suggest to a possible prospect that he should make the church a beneficiary in his will. At the same time there are limits which surround such an appeal. The courts have been fairly consistent in ruling that "moral coercion" is ground for voiding a will or a portion of a will.

With the abundance of money in our nation today there should be possibilities of securing funds through this source which can serve the church of the future. Keep in mind that the wealth is to serve and not to impoverish the members. Too much endowment can kill the sense of stewardship which is so necessary for the spiritual life of every Christian society.

Stewardship and Finance

APPLEGARTH, M. T., *Twelve Baskets Full*. Harper, 1957.
CASHMAN, R., *The Finances of a Church*. Harper, 1949.
CRAWFORD, J., *The Stewardship of Life*. Cokesbury, 1929.
CROSSLAND, W. F., *How to Increase Church Giving*. Abingdon, 1946.
CUSHMAN, R. S., *The Message of Stewardship*. Abingdon, 1946.
ELLIS, H. W., *Christian Stewardship & Church Finance*. Zondervan, 1953.
GAMBLE, C. W., *How to Raise Money*. Association, 1942.
LEACH, W. H., *Church Finance*. Cokesbury, 1928.

Lumley, A. W., *Raising Money for Church Building Projects*. Abingdon, 1954.

Pendleton, O., *New Techniques for Church Fund Raising*. McGraw-Hill, 1955.

Schwarz, J. D., *Financial Security for the Synagogue*. American Hebrew Congregations, 1935.

13 CHURCH PUBLIC RELATIONS

CHURCH PUBLICITY HAS NOW BECOME CHURCH PUBLIC relations. If you will examine the books on the subject you will find that printed publicity still has a large place in the literature on the subject, but the new title is good and more inclusive than the old. It includes more tools with which to work.

A continuous "selling" job must be projected to keep the church in a position of influence. The multiplicity of present day organizations and the appeals of a thousand other activities require all of the genius available to keep the church in the position of leadership that it has occupied during the life of our nation.

Public relations has been defined as the total impact that one makes upon the community. This would include personal contacts, physical appearances, the printed message, and every other phase of activity which influences individuals and institutions. Among these institutions will be the local church itself. One of the most difficult tasks of public relations which the local church has is to keep its own members informed sufficiently that it constantly has their loyalty. Many times a discouraged minister will say: "Things are going fine; now if I could only get my church to see the value of the program."

In general there are four areas in which the public relations efforts should be directed: the local church; the immediate community; the city in which the church is located; and the world beyond. The local church has assets and techniques to reach these groups.

THE LOCAL CHURCH

Traditional reputation of the local church
Personality of the minister

243

Physical property
Quality of worship services
Quality of educational program
Long-term objectives
Telephone contacts
Printed materials
Projected materials
Outdoor bulletin board
Newspapers
Bells and chimes

THE IMMEDIATE COMMUNITY

Traditional reputation of the local church
Personality of the minister
Physical property
Long-term objectives
Printed materials
Outdoor bulletin board
Inter-church cooperation
Club and lodge contacts
Newspapers
Radio and television
Bells and chimes

THE LARGER COMMUNITY

Traditional reputation of the local church
Personality of the minister
Physical property
Newspaper publicity
Lodge, club and committee contacts
Inter-church cooperation
Radio and television

THE NATION

Traditional reputation of the local church
Personality of the minister
Denominational press
Participation in conventions and conferences
Articles in magazines of national coverage
National radio and TV programs

Two things will at once interest the reader. First the local church is one of the areas toward which public relations should be projected; the second is that the personality of the minister is placed second from the top in each of the various classifications. The reasons for both of these are sound. If the local congregation is not thoroughly sold on the worth of the church program, it will be very difficult to sell it to anybody else. The membership needs to know the purposes and details of the projected program. An informed congregation is the first step toward a good public relations program. As growing businesses have found it necessary to create house organs to strengthen the morale of their own employees, similarly churches must have some techniques for this purpose.

The pastor has always been high on the public relations list of the local church. This was true before the term *public relations* was used. Popular pastors mean full churches, but popularity does not necessarily entail huge physiques and a broad smile. More often the man who is thoroughly consecrated to his job will win the hearts of his congregation by his sincere ministry. The congregation must think well of their pastor and believe that he is indeed consecrated to his work. Our generation has torn the cloak of divinity from the ministry and seeks genuine worth in the character of the man himself. The period through which we have been passing has been a difficult one for clergymen who have relied upon traditional deference toward the minister. Some men have resisted the breakdown of the old separation between priest and people, but these are rich days for the ministers who welcome the opportunity to meet people on a common level. The result has challenged the old concept that "familiarity breeds contempt." It has demonstrated that where the minister is ingenuous, familiarity wins respect.

Next to the minister himself the greatest asset the local church may have for public relations is the physical appearance of its property. An attractive church building situated on a well kept lawn is an asset worth many dollars in wooing friendship and good report. This does not mean a huge building. Churches today do not sell themselves on size; their appeal is on friendliness and quality of the service. But church property should be well kept. If the church is built of wood, it should be clean and well painted; if of brick and stones, the mortar between the blocks should be cleanly pointed and dark stains from gutters removed. Broken steps or sidewalks always affect church property adversely. If there is a lawn, a good bed of grass helps. Carelessly kept property indicates a church which is untidy in its worship of God.

As far as the local congregation is concerned this same care goes into the interior of the building. The worshipper has a right to expect to worship in a building which is clean and well ventilated. A small proportion of the churches today are air conditioned but practically every church can be well ventilated. There is no excuse for dusty pews and hymnbooks except neglect on the part of the church officers who have not insisted that the custodian do an honest job.

The tremendous building program of new public schools has forced churches to buy adequate and clean educational rooms. Mothers of young children demand that the classrooms in church school buildings compare favorably with those in the public schools. New families shop around for churches of quality. The quality of the building and the program means more to some of these families than their earlier denominational affiliations. Their quest goes beyond the appearance of the building and the worship service. They want to know just what the purposes of the church and its program are. Is it interested in character building? Is it working with community forces for a better neighborhood?

The physical property is a medium of public relations that will project itself. If the appearance is pleasing to those who pass its doors it has told its message. The long term program of the church is not quite so tangible an asset. It is here that the church must call to its aid the mediums of publicity.

Reverend J. Hugh Evans in *The New Christian Advocate* for December 1956 gives the following sources for good public relations: 1) well kept property; 2) bulletin boards; 3) weekly bulletin; 4) church newspaper; 5) letters; 6) commercial newspapers; 7) telephone; 8) movie slides and strip; 9) chimes and bells; 10) literature rack; 11) radio and television; 12) brochures and leaflets; 13) friendly atmosphere.

The Outdoor Bulletin Board

The outdoor bulletin board has become an integral part of the physical property of the church. Attractively made and located advantageously, it can become a very valuable part of the public relations program. There are two main types of these boards. First is the changeable letter bulletin board. This is used for the most part in announcing the time of meetings and sermon topics.

The second type is a custom built board large enough to take special posters and general invitation announcements. Several houses now provide sentence sermons and illustrated posters for such a board. Neither type of board will work itself; the proper use requires care and planning. If sentence sermons are used they should be well selected. If sermon topics are used they should be changed as occasion requires; when pictorial or sentence sermons are displayed, do not leave them for too long a time; replace them with new messages so that the board will have a constant appeal.

Keep the board fresh with new paint as necessary. If the letters are of steel, watch for rust which will show through the paint. A shabby board is hardly an honor to any church.

Bells and Chimes

The angelus of the old church is with us again with electric chimes, tubular chimes, and swinging bells. Thousands of churches are now equipped with dulcet carillons which ring out their pleasant messages, but a word of caution seems advisable. There should be definite hours for playing these bells. They lose their appeal if they are continued hour after hour. Sweet music at sundown seems a natural.

Another caution—when every church is equipped with playing bells, there must be some cooperation. To have one church playing *Adeste Fideles* while another across the street is playing *Consolation* challenges the good nature of any man. Some communities are legislating restrictions for these tower carolers. They are a great public relations asset but they must not be overdone.

There are several gradations of chime playing devices. Lowest in cost and acceptability are record players using discs. Their message is amplified through loudspeakers placed on the roof or in the tower; next is the magnetic wire carillons played from a keyboard. These reach a high degree of accuracy in pitch. Third would be the amplification of organ tubular chimes played from the organ console; fourth, the larger tubular chimes hung in the tower. The most costly and most desirable are cast bell carillons.

The telephone mentioned as one of the necessary office machines for the church office is more than a machine, it is a medium of communication. Formerly a minister had just two media for reaching his congregation. One was the voice from the pulpit, used as a medium of both education and publicity. The percentage of membership participation in the old church was high and an announcement made from the pulpit was effectively publicized. But as attendance and loyalty declined, the pulpit announcement lost its force.

The second medium of publicity was the pastoral call. A practicable, system of pastoral calling brought the pastor face to face with each family in his parish. Increasing duties placed on the clergy has limited his time for pastoral calling and the length of each pastoral call. The almost universal use of the telephone gives the minister immediate voice contact with nearly every home in his parish. This is good as a medium for reaching individuals but for mass communications we must seek other media such as the printed word, radio, and television.

The Printed Word

LITERATURE RACK. An attractive literature rack placed at a convenient spot in the narthex can be a most effective stimulus to good religious information.

THE PASTOR'S LETTER OR CARD. The minister can easily reach the families of his congregation through a personal letter duplicated on personal or church letterhead. These letters can convey any idea the minister has in his mind from a note of thanksgiving for recovery of health to the announcement of a series of sermons. Preferably, letters from the minister, even though duplicated, should go in a sealed envelope by first class mail.

Attractive postcards offer a splendid contact for the minister. Birthday cards, cards of cheer in times of illness, congratulations on graduation, promotion, and similar pleasant occasions, and condolences in the hour of death are always appreciated and have a place in the program.

THE SUNDAY CALENDAR. This weekly guide to worship carries announcements of items of interest for the weeks ahead. Patented covers are now available so that even the smallest church may now have an appealing calendar. In the church service, it serves a dual purpose and can very easily be given a third and a very important duty, that of informing the absentees.

The churches are very few today which have a Sunday attendance equal to the number of enrolled members. If the announcements printed on the calendar reach only those who attend the Sunday services, they are as limited as a pulpit announcement. If the church possesses an addressing machine, the program may be easily sent to the absentee congregation. If the pastor writes a personal note expressing regret that those absent were not able to be present, the envelope should be sent by first class mail; otherwise, it can be sent as third class mail.

There are several ways of securing the list of absentees necessary to complete the mailing of the calendar. Perhaps the most effective way is through the use of registration cards for those present at the services. A very popular form is the "Ritual of Friendship" in which a formality is made of the signing by the worshippers. By checking these cards against the membership list one can quickly get the names and addresses of absentees.

A second way is to give a list of the membership to the ushers and let them check off the members as they come into the church.

This will probably be effective only in the smaller churches and even then some ushers will not meet the responsibility.

A third way can be used in the average sized congregation. The minister usually scrutinizes his congregation. When the service is concluded he knows pretty well which families were there. If he will go immediately to the addressing machine and start addressing envelopes, he will find it quite easy to pick out and throw away the envelopes of those who were present, leaving for mailing only those of absentees.

A Church Paper

The Sunday calendar mailed to the absentees as well as distributed to the worshipper is to all effects a church paper. Announcements can be expanded, sermonettes and financial reports included so that it will have general interest. Some churches, however, prefer to have the calendar as a worship guide and issue a weekly or monthly periodical as a special church project. This may range anywhere from a four page sheet to a magazine of fifty or more pages. A church publication can be a large help to the average sized church. It offers a good project for a young peoples' group or any other organization in the church which may be publicity minded. The editor of such a publication can render a great service.

All groups of the church should have representation on the editorial board. It should not be a journal for the reprinting of the Sunday sermons but should include personal items, new events, denominational items, and other things of interest. If the magazine is at all pretentious the editor must have a closing date which is rigorously enforced. He will have the responsibility of editing the copy and preparing it for the press, the selection of suitable pictures for publication, and arranging for necessary engraving. He will also have the responsibility of reading the galley proofs and of making the dummy which serves as a pattern for the printer.

Printed material is not inexpensive these days, so if the magazine is to be printed it will be well to ask for competitive prices

Many churches now issue weekly or monthly periodicals.

based on the size, the amount of composition, and the quality of paper to be used. Funds must be available to pay for the printing. There are reputable printing houses which specialize in this kind of printing and their prices are competitive with other printers. In addition they supply editorial aid in format and fillers.

The funds for the church periodical come from a number of sources. Occasionally a church will subsidize the publication on the grounds that as a medium of public relations it is worth all that it costs. A second method which is used a great deal is to have the annual pledge card carry a line which says: "It is understood that fifty cents of this pledge is to pay for a year's subscription to *The Wesleyan Broadcaster*." This fifty cents or whatever price is agreed upon is turned over to the paper committee and partially pays the cost of publication. There is an advantage in having this subscription provision included in the mailing costs. It will make it possible to have it entered as "second class mail" which gives the lowest postal rate available to any publication. These rates are available only to publications which have a genuine paid subscription list.

A third source of income for a periodical is advertising. There may be financial profit in this or not, depending on several considerations. There is also an ethical question involved. Commercial publications charge rates for advertising based on the number of copies distributed and the character of the readers. A church publication in seeking advertising should be as ethical as a business organization. If it does not have a profitable circulation, any effort to sell advertising is simply a request for a donation. If it does have a real field for the advertiser, it has the right to ask honest rates for its space.

If rates are too low, advertising will hinder rather than help the financial returns of the publication. A half dozen pages of advertising at ten dollars per page may be a financial debit rather than a gain. The publisher or church should consider very seriously seeking this kind of aid. Better to let the magazine stand as a house organ and justify it as good public relations if it cannot honestly command a good price for the advertising space.

THE CHURCH DIRECTORY. Another good medium for printed public relations is the church directory which lists the names and addresses of the members, the organization and officers of the various groups, dates of meetings, etc. This directory placed in the hands of the members will be the most consulted publication of the church. The minister will find its convenience invaluable in carrying on his own work.

The Community Newspaper

Outside of the local congregation most people will have their chief contact with the minister through the local press. The newspapers of the community usually recognize the value of church news, but no church should take too much for granted. The church helps the papers by providing news items, but the space given the church by the newspaper spells prosperity for the church as well.

The church has an obligation to become familiar with the newspapers in the local community. These may vary from the small country weekly to the great metropolitan daily. In the great cities there are usually sectional papers which are largely advertising sheets serving the individual communities. All these are public relations media for the church. Many papers like to carry formal church announcements each week. The minister is selected publicist and should know these periodicals. Some of the suggestions which will be helpful are:

1. Know the papers and the editors. No typed or printed message is as valuable as personal contact. Having established the contact, do not overdo it.

2. Honor the deadlines. Every editor has respect for the correspondent who gets his material in on time.

3. Honor the space limitations. Remember that your sister churches are entitled to space.

4. Make sure that your copy is accurate. This is especially true when names of speakers are used. Be sure that the initials are correct and that the names are correctly spelled.

5. If you mail the copy to the paper, make sure that the

church is properly identified and be sure to sign your own name so that the editor will know the source of the information. He may want additional information.

6. Keep your eyes open for stories which may be worthy of more than announcement space. Remember that all of the news of interest does not concern the minister.

7. Don't insist that the editor "print this as is, or not use it at all." Be patient with the paper when your copy is omitted or changed. Remember, you have probably made the same errors.

8. More and more the daily papers are giving space to sermons or selected portions of sermons. When you think you have an especially good sermon, let the paper know of it. Do not submit the entire manuscript and expect the editor to cull the portions he wishes to use. Give it to him either very much condensed or better yet quote in full the very few paragraphs which you think have the real message. Then place above the copy some lines such as: "Mr. Brown said in part. . . ." Let the editor decide whether the paragraphs quoted are worthy of the space.

The Denominational Press

One of the most effective ways of helping churches of your own denominational affiliation to know about your words is to send occasional news items to the denominational press. The periodicals will be glad to have stories about successful programs and personal notes on the relationship of prominent people to your congregation. Ground breaking services, cornerstone layings, and dedications are always good news. Anniversary services are important. If you have someone who has not missed a church service or church school for fifty years, that is news.

The minister who has the yen to write can utilize this method to sell his own personality as well as the program of the church. If he has a real desire to break into the writing field, he will find here a wonderful apprenticeship.

Projected Materials

The use of still and motion picture projectors give a splendid medium for selling the program of the church to the local congregation. The use of projectors in annual meetings, club, and class programs can be a most powerful factor. Use of projectors is more thoroughly discussed in the chapter on religious education.

Radio and Television

Here is the tremendous new field of mass communications. The only real competition it has is the daily press. Wisely the papers have integrated themselves into the electronic field so that there is more cooperation than competition.

Individual churches in some communities have their announcements made in the religious hour on the radio, less often in a televised program. While both the radio and television agencies have a responsibility to give time to organized religion they are naturally confused by the large number of churches, denominations, and religious faiths. They ask that churches approach them through the ministers' associations, the city council of churches, or some other cooperative agency.

Individual radio and television appearances, if one has the facility to interpret religious news, will be welcomed. Forum discussions are another form of public relations which may be open to churches. One small church has been holding a religious kindergarten on television. Several ministers in different parts of the country have acquired good reputations as pastoral counselors by radio and television. Daily devotional services are given by hundreds of radio and television stations across the country.

Some churches are able to broadcast their Sunday morning services. A charge for time and wire facilities is legitimate if the station wishes to make it. Now and then an exceptional church has its own broadcasting station. We feel, however, that the day of the individual church broadcasting station is over.

The National Council of Churches has a department in this field as do several of the denominations. These agencies provide scripts, tape, and disk recordings and aid local communities in many ways. Since television requirements are rather severe, these recordings are often preferred to live progams by local stations. The Missouri Synod Lutheran Church has been a leader in both the fields of radio and television. An effective use of television or radio is through the use of a closed circuit so that overflow audiences may hear and see the services.

Force of Total Impact

The total impact of the churches upon our society is very impressive. It has focused attention upon religion and helped to bring new religious interest to the America of today. All individual churches profit because of this. At the same time, every church has the responsibility of doing its bit to give the message of faith to its community and to the world. It is a case of all for one and one for all. The program has been bringing together not only churches of various Christian denominations but also churches of varying religious faiths.

Administering the Program

How is this program of public relations to be organized in the local church? Several ways are now being used. A committee may plan the broad program, decide on the types of publicity to be used, and assign the tasks to various individuals. Each organized group should appoint someone to feed publicity items into the central bureau. This is a good standard form for the average church.

Other churches prefer not to follow this pattern. In some instances the minister has a genius for publicity and he deals directly with the newspapers. In other instances the task is given to a church secretary. Publicity is a sensitive thing and good reporting is almost an instinct. News which must be used immediately cannot await committee action. Valuable space can be secured by having someone immediately on the job.

Several churches employ professional publicists to get space in the daily press. One church pays a woman of the congregation a small monthly fee to watch for stories which will get local coverage. Definitely, however, a church should have some orderly way of securing items of interest about its own members. This is the reason for a publicity committee member in every group.

Space Advertising

Paid advertisements in the daily and weekly press are valuable. Most churches do not use great display space listing the address, hour of services, name of the minister, and sermon topics. Probably the use of paid space combined with the feeding of new items is a paying combination. The small investment pays off. In this program do not concentrate on the big dailies but give the community periodical a break. Big display space is valuable for certain types of services—evangelistic and cooperative—but for one church to use a third of a page in a metropolitan paper while its neighbors use two inches creates a bad reaction.

Public Relations

BRODIE, W. A., *Keeping Your Church in the News*. Revell, 1943.

———, *Keeping Your Church Informed*. Revell, 1944.

FORTSON, J. T., *How to Make Friends for Your Church*. Association, 1943.

GARRISON, W. B., *Improve Your Church Bulletins*. Revell, 1957.

HARRELL, S., *Public Relations for Churches*. Abingdon, 1945.

HENRY, C. F. H., *Successful Church Publicity*. Zondervan, 1943.

LEACH, W. H., *Church Publicity*. Cokesbury, 1931.

LESLIE, P., *Public Relations Handbook*, Prentice-Hall, 1950.

PARKER, E. C., *Religious Radio*. Harper, 1948.

STUBER, S., *Public Relations Manual for Churches*. Doubleday, 1951.

WOLSELEY, R. E., *Interpreting the Church through Press and Radio*. Muhlenburg, 1951.

14 | THE SERVICE OF WORSHIP

THE SERVICE OF WORSHIP IS NOT ENTIRELY A MATTER OF sermons, prayers, and music. It is, as well, a program which requires skill in organization and physical facilities. No doctrine was given by the apostolic age as to just what type of a building is satisfactory for the Christian church, nor did the age give us instructions about the organization of a congregation for the greatest satisfaction in work. One of our struggles in the present day is to convince Christian people that a service is for worship as well as preaching and that the services require a sanctuary rather than an auditorium.

It is most important to appreciate the brevity of the worship service. In many churches, the time is limited to one hour. In that period of time, the church must organize to welcome and seat worshippers; the ministers and choir must enter; an offering must be received; the scriptures must be read; the appointed liturgy recited; a sermon preached; and in some churches, the Holy Communion observed. Only the highest skill of organization can induce a feeling of relaxation, worship, and satisfaction in this period of time. One hour must open the windows of heaven to let in the sunlight of God for an entire week.

Building Facilities

We have learned that a rectangular unit is most desirable for worship. This shape offers much better opportunities for personal reaction than the old square or circular room.

The entrance to the nave will then be at one end. From the out-of-doors, the worshipper first enters a foyer sufficiently large so that the people may gather and greet those they know before entering the nave. Economy on the size of the foyer is seldom justified. The larger space pays well in fellowship and gives an outer court where the discussions of the day can be laid aside with the outer wraps and individuals can prepare to enter the Holy of Holies. The foyer is the place for coat racks provided—and only then—the ushers have instructions to watch these items which are frequently sought by the dishonest.

Proper hangers for coats and hats is one of the real problems for churches in the northern states where outer wraps must be worn for several months each year. A checkroom is not the answer, rather sufficient space in the foyer for the hanging of the garments. The checkroom savors too much of the commercial and requires dependable attendants. A small checkroom without an attendant creates more problems than it solves.

Front Entrance

Every church needs convenient exits. Some churches provide these at the sides near the chancel. In other churches, doors open to the social rooms or the educational building. Such doors could be reserved for exits and the worshipper could enter the worship service from the narthex, either at the center aisle or at one of the side aisles. Having freed himself from conversation, he will be ready to enter the inner court of the church.

Timing

The Sunday services need to be set at a convenient time for worship. Traditionally in this country, the time of worship has been a late morning hour. With the new influx of worshippers, many churches have been obliged to plan two services for each Sunday morning, and in some instances three. This creates a new problem for Protestants.

The ten-thirty and eleven o'clock hour doubtless was the most convenient time for our grandfathers. They were rural folk and had to milk the cows and care for other animals before they could start for church. Our new requirements give worshippers a choice in the matter.

In a recent survey conducted by *Church Management*, seventy-nine churches were holding duplicate services each Sunday. Only sixteen of the seventy-nine reported that they had held such services five years ago. The most popular hours for the two services were nine-thirty A.M. for the first service and eleven A.M. for the second. Where three services were held, the first service was held at eight A.M. In one instance, the final service was held at noon, but most churches preferred to have all of their services concluded by then.

One very interesting thing shown in this survey was that the early hour increased in popularity as the warm weather came; others pointed out that for the first few months, the early service was poorly attended but as the months went by, the interest in that service increased and a large number found the early hour a convenient one. There was universal agreement that adding a second service brought to the two services more people than had attended the single service. Some who still mourn the passing of the evening service in Protestantism can now be consoled in that the church has regained the loss through the installation of duplicate services for Sunday morning.

The real challenge of the duplicate service seems to be in the department of music. Clergymen have not found the second service much of a strain but choirs have been reluctant to carry double responsibilities. This is as true of the professional choirs as the volunteer ones. Regardless of the hour of service, it is important that the organ voluntary start promptly. Then the service must move on schedule from item to item. The minister has the responsibility to see that the reading, liturgy, sermon, and music fit into the schedule.

Preparation of the Building

Heat, light, ventilation, and cleanliness certainly need to be discussed here. When the first worshippers arrive, the church should be at the right temperature, the seats should have been dusted, and the warm air should be fresh air. If flowers are to be displayed, they should be in place before the organ starts its first note.

The choir needs its instructions before the hour of the service and the practice of rushing to the choir stalls to gather books or to place music for special numbers on the organ should be taken care of before the start of the service. The ushers who have a tremendously important role to fill should plan to be at the church a half hour before the opening of the service.

Tips on Good Ushering

COMMISSIONING OF USHERS

At the beginning of another year, we give you this fresh commission, new and yet old. Bestill the incarnate hospitality of this church. Clothe our services of worship with human friendliness. Have mercy on us strange human beings, part body and part soul, part physical and part spiritual, and so care for our physical convenience and comfort that our spirits may be free and at leisure from the body to enter into the significance of worship. And among ourselves continue to be such good friends, that you may be, as you have been, not so much a board of ushers as a fraternity. (*From a commissioning service in The Riverside Church, New York City, as used by Dr. Harry Emerson Fosdick.*)

SOME THOUGHTS ON USHERING

Ushers in a very peculiar sense have the responsibility of acting as hosts to worshippers at the services of the church.

Their personal appearance is important, but their spiritual and social attitude are the things which really count. Let them wear distinctive dress so they may be recognized but the art of graciousness is more important.

Let them be at their posts at least twenty minutes before the organ begins its prelude. Keeping in mind that they are the hosts, they should check the physical conditions of the room, including temperature, ventilation, cleanliness before people arrive for the service.

Traditionally, their tasks have been to greet the worshippers, lead them to their seats, see that they are supplied with hymnal, prayer book (if one is used), and have a good seat.

Some ushers can be assigned to the out-of-doors to help in opening the doors and directing the drivers to a parking area.

Brusqueness and tenseness should be avoided in all his actions. An individual needs to be in a mentally relaxed condition for worship. Ushers can do much to help in this respect. Learn to direct people without ordering them. "Will you please wait here until after the prayer" is more effective than "You can't go in now." "Will you kindly go up the side aisle" is preferable to "You'll have to take the side aisle."

The worshipper is entitled to the best seat available. The usher should know the relative value of the various areas. There are restrictions in some churches which still rent pews. There are other seats which have been reserved through tradition for individuals. The ushers should know which these are in order to save worshippers from embarrassment by placing them in one of these pews.

The usher should watch for any worshippers who are handicapped by physical disability. If he sees evidence of lameness, the worshipper should be seated where he will not be pressed by others. If he is deaf, he should be led to a pew where there are phones for the deaf. The blind should be permitted to take the usher's arm to be led to his position.

The *shuttling* method of ushering is being replaced in the large churches with *fixed post* ushering. The shuttling method requires that the usher walk ahead of worshippers to show them to their seats. In the fixed post system, the ushers are stationed by section. Head ushers direct the worshippers to the aisle and the usher at the post indicates the pew which each will occupy.

Ushers should recognize individual temperaments. Few people like an empty church for worship. At the same time, they do not like to be unduly crowded. Architects usually specify eighteen to twenty inches per person in the church pews. To unduly crowd a pew makes worshippers self-conscious and uncomfortable. In seating the congregation in a church which is too large for the congregation, the ushers will judiciously seat them in such a way that the church will appear to be filled. In case of a crowded congregation, it is better to bring in chairs than to crowd groups in single pews.

Protect the individuals who arrive early for a few minutes of prayer and communion. Ushers should strive to keep the sanctuary free of conversation before the formal beginning of the service of worship.

Every church has the individual who takes his place at the aisle end of the pew. In seating him, the usher can suggest that he move to the center so others may be seated. Or, if it seems preferable, wait until the others are to be seated and then suggest, "Will you move over so that these friends may be seated?"

The processional for the offering should be lined up in the narthex. The usual custom is for the shorter men to lead and the taller ones bring up the rear. If there is a center aisle, always use that for the processional. After the offering has been received, the return to the altar for consecration should also be through this aisle. Some churches do not require the entire group to return to the altar.

A system of buzzers will help the ushers in their tasks. It will help if they know that the organist is to begin the voluntary; that the offertory anthem has been completed so the march to the altar can again begin. Times in the program when doors should be closed for prayers can be learned from the calendars of worship.

It helps the attendance of individual ushers if their names are printed on the worship calendar on the date they have appointed to serve.

Ushering will assume greater importance if there is a definite organization of a Board of Ushers. In case of weddings, the party will provide its own ushers but a representative of the Board should be present to help them in their organization and conduct. In case of a small funeral, the mortician will attend to the ushering; in a large one, the church ushers should serve.

Ushers need to be prepared for many kinds of emergencies. Sometimes the electric power is off. Result—no lights and no organ. The next time it may be a person fainting during the service. A third time it may be a drunk who is seeking admission. Whatever it is, the ushers must seek to handle the situation without noise or confusion.

Finally, ushers should play no favorites. In a congregation there is plenty of work for the ushers. One should not turn from his duties for long conversations with friends or acquaintances while worshippers are being neglected.

Remember, you are door keeper in the house of the Lord.

USHER'S MANUAL

1. Four ushers should be on hand for each Sunday morning service, ready to take up their duties, not later than ten-twenty o'clock. The morning service begins at ten forty-five o'clock.

2. On arrival, the following matters should be immediately cared for.

a. Temperature of sanctuary. If the atmosphere is musty or close, or the temperature more than sixty-eight degrees, open the windows wide, for a quick airing. Three to five minutes should be sufficient. The windows should be closed again, unless the weather warrants leaving some of them open.

b. Lighting. If it is the least bit dark or gloomy in the sanctuary or hallways, turn on the proper lights.

c. Hymn books. Each section should have at least three hymnals, except the very front pews.

d. Bulletins. See that these have arrived and are ready for hand out.

e. Assignment of duties for each usher.

1. Two to greet people at the head of the stairs and hand out bulletins.

2. Two to usher people to their places, or stand in readiness to otherwise serve.

3. Points on ushering.

a. You are the official reception committee for the church. Greet people cordially, whether you know them or not. Let them know they are welcome.

b. Make it a point to usher all newcomers, and all others who desire it, to a seat. (Older people should generally be taken towards the front.)

c. Five people can be seated comfortably in each section. Do not attempt to crowd six in a section.

d. It is the ushers' business to see that no one enters the sanctuary during the following parts of the service: Invocation; the Lord's Prayer; the Scripture reading; the anthems or solos; or the pastoral prayer.

e. After the service begins, no one should enter the sanctuary unless conducted by an usher.

f. Generally speaking, late comers should be seated towards the rear of the sanctuary. Try to save a rear pew for this purpose.

g. Have the congregation evenly distributed. Endeavor to eliminate crowding towards the back, by taking people further front.

h. All ushers must be alert for any disturbances in the sanctuary; the downstairs part of the church or parish house; or immediately outside the church windows. Steps should be taken immediately to restore quiet if possible.

i. Be especially sensitive to the physical comforts of the congregation. Watch out for drafts from open windows or doors. If the sun is shining directly into the pews, adjust the shutters. Be alert to help anyone who feels sick or faint.

j. Always be courteous, even when guests are unresponsive. If possible, call people by their name. Say, "Good morning, Mr. Smith, may I show you to a seat."

k. Ushers should never speak loudly, or otherwise call attention to themselves. Do not attempt to hold conversations, or conduct business while ushering. Guard against over-familiarity.

4. The offering.

a. The offering should be taken in a dignified and orderly fashion. There should be no sense of hurry.

b. No group of ushers should attempt to take the offering without a thorough rehearsal beforehand.

c. At the Amen of the prayer hymn, the four ushers should stand in readiness, in the rear of the sanctuary. After an offertory sentence, they should come forward, two together, in step, and stand four abreast, and receive the plates at the foot of the chancel stairs. Then, all should turn outward, two to collect from the center aisle, and the other two from the two outside aisles.

d. The first collector to finish his section should take his plate up to the balcony to receive any offering from those seated there.

e. The collectors should reassemble at the rear, and await the nod from the organist, to bring the offering forward. They are to remain holding it at the foot of the chancel stairs, until it is received by the minister after a brief offertory prayer.

f. After the prayer, all turn together, and return down the center aisle in the same manner as they came forward.

g. Following the offering, one usher should remain in the Tower Room or rear pew, ready to meet any need that might arise during the rest of the service.

5. Counting those present.

a. Keep in mind that each usher is to count the people seated in his section as he takes the offering, and to give the count to the head usher. To this count, the head usher will add those present in the chancel, and among the ushers, for the total count.

b. The head usher should record the total attendance on the attendance chart in the office.

6. Head Ushers.

a. There are four head ushers. One of these should be on hand each Sunday, to work with and direct the others.

b. The efficient working of the ushers corps is the responsibility of the head usher, as well as each usher.

c. The head usher should be especially attentive to newcomers to town or strangers. Greet them, ask their name, introduce them to others; and, if possible, ask some one to act as their host who will give them friendly attention. At the close of the service, he should seek them out, and invite them to come again. He should be sure that they are introduced to the pastor.

7. General matters to which ushers should give attention.

a. It is a good policy to lower the windows each Sunday during the singing of the prayer hymn. These may be closed during the singing of the last verse of the hymn, or just before the sermon, depending on the weather. Windows should not be closed during the singing of an anthem or solo.

b. During the colder weather, an usher should go down stairs shortly after the opening hymn to see that the outside doors at the church entrance are closed. If these doors are left open, those sitting in the rear of the church may feel a draft.

c. Unless the church is crowded, do not allow children or others to sit in the balcony sections toward the front of the sanctuary where their presence might prove distracting.

d. Ushers should endeavor to keep the balcony closed on Communion Sundays.

e. Ushers should tell parents bringing small children to church that there is a Church Hour Class for children, meeting in the parish house; and if possible, direct them there personally, or have someone do it.

f. If an usher cannot be present for a service, he is to let the head usher know, or make arrangements for someone to take his place.

g. The ushers' list and the Sundays they are to serve, is posted on the bulletin board in the church office.

CONCLUSION. The Bible speaks of "the doorkeeper of the house of the Lord" as a high calling. It is to that service you are called, in performing the duties of usher in this church. You are the official reception committee of the church. People oftentimes receive a favorable, or unfavorable, impression of a church by the way they are greeted on first entering. You are helping or hindering the work of your church by the way you conduct yourself as "doorkeeper in the House of the Lord."

Add to the foregoing lists, the additional responsibility of the ushers for the parking of automobiles. Each church which maintains a parking lot should have a corps of ushers in attendance. It is their duty to place the cars in position and assist the worshippers, directing them to the proper entrance of the church. One church provides armbands for these ushers. Their services are appreciated.

The Service of Worship

In the single hour service of worship is combined the skills of artist, theologian, preacher, priest, musician, dramatist, liturgist, and psychologist. Many physical elements enter in. Our book deals neither with homiletics nor theology. We are concerned here simply with the organization of the service to make it most effective.

Of course the preparations started many years before the actual service. The architect who designed the building was working to this end; the builder who made the organ was working for this purpose; the artisan who installed the lights helped in the preparation.

But the contemporary participants have the larger part in making the service the inspiration it should be. Custodians, ushers, choir, organist, and worshippers all make their contribution. The minister's influence is the most important item; while he is not the only participant, he occupies the central position. In addition to his personal appearances, he has the responsibility of planning and advising in every part of the service.

Sunday is the Sabbath of God; the service of worship is God's hour. This service of worship should not be considered as a flash from the sky. It is not a single picture placed upon the wall. It is a drama which has progression. It has a beginning and an ending. Worshippers come with heavy hearts and they should leave with their burdens lightened.

The service of worship does not consist of a preacher and listening people. These are essential but the service is broader. It seeks to dramatize human experience. There have been many changes in the concepts of worship during the Christian centuries. In the apostolic era, the love feast and the eucharist were combined. Later these were separated. A preparatory service was made a separate institution from the service of the Lord's Supper. The progression for ecumenical worship developed around the growth of Christian living and experience.

The progression of this service ran something like this:

1. THE INTRODUCTION. This would include the call or announcement of worship; the confession of sins; the assurance of pardon.

2. THE LITURGY OF THE CATECHISMS. Important here was the

instruction which included the "Little Entrance" in which the clergy bore to the chancel the Old Testament and the Epistles. Included also were the *Gloria Patri*, *The Kyrie*, the *Gloria in Excelsis*, the collect for the day, the epistle for the day, the Gradual, the Gospel for the day, recitation of the Nicene Creed, the sermon, and a hymn.

3. THE LITURGY OF THE FAITHFUL. This opens with the "Great Entrance" in which the gifts of bread and wine are placed on the table and the eucharistic prayer is given, the distribution to the faithful.

4. THE DISMISSAL. A hymn and benediction.

This plan of progression has passed to other forms. Few of our churches offer communion at every service. The offertory has been changed to now mean the presentation of gifts and the whole drama based on a cycle in the life of a Christian. The Roman Catholic Church and some other historic churches have preserved the mass with its dramatization of the last supper and the death of our Lord. Except in the occasional services which celebrate the Holy Supper, other churches follow a different drama and progression.

To visualize it, think first of an individual burdened with the thought of his spiritual needs, seeking help through the service of worship. The note of the organ voluntary gives the invitation for him to come into the presence of God. The minister opens his service with the announcement or invitation, "The Call to Worship."

How does the honest worshipper come to the service? Quietly and modestly conscious of his own needs. He comes as a sinner and seeks pardon for his sins and help for his life. So at this early part of the service, we have a confession of sins. The minister as a priest of God accepts the confession and gives him "Assurance of Pardon."

The next step is that of instruction in which the scriptures are read, sometimes by the clergy, at other periods by clergy and congregation responsively. The pastoral prayer is made for enlightenment.

Following the offering of prayer, the congregation makes its offering in money for the work of the local church and its world-wide mission. While the term "Offering" is to be preferred to that of "Collection," it is well to point out that traditionally the offering is the bearing of the bread and wine to the priest that it may be consecrated for its holy use. There is some justification for the use of the term, however, as it seems that the ecumenical church did accept gifts and offerings from the worshippers at the time of the "Great Entrance."

Next, the Sermon, to the minister and people may be the climax of the hour of worship. It gathers up the thoughts of the confession, the creed, and the assurance of pardon. In its best form, it is inspiration as it seeks to answer the questions which are raised in men's hearts. Then the dismissal with the hymn and benediction.

It is well to note the need of a progression in the hymns used in the service. The opening hymn should be one of adoration. The people at that stage need to proclaim their faith in God and church. *Come Thou Almighty King, Holy, Holy, Holy, Lord God Almighty, Worship the King, All Glorious Above,* are good hymns for this period.

The hymn which follows the general prayer is rightly selected for Christian fellowship. It is to lead the worshipper into an intimate relationship to God the Father and with fellow Christians. Some churches prefer that the congregation be seated during this hymn. Suggestions would be *O Love That Wilt Not Let Me Go, My Faith Looks Up to Thee, Immortal Love Forever Full, For the Beauty of the Earth,* and similar themes.

The concluding hymn, if one is sung, should be determined by the theme of the sermon. Thus, it could be one expressing security, offering challenge, missionary appeal or any appropriate theme. Tradition is for a final hymn, but many churches are omitting it. Sometimes the minister is responsible, feeling that it may take away from the effect of his sermon. Rather he should select a hymn which builds his theme for the day and gives the worshipper a chance to say "Amen" to the sermon.

A Progressive Service of Worship

The following service is a good illustration from the Call to Worship through the Benediction. It is taken from the book *Public Worship of God* by J. R. P. Sclater (Doran, 1927).

ORDER OF SERVICE

I. THE APPROACH (OR PREFACE)

    1. The Call — MINISTER. *O come let us worship and bow down, let us kneel before the Lord our Maker; for He is our God.*

    2. The Realization — PEOPLE. *Holy, holy, holy is the Lord of hosts, the whole earth is full of His glory.*

    3. The Cry for Help — MINISTER. *Almighty God, unto whom all hearts be open, all desires known, and from whom no secrets are hid: cleanse the thoughts of our hearts by the inspiration of the Holy Spirit, that we may perfectly love Thee, and worthily magnify Thy Holy Name; through Christ our Lord. Amen.*

II. THE WORSHIP — PSALM. *All people that on earth do dwell.*

    1. Vision and Humility — Prayer of Confession, and for Pardon and for Cleansing.

    2. Vision and Deepened Humility — THE LAW. Deut. 6:1–9.
THE ANTHEM. *Incline Thine ear* . . .

    3. Vision bringing Vitality and Illumination — THE LESSON. Romans 8:31–39.
Hymn of Thanksgiving, *All Hail the Power of Jesus' Name* . . .

Thanksgiving, Intercession and Dedication

Prayer of Thanksgiving, Intercession and Lord's Prayer.
Offertory.
MINISTER. *Receive these symbols of Thy people's labour, Lord, and be pleased to use alike them and us for the Kingdom of Thy Son, for His Name's sake.* (Announcements, if any.)

4. The Particular Vision
Illumination

HYMN. *Oh Master let me walk with Thee.*
SERMON. Psalm 23:3.
(Brief Prayer.)

5. The Final Vision
Gift of God.

HYMN. *The King of Love My Shepherd Is.*
THE BENEDICTION.

Minister and Choir

How can the minister properly prepare for this drama to make it most effective. First, he can make his preparation carefully in advance and assure himself that his co-workers are to be trusted. The minister should seek to free himself from all other duties so that he may have time before the service for prayer, meditation, and thought. In the meantime, the choir is organizing for its part of the work. Some ministers plan a meeting with their spiritual officers before the service. These men and women come to the study to help him adjust his vestments and join with him in a prayer for the service. Often the choir waits for the minister who then fully vested meets with them for the opening prayer. These should be concluded when the organ voluntary starts.

If the church uses a processional, the clergy will follow the choir. The congregation should rise as they enter and remain standing during the call to worship and the invocation. If there is no procession, the choir should be seated before the minister appears and rise with the congregation when he makes his appearance.

Each item of the service should proceed without interruption.

Announcements are sometimes necessary but usually they can be printed on the order of worship for the day so no disruption is necessary during the service. The choirmaster should have his music timed so that a minute by minute schedule may be set up for the service. While a schedule is necessary, neither the minister, the choir, nor the ushers should give any indication of tension because of the lack of time.

The benediction may be given from either the chancel or at the door of the narthex. If there is a recessional, the minister will follow the choir to the exit. If not, he may elect to remain on the congregational level near the chancel.

Ushers are as important at the close of the service as they are at the beginning. If they have spotted strangers, they can give them a handclasp and ask them back, introduce them to the ministers, and serve in other ways. A coffee hour at the close of the service has helped many churches to welcome their guests. The ushers may be an important factor here.

Check List for the Evaluation of Public Worship

QUALIFICATIONS OF THE LEADER

1. Does he create a worshipful mood among those whom he leads?
2. Is he interested in developing the best possible worship service?
3. Does he make thorough personal preparation?
4. Does he make a study of worship?
5. Does he appreciate the fact that he is to lead his people in the worship of God?
6. Is worship a vital, dynamic experience with him?
7. Does he have a vital, personal devotional life?
8. Is his personal bearing conducive to worship on the part of those who follow him?
9. Does he have a sense of propriety?
10. Is he dignified, calm, poised?
11. Does he have pulpit mannerisms that are distracting?

12. Does he leave the pulpit on errands after the service begins?
13. Are his clothes conservative, clean and pressed?
14. Does he appreciate great hymns?
15. Does he select the best hymns available?
16. Is he familiar with great poetry, prayers and scripture?
17. Is he constantly trying to improve himself in the art of conducting public worship?
18. Does he keep a record of hymns used?

AIMS

1. Do you have specific aims for your worship services?
2. Are your aims Christ-centered?
3. Do you take into consideration the experience of your people?
4. Do you take into consideration the needs of your people?
5. Do you discuss your aims with the organist, choir and others?

BUILDING AND EQUIPMENT

1. Does the sanctuary help to create a worship mood?
2. Is a simple cross, a beautiful picture of Christ, or some other appropriate symbol used at the center of the sanctuary to create atmosphere, focus the attention of the worshiper, and make the worship Christ-centered?
3. Is the sanctuary clean and orderly?
4. Is the building properly heated and ventilated?
5. Is the lighting good?
6. Does the sanctuary possess a good musical instrument?
7. Is there an adequate number of good hymn books?

CONTENT OF THE SERVICE

1. Does the service have order, movement, climax, theme?
2. Does the minister use brief transitional sentences to introduce each part of the service and to tie all parts together? For instance, call to confession, call to praise, call to prayer, offertory sentence.
3. Is the pastoral prayer carefully prepared and appropriate?
4. Are the unison prayers varied from time to time?
5. Is the offering an impressive and worshipful part of the service?

6. Are the hymns worshipful?

7. Do the words and music of the hymns used adequately express the sentiments of the worshiper?

8. Do you give recognition to special days in hymns, prayers, responsive readings and sermons?

The following questions have to do with the content and the psychological sequence of the service. The stars designate those parts that are necessary in a brief service.

1. First, do you have a *prelude* that helps to create a worshipful mood?

2. Is the prelude followed by a *call to worship* that makes people conscious that the purpose of the service is the worship of God?

3. Is the call to worship followed by a general prayer of *confession of sin?*

4. Do the people have an opportunity to praise God through participation in some of the following: singing the doxology, reading from the psalter, singing the Gloria?

5. Do you instruct the people through the reading of the scriptures?

6. Do the people have an opportunity to express their faith by reciting a creed?

7. Are the worshipers brought to a fresh vision of God and his way of life and to a new dedication of life to God through the pastoral prayer, the offering, the hymn, the sermon and the benediction?

8. Is the postlude in keeping with the quiet dignity of the benediction?

ORGANIZATION AND CONDUCT OF SERVICE

1. Is the entire service planned to the smallest detail before the service begins?

2. Do all participants maintain a worshipful attitude?

3. Is the entire service so conducted by minister, organist, choir, ushers and congregation so that it is apparent that it is for the worship of God?

PARTICIPATION OF THE PEOPLE

1. Do a large percentage of those present (over 75% actively participate in the services?

2. Do the worshipers know the meaning of the materials which you use?
3. Do you have a plan for teaching worship materials outside of worship services?
4. Are people given opportunities to make decisions for Christ and his way of living?
5. Are people given opportunities to make decisions concerning some *specific act or area of Christian living?*
6. Do others than the minister participate in the planning of worship services?

RESULTS ACHIEVED

1. Are any attempts made to check up on the results achieved?
2. Is there a greater spirit of reverence?
3. Is there an increasing appreciation of the better type of worship service?
4. Do a larger percentage of those attending the services participate?
5. Are more people appreciating the better type of hymns?
6. Have the services resulted in better character and living in the participants?
7. Has the building been made more worshipful?

P. Henry Lotz

Worship

An Outline of Christian Worship, Its Development and Form. Oxford (London), 1936.

BLACKWOOD, A. W., *The Fine Art of Public Worship.* Abingdon, 1939.

BRENNER, S. F., *The Way of Worship.* Macmillan, 1944.

BYINGTON, E. H., *The Quest for Experience in Worship.* Harper, 1929.

COFFIN, H. S., *The Public Worship of God.* Westminster, 1946.

GARRETT, W. O., *The Church Ushers Manual.* Revell.

HEIMSATH, C. H., *The Genius of Public Worship.* Scribner's, 1944.

HEDLEY, G., *Christian Worship; Some Meanings and Means.* Macmillan, 1953.

LANG, P. H. D., *Church Ushering.* Concordia.

LOWRIE, W., *Action in Liturgy.* Philosophical, 1953.

PALMER, A. W., *Aids to Worship*. Macmillan, 1944.

――――, *The Art of Conducting Public Worship*. Macmillan, 1939.

Principles of Church Ushering, Church Ushers Association of New York, 1953.

SCLATER, J. R. P., *The Public Worship of God*. Harper, 1930.

15 | THE MUSIC OF THE CHURCH

THE ORGANIZATION OF THE CHURCH MUSIC SHOULD START with the appointment of a Music Committee by the proper official body. This need not be a large committee, but it should be representative of the men and women who appreciate both music and liturgy. Subject to the official board of the church this committee will take upon itself the responsibility of seeing that there is a choir; that the choir has the physical properties necessary for its work; that there is a suitable instrument for the services; and that there are financial resources for providing music, vestments, organist, choir director, and such professional singers as are deemed desirable.

The committee will be the functioning executive link between the official board and the choir; it will have the authority to hire such professional musicians as are authorized by the board and will have general direction of the entire program. It will make recommendations concerning the type of choirs to be used— whether a quartet, chancel choir, or larger program using graded choirs throughout the church. It will have as its responsibility the recruiting of such singers as are needed.

The committee needs a chairman, a representative from the governing body of the church, a representative from each of the choirs in the church, and a sub-chairman in charge of vestments. If the choir is to finance itself either partially or totally, it will need a sub-chairman in charge of finance as well. As is usually true in most church executive committees, the minister should be an ex-officio member that he may know at any time just what the situation is in that department of the church.

The minister has a very important place in the music program of the church. He is directly in charge of every service of worship and should select or at least pass on the hymn selections. He should know what anthems or special music are to be presented that he may judge its acceptability. He should be willing to recommend music for any particular service. He must work very closely with the choir director and organist. Moreover, he is the head of the local church and has the responsibility for the religious training of the youth and adults of the church and should be in a position to control the quality of music, including its theology, as it is presented to the congregation.

We cannot condemn too strongly the practice of dividing the worship service into various parts, each one separated from the others. Some ministers will insist that they will take care of their part and will let the choir take care of its program. The church service is definitely one place where all persons should work together for the glory of God.

Director and Organist

Perhaps the most important task of the music committee is to select the choir director and the organist. Sometimes this means an organist-director, otherwise it means an organist and a director. Here is one place where the final judgment must rest on the local church. Some of the advantages of the organist-director are:

1. One person is made responsible for the administration of the music in the church.

2. It avoids temperamental clashes between two individuals.

3. There is greater flexibility in making minor adjustments to adapt music or program to the local situation.

4. The combined office would eliminate the sight of a director with his back to the congregation beating time to the music. From a console visible to the entire choir, he can direct with a wave of the hand or a nod of the head.

The matter is not entirely one-sided. Some good arguments can be offered on the other side.

1. There are good directors who are not organists, and there are some very good accompanists who are not qualified to direct.

2. In rehearsal, when the offices are separate, the director has the opportunity to walk around the choir making suggestions to individuals and groups.

3. Any director needs to hear the choir and organ balance at times. This he cannot do if he is playing the organ.

4. If one person has the dual positions, a special placement for the console is necessary so that the director is visible to all singers but invisible to the congregation. A hand-waving organist-director, visible to the congregation, is as objectional as a baton-waving director standing between the congregation and the choir.

5. There is less temptation to seat the choir in tiers; a practice to be deplored.

The Position of the Choir

With the present trend to an open or divided chancel and a center aisle, the tendency has been to have the choir divided, sitting on opposite sides of the chancel in stalls or seats parallel to the walls. The space between is the approach to the altar. This placement has some advantages. The congregation has unobstructed vision of the altar or communion table and the choir ceases to be the focal center of worship. If the processional is used, this type of seating gives the balance necessary for an orderly service.

There are some directors who insist on having the choir in one unit. They feel that this is necessary for a balanced choir. If the chancel position is used the choir has the most conspicuous position in the church and the members sit facing the congregation. Most leaders are aware that this is undesirable and impose a screen or grill between the choir and the liturgical part of the chancel. The choir is seen "yet darkly" in the apertures of the grill, but are not as conspicuous as when spread out in front of the congregation.

Some churches prefer the rear balcony for the choir. This is a position *par excellence* for the director. He can direct with

arm and body and has full control over his choir, but it elimi-
nates a processional of any liturgical significance.

Lutheran churches more and more are placing the choir at
a one or two step elevation in the front and to one side of the
nave. The transept is frequently used. This permits the choir
to have an active part in the liturgy and yet not receive the
focus given when seated in the central position in the chancel.
It offers a good location from which to lead the congregation
and a processional is still possible if desired.

With the coming of graded choirs extra space is needed if
choirs are to be massed as part of the service. Sometimes the
extras are placed in chairs in front of the chancel. A better
position would be to have the nave so designed that one of the
transepts can be used for seating the extra choir members.

The location of the choir is very flexible at the present time
and can be adapted to any one of several positions. If, as some
prophesy, there will be a greater interest in congregational singing, it is quite possible that the movement will be to place the
choir much closer to the congregation.

Choir Rehearsal Rooms

The placement of the choir is giving church architects a
headache, but even more so is the question of practice rooms
for the choir or choirs. The local church must build according
to its program and if that involves the organization of several
choirs, it must plan to care for them. Choir rooms become one
of the necessities of the building.

The choir area should offer a room for practice, cabinets for
vestments, filing of music, hangers for singers' garments, and
an office for the director of music. It should be equipped with
a piano. One choir needs considerable space and when the
church has three, four, five or more choirs, the space demands
grow very large.

One problem is that of soundproofing. Directors are asking
that their chancel choirs meet for practice before the Sunday

morning service. That is usually the time of the church school so the choir rooms cannot be shared with the school classes and must have such a location and be so reinforced with sound-proofing that the classes are not disturbed. One way is to have the choir space in the basement. The present resentment against basement rooms is shared by the choirs. The recent request of one church which has nine choirs was for one-hundred twenty-two thousand cubic feet of space for its various practice rooms. However, a program whereby the choirs agreed to share some rooms reduced the space to reasonable proportions.

There are many advantages in having the choirs practice in the smaller rooms rather than in the church itself. The seating of the practice room can be arranged to fit the desires of the director. If he wishes elevated seats, they are available. One of the best reasons is the convenience of having music and books at hand and directors will tell you that a piano is preferable to an organ for practice sessions. In addition a chancel, beautiful as it may be in its Sunday clothes, lacks something on a cold winter evening when but a small portion of the church is lighted and heated. The choir room is also used for the vesting ceremony. It needs to be in a location with easy access to the narthex or the chancel, depending on local practice.

The Entry of the Choir

Just how shall the choir come to the chancel? Shall it be by means of a processional through the long aisle of the church or shall the members quietly take their places and await the entry of the minister? Shall the minister precede the choir or follow it into the chancel? If the verdict is for a processional is it to be a marched processional with the regularity of step of the percussion band?

The tendency today is to the processional and many of the newer church buildings include a center aisle for that purpose. It is not the best reason, however, and some authorities in worship will insist that it lacks the support of Christian tradition.

For instance, Scott Francis Brenner in his work, *The Way of Worship* (Macmillan) says:

> The entrance of the clergy or clergymen is quite a different matter from the entrance of the layman, and is supercharged with the possibilities of folly and vulgarity. It should not need to be said that the way for the choir to go to its accustomed place is by the shortest route, and in the most inconspicuous manner. Every choir room should have on its walls a framed and adorned copy of Euclid's theorem which reminds us that a straight line is the shortest distance between two points. Let the clergy or the clergymen, together with attendants, if there are any, go into the chancel by the nearest entrance, and after taking their places either within the sanctuary or the choir, reverence the altar. Meanwhile the congregation will arise in honor of them and the corporate worship will begin at once.

On the other hand Andrew W. Blackwood in *The Fine Art of Public Worship* (Cokesbury) after observing the choir processional in the Gothic chapel of Princeton University has this to say:

> In the Gothic chapel of Princeton University he (the minister) may have witnessed the awesome procession of the Westminster Choir College with a hundred-fifty singers, arrayed in robes of "wine and cream." But if he asked for anything of the sort in the modern church at the crossroads, the officers might think that he was beside himself. "Plain horse sense" would tell them that a procession is an orderly way of getting a large group of singers from the robing room into the choir loft without interfering with the devotions of the waiting people.

Donald D. Kettring in *Steps Toward A Singing Choir* (Westminster) takes a moderate position. He is not an active pro or an insistent anti. He is against some of the abuses of the processional. He dislikes the trappings often seen, but sees virtue in an orderly processional.

Mr. Kettring points out that one of the advantages is the triumphant and commanding opening to the service. He has found that the pageantry of the processional and the recessional appeals to many, especially to those in the children's choirs but he adds:

> If a choir wanders circuitously through dark, subterranean recesses of the church simply to reach a place from which it can march, it invites criticism.

Another criticism is that the processional usually organizes in the narthex of the church when the space is most needed for worshippers. This congestion would be eliminated with a more simple entry to the chancel.

He is definitely against the marching choir requiring a tempo which is often overworked. However, it need not be pompous or military but can be stately and dignified. At the other extreme are the few instances in which the hesitation step is introduced into the processional for worship services as it has been for weddings.

Mr. Rupert Sircom, of Minneapolis is quoted as saying:

> There exists a world wide practice of walking slowly—but not marching. There is no ecclesiastical basis for the marched processional or the marched processional hymn. There is, however, an established ecclesiastical authority for the other type . . . the beauty of the unmarched processional is far greater than that of the other type because it is less aggressive, smoother and of more gentle progress; greater dignity and reverence are to be found here, and these qualities are consistent with worship and self-effacement.

If there is a processional the clergy will follow the singers; the choir will remain standing with the congregation until the opening part of the service is concluded.

The Organization of the Choir

It is generally conceded that the choir should be organized, but just how much organization is desirable is debatable. Charles

L. Etherington, a choir director, in his book *The Organist and the Choir Master* (Macmillan) feels that even one officer or committee may be too much. The purpose of the choir is to provide music for worship and to follow the instructions of the director.

> The average choir has little business to transact—nothing that cannot be brought to the members' attention by the choir master (who will be anxious to get on with the rehearsal) and speedily disposed of.

Mr. Etherington likewise sees no need for a music committee, contending that an inactive one could be tolerated but an active one could interfere with the music of the church and get in the choir master's way.

On the other hand Donald Kettring, now minister of music at the East Liberty Presbyterian Church, Pittsburgh, Pennsylvania recommends a pretty thorough organization including President, Vice-President, Treasurer, Librarian, Vestment Secretary, Attendance Secretary, Property Secretary, and an Historian.

The difference reveals two concepts of church music. Mr. Etherington works with a church in which the choir is closely associated with the singing of liturgical music. One does not think of this choir except in connection with worship. Mr. Kettring is a leader in the new concepts of graded choirs in the church which involves several choirs, many leaders, workers and singers. Close organization is essential.

Many things concern the choir which should not be the sole responsibility of the director. Certainly a librarian who keeps the music classified and filed has an important position. If an attendance record is to be kept a secretary is definitely needed and a vestment secretary has a big job. The historian keeps a scrapbook of the services of worship, newspaper releases of interest, photographs, etc. Perhaps these are not vital to the music of the church but well worth preserving.

Choirs down to the earliest ages should have their own organizations. Choir mothers appointed by the music committee will have most important functions at the beginners' level. The choir mothers have the assignment to attend every rehearsal session of the choir and where there are several they can arrange their schedules so that at least one will be present. If fees are charged, they will make the necessary collections and keep the account. They will keep the attendance records which are rather important in children's choirs. If the director is called from the room they will have charge of the discipline. They will care for the vestments and assist in the distribution of the music. They will watch for signs of illness and help the child to return home if that is desirable. They will have charge of any social activities of the children's groups. If the children's choir is placed in the balcony, the mothers may sit with the children. These women need to understand both music and children. They should have the respect and confidence of the mothers of the children in the choir.

Financing the Music Program

Every church of any resources whatever will provide a place in its budget for the church music. Funds must be provided for choir director, organist, soloists, vestments, and organ upkeep. It is not at all unusual for the amount appropriated to fall short of the total amount needed. The choir may require some special music after the church budget has been exhausted or vestments may need replacement. There are several ways of meeting such an emergency.

A direct appeal to the congregation may be announced in the Sunday bulletin and supplemented with choir envelopes in the pews. Permission for the use of this appeal must be received from the governing board of the church. Some churches have inclusive budgets and will not permit extra appeals of this kind. Another method is to present some kind of musical entertainment for which a fee is charged or at least an offering taken, proceeds going to supply the need.

A third method of raising special funds is the use of a membership fee. Two or three dollars per year may supply the needs and the fee idea has other virtues beside securing extra funds. It immediately announces that the person who joins the choir is taking the task seriously. The plan may be especially effective where the church has children's choirs. By charging a fee and keeping records, we find that parents respect the training that their children receive in the choir. It prompts respect and loyalty. When a church has set up a program of church music under a full time director who gives much of his time to the development of individual voices, the value of such training more than outweighs the small fee which is paid.

Enlisting Choir Members

One unfortunate method of securing members is an appeal either from the pulpit or the choir director that more voices are needed and asking any one who can sing to come to the Thursday evening rehearsal. The choir needs voices but it needs voices which are qualified or can become qualified for the presentation of good music. Good prospects must be invited in person or by phone to discuss the matter with the director.

Lucky is the director who has a church with a sufficient number of good voices that he may mention the subject of "audition." Many have to accomplish the personal appraisal of voices in a more subtle way, but the director does need to know the voices which he is to develop for his task.

One church used a parish survey based on the every member canvass idea. The visitors went to each home for a music survey. They used a card for listing the names of each adult and child in the family and listing their musical experiences and ambitions. They indicated if they played an instrument, sang in choruses, etc. From the returned cards, a prospect list was built from which names were taken for auditions. There are obvious dangers in the plan and in a large parish a great many names will be returned. The director will have an avalanche of material on his hands. Yet, there should be an opportunity for such a survey in any church organizing a new choir program.

Members of the music committee and teachers in the church school may give the names of those they have found qualified for choir service. The director might ask to meet the various age groups in the school and have them sing for him. In this way he may select prospects who seem to offer choir material. The auditions offered are not to find musical experience and great talent. Instead they seek singers who have normal pitch and will be responsive to direction. A good director, if he has the time available, will welcome the opportunity to work with children, young people, or adults who have native ability.

Necessity for Rehearsals

In any musical program rehearsals are the very essence of success. To the uninitiated the long hours spent by musicians to perfect their presentations is challenging. The good choir singer will welcome the rehearsal rather than look for a chance to get out of it. As the quality of the singers improves the desire for rehearsals grows and a professional choir will spend more time in rehearsal than an amateur group.

There is a growing recognition that one rehearsal during the week is the very minimum and added rehearsal on Sunday morning before service is desirable. One evening a week, plus the Sunday morning rehearsal, plus one or two extra evenings a month is better. If complete attendance is impossible the choir may rehearse in sections, but complete rehearsals are necessary for the best possible performance.

Suggestions for Small Churches

Most of this chapter is directed to growing churches which are expanding in many directions including the music program. There are, of course, more small churches than great churches. These smaller churches have their own choir problems. The idea of individual auditions may seem peculiar; the director would be glad to fill his seats with anyone who can sing at all, let alone one with proper tone.

However, many of the suggestions apply to the small church.

The director definitely needs a music committee to help plan his program. He can throw much responsibility on this committee. The choir in the small church can gain much through organization and the small church certainly needs training in music and liturgy. The choir of the small church needs to put its trust in the quality of its work and not in the external trappings. Good music is more important than a processional, though a processional need not be barred.

The small church is limited by time of its director and organist. On the other hand it may have leaders whose first love is music and their consistent leadership compensates for the lack of time. Both small and great churches need to learn that the best way to secure applicants for their choirs is to present the best in sacred music and not merely to fill the chairs.

The Minister and the Choir

While the organization and training of the choir is the responsibility of the choir director, the minister of the church is responsible for all parts of the worship service. Pastors today are giving much more attention to the choir and organ selections than did their fathers. Many will prefer to select the hymns for the service of worship, and many avail themselves of the privilege of previewing the selections to be used by the choir and organist. As clergymen are learning to select their sermon subjects in advance, so choir leaders and organists are selecting their material well in advance. Some ministers plan to sit down with the organist and choir director to select material for the entire year. This tendency is good, for worship combines music, prayer, liturgy and instruction, and when they are brought together in a Sunday service there should be a spiritual harmony. Denominations are helping this trend by publishing recommended choir anthems and organ numbers for the entire year.

Organization of Church Music

CONWAY, M. P., *Church Organ Accompaniment*. Macmillan, 1952.
———, *Playing a Church Organ*. Macmillan, 1949.

DOUGLASS, W., *Church Music in History and Practice*. Scribner's, 1953.

ELLENWOOD, L., *The History of American Music*. Morehouse, 1953.

ETHERINGTON, C. L., *The Organist and the Choirmaster*. Scribner's, 1952.

GILBERT, H., *Gilbert's Manual for Choir Loft and Pulpit*. Scribner's 1939.

HALTER, C., *The Practice of Christian Music*. Concordia, 1955.

HJORTSVAG, C., *The Amateur Choir Director*. Abingdon, 1941.

KETTRING, D. D., *Toward a Singing Church*. Westminster, 1948.

SHIELDS, E. M., *Music in the Religious Growth of Children*. Abingdon, 1943.

SIMS, W. H., *Instrumental Music in the Church*. Convention,   .

SWARM, P., *Guideposts for the Church Musician*. Church Music Foundation, 1949.

THOMAS, E. L., *Music in Christian Education*. Abingdon, 1953.

WHITTLESEY, F., *A Comprehensive Program of Church Music*. Westminster, 1957.

WILSON, H. R., and J. L. LYALL, *Building A Church Choir*. Hall & McCreary, 1957.

16 | CHURCH SCHOOL ADMINISTRATION

THE CHRISTIAN CHURCH IS A VERY OLD INSTITUTION BUT its child, the church school, is a mere infant. From the earliest days of Christianity the candiates for church membership were required to pass certain tests. The catechumens did not find it easy to come to full membership. The baptistery was found outside the doors of the church. The baptism was a symbol of stature and they had to qualify before they could enter the church building and assume the responsibilities.

As the church developed, the catechism became the basic study curriculum in the church. The practice still persists and in some instances provides the material of study for church membership. One could easily assume that the church school was an evolution from these earlier doctrinal instruction classes, but the explanation is quite to the contrary. The Sunday school forced its way in from the outside and its origin is more social than religious. The work originated with a socially minded British editor, Robert Raikes, about 1780.

Raikes was distressed because of the illiteracy and lawlessness of the children of his city, Gloucester. England was passing through the beginnings of an industrial age and the children of the poor were forced into the factories to help keep their families alive. The poet Irwin Granich describes the period.

> Sadly through the factory doors
>   The little children pass,
> They do not like to leave behind
>   The morning sky and grass.
>
> All day the wheels will eat their joy
>   And turn it into gold,
> And when they pass the doors again,
>   The world will seem so cold.

But England was a Sabbath-observing country and these factory children were free on Sunday. They crowded the streets, stole sweets and food, fought among themselves, and were a general nuisance. Raikes dreamed of a school on Sunday, the only day of the week available which would help these waifs. He felt some provision should be made for their character training and an elementary education which was not provided by the state. He gathered around him a few like-minded individuals. They invited a group of these youngsters to meet in the Raikes home for what was called a "Sunday school." In this school they were taught to read and to write and they did receive some elementary instruction in the principles of the Christian religion.

The movement caught fire in England. Soon, teaching in the Sunday school became a fashionable avocation for the well-to-do who needed an outlet for their philanthropic inclinations. It is estimated that within four years of the founding of the first Sunday school there were four hundred boys and girls enrolled in the various schools.

British churches with the exception of the Wesleyans were not much impressed by the movement. Many clergymen openly resisted the movement and church doors were closed to it. The Archbishop of Canterbury called a convocation to find some method of stopping the movement. Despite this, it continued to grow but it was a lay movement, not a church one.

In its transfer across the sea to the United States, it lost its lowly origin but the ministers as a whole were definitely unfriendly. There are several instances of the persecution of those who sought to inject the Sunday schools into the churches. In one instance in New England a young lady with the dozen children she had won for a Bible class were driven from the church by an angry minister who screamed at them as they ran: "Ye imps of Satan; why will you desecrate God's house?" There were exceptions, of course. In 1827 the Methodist Sunday School Union was organized and three years later it reported twenty-four hundred schools and one-hundred-fifty thousand pupils. We must wait until the years which followed the Civil War before we see the full fruition of these efforts.

The early schools may be seen through one of the texts which were used. The three "R's" were included in the curriculum. One of the early texts, published by the Sunday School Union carries a picture of children gathered before a chart on the wall. The chart has pictures of each letter in the alphabet and the numbers from one to ten. Under the chart is a verse for the children to sing.

> Here in a pleasant row we stand,
> Of boys and girls a happy band,
> Some times we sing, some times we play,
> But now our ABC we say.

Following the War Between the States most denominations had been won over to the Sunday school. Ministers were giving it more consideration. Several denominations led by John H. Vincent, secretary of the Sunday School Union of the Methodist Episcopal church, got together and worked out courses of study. Until that time all lesson material had been published by independent printers. These publishers were asked to revise all of their material so that there would be "uniform" lessons for all denominations and age groups.

The significance of this ecumenical move is not sufficiently appreciated in our own day. It was a marvelous example of interdenominational cooperation. It gave the impetus to the Sunday school movement which lifted it to great heights of interest and participation. Lesson materials poured from the presses; the aged and the young crowded the churches for Bible study. Daily papers found a demand for lesson interpretations. The enthusiasm for church schools became so great that it influenced a new type of church architecture, called the Akron Plan, which we have discussed in the chapter on church buildings.

Through all of this period the Sunday school was a laymen's movement. Great conventions were held with laymen presiding. They devised methods of instruction, methods for promoting attendance. The work of the pastor in this movement was usually limited to the teaching of a class in the local church. Many ministers felt that the Sunday school was a competitor, not a part of the church. That this has not been completely resolved even to this day may be seen by reading an article by William Esler Slocum in *The New Christian Advocate* (February 1956) entitled "Are Sunday Schools Competing With the Church."

There were some noble laymen in control of the Sunday school at the beginning of the present century. Among these were the great merchants John Wanamaker and H. J. Heinz, founder of the company which bears his name, Russell Colgate whose name is still associated with the great soap and cosmetic company. President William McKinley was the superintendent of the Sunday school of the First Methodist Church of Canton, Ohio where he lived. Old timers still recall the picture of this famous man on the way to his church with a Bible under his arm. His two-time opponent for the presidency, William Jennings Bryan, was proud to be a teacher in the local Presbyterian church and also was a Bible-carrying man.

It was a period of great Sunday schools, great leaders, great conventions, great enthusiasms. Bible-carrying became the Sunday habit. Instruction was by laymen whose Bible knowledge came from familiarity with the book itself and the helps offered in the form of "quarterlies." Dozens of churches today carry the name of Marion Lawrance, the great Sunday school leader. The reservations of the clergy were based on the fact that these devout men and women were amateurs and did not have the finer qualities of theological education. Some of the independent publishing houses which provided materials for the curriculum were controlled by laymen who sought to serve the cause in accord with their talents.

The spectacular days of the church school were to pass into the period, which came very early in our century, when came the desire to advance from the Sunday school to some plan of

"Christian Education." Magnificent as it was, the old Sunday school was more of a social institution than one of education. American public schools were developing into what may be the finest educational system in the world; religious leaders felt that the Sunday school should advance in the same way. The denominations began to place more emphasis upon their boards of education. The number of personnel increased; the amount of money spent was expanded.

A conflict started between the old and the new as might have been expected. The old ridiculed the new as being "high-hat" and insisted that the plans suggested were way over the heads of the people. The new replied that the teaching methods of the old were antiquated and ineffective and that proper methods of education would better serve its generation. New materials began to flow from the denominational presses. Local teachers were confused by the changing concepts. The graded lessons which made their appearance about 1900 hit the churches with too little preparation. From one minister who took his first church in 1911 I have this story.

> I came to my first church in 1911 with the ambition to develop a great church school. The graded lessons seemed the logical thing for me. I insisted that my church throw out the international lessons and put in their place the new graded series. It took me six months to do this but it was a great achievement. After three years, I moved to another church. It took the church I left just three weeks to throw out the graded lessons and to reinstitute the international lessons.

The transition has not been easy; in fact it has not been achieved. The new ideal required more training for teachers and not every school was able to provide it. It has meant new building arrangements and very few churches have been able to provide them. We are now well into the second half of the twentieth century and we have not reached the promised land predicted by Athearns, the Betts, the Bowers, the Munros, and others.

Professor Wesley Shrader of Yale Divinity School wrote in *Life* magazine in 1957 that the average Sunday school is the most wasted hour in the week. In 1931 Harold C. Munro wrote in *The Pastor and Religious Education* (Pilgrim):

> Out of every hour which Johnnie spends under the influence of a teacher, fifty-nine minutes of it are spent with the public school teacher.

This proportion of time between the church school and the public school would be true today. It shows that the last thirty years have brought little progress in our religious education methods. Indeed there has been somewhat of a retrogression as what once looked like a splendid weekday system of religious educational instruction has lost much of its vigor. At the same time, the three hour period for religious education—once a hope —is disappearing from our churches.

There have been some gains. Many more churches have full time directors of Christian Education. A good proportion of these have training at the graduate level. These directors, however, find that the integration of educational ideas into the complexity of the modern church is a slow process. They find it very difficult to get trained leaders at the local church level.

One very important gain is the idea that the entire church belongs in the educational program. The various organizations are encouraged to use educational methods in their programs. At least people are beginning to use educational terms. The Board of Education has become a policy-forming group not alone for the church Sunday school but the entire church program. Churches more and more talk educational terminology.

Organization for Religious Education

The following plan outlines the normal requirements for local church organization in education. There will be variations in denominations. You must recognize that the church without a professional director needs to operate differently from one with the professional director.

Board of Education

This is the board which will oversee the educational program of the entire church. Its membership will seek to inject the educational attitude in all organizations. It need not be a large committee. Three, five, or seven members will be sufficient with the minister as an *ex officio* member.

DUTIES OF THE BOARD

1. To survey the educational possibilities of the entire church.
2. To survey the educational literature not alone for the church school but for other groups as well. It will recommend study courses and texts.
3. To select teachers and officers for every educational agency of the church.
4. To make recommendations to the church council where educational problems are involved.
5. To mediate between the local church and denominational and interdenominational agencies; also to be the intermediary between the local church and county, state, and national agencies.
6. To coordinate the work in the local church.
7. To survey the social and educational background of each child in the church school to seek direction in the curricula and instructional methods.
8. To hire an educational director at such a time as the budget for that purpose has been approved.

The Director of Christian Education

In the selection of a director, the board should undertake the same careful exploratory work as the average school board in selecting a superintendent of schools. In some churches the director will also be the superintendent. Others prefer to select a layman for the superintendency, leaving the director as the executive officer coordinating all sides of the work.

In case the church is not financially able to provide a director of Christian education, the board should use its authority to suggest to the committee seeking a new minister that he be one who

Teacher's Agreement

By and Between

--and the

-- Church

--, Pastor

In view of my acceptance of the privilege and duty of co-operating with others in the educational program of the above church and with the desire of becoming a workman who does not need to be ashamed, I agree to maintain the following standards, to the best of my ability, during the period covered by this agreement, namely, from_____

_____to_____.

As a teacher, I will endeavor to:

1. Be regular in attendance.
2. Be present early to greet the pupils upon their arrival.
3. Keep the records carefully.
4. Maintain discipline.
5. Spend adequate time in general and specific preparation for each lesson (not neglecting the cultivation of the devotional life).
6. Worship with the pupils during periods in which they are expected to hold communion with God.
7. In case of unavoidable absence, notify superintendent and aid in getting a substitute.
8. Improve my teaching by attending special training courses, when they are available, and by reading approved literature on the subject of leadership.
9. Follow up absentees and visitors.
10. Live an exemplary life in both moral and religious matters.
11. Attend monthly workers' conferences.
12. Understand the pupils and their background.
13. Consult with my superiors before substituting new curriculum materials for that which has been approved.

(*Created by the late Norman E. Richardson.*)

Agreement between a church and its teachers.

has training for leadership in Christian education and that he be hired with the expectation that he will take leadership in the church school. He should not, however, be the presiding officer, that task to be assigned to the traditional lay superintendent.

In addition to these officers, the school should have a secre-

14. Be alert to make friendly contacts with pupils outside of the class room.
15. Co-operate, cheerfully, with other teachers and with the officers of the school.

Obligations of the Church

The above church, recognizing its responsibility for nurturing the religious life of its present and future members, agrees to facilitate the work of the teacher in the following ways:

1. Provide a meeting place for the class, with as great freedom from distraction as possible.
2. Provide adequate heating, lighting, ventilation, and cleanliness.
3. Provide helpful lesson materials, maps, blackboards, and other aids in teaching.
4. Conduct helpful workers' conferences.
5. Provide moral support and backing for the teacher.
6. Provide textbooks and other literature to aid in preparation and study of the lesson materials.
7. Make available suitable magazines and other materials needed for the teacher's general improvement while in service.
8. Provide sympathetic supervision and counsel.
9. Encourage parents and guardians of children to co-operate.
10. Co-operate with other churches, when advisable, in maintaining a leaders' training school or courses.
11. Make available whatever money is needed to pay the cost of maintaining the school.
12. By prayer and social recognition, to aid the teacher in every possible way.

--, Teacher

------------------------------------, Church Representative

tary, a librarian, a financial secretary, and such assistants as seem desirable. For the direction of the church school, an educational committee should be set up. It should include the members of the educational board, general officers of the church school, officers of societies under direction of the church educational committee, teachers of all departments, departmental superintendents, two representatives from each society which is included in the educational program, the church librarian, and the leaders of the school music.

The qualities of the director of Christian education are most important. He is not only the general overseer of the entire educational program, he must also be the authority on curricula and organizations. In some way the usual plan of having a lay superintendent and a professional director is unfortunate. When the director arrives, it will be necessary for the superintendent to surrender some of his authority and responsibility. On the other hand, he has the prestige of years and the director may feel handicapped in making decisions necessary in the transition of a Sunday school to a school of education.

The director's emphasis will be put on curriculum and methods of instruction while the lay superintendent may be thinking of attendance and lively music. The director after a few months trial work may find that the superintendent upon whose cooperation he should depend has joined the ranks of those who prefer the old order. Some churches have been brave enough to face the situation and to give the director authority comparable to that which is given a superintendent of schools. This type of organization has not become general.

The church school needs office space not only for the director but for the financial secretary too. If the school has complete autonomy it will need a treasurer to care for the funds. The plan usually recommended is that the church school collections be delivered to the church treasurer who on the receipt of vouchers from the director or superintendent issues checks to pay the bills.

An office for the secretary and proper systems for recording attendance and offerings are a "must." The librarian needs space for the text books that are available and for the distribution of Sunday school literature to the various classes and individuals. A room for this purpose will give order to the entire system. Bundles from the church office and the superintendent's home will get into the right rooms and a check of the quantity of materials received will make it possible to increase or lower the order as the occasion demands.

Department Organization

After a few years of experimentation, church educators decided on a departmentalized organization for Sunday schools. This of course is much different from public school organization which is graded. Doubtless the reason for the departmental organization is that most Sunday schools do not have sufficient enrollment to base their work on the grades. The conventional department which has been in use for two generations divides in the grades and age groups listed below.

THE CRADLE ROLL
From birth to the age when child enters an active department.

PRE-SCHOOL GROUPS
Toddlers (Nursery Roll), ages 1½–2
Nursery, age 3
Kindergarten, ages 4–5

PRIMARY DEPARTMENT
Grades 1, 2, 3; ages 6, 7, 8

JUNIOR DEPARTMENT
Grades 4, 5, 6; ages 9, 10, 11

JUNIOR HIGH DEPARTMENT
Grades 7, 8, 9; ages 12, 13, 14

SENIOR HIGH DEPARTMENT
Grades 10, 11, 12; ages 15–20

YOUNG PEOPLE'S DEPARTMENT
Beyond school age

ADULT DEPARTMENT
Ages 22 and up

This plan of departmentalization has not been questioned until recent years. Now some leaders prefer two-grade departments. This is based on the thesis that there is much closer integration between two grades than three. The suggested plan keeps the same pre-school departments, then the division is made as below. Note that this advances the ninth grade from association with the eighth graders to one with the tenth graders. The use of the two grade department is growing. Several denominational boards now provide lesson material edited to this division of ages. When the church wishes to identify the departments by group names Department One is called Primary; Department Two, Lower Junior; Department Three, Upper Junior; and Department Four, Intermediate. Yet in the case of the larger Sunday schools, the two grade classification hardly meets the need. When each grade has an enrollment of thirty or more, some leaders now prefer to have each grade organize its own department.

The division of the educational and social activities work into divisions, each division including several departments, is also practiced in some denominations. The children's department would include all children from one to eleven years of age; the youth department, all groups from twelve to twenty-three years, and all above twenty-three years, the adult division.

In our listings above, we have not included the home department. In actual practice this may be—and usually is—a part of the nursery department. This gives the nursery department the responsibility for all children of the church from birth until they pass to the beginners. There will be necessary flexibility in any plan for dividing the school dependent upon the enrollment of the local school, local leadership, and the rooms which are available for instructional purposes. Some churches will omit the beginners' department and place two-year olds and three-year olds in the nursery; then the kindergarten takes those of four and five years.

John Scotford in his book *When You Build Your Church* (Doniger & Raughley) compresses in a single paragraph the interpretation of this philosophy.

. . . we are convinced that next to the place of worship, the accommodations for small children are the most essential facilities for a church. Here is where a liberal investment will pay the largest returns both in lives and in dollars. As we have already pointed out, the little child must be brought to church. If he is there his parents will be with him. The older a child gets, the less likely this is to be the case. By the time they get to high school young people are prone to go one way and their parents another. The time to claim the parents for the church is when the children are small.

Organizing the Departments

The nursery and kindergarten departments have the right to claim the best space. It should be above ground on the first floor, with plenty of floor space for self-expression, coat racks, cases for lesson helps and equipment, and the basic play facilities so necessary for children. Cleanliness is essential. Where cribs are provided they must be sterilized periodically and oftener when an emergency arises. Unless a church is financially equipped to take care of the city requirement for a sanitary nursery, it is better that it does not try to maintain one. City health codes are becoming increasingly severe in this respect. The interdenominational code says that the children in the nursery, beginner, and primary departments need from thirty to thirty-five square feet per child.

For little children, the room should be large, on the ground floor with plenty of windows. If possible, an outdoor exit on ground level is desirable. Little tots should not be brushed and pushed through the crowded corridors when dismissed from their study period. The room must have warm floors. The little children will be on the floor much of the time, even during the story-telling period. This will usually mean radiant heating of some kind with a carpet over the tiled or wooden floor.

While it is desirable that each department of the school have its own rooms surrounded by permanent partitions this is especially important in the pre-school groups. At the same time economy demands that we have multiple-purpose rooms. The little children's rooms will have equipment such as slides, horses, sandboxes, etc., which cannot be crowded under tables or pushed in a cloak room. It will have religious pictures on the wall which should not be removed during Sunday.

However, in actual practice in many churches the rooms are used several ways during the week. When the women's organizations meet, the room is available for the entertainment of little children. Thousands of churches are operating weekday nurseries, keeping the facilities in use. With the modern mother forced into business to help with family expenses, this program seems most advisable.

A problem in many schools is the confusion which comes because the building was not planned to take care of the "extras" which are sure to come. There must be a place for hanging wraps and the children should be responsible to see that their coats and hats are hung in the proper place and that their boots are placed under their wraps. The present trend is for hooks to be on one of the walls in the rooms rather than in the corridor or in a cloak room. The corridor space pushes the little children into the moving mass of people and the small cloak room is a point of congestion. This is discussed more thoroughly later.

The Primary Department

We advance to the Primary Department where the system of organization becomes more formalized. Worship is introduced as a part of the curriculum and the arrangement of the rooms for graded work becomes more apparent. It will be necessary to provide space for the worship assembly and also for at least three classes. The policy of separate classes for boys and girls means six classes. The trend, however, is to follow the public school plan and have mixed classes throughout the school.

Departmental worship is very desirable, almost essential. The old time assembly for the entire school is no longer desired and few leaders recommend it; departmental assembly for worship has become the practice.

The code book says that children in the primary department need twenty to thirty square feet per child. This would mean a minimum of three rooms plus a room for the worship assembly.

The problem of investing in so much space for a few minutes use on Sunday will challenge the trustees of any church. So we come to the problem of multiple use of the space.

For most effective work, each department should have its own space surrounded by solid walls. This space may be within the church or in a separate building. Churches today are turning again to separate buildings. The Good Shepherd Lutheran Church, Easton, Pennsylvania plans a separate building for each department of its school.

To offset the exclusive use of rooms they may be planned so that the same space will be used for three purposes; first for a departmental assembly; next the space is divided into classrooms for the class period. Then in the third place, it is used for any social meetings of the department during the week. The fact that the rooms are large enough for the entire department means that they are large enough for other purposes so that they may be still further used.

Churches have found the old system in which each department has an assembly room and each class its own individual classroom most expensive. They are usually too small for any purpose except for the classes and combined they take a great deal of space. In our chapter dealing with church building, we present layouts of multiple-purpose rooms and show the contrast with the old style. The small "cubby-hole" rooms came from a period when educators felt that classes must be small. Today's leaders are encouraging larger classes. A class of twenty with two teachers would seem better than two classes of ten each.

While the interest has been growing for departmental rooms with solid walls, the older idea that each class must have its own room is weakening. In addition to the concept that larger classes are desirable there have developed better methods of controlling acoustics. According to John R. Scotford:

> The public schools report that four reading classes can be
> conducted at the same time in an acoustically treated room

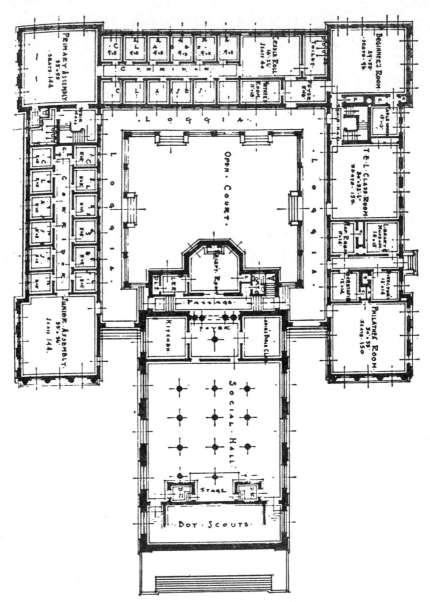

The passing departmental plan. The departments are segregated. There is a large room for the assembly, and many small rooms for individual classes, which will be limited to ten or twelve pupils each. Note the wastefulness of this plan. The small rooms are usable for but one purpose—a class on Sunday.

without interfering with each other. After installing an acoustical ceiling in a parish hall where a number of classes had been meeting separated by moveable screens, the rector of a Rochester, New York church reports, "We no longer bother to set up screens!" (*When You Build Your Church*, Doniger & Raughley)

For the best administration each department needs its own enclosed space. Within this area classes may be separated by screens, folding or solid partitions, or contrary to practices of the past few years, they may meet in the open space of an acoustically treated room.

What we have said about the primary department applies as well to the junior, intermediate, or other departments. The code shows that the need for floor space decreases as age increases. For juniors, twenty to thirty square feet is recommended; for the intermediate (junior high) fifteen to eighteen feet is desirable, the same for senior high; and for adult classes, ten square feet per person seems to be sufficient. The primary and junior departments should have housing similar to that discussed for the primary.

As space requirements are less, the high school housing requires a different approach. Most churches experience a decline in attendance following the junior years. It is an exceptional church which has a strong high school department. Because of fewer number, it is often wise to consider the junior and senior high as one group in planning the building. The center of this may be called a "youth center" which is designed as both a social and assembly room. It will also be used as classrooms which, when combined with other space available, will house the junior high and senior high classes. Some prefer to call the youth center a youth lounge. It is more or less a luxury room which is available for week-night meetings and should be equipped with a kitchenette so that it will not be necessary for the young people to use the church kitchen for their snacks.

Looking over the chapters dealing with the housing of the educational departments one cannot help but be impressed by

A fairly large graded school without departmental assembly is shown here. ▼

A floor plan showing a suitable arrangement for a school based on two-grade departments. ▶

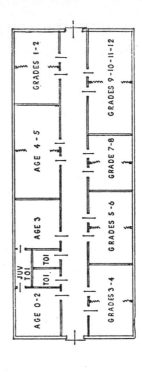

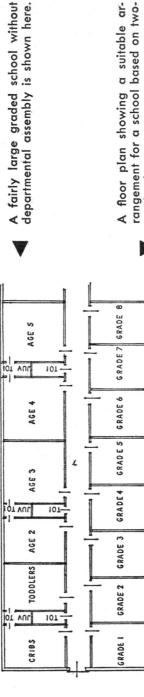

one feature. The entire plan is based on the principle that each age group has a place in the church which it can call its own. In these rooms is found equipment planned definitely for the age. Toilet facilities are conveniently near. The pictures on the walls are adapted to the age group. The child is actually a part of the church itself. No makeshift arrangement in a dining room or balcony can make up for the lack of space.

Churches have grown accustomed to women's organizations which insist on their own rooms—parlor, kitchen, etc. They insist that they must have the keys and full control of equipment. Is it not just as natural that the children's groups can develop church loyalty by having quarters which are their own? This does not mean that others cannot use the rooms, but it does mean that other groups using the space are using the junior space or the junior high school space. The departments should feel that it is their room which is being loaned for other work. The willingness to share with others may be a good lesson for the children and for adult organizations in the church.

Space will not permit a discussion here of curricula for the various departments. We feel that the denominations are doing a wonderful job as far as this is concerned. Our emphasis is on organization and equipment. Curriculum may be most important; space is close to that and then follow closely equipment and projects. One reason rooms are larger than formerly is that teachers more and more are insisting on material equipment and definite projects and these require space.

Double Services

One of the interesting signs of new religious interest is the number of churches which are finding it necessary to hold duplicate services on Sunday morning and, sometimes, duplicate church school sessions. It is one of the methods churches are using to meet the high cost of building and equipment. The least expensive way to get an extra five thousand square feet is to use the available five thousand square feet twice.

Two services of worship while the school has but one session presents some problems; two church school sessions and one church service of worship likewise has its difficulties. If both the worship service and the church school session are offered twice on Sunday, church families can more conveniently adjust themselves to the program.

Most families drive to church. The number of adults who attend the worship service is much greater than those who attend both the service of worship and the church school session. If two sessions are offered for each area of service, the family can elect the one which it will attend. If there are adults who wish to attend both services or children who wish to attend both, it can easily be arranged.

Some churches have tried to divide school in two units. Under this plan the children through the primary department will attend the first session of school and departments from the Junior on will attend the second session. This divides families and makes it necessary that a family car appear before the church twice to pick up the various members.

So many churches have had pleasant experiences with two services for both the worship services and the church school that the resistance earlier experienced is rapidly passing. Few churches having tried the plan would want to go back to a single service. Of course it must be understood that there are some churches so small in size that duplicate services are both unnecessary and undesirable.

Audio-Visual Aids

The wonderful helps now being offered in projected pictures makes it almost essential that the church be equipped for audio-visual aids. The motion picture machine, the film slide projector, and the slide projector are servants of the school. When a record player is added to these, the church is much better equipped to teach.

To make full use of these facilities the church should be so wired that the audio-visual equipment can be used in each room. This requires the proper outlets for electric current. Some churches prefer a single projection room where the class may meet for the pictorial presentation. Even when that is desirable the outlets should be installed in the individual classrooms for record players.

In this sketchy chapter should be included a reference to the Vacation Bible School which is conducted so successfully by thousands of churches each summer. Program materials are available for departments from the kindergarten through the junior high. Most of the instruction parallels somewhat the work done in the Sunday school except that hand projects have more emphasis than in the average school. Many children revel in the vacation school because it offers the opportunity for play-study which is thrilling to them. We suspect that the most ardent admirers of the work are the tired mothers who are glad to be released from the supervision of little children for at least a few hours each week.

The entire program of religious education is too broad a subject to be confined within one chapter in a book of this nature. We continue it in the next chapter by discussing groups at work in the church. The adult department of the church school will be treated in that chapter.

Perhaps problem number one in religious education is to find the time for adequate instruction. Most schools today are limited on Sunday to one hour, or one hour and fifteen minutes. The departmental assembly usually takes thirty minutes. Allowing time for traffic, wrap-hanging, etc., the actual instruction probably averages less than one-half hour per Sunday, which in most instances, means one-half hour per week. Allowing for absences and illnesses, it has been estimated that the average Sunday school pupil spends but three and one-half days in his life up through junior department in actual instruction. Even the construction of beautiful new educational buildings cannot atone for this deplorable situation in Protestantism.

A generation ago school leaders thought the three hour program on Sunday might bring the desirable time. The hours were set up in this way.

9:30 A.M.– 9:50 A.M.	Departmental Worship
9:50 A.M.–10:20 A.M.	Period of Instruction
10:20 A.M.–10:50 A.M.	Period of Expressional Work
10:50 A.M.–11:00 A.M.	Recess
11:00 A.M.–12:00 or 12:15	Church Worship

The idea was that the entire family would participate in both the instruction and the worship. In case the family did not desire to do that it could select for the various members the services each preferred. It looked like a good idea and had much backing but three-hour sessions are difficult to find today.

There must be some way to make the time more effective. Many are questioning the value of the thirty-minute worship assembly. It has some of the faults of the old time general assembly of the entire school. Many superintendents take too much of the hour with their speeches rather than leading the group in an expression of worship. Too many amateur educators want to be preachers. It is now suggested that the one hour be lengthened to one hour and fifteen minutes and that this time be divided as follows.

9:15 A.M.– 9:30 A.M.	Worship Assembly
9:30 A.M.–10:00 A.M.	First Study Session
10:00 A.M.–10:05 A.M.	Recess
10:05 A.M.–10:30 A.M.	Second Session

By this simple adjustment we may gain nearly double the time for actual instruction and expressional work.

Equipping the Classroom

We have mentioned a number of items which belong in the departments. A general treatise on the subject of church school equipment by William S. Hockman appeared in one of the issues of *Church Management*. The article gives a good picture of the broad needs. We are condensing it for our pages.

STORAGE. Always important, the need for storage space becomes increasingly necessary in our day with the emphasis on the multiple use of rooms. In one particular church, the scouts were assigned the kindergarten and a special room provided for the storage of their equipment. But no provision was made for the storage of the kindergarten material while the scouts used the room.

CUPBOARDS. It is wise to have cupboards built into the rooms; however, if this is neglected, portable cupboards will be satisfactory. The shelves should be wide enough to accommodate flat pictures and large books. It is preferable that they are not built directly from the floor. Cupboards and drawer space should, with some exceptions, be sufficient for the storage of all of the toys and playthings of the little children.

WRAP-HANGING. Coat-hanging facilities for the little children through the fourth grade should be integral with the department and classrooms; above the fourth grade children can hang their own wraps in hallways or coatrooms. For the younger children, wall-hanging is preferable to cloak rooms which cause congestion. Parents who come into the room to help their children can move more freely with the installation of wall-hangers.

CHALK BOARDS. These should be tailored to fit the age groups. Little children do not need much chalk board space but what they do have should be low enough for their scribbling. The teachers should have their boards high enough for convenience. Hence two boards in each room to suit the ages. From the fourth grade up, chalk boards two by eight feet are sufficient. Composition chalk board is cheaper than slate and is very satisfactory. Black still outsells green, but the green is catching up.

PIN-UP AND BULLETIN BOARDS. The least expensive and most satisfactory are constructed by pasting the unframed cork directly to the wall. Use linoleum paste and finish with a molding if that is desired. The little children require more pin-up boards than the older grades because they use more pictures. Framed pin-up boards which can be placed on a standard or stand for special exhibits come in handy. There is no substitute for cork.

CLOCKS. Important and many times forgotten.

TOILET FACILITIES. Installed for age sizes, of course, but just as important is sufficient space so that mothers and teachers may enter the room with little children. The installation should be related to age groups and so placed that the children may easily locate them.

CHAIRS. Rigid chairs are preferable. The increasing quality of folding chairs has made some of this kind commendable but judge carefully. Chairs should be comfortable. One man has said, "The chairs my children sit in when they are trying to learn of God should be just as comfortable as the chairs they sit in when they are learning arithmetic." Chairs must conform to the size of the individual child. In a closely graded school the following sizes are recommended.

AGE	GRADE	SEAT HEIGHT
2		8"
3		10"
4	Kindergarten	11"
5	Kindergarten	11"
6	First Grade	12"
7	Second Grade	13"
8	Third Grade	14"
9	Fourth Grade	16" (15" optional)
10	Fifth Grade	16"
11	Sixth Grade	16"
12	Seventh Grade	17"
13	Eighth Grade	17"
14	Ninth Grade	17"
15 and over		18"

Where a departmental pattern prevails, the chairs of these sizes will suffice. Nursery, ten inches; kindergarten, eleven inches; primary, twelve inches; junior, fifteen inches; junior high, seventeen inches; senior high, seventeen or eighteen inches. Table armchairs are the thing if much written work is required.

TABLES. Most necessary are substantial legs. Next is a top made of such material that it will resist scratches and remain smooth. Many sizes and shapes are available but the rectangular table seems to be the most popular. Heights should vary with the ages; some modern tables are adjustable to size. Proper height for a table is ten inches above the chair on which the child sits. For example if a second grade child sits on a chair thirteen inches high, the table top should be twenty-three inches from the floor.

PIANOS. Churches should make a move toward the extermination of old, moth-eaten pianos, adding good new ones as the budget permits.

AUDIO-VISUAL EQUIPMENT. Motion picture machine, film strip projectors, slide projectors (or combination), screens, and shades for darkening the room are necessities.

ADDITIONAL ITEMS. Teachers should not be expected to use the same chairs and tables as those used by the children. Maps are important but should be dispensed from a central location—there is no need of duplicating them in each department. While each classroom has its permanent chalk boards, there is need for several portable ones which should be dispensed from the central storing area.

All purchasing, care, replacement, and repair of all equipment should be the responsibility of a committee responsible to the board of Christian education. This committee must develop policies which will determine what equipment should be locked, what may be loaned to members, what may be borrowed by other churches. It should estimate repair and maintenance cost and insist on a budgetary allowance. Only through some provision such as this can the furnishings and equipment of the school be kept in constant repair. More and more we see the necessity for a central storage area from which all parts of the building may be serviced.

Graded Pictures

Two reasons for rooms enclosed by solid walls are chalk boards and pictures. These are essential in good educational rooms. Many presentations of pictures are suitable for various age groups and from these we have selected the following as good examples for display in the various grades and departments. They are time-tested pictures.

FOR NURSERY

Spring of the Year—Muriel Dawson
Floral Procession—French Foster
Christ Blessing Little Children—Plockhorst
Spring Song—Glucklich
Song of the Bluebird—Kenyon
Madonna—Partridge
Suffer Little Children—Tarrant
Madonna and Child—Raphael
Christ with Children—Vichon
Dignity and Impudence—Landseer
Feeding the Hens—Millet
Brittany Sheep—Bonheur

FOR KINDERGARTEN

(Any of the above)
Morning Carol—Tarrant
All On A Summer's Day—Muriel Dawson
Children's League of Nations—Moddorigh-Bokhorst
Youthful Gardeners—Moddorigh-Bokhorst
Rabbits—Muriel Dawson
Arrival of the Shepherds—LeRolle
The Age of Innocence—Reynolds
Piper and Nutcrackers—Landseer

FOR PRIMARY

When the World Was Young—Tarrant
Spring—Cizek
Workshop at Nazareth—Briggs
Mary and the Shepherd Boy—Scheurenberg
Jesus and the Children—Katz
A Helping Hand—Renouf
Milking Time—Dupre
Shoeing the Horse—Landseer
The Sower—Millet

The Song of the Lark—Breton
The Angelus—Millet
Pilgrims Going To Church—Boughton

JUNIOR DEPARTMENT

St. Francis Preaching to the Birds—Giotto
The Children's Hour—Taylor
Christ and the Doctors—Hofmann
The Harvest Moon—Tarrant
Reading Wycliffe's Bible—Clausen
Christ at Twelve—Hofmann
Christ and the Fisherman—Zimmerman
Jesus and the Children—Copping
Christ and the Rich Young Ruler—Hofmann
The Boy Jesus—Murillo
Washington Crossing the Delaware—Leutze
The Capitol Building at Washington
Statue of Lincoln—St. Gaudens
The Coliseum
Pyramids and the Sphinx
St. Michael and the Dragon—Reni
Westminster Abbey
St. Peter's (in Rome)
Cologne Cathedral

YOUTH

Calling of Matthew—Bidd
The Presence—Borthwick
Peter and John—Burnand
Christ of the Andes—Cimabui
Jesus and the Newsboys—Copping
The Hope of the World—Copping
Jesus Weeping over the City—Flandrin
The Last Supper—Leonardo
Jesus Christ—Max
The Return of the Prodigal—Tissot
Sermon on the Mount—Wood
Man with the Hoe—Millet
Moses—Michelangelo
Sir Galahad—Watts
Breaking Home Ties—Hovenden

The Appian Way
United States Supreme Court
Capitol at Washington
The Lincoln Memorial at Washington
The Statue of Liberty
Panoramic View of Jerusalem

Other Activities

No discussion of the educational program of the local church would be inclusive if it failed to mention three additional activities—the daily vacation Bible school, religious drama, and summer camps and conference. They are not found in every church but are recognized as legitimate activity for the church school.

Vacation Bible School

There is more general recognition of this activity than the other two. Few communities are without a summer vacation school running three, four, or more weeks. Practically all of the denominations publish curriculum material for these schools. In many communities the vacation schools are cooperative ventures with other churches joining in. The curriculum used divides the time between play, handcraft work, religious drama, and formal instruction. In a true sense, it is a vacation school. Teachers, parents, and children recognize that. No homework is required. But the social assets found in a school running five days a week over a period of time are great.

Religious Drama

Religious drama has an important part in the program of most churches. It is an effective method in religious education from the earliest years. The need for a large stage for public presentations does not seem to be as important as we once thought. Many truly religious plays can be better presented from the church chancel.

The increasing cost of church building has played its part in limiting stage space. This situation is a result rather than the cause of decreasing interest. Where a production is given but two or three times a year, the reservation for stage space and dressing rooms comes pretty high. Bethany Union Church, Chicago, Illinois has met this problem by having a removable stage. When needed for dramatic productions the stage is erected and the wings and curtains extended from the ceiling. In a few hours, one end of the large dining room is converted into a complete stage for drama. If drama becomes an important part of the program of the church there should be a return to the permanent stage to permit rehearsal periods.

Summer Camps and Conferences

These have become increasingly important in the life of the church. The conference is a successor to the old camp meeting. It provides drama, music, and religious inspiration. Good programs are maintained by denominations during the summer season. The camps are closer to the local church area. There are few churches which do not offer summer camp facilities to its children and young people. Many local churches now own their own camps. Others cooperate with the regional denominational bodies such as synods, presbyteries, conferences, or associations.

There is offered a contact with the out-of-doors, association with others with Christian ideals. Through play, fellowship, and instruction they are offering great opportunities to the church youth of America. The camp offers twenty-four hours a day of group living in the out-of-doors and the children come in close contact with consecrated counsellors. The skill of the hands, study of the Bible, and Christian fellowship work together for spiritual experience. It has been described as an experiment in living at its best.

Religious Education

BOWER, W. C., *Christ and Christian Education*. Abingdon, 1943.

CHAVE, E., *A Functional Approach to Religious Education*. University of Chicago, 1947.

CROSSLAND, W. F., *How To Build Up Your Sunday School*. Abingdon, 1948.

CUMMINGS, O. De W., *Christian Education in the Local Church*. Judson, 1942.

FRANZBLAU, A. W., *Organization, Supervision and Administration of the Jewish Religious School*. Hebrew Union College, 1935.

HARNER, N. C., *The Educational Work of the Church*. Abingdon, 1939.

JONES, P. R., *The Church School Superintendent*. Abingdon, 1939.

KEAN, C. D., *The Christian Gospel and the Parish Church*. Seabury, 1953.

LOBINGER, J. L., *The Better Church School*. Pilgrim, 1952.

LOTZ, P. H., ed., *Orientation in Religious Education*. Abingdon, 1950.

MILLER, R. C., *Education for Christian Living*. Prentice-Hall, 1956.

Plays for the Church. National Council (a leaflet), 1957.

SHERRILL, L. J., *The Rise of Christian Education*. Macmillan, 1944.

SMART, J. D., *The Teaching Ministry of the Church*. Westminster, 1954.

AUDIO-VISUAL AIDS

ABC's of Visual Aids and Projectionists' Manual. M. O. Publishers.

BACHMAN, J. W., *How To Use Audio-Visual Materials*. Association, 1956.

DALE, E., *Audio-Visual Methods in Teaching*. Dryden, 1948.

Educational Screen (magazine). 64 East Lake Street, Chicago.

HAAS, K. B. and H. Q. PACKER, *Preparation and Use of Audio-Visual Aids*. Prentice-Hall, 1950.

HOCKMAN, W. S., *Projected Visual Aids in the Church*. Pilgrim, 1947.

RIGERS, W. L. and P. H. VIETH, *Visual Aids in the Church*. Christian Education, 1946.

TOWER, H. E., *Church Use of Audio-Visual Aids*. Abingdon, 1940.

WALDRUP, E., *Using Visual Aids in a Church*. Broadman, 1949.

DAILY VACATION BIBLE SCHOOL

BLAIR, W. D., *The New Vacation Church School*. Harper, 1939.

RISTINE, E., *The Vacation Church School*. Abingdon, 1947.

The How of Vacation School, National Council.

WEEKDAY CHURCH SCHOOL

DAVIS, M. D., *Weekday Classes in Religious Education*. Bulletin 3. U. S. Office of Education, 1941.

MOEHLMAN, C. H., *About the Church as an Educator*. Hinds, Hayden and Eldredge, 1947.

MOON, A., *Planning the Weekday Church School*. Methodist, 1941.

SUMMER CAMPS

Campcraft ABC's. Girl Scouts, 1941.

CARLSON, R., *Day Camping for Your Church.* Judson, 1948.

DIMOCK, H., *Administration of the Summer Camp.* Association, 1948.

GRAHAM, A., *Working at Play in Summer Camps.* Woman's, 1941.

OTT, E., *So You Want To Be A Camp Counselor.* Association, 1946.

17 | USING THE CHURCH YEAR

NO PERSON REALLY GETS THE "FEELING" OF CHURCH AD-
ministration until he has been initiated into the mysteries of the
church seasons of the year. The liturgist needs to know the historical church calendar to follow the liturgy, arrange the altar
and the music. The minister needs to know both the church and
national calendar for emphasis in his preaching ministry. The
administrator needs to know the best seasons for financial efforts, the months when evangelism may best be promoted, the
periods when you "just cannot" expect great congregations.
The youth leader must be familiar with the school terms, the
vacation seasons, the camping dates. All of these varieties of
calendars come into the functioning of the present day church.

Traditionally, the church year begins with the season of
Advent. Though introductory to Christmas which is a fixed
date, the date of Advent is determined by Easter. With the first
Sunday in this season the church year really begins. St. Andrew's
day is a fixed date, November 30; the first Sunday in Advent is
the Sunday nearest to this date.

This introductory word shows at once some of the difficulties
in the church calendar. Some of the Holy Days are fixed; some
are movable. There are other factors which increase the confusion. The church year is a development of many centuries and
the dates used in the present generation are not identical with
those used five hundred years ago. The Lenten season has been
shortened and the great fifty days, Easter to Pentecost, the first
recognized season of the early Christian church has become less
important. Right now there is an effort being made to recover
this particular season. This is not alone for continuity of observance but to help in the promotion of religious interest in the

post-Easter season. Churches have found it difficult to sustain
the spirit of Easter through the period from Easter to Pentecost.
As this is the season when the church was organized and really
marks the birth of the Christian church, it is important to recover the significance of these days.

There have been differences in the dates observed by the Eastern and Western divisions of the church. In the West, Christmas
is celebrated on December 25. In the East, the date has been
January 6. Recently it has been noticed that the immigrant
orthodox churches are swinging to our date for both Christmas
and Easter.

As far as the Roman historic calendar is concerned, the days of
the year, starting with Advent would be divided in these divisions.

First Half of Year

ADVENT
Starts on or about November 30 and continues until Christmas
Eve. Four Sundays.

CHRISTMASTIDE
This period starts with Christmas Eve and continues through
Twelfth Night (Epiphany Eve).

EPIPHANY
Starts with Epiphany and continues to Ash Wednesday. From
four to nine Sundays.

LENT
From Ash Wednesday to Easter. Forty week days plus six
Sundays.

EASTERTIDE
Easter to Pentecost. Fifty days including seven Sundays.

Second Half of Year

WHITSUNTIDE
Pentecost to Advent. Twenty-three or more Sundays.

It is evident from a mere glance that the first half of the
church year is crowded with special days while the second half

lacks much of the dramatic appeal. The Sundays are listed as "First Sunday after Trinity," "Second Sunday after Trinity," etc., in the Lutheran and Episcopal churches but in the Catholic churches the designations are "First Sunday after Pentecost," "Second Sunday after Pentecost," etc. These designations are continued up to the Sunday before Advent in the Episcopal calendar; in the Lutheran calendar it is termed "The Last Sunday after Trinity." The length is variable and may include from twenty-three to twenty-six Sundays.

This very much condensed calendar shows one of the reasons why the Committee on Worship of the National Council of Churches has recommended many additions and changes in the historic church year. The changes are based on special days and seasons which have already been accepted by many communions. First of all the recommendations is that the Pentecost season known as Whitsuntide be divided; the first period to include the period from Pentecost to the last Sunday in August. The balance of the season is to be known as Kingdomtide. The first section emphasizes the Holy Trinity, Kingdomtide emphasizes the doctrine of the Kingdom of God.

Kingdomtide starts with the Festival of Christ the King and continues until the Sunday before Advent. Denominations which use the historic calendar may continue to list the Sundays —"Sunday after Trinity or Pentecost." Some may prefer to number them as "First Sunday in Kingdomtide," "Second Sunday in Kingdomtide," etc. After this division the Sundays of the year are divided as follows.

ADVENT

First through Fourth Sunday (The Sunday before Christmas) in Advent.

CHRISTMASTIDE

First Sunday (The Sunday after Christmas) and Second Sunday (New Year's) in Christmastide.

EPIPHANY

First through Ninth Sunday's after Epiphany.

LENT

First through Fourth Sunday's in Lent, followed by Mission Sunday and Palm Sunday.

EASTERTIDE

Easter Sunday, First through Fifth Sunday's after Easter, and Sunday after Ascension Day.

WHITSUNTIDE

Whitsunday (Pentecost), First Sunday (Trinity) through Fifteenth Sunday after Pentecost.

KINGDOMTIDE

Festival of Christ the King, Seventeenth through Twenty-eighth Sunday's after Pentecost.

The continuity of the church year follows the traditional calendar. The second recommendation of the committee was that there be placed in the calendar, near an appropriate Sunday, the special days which the church, through practice, has been observing in recent years. The calendar as proposed in a recent issue of the Handbook of American Churches would be as follows. The special days are named in the parentheses, and are placed with that Sunday on which they are customarily observed.

ADVENT, THE SEASON OF EXPECTANCY

First and Second Sunday's in Advent (Universal Bible Sunday), Third and Fourth Sunday (Sunday before Christmastide) in Advent.

CHRISTMASTIDE, THE SEASON OF THE NATIVITY

Christmas (The Birth of our Lord), Sunday after Christmas (New Year's Eve) (Watch Night), Festival of the Christening, Second Sunday in Christmastide (Twelfth Night) (Epiphany Eve) (Universal Week of Prayer).

EPIPHANY, THE SEASON OF THE EVANGEL

Epiphany, First and Second Sunday's after Epiphany (Missionary Day) (Church and Economic Life Week) (Youth Week), Third and Fourth Sunday's after Epiphany (Presentation of Jesus in the Temple), Fifth Sunday after Epiphany, (Race Relations Sunday), Sixth Sunday after Epiphany (Universal Day of Prayer for Students) (Brotherhood Week), Seventh Sunday after Epiphany (The Transfiguration—also August 6), Eighth Sunday after Epiphany.

LENT, THE SEASON OF RENEWAL

Ash Wednesday (World Day of Prayer), First through Fourth Sunday's in Lent, The Annunciation, Passion

Sunday, Holy Week, Palm Sunday, Maundy Thursday, Good Friday, Easter Eve.

EASTERTIDE, THE SEASON OF THE RESURRECTION

Easter, First and Second Sunday's after Easter (National Christian College Day), Third and Fourth Sunday's after Easter (May Fellowship Day) (Rural Life Sunday) (Youth Sunday—one of the Sundays after Easter) (National Family Week) (Festival of the Christian Home) (Mother's Day), Ascension Day, Sunday after Ascension Day (Memorial Day).

WHITSUNTIDE, SEASON OF THE HOLY SPIRIT AND THE BIRTH OF THE CHRISTIAN CHURCH

Whitsunday (Pentecost) (Birth of the Christian Church) (Christian Unity Sunday), Trinity Sunday, Second Sunday after Pentecost, Children's Sunday, Third and Fourth Sunday's after Pentecost (Nature Sunday), Fifth Sunday after Pentecost (Independence Sunday), Independence Day,

Sixth through Ninth Sunday's after Pentecost, The Transfiguration (also last Sunday in Epiphany), Tenth Sunday after Pentecost.

KINGDOMTIDE, SEASON OF THE KINGDOM OF GOD ON EARTH

(Festival of Christ the King), Eleventh and Twelfth Sunday's after Pentecost (Labor Sunday) (Labor Day), Thirteenth through Nineteenth Sunday's after Pentecost (Christian Education Week), Twentieth Sunday after Pentecost (World-Wide Communion) (Men and Missions Day) (Churchmen's Week), Laymen's Sunday, Twenty-first Sunday after Pentecost (World Order Sunday) (World Temperance Day) (Reformation Sunday) (Reformation Day), Twenty-second Sunday after Pentecost, All Saints' Day, All Souls' Day (World Community Day), Twenty-third through Twenty-seventh Sunday's after Pentecost, Stewardship Day (Thanksgiving Sunday) (Thanksgiving Day).

As a book of this type serves many years, it was not thought wise to place dates in the calendar above. The following tables give the information which will be helpful in making the calendar for the local church. Source of information is *The Church Year* by Fred Winslow Adams, a booklet distributed by the National Council of the Churches of Christ in America.

FIXED FESTIVALS

Christmas Eve—December 24
The Nativity—December 25
Festival of the Christening, New Year's Day—January 1
Twelfth Night, Epiphany Eve—January 5
Epiphany—January 6
Presentation of Jesus in the Temple—February 2
The Annunciation—March 25
Reformation Day—October 31
All Saints' Day—November 1
All Souls' Day—November 2

MOVABLE FESTIVALS

Advent. The Sunday nearest November 30th.
Christmas Sunday. The Fourth Sunday in Advent, or as in the Episcopal and some other churches, the next Sunday after December 25th.
The Transfiguration. Last Sunday in the Epiphany Season.
Ash Wednesday. The beginning of Lent, forty-six days before Easter.
Passion Sunday. Two Sundays before Easter.
Palm Sunday. The Sunday before Easter.
Maundy Thursday. In Holy Week.
Good Friday. In Holy Week.
Easter Day. Always the first Sunday after the full moon which happens upon or next after March 21st.
Ascension Day (Holy Thursday). Forty days after Easter.
The Sunday after Ascension Day. Next before Whitsunday.
Whitsunday or Pentecost. Fifty days after Easter.
Trinity Sunday. The Sunday after Pentecost.
Festival of Christ the King. Beginning Kingdomtide, the last Sunday in August.

OTHER SPECIAL DAYS

Universal Bible Sunday. The second Sunday in Advent.
Missionary Day. The second Sunday after Epiphany.

Race Relations Day. The Sunday nearest February 12th (Lincoln's Birthday).

Brotherhood Day. The Sunday nearest February 22nd (Washington's Birthday).

World Day of Prayer. The first Friday in Lent.

Day of Prayer for Students. The third Sunday in February.

Stewardship Day. The fourth or some Sunday in Lent. In 1940 the United Stewardship Council for the first time designated a Stewardship Sunday, selecting November 24th.

Rural Life Sunday. The fifth Sunday after Easter.

Youth Sunday. Some Sunday in Eastertide.

Festival of the Christian Home. The second Sunday in May.

Christian Unity Sunday. Whitsunday (Pentecost).

Children's Day. The second Sunday in June.

Nature Sunday. The last Sunday in June.

Labor Sunday. The Sunday before Labor Day.

World Temperance Day. The Sunday nearest the first day of November.

World Peace Sunday. The Sunday before Veterans' Day, November 11th.

Thanksgiving Sunday. The Sunday before Thanksgiving Day.

Thanksgiving Day. The fourth Thursday in November or such Thursday as is designated by Presidential Proclamation.

SPECIAL WEEKS

Week of Prayer. The first week in January.

Holy Week. The week preceding Easter.

Religious Education Week. The first week in October.

The Use of Seasonal Colors

The use of liturgical colors is increasing along with the general trend to add decorations to vestment and altar. The practice of using seasonal colors has no tradition in the early church. The first mention of any altar color with the exeption of white came in the twelfth century when red was introduced in Pentecost.

The rise of liturgical guilds in our churches has increased the interest in color and they are considered in many areas impor-

tant to the proper observance of Christian worship. There is of
course a symbolism in color which fits into the church calendar
for the year. Red, the color of blood and fire, is proper for the
days which commemorate the deaths of martyrs. Violet and
black are the colors for penitence and mourning, hence the

	EPISCOPAL	LUTHERAN
First Sunday in Advent	Violet	Violet
Second Sunday in Advent	Violet	Violet
Third Sunday in Advent	Violet	Violet
Fourth Sunday in Advent	Violet	Violet
Christmas Day	White	White
Second Sunday after Christmas	White	White
First Sunday after Epiphany	White	White
Second Sunday after Epiphany	Green	White
Third Sunday after Epiphany	Green	White
Fourth Sunday after Epiphany	Green	White
Septuagesima Sunday	Violet	Green
Sexagesima Sunday	Violet	Green
Quinquagesima Sunday	Violet	Green
Ash Wednesday	Violet	Violet
First Sunday in Lent	Violet	Violet
Second Sunday in Lent	Violet	Violet
Third Sunday in Lent	Violet	Violet
Fourth Sunday in Lent	Violet	Violet
Passion Sunday	Violet	Violet
Palm Sunday	Violet	Violet
Maundy Thursday	Violet	Violet
Good Friday	Black	Black
Easter	White	White
First Sunday after Easter	White	White
Eve of Second Sunday after Easter	Red	White
Second Sunday after Easter	White	White
Third Sunday after Easter	Red	Red
Fourth Sunday after Easter	White	White
Fifth Sunday after Easter (Rogation Sunday)	White	White
Sunday after Ascension	White	White
Whitsunday (Pentecost)	Red	Red
Trinity Sunday	White	White

natural colors for Lent. Green, the color of nature, was proper for ordinary occasions. White is still the color to be used on Christmas and Easter.

Checking the church year of the two traditions, Roman-Episcopal and Lutheran, we find some differences still persist.

From this point all the Sundays run numerically until the First Sunday before Advent is reached. The liturgical color for each Sunday, in both traditions, including the Sunday before Advent is green.

Interspersed throughout the year on week days are what are called the days of the martyrs. The liturgical color for these days is red. In the Episcopal church, black is the color for mourning and funerals, white for weddings, confirmations, and ordinations. In the case of baptisms the priest may wear a violet stole until the renunciation of Satan and then reverse it to reveal the white underside. In the Lutheran Church the color for the day is followed regardless of the particular service.

The Minister's Executive Calendar

Throughout this chapter we have kept the order of the historic church calendar, starting with Advent around December 1. But there are two others which must have consideration. One is the calendar under which the business affairs of the nation are conducted. This starts with January and ends with December.

If one is to do business in our land it is necessary to recognize this calendar and very few churches use the church calendar in their business affairs. In recent years even the publications of the liturgical denominations are listing the annual dates in the order of our national calendar rather than the traditional church sequence. The historic days are set in a modern continuity.

Salary payments are made on the workday calendar and contracts must be dated by such calendars. While the church calendar will probably be continued as the historic form for worship, it will exercise a decreasing influence in other areas of life. Even the immigrant churches tend to change their religious dates to conform with Western practices.

Another calendar is very important in the church and may very well control the program of the church. Certain seasons are adapted to specialized activities of the church. The successful church learns to use these natural seasons. Take the summer time, for example. Most parts of our country swelter in the heat during parts of the summer. This means summer vacations and falling congregations. Churches can resist these tendencies. Some have found a way to sustain large attendance during the summer seasons; others have done wisely and changed their program to meet the weather.

Services are maintained during the warm months of course. But the season has been found to be very profitable for summer camping, vacation Bible schools, summer conferences, and exploratory trips. Neglected for many years in the church, here is work which blossoms into great promise as a warm weather program. There is no provision for this in the historic calendar.

To all appearances, the church year starts with early fall when the families get settled from their summer vacations. Rally Day of a generation ago was the day when the church and the school started for the new year. Formerly held in September, it has been pushed farther along and at the present time probably coincides with World Communion Sunday.

The appearances, however, are deceitful. The year really started with the planning period which probably occurred before the vacation months. The minister should have his fall program well in hand before leaving for his annual vacation. He will keep turning it over in his mind and checking it at every point so that the plans are mature when he returns in early fall. World Communion Sunday is a good pivotal date to start the fall program.

September, October, and November are naturals for getting started. November is the ideal time for the every member canvass, especially if the fiscal year starts January 1. The fall months are the time to get all committees started on their work. The people have been psychologically prepared for this season. Not only financial campaigns but the school, women's society, and young people must get their work started. This brings us to Christmastide which plays such an important part in the church year. It can easily climax the fall months. Committees for the celebration should be appointed in October so there will be time for adequate work.

The church calendar in the foregoing pages places the week of prayer early in January. It fits well into the program. In the period before Lent begins, meetings for prayer and evangelism can be effective. The Christmas spirit is still abroad and people are eager to hear the message. Youth week begins the last week of January. This also is in the proper place.

Time runs on to Lent. In contrast to January which is ideal for evangelism, Lent is a time for deepening the spiritual life. The messages of the pulpit and any extra services should be directed to this end. The end of such services is the development of humility and devotion to the spirit of Christ.

This reaches its climax in Good Friday which is followed with the joys of Easter. Having been through the darkness of the night the Christian can now share its joys. Unfortunately many churchmen feel that the joys must be experienced outside of the church services and attendance suffers during the weeks following Easter. We must make every effort to correct this situation. Our people need to understand that these days celebrate the birth of the Christian church. The minister needs to include the special days of this season for education—to bring knowledge of the historic church, the contribution made by the Apostles and early Christians.

Next is Pentecost or Whitsuntide from which we rush rapidly on to summer. In the weeks between Easter and Whitsunday, plans should be formulated for the summer to keep the church open and supplied with good ministers. Do not pressure people into attendance. That policy should pass with Whitsunday. Rather work on extracurricular activities. Use the out-of-doors for camping, summer conferences, and schools. Tie the church program up with nature.

Start the plans for the next fall when people will again return

THE MOVABLE FESTIVALS OF THE CHURCH YEAR
1955-1979

YEAR	1955	1956	1957	1958	1959
Sundays after Epiphany	4	3	5	3	2
Septuagesima	Feb. 6	Jan. 29	Feb. 17	Feb. 2	Jan. 25
Ash Wednesday	Feb. 23	Feb. 15	Mar. 6	Feb. 19	Feb. 11
Easter	Apr. 10	Apr. 1	Apr. 21	Apr. 6	Mar. 29
Ascension Day	May 19	May 10	May 30	May 15	May 7
Pentecost	May 29	May 20	June 9	May 25	May 17
Sundays after Trinity	24	26	23	25	26
Advent Sunday	Nov. 27	Dec. 2	Dec. 1	Nov. 30	Nov. 29

YEAR	1960	1961	1962	1963	1964
Sundays after Epiphany	5	3	6	4	2
Septuagesima	Feb. 14	Jan. 29	Feb. 18	Feb. 10	Jan. 26
Ash Wednesday	Mar. 2	Feb. 15	Mar. 7	Feb. 27	Feb. 12
Easter	Apr. 17	Apr. 2	Apr. 22	Apr. 14	Mar. 29
Ascension Day	May 26	May 11	May 31	May 23	May 7
Pentecost	June 5	May 21	June 10	June 2	May 17
Sundays after Trinity	23	26	23	24	26
Advent Sunday	Nov. 27	Dec. 3	Dec. 2	Dec. 1	Nov. 29

YEAR	1965	1966	1967	1968	1969
Sundays after Epiphany	5	4	2	5	3
Septuagesima	Feb. 14	Feb. 6	Jan. 22	Feb. 11	Feb. 2
Ash Wednesday	Mar. 3	Feb. 23	Feb. 8	Feb. 28	Feb. 19
Easter	Apr. 18	Apr. 10	Mar. 26	Apr. 14	Apr. 6
Ascension Day	May 27	May 19	May 4	May 23	May 15
Pentecost	June 6	May 29	May 14	June 2	May 25
Sundays after Trinity	23	24	27	24	25
Advent Sunday	Nov. 28	Nov. 27	Dec. 3	Dec. 1	Nov. 30

YEAR	1970	1971	1972	1973	1974
Sundays after Epiphany	2	4	3	6	4
Septuagesima	Jan. 25	Feb. 7	Jan. 30	Feb. 18	Feb. 10
Ash Wednesday	Feb. 11	Feb. 24	Feb. 16	Mar. 7	Feb. 27
Easter	Mar. 29	Apr. 11	Apr. 2	Apr. 22	Apr. 14
Ascension Day	May 7	May 20	May 11	May 31	May 23
Pentecost	May 17	May 30	May 21	June 10	June 2
Sundays after Trinity	26	24	26	23	24
Advent Sunday	Nov. 29	Nov. 28	Dec. 3	Dec. 2	Dec. 1

YEAR	1975	1976	1977	1978	1979
Sundays after Epiphany	2	5	4	2	5
Septuagesima	Jan. 26	Feb. 15	Feb. 6	Jan. 22	Feb. 11
Ash Wednesday	Feb. 12	Mar. 3	Feb. 23	Feb. 8	Feb. 28
Easter	Mar. 30	Apr. 18	Apr. 10	Mar. 26	Apr. 15
Ascension Day	May 8	May 27	May 19	May 4	May 24
Pentecost	May 18	June 6	May 29	May 14	June 3
Sundays after Trinity	26	23	24	27	24
Advent Sunday	Nov. 30	Nov. 28	Nov. 27	Dec. 3	Dec. 2

from their vacations. Before leaving the parish for the vacation weeks the minister should check every department of church work to make sure that they have their committees appointed and that some meetings will be held before the autumn months. This can be, from the executive point of view, the most important contribution in the weeks between Whitsunday and Labor Day.

Some churches follow this emphasis on the seasons of nature so far that they divide the church year still further. The weeks starting July 1 and continuing until the eve of the last Sunday in August are called "The Season of Refreshment and Rest." Kingdomtide starts with the last Sunday in August.

The Church Year

Book of Common Worship of the Protestant Episcopal Church.

Easton, B. S. and H. C. Robbins, The Eternal World in the Modern World. Scribners, 1937.

Gibson, G. M., The Story of the Christian Year. Abingdon, 1945.

Horn, E. T., III, The Christian Years; Days and Seasons of the Year. Muhlenberg, 1957.

Newland, M. R., The Year and Our Children. Kenedy, 1950.

Scudder, V. D., Social Teachings of the Christian Year. Dutton, 1918.

Strodack, P. Z., The Church Year. United Lutheran, 1924.

Walker, C., The Christian Year. Longmans, 1947.

Wallis, C. L., Worship Resources for the Christian Year. Harper, 1954.

Yearbook of American Churches. National Council, annually.

18 | MINISTERIAL ETHICS & PRACTICES

MANY CHANGES HAVE TAKEN PLACE IN CHURCH PRO-
grams, methods, and practices, but no area has seen more
changes than the ministry itself. Some requisite qualities of the
clergy have existed since New Testament days. Others have
been added to meet the changing world and some old thinking
has been dropped from the ministerial concept. The minister
enjoys a freedom from congregational supervision quite different
from that of a generation ago. Churches recognize that the
parsonage or manse is the home of the minister and they permit
him privacy in his home life. Writers formerly warned ministers about the dangers of private counselling. If the client should
be a woman, the pastor was asked to have a third party present
to prevent any suspicion of immoral thoughts or acts. Today
our congregations seem to have more confidence in their spiritual
leaders. Finding a minister with a baseball bat in his hand does
not result in a warning to keep from all appearances of evil.

The minister of thirty years ago often found his salary in
arrears, but that is unusual today. Churches appreciate that the
laborer is worthy of his hire and decency demands payment at
regularly stated intervals. My own Methodist father faced an
angry official board when he took his sons to see the circus. The
recreation of the minister and his family is no longer dictated
by the whims of the congregation.

Churches are morally tolerant on theological and intellectual
issues. Heresy trials are now unknown but we should examine
the theology of the pastor lest he be dragged before his congregation to answer questions regarding his interest in athletics,
psychic research, or attending the movies. Ministers, however,
were conscious that theirs was a changing profession and a

popular subject in ministerial meetings was professional ethics. The resulting codes were printed in a volume, *Ministerial Ethics & Etiquette* (Cokesbury, 1928), edited by Nolan B. Harmon, now a bishop of the Methodist Church.

Others included "The Congregational Code" produced for New Haven, Connecticut; "The Methodist Code" adopted by a conference of Methodist ministers in 1926; "The Presbyterian Code" adopted by the Presbytery of New York in 1926; and "The Unitarian Code" adopted by a ministerial association in Boston. These make interesting case studies but would hardly be news at the present time. They do, however, make good copy for comparison with our day. From a book of my own authorship, *The Making of a Minister* (Cokesbury, 1938), the following lines may give insight into an era now past.

> Crowded churches among Protestants are not common in this day.
>
> Falling church attendance has had its reaction on church giving. The per capita giving of Protestant church members in 1928 was $23.30; in 1934, it had fallen to $12.06; in 1937, it had risen only to $13.25. Yet 1937 saw business well back to the predepression figure.
>
> Religion in our land no longer speaks with authority.
>
> The preacher has lost much authority; the age is not against him; it merely takes him for granted.
>
> The ministry, today, is a white collared job, expecting much from the preacher and offering him little in material reward.

In many ways, 1938 may have been the turning point for churches, for I find this paragraph in the analysis:

> At the time this is being written there are some indications of religious recovery. During the first months of 1938, the churches were able to sustain the same rate of giving as in 1937 though national income was very low. Attendance at services is averaging considerably more than the preceding year. If this tendency can be maintained and expanded, we may be in for a period of enlarging church influence.

As a matter of fact this was the turning period. Judged by the records of the years, increasing attendance and increased giving started in 1938. Each year since has seen further advances. In the period between 1938 and the present, we have seen unprecedented church growth and new concepts of church program, church building, and changing ideas of ministerial responsibilities. From this point of view we still discuss the minister, his personal responsibilities, and some of his pastoral practices.

Ministerial Ethics

The ethics of the minister seem to fall in the following classifications: the man, his family, his church, his profession, and his community. We will take up the subjects in that order.

The Man

We put the minister as a man first in this list, not because of any selfish ministerial ambition but because every category begins in the man himself. In his desire to be fair to every one, he must include his own life. Not every minister is an executive, but only with difficulty can he pass on responsibilities to others. Most ministers are general practitioners, not specialists.

In every phase of ministerial activity, one quality stands above all others—sincerity. He not only proclaims the truth of the Lord Jesus Christ, consciously or unconsciously he day by day proclaims the truth in himself. What he is will speak so loudly that those who know him may not hear the words he is saying. To the novice preacher sincerity may appear to be a very meek quality, but ministers of maturity know through personal experience the difficulty of being true to oneself over a period of thirty to forty years.

There are many methods of publicity available to the minister, and tricks of the platform urge him to utter half truths. Techniques of administration may help him to win people, but in every private and public activity he needs this basic quality of simple honesty. This does not mean that he should hide his light under a bushel or refuse to accept preferment. Ambition in the ministry is not an evil thing. A minister is entitled to aspire to a better church or denominational position, but trickery and deceit must be put aside in such an ambition.

> To thine own self be true and it will follow as the night the day, thou canst not then be false to any man.

Closely allied to the quality of sincerity is that the Christian minister should in every respect qualify as a gentleman. This implies the tolerance, courtesy, kindness, and decency which we expect from every Christian. He should be free from boastfulness and should know how to control his tongue. He should keep apart from gossipers and slanderers. He should try to free himself from the desire to accept all of the benefits from the profession and the glory in his distinct vocation. There are numerous passages in the New Testament which describe these qualities.

> Let love be without dissimulation. Abhor that which is evil; cleave to that which is good. Be kindly affectioned to one another with brotherly love; in honor preferring one another; not slothful in business; fervent in spirit; serving the Lord. Romans 12:9-11.
>
> Mind not high things but condescend to men of low estate. Be not wise in your own conceits. Romans 12:17.
>
> For a bishop must be blameless, as the steward of God; not self-willed nor soon angry, not given to wine, no striker, not given to filthy lucre. But a lover of hospitality, a lover of good men, sober, just, holy, temperate. Titus 1:7-8.

The man to be true to himself will try to keep his own health and the health of his family. He preaches Sabbath observance, yet he must spend himself on Sunday. The law of a day of rest applies to him as it does to his neighbor. To offset the Sunday exertions, he selects some other period of the week for his rest period. Monday has been the minister's traditional day of rest, but changing conditions may indicate a change. Charles E. Jefferson preferred Saturday as his rest day and prepared his required two sermons by Friday evening which meant an advanced schedule. James Elmer Russell suggested that a half day taken Saturday afternoon and a half day taken on Monday morning helped him best.

How Many Hours?

Just how many hours a minister should put in at his task is difficult to determine. Most men work more than the industrial forty hours, but even a special day set aside and publicized cannot be inflexibly observed. Emergency calls will arise which no sincere minister can pass by.

Because it is well nigh impossible to separate his professional life from his home life, he will find it necessary to get much of his rest in vacation weeks away from the parish. But even then, no honest minister will blankly say no to a request for his services by those in trouble. The author served for two short periods of time as the guest pastor of the Old Stone Church, Cleveland, Ohio. Before Dr. Robert B. Whyte, the pastor at the time, left for his summer vacation we discussed any possible situations when he might be called back to the parish. His instructions as I recall them were these:

> In case there is a request for my services for a funeral, wedding, or an emergency, try and ascertain just how important it is that I return. If you feel I am needed, indicate that I shall be glad to return. At the same time, point out what the actual cost of transportation and other expenses of the return will be. Give the family an opportunity to offer to assume these expenses. If they feel they can do that, fine. If, on the other hand, they feel that they cannot provide the expense money and you are convinced that my services are desirable, you may advise them I shall be glad to return for any service I can render.

There are opportunities for conserving the minister's health even during the weeks while he is busy. Most communities now provide golf courses where, with his fellows, he can enjoy a few hours of joyous relaxation. Most cities provide health clubs and YMCA's which give an opportunity for exercise, rubdowns, and massages. Work in a garden, however small, relaxes a man and an occasional day at a circus or amusement park with his children or grandchildren is a good tonic.

Close to physical health is mental health and intellectual growth. The ministerial codes of a generation ago never considered the mental health of the minister, except as related to reading and study. Yet, by his very calling the minister is subject to mental hazards. Few people outside of the profession know how difficult it is for the clergyman to keep his optimism in a world which offers so many examples of brutality, immorality, and suffering. Many nights he prays for a faith strong enough to keep his belief in an all-loving God despite the signs of unwarranted suffering in his own community. He sees evidences of unbelief in the very people who proclaim their faith in vigorous terms. He witnesses avarice which disregards the sanctity of individual personality. Marital infidelity is met on every side. Parents ignore their responsibilities to their own children and children turn their aged parents over to public institutions. Yet, in all these situations he must sustain his faith that God is just and that His way is best.

Sometimes, he finds himself involved in local bitterness without cause. His best friends for some unexplained reasons will turn against him. Those in his own home fail to understand him. Physical exercise may keep him physically strong in tests such as these, but it requires more than this to maintain a hold on faith and life.

He can find help in counselling with other ministers who understand his situation; he can help himself by the reading of good devotional books. He may seek help from a doctor or psychologist and he always has access to God through the avenue of prayer.

When the great poet and humanitarian William Blake was subject to severe criticism because of his social attitudes in a world resisting change, his good wife Catherine, alarmed, asked him: "Now what can we do?" Blake replied: "You know what the cure is Katie; we can pray." More things are still being wrought by prayer than this world dreams of.

Place of Reading

But the second side of mental health is that which deals with the mind kept alert through the ministry of books and supplemental training. The minister still needs to protect his mental health by setting aside certain hours every day when he will engage in serious reading. The reading may be roughly divided into three classifications: (1) enlargement of the mind; (2) homiletic material to strengthen the quality of his sermons; and (3) reading for relaxation.

How can the minister protect his time for reading and study? There is a growing appreciation of the tasks of the ministry and most church boards realize that a minister needs time to study. They are more than anxious that he set up definite study periods, that he close his door and give three hours or more a morning to reading, study, prayer, and writing. We are not as dogmatic about the period as some advisors. The minister finds that he must fight to maintain this period. The fight, however, is not against his congregation, but against his own conscience. Appreciating the heavy responsibilities of parish duties, he weighs carefully the many burdens of his work and tries to judge objectively which things must come first. He can hardly refuse to see a grieving husband who comes to arrange for special burial services. He finds it difficult to close the door in the face of a young man with a serious problem. A sermon seems less important when weighed against the tragedies of every day life.

William P. Merrill, once minister of the Brick Presbyterian Church in New York, helps some of us to understand a basic principle. Dr. Merrill did not invite visitors during the study hours. His secretary was instructed, however, to admit any who really needed help.

"Doesn't that mean poor sermons?" we asked him.

"Undoubtedly," was his modest reply, "but it also means more human sermons."

Then he added, "It also means better congregations."

The quality of reading in the study hours is important. The wise man will put ahead of speed in reading, the ability to read thoroughly. Some years ago a well known minister lectured to his fellowmen across the country on the need of reading many books. Giving himself as an example he insisted that he read a book a day. More recently a distinguished Bishop asked that a man read a book a week. It is much more important to select well the books to be read and to give them sufficient time to reveal their meaning. Good books require digestion.

As a young man I went into the publishing house of the George H. Doran Company of New York City which at the time was one of the greatest religious book publishers of the United States. I found that my task as editor of religious literature required the appraisal of several book manuscripts each day. One can acquire the ability to do this and it consists of a sort of spot reading to find how much the author knows about his subject, his accuracy of statement, and his facility of expression. From this spot reading manuscripts were selected for further study. I suspect that many ministers who boast of the number of books they read are doing spot reading which may be the technique of the reviewer and editor but certainly does not have the compensations of thorough reading.

Personal Finance

The minister needs to be fair to himself in preserving his reputation of dealing honestly with the problems of personal finance and fees and discounts. Here is a perilous valley for ministers and many have fallen into the temptations which it offers. Some have allowed themselves to become embroiled in personal debts they find difficult to pay. Others have taken advantages of ministerial discounts and exemptions to the point of embarrassment.

There are many reasons for going into debt. Probably most homes now being established are founded upon indebtedness. There is nothing dishonorable in buying an automobile on time, or carrying a charge account for groceries or other necessities. There are emergencies which require large investments in hospital and doctor bills. Children's education is a pressing matter. There is also such a thing as accounting and the minister must try to keep his expenditures within his income. If he does not, the dealer may seek to collect the money from the church which is not good publicity for either the minister or the church.

The trials of the minister in a time of inflation may be very heavy. It will be especially hard with the younger men and women who are establishing their families. While it is not usually desirable that a minister shall supplement his church salary with outside work, that is preferred to permitting him to be loaded with unpayable debts.

Some ministers have found themselves in difficulty not because of their own obligations but because they have been drawn into a bad situation by the debts of others. Frequently the minister will be asked to endorse a note for some needy individual. Many of those asking for this financial help are individually honest. Some, however, lack the resources to meet the obligation when the payment comes due. It is hard to decide who is and who is not responsible. If bankers with years of experience fail, how can the minister make sure that he is a good judge of credit risks.

It is wise for the church to provide some kind of social service fund, sometimes known as the minister's discretionary fund, which the minister can use in these emergencies. The church in the city seems to invite stragglers of many kinds. Some need only a meal to help them to their next stop; others make larger requests. The minister can be more objective if he is handling the money of the institution and not his own purse.

Most clergymen have, at times, forgotten all injunctions of caution and used their own resources to help others in emergencies. Some of these experiences have been pleasant, but more often they bring disappointment. No one can say that the minister should never offer aid, but it should be done with much deliberation.

Ministerial Discounts

There may be little moral danger in accepting ministerial discounts or free club memberships, but asking for these concessions as a ministerial right is a different matter. Discount buying is very popular in our day. Trade restrictions against price cutting are breaking down and many people never pay the listed or advertised price. They know the way to the nearest discount house. A minister who follows the procession is not to be too much condemned, but he should avoid the feeling that because he ministers the Gospel he has a right to these financial benefits.

One man immediately upon moving to a new city called on the manager of the country club for his free ministerial membership. Another minister developed a technique of enjoying the television sets of the church members on whom he called until they caught the idea and combined to supply one for his home. The "poor mouth" has too often characterized the Christian ministry.

Wedding, baptismal, and funeral fees are an important factor in the minister's financial income. One minister may consistently refuse to accept them at some embarrassment to himself; a second judges each instance by itself; a third tries to keep his conscience clear by giving the money to some worthy cause; others think the most worthy cause is the minister's wife and family. This individual matter must be decided by each person and the mere fact of many different ideas on the matter shows some troubling of the conscience. After one accepts payment for such services, the income received must be accounted for in his income tax. Failure to include this as income would be both immoral accounting and dishonest.

Many ministers are troubled ·by civic exemptions given because of their profession. Ministers may be exempted from jury duty and the Federal government excuses them from military service in time of war. This may be a more serious thing than taking commercial discounts.

Almost everybody takes some kind of discount. Discount stores are thriving in many cities; advertised products may be purchased at a twenty-five to forty per cent reduction. Store employees receive a discount and professional men permit discounts among themselves. Gasoline discounts are permitted heavy users, but war service claims most able bodied men.

Only a few of the many denominations have been traditionally opposed to war. In fact the Christian church through history has been a war-making agency—we don't mean defensive wars either. Just why a clergyman who feels that a war is just should not participate as a combatant is difficult to understand. The religious man of faith should be among those to accept the responsibility.

The opportunity to serve on the jury is a privilege which the clergymen should seek. Not alone is he giving himself to a necessary task but the experience will be a vital one, enlarging his vision. While most states permit the release of a clergyman from this service, each will permit the minister to waive the exemption and permit him to render this service if he desires.

Adding up all of the qualities, it would seem that the minister needs all the qualities of a fine gentleman. He does not intentionally give offense; at the same time, he will refuse to be a suppliant of any who may wish to use him for their own ends. He need not play the part of the fawn asking for favors. He is worthy of his hire and like Kipling's hero, he must be able to:

> Talk with crowds and keep his virtue
> Or walk with kings nor lose the common touch.

A big job, indeed!

In this same category we find the many instances of discounts allowed men of the ministerial profession. Clergy discount tickets are available on many railroads and buses. Various stores permit what is called a ministerial discount of ten per cent. In some communities, doctors serve the minister's family without a charge. Lawyers and other professional men may make a discount available. What should our attitude be?

One doctor explained his free services by saying that he felt a pressure to help the work of the Christian church. Inasmuch as he could not serve the church in a professional capacity, he felt that serving the minister gave him the opportunity. That satisfied the minister but some might challenge the theory by suggesting that he make a contribution to the church and that the minister's living is paid by the church.

The late Dr. William C. DeWitt, one time president of Western Theological Seminary, Chicago, attempted in his book *Decently and in Order* (Morehouse, 1914) to show that the physician gained in prestige in serving the rector's family and that might justify the free service. He writes:

> Practically, it would be to the man of small practice, quite an advertisement to be known as the rector's physician. To the man of commanding practice, it might be a cause of chagrin if he were not invited to this responsibility.

It is well that this statement is dated. I am sure that in the crowded life of today a clergyman or two as a free client would not add much or take away from a physician's prestige. We like much better what he says on another page of the same chapter:

> As social conditions have become better organized, it has come to be much more desirable for all parties concerned, that save under exceptional circumstances, the physician should send in his bill, and that the minister should be paid a salary, supplemented by honorariums for services rendered at marriages and funerals.

> I venture to say that in a small town a clergyman pays a big price, directly or indirectly, for every gift he receives—even the chicken or turkey sent for Thanksgiving Day by the butcher.

What then should the minister do? Should he flatly refuse all of the discounts and gifts and embarrass himself and others?

We think not. The better plan is to accept courteously the gifts offered but never ask or expect them. Don't expect every layman who takes the minister to lunch to pick up the check. Let the minister pay the bill once in a while. It may crowd his financial resources but it will be good for his morale.

Ministerial Ethics

CAIRNS, F., *The Prophet of the Heart*. Harper, 1935.

CLARK, W. C., *The Minister Looks at Himself*. Judson, 1957.

DOLLOFF, E. D., *Maturing into the Ministry*. Round Table, 1938.

DOUGLAS, L. C., *The Minister's Every Day Life*. Scribner's, 1924.

FARMER, H. H., *The Servant of the Lord*. Scribner's, 1942.

FREEMAN, J. E., *The Ambassador*. Macmillan, 1928.

FOOTE, H. W., *The Minister and His Parish*. Macmillan, 1923.

HARMON, N. B., Jr., *Ministerial Ethics and Etiquette*. Abingdon, 1956.

HEDLEY, G., *The Minister Behind the Scenes*. Macmillan, 1956.

JEFFERSON, C. E., *The Minister as a Shepherd*. Crowell, 1912.

LEACH, W. H., *The Making of the Minister*. Cokesbury, 1928.

McAFEE, C. B., *Ministerial Practices*. Harper, 1928.

PALMER, A. W., *The Minister's Job*. Willet, Clark, 1937.

SCHUETTE, W., *The Minister's Personal Guide*. Harper, 1953.

SLEIPMAN, R. M., *We Ordinary Preachers*. Vantage, 1957.

TRUMBULL, R. G., *A Minister's Obstacles*. Revell, 1946.

19 | THE ETHICS OF THE PARSONAGE

THIS CHAPTER DEALS WITH THE MINISTER AND HIS FAMily in their social relationships. Most ministers marry and the majority of them have children. They live in parsonages, manses, or rectories. The family of the minister has a very definite relationship to the church which he serves. Much has been said about this relationship, but surprisingly little has ever been written about it.

We could lengthily discuss the advantages and disadvantages of marriage and family for a minister. Unmarried, he has an economic freedom which the married man cannot possess and in a day of pressing economic conditions this may mean a great deal. Obligations are quite apt to still the voice of the prophet. On the other hand the unmarried minister may have a very lonely life. For every idealist who is involved with practical affairs some retreat or a place of understanding and sympathy is necessary for existence.

A happy marriage, one in which there is understanding of the purpose of the church and the intent of the ministry coupled with a desire to help both the husband and wife reach the highest desire of happiness in human service, is the objective to be sought. Some marriages approximate this and some fall far below it. There are ministers who are sufficiently strong to rise above unsatisfactory marriages, but the average minister is a better preacher and pastor because of a congenial home.

A wife must try to understand her husband and the work he is doing. Equally important, the husband should try to understand the position of his wife and try to help her to realize her ambitions. If many ministers' wives will read this book, they will appreciate this word put in for a two-way appreciation.

Thousands of wives of ministers read *Church Management*. Occasionally one sits down and writes the editor a letter that indicates understanding and sympathy with the situation. As a class, ministers' wives must be noble women.

One woman wrote a letter in which she discussed the problems of a wife. Her analysis is so correct that a few lines must be quoted.

> First of all, let me say that the life of the minister's wife is a lonely one. She must not have intimate friends within the congregation. Her husband is a busy man with little or no time to give to her or the family. Because of her position she can never be a real part of any group within the church; they never can seem to forget that she is the minister's wife.
>
> It takes so little to keep most ministers' wives happy. They knew what kind of a life they must live before they married. They married because they loved the man. They will be content and happy so long as the man makes them feel that he loves and needs them.

Ministers usually do not have much in worldly goods or social standing to give the women they marry. The minister is the servant of the church and restrictions are necessarily placed upon the wife and children of the parsonage. What other reason than love can any woman have to marry a minister? Perhaps, though, there is another one. She will care for the church and have an affection for its work.

What kind of a woman is best suited to be the wife of a minister? That depends entirely upon the minister and no cut and dried formula will work in every case. Need she be young, or mature? Should she be rich, or poor? Should she be aggressive, or retiring? No one can give specific answers to these questions. A seminary professor of mine made it a point to lecture once each year on the preparation for marriage. He never missed this particular item: "Young gentlemen, always marry for love—that is the first time."

In Scotland, Lord Sands pleaded that the parson seek a woman of means so that the parsonage might have some furnishings which the poor parish could not supply. Wealth should not stand in the way of a happy marriage, but we can repudiate any suggestion that the preacher should follow, as a principle, the advice of Lord Sands. There are situations where a wife of wealth might be more of a liability than an asset.

Essential Qualities

The minister's wife should believe in her husband and in his work. Some ministerial marriages do not have this foundation and the result is usually discouraging. Both husband and wife try to brave the thing through. They may assert that the church hires the minister but has no claim on the wife, but this position is untenable. The minister who tries to face the world with a wife who has no confidence in the work of the church will have a difficult time.

Her own life should express those qualities of character and sympathy always vital in a life of culture. Like Caesar's wife, she should be above suspicion. The qualities may express themselves in leadership, but much more they will be reflected in the life of her husband and her children. Her emotional life should be so well established that she is free from the bitterness of prejudice and hatred. Unquestionably the minister should confide in his wife, but he can do so only when he is sure that she is emotionally stable enough to help him with his problems. She should have the ability to look at the parish objectively and not to become the center of any parish rancor.

She must have some ability as a housekeeper, for even if the income permits the employment of a servant the burden of housekeeping will fall upon her. She should have some degree of education and the culture which such education usually indicates. She need not be a scholar of the Bible or church administration, but her instinct and her training should equip her with an understanding of the preaching and pastoral tasks which lie upon her husband.

She should like people, but not in the sense that she patronizes them. If she has a genuine affection for humanity she will find her place in the church whether or not she becomes the president of any of its societies. She should have some degree of versatility because she will certainly have many opportunities to display it during her career. She should enjoy using it. She will probably also have occasion to use it to help her husband out of some mistakes he makes.

The kind of work she should do in the church depends on the church. That is where her versatility comes into play. She will not always play the organ or lead the choir, yet in many instances she may do one or both of these. There will be times when the minister's wife should be excused from any specific duties so that she may give her time to her own babies and her home. She must be a mother first and a church worker second.

She must be a pleasant hostess for there will be guests. Even the poorest parsonage must entertain occasionally. Playing the part of the hostess is not a matter of having much, but rather having a ready smile and a spirit of cheer.

The Family in the Parsonage

Our subject is much broader than merely the discussion of the qualities for the wife of the minister. It involves the family in the parsonage, including the preacher, the wife, and the children. It includes the attitude of the congregation toward the minister's family and their place in the communal life.

The children of preachers have usually given a pretty good account of themselves. The list of illustrious men and women who claim ministers for their fathers is long. Nobody has ever tried to compile a list of children of ministers who have gone wrong, and perhaps if this were done the halo of parsonage life might be somewhat dimmed.

The editor of a metropolitan daily once confided that the years he lived with a relative, a minister, gave him a definite prejudice against religion. A professional singer has volunteered that she spent so much time in church as a child that she never goes now. A professed atheist has confessed that his resolution to dispute religion came from the arbitrary manner of his ministerial father in denying the right of free discussion in the home.

The truth of the matter is that ministers' offspring are influenced by the same psychological laws as other children. The parents hold the destinies of children in their hands. Perhaps a heavier burden rests upon the preacher and his wife to give their children a normal opportunity for expression than is found in some other groups. Honesty and genuineness are necessary in family life. Children cannot but react unfavorably to repressions placed upon them for effect.

"You mustn't do this for the congregation will not like it" is the kind of advice which will be resented by any normal child. Restrictions based upon sane grounds of morality make quite a different proposition. The advice that the child must so live that offense shall not be given to the most insignificant person in the congregation cannot build character in the youth. The parents owe it to their children that they be free from this hypocrisy.

There are some people who feel that they are self-appointed guardians of the Almighty to see that the minister's children do not injure the property in any way. The minister must not permit such persons to dominate the situation so that the natural freedom which is the birthright of the child is lost.

Statistics show that the parsonage child has a better than even chance for success and happiness in this life. He is reared in a good moral atmosphere. He is surrounded with good literature. He has the opportunities to meet good people. There are limitations, of course. The most serious ones are found in the pressures placed upon him to conform to the mores of the local church community while his dreams are taking him to other entrancing areas. Even the great Albert Schweitzer rebelled against the caste system of his native Germany which placed him, as the son of a clergyman, above the tradesmen of his community.

One great asset is the advantage which comes to the children of ministers through social contacts with guests who may come to the parsonage. From all parts of the world, they come and the children sit at the table with them and participate in the table talk. Many ministers make it a point to have their children take a part in the conversation. This asset is almost sure to bring to youth a "larger view."

The relationship of the parsonage to the minister is quite simple. The church owns the home which it places at his disposal. It is given in part as compensation for his services. He has the same relationship to it as he would to a house he might rent. But, on the other hand, he should have the same freedom for security in family life. Church and minister can be agreed on this.

But common courtesy decrees that the hospitality of the parsonage should be extended to aid the program and work of the church. Many churches abuse this courtesy. During social functions at the church, women may run into the parsonage, taking whatever fancy desires and playing havoc with personal possessions. It is embarrassing to protest, but no wife likes to see a cherished bit of china carried carelessly across the church lawn and placed in a hazardous position on a shaky table. Many times it requires some strategy to keep this from happening. Where strategy fails, a good lock and key may succeed.

The solution to many of the abuses lies in the presence of some understanding individual who can explain, much better than the members of the minister's family, that the private possessions of the family must be respected as the private possessions of others. Perhaps too much space has been given to this side of the picture. The abuses are not as many as some would have us believe. Most wives of ministers will testify to lasting friendships formed with members of the congregation. These friendships more than compensate for the few abuses of privacy which may have been experienced.

Family Privacy

It is more difficult to protect the private life of the family than their chairs and dishes. The minister may be the servant of the church, but before he became a minister God made him a man and his first responsibility before God is to protect that manhood. He is a husband and father as well as a minister and he has the obligation to fulfill the functions of that relationship. Ministers are busy men in these days, but the minister who allows himself to become so busy that he cannot play the part of a husband and father is just too busy.

Some ministers make it a point to reserve one night each week which is spent at home with the members of his family. Perhaps the minister and his wife spend it together. The children may be included. If the home is sufficiently secure from intrusion, the time may be spent there. No committee meetings should interrupt and only emergency calls should be permitted to intrude at this hour.

There are vacation weeks when family ties can be still further strengthened. They are threatened, however, by the new emphasis on summer training schools for ministers. It is not an easy matter to balance the time between church and family. Yet the obligation rests upon the preacher to organize his time so that his family shall never feel that they are merely incidental in his ministry to the congregation.

I was once the Sunday guest in a rather modest parsonage. There were four small children ranging from two and a half to ten years of age. The wife had no maid to help her with her work and her husband was busy with the affairs of the morning service. I was surprised to find the children neatly washed and dressed at the breakfast table. The service was in good taste and orderly. I excused myself as soon as I could and went to my room. When I entered the church for the morning service, I found the wife attractively dressed, sitting in her accustomed pew. The children were in their respective classes in the church school. To my mind this was a modern miracle. How could any woman do what this one did?

Few could. I wonder if anyone has the right to expect it. Economic restrictions do not always permit help in the home. In such a case, one may expect the wife to do the almost impossible. Where there is no money to pay for help, various short cuts must be used. The husband may have to don an apron and help with the dishes or he may take his turn at the washing machine. Running the washer is hardly compatible with the dignity of the clergyman, but who in the congregation can object if his pay is insufficient to employ help to aid his burdened wife?

Many times the solution is found by taking someone into the home for a period of time. It may be a schoolgirl who needs a home while completing her courses. Or it may be a widow without resources who can give sufficient help to justify the expenditure for food and lodging. These are not ideal solutions, but they do fill the gap. These are very necessary if the wife is expected to share in the pastoral tasks of her husband.

Entertainment in the Parsonage

The most modest parsonage has the responsibility of social entertainment from time to time. Various groups from the church will come as guests for business and social meetings. The spirit of hospitality must prevail, but there is no need to feel that a heavy investment must be made in refreshments. Wafers and coffee or, in the case of the young people, wafers and chocolate milk can add to the friendliness of the occasion.

It is well to open the parsonage once each year for an "open house." New Year's Day is a splendid time for this. For most people it is a holiday. The open house may be conducted from three to five in the afternoon and from eight to ten in the evening. A committee from the women's organization in the church may very well help the ministerial family with the preparations and the execution of the plans.

Some ministers make a practice of having the official board at the parsonage once each year for a more formal dinner. This is almost impossible without outside help. A good caterer or experienced cook and server can usually be employed for the day to help with the service.

Then there are the many little informal committees and

groups which naturally gravitate to the minister, his wife, or his children. They do not require much in preparation. Their visits mean friendship, laughter, and good fellowship. Out of such gatherings intimacies grow. They are to be encouraged, for it is in groups like this that we find the qualities which make life worth while. One may argue against a minister's family showing partiality, but normal social progress almost demands these close friends who understand our problems. They help the preacher's folk to be "folks."

Compensation of Family Love

Perhaps we have put too much emphasis on the lack of material wealth in the preacher's home. There are always compensations where there is mutual understanding and trust. In a past issue of *The Ladies' Home Journal*, Dorothy Thompson gives two sides to parsonage life. First she emphasizes the poverty; next she mentions its beauty and its warmth.

> I think very often, these days, of my own childhood in an upstate New York Methodist parsonage. According to the standards of today, it was a childhood extremely limited, and even impoverished. I am sure, for instance, that the food that we had to eat was deficient in the properties which are recognized today as essential for a "minimum standard" of nourishment for relief cases. A green vegetable in winter was unknown, and an orange was a Christmas treat. We shuddered through the winters with continual drippy colds, sheltered in stove-heated houses, or houses warmed by hot-air furnaces that concentrated the warmth in the lower floors and left the bedrooms icy. And the preacher's children suffered many a school humiliation from having to wear unbecoming clothes, cut down from their elders', or handed down by a distant cousin.
>
> Yet my own childhood was bathed in warmth and light, which was nothing but the irradiation of a beautiful personality, a man whose whole being was warmth and light: my father. His intimate belief in the goodness and justice of God, his unconquerable faith in the inherent decency of men, made him a creature radiating cheerfulness, even gaiety, turning every misfortune into a challenge or an only half-rueful joke; or, if it were a *real* misfortune, like the death of my mother, accepting it with a sweetness that was eternally impressive. And when he

died, hundreds of people came to his funeral, not because he was "successful" and a celebrity—he never was—but because they loved him. His was the liberal spirit. Liberal, in the sense that we use the word when we speak of "liberal arts." Humane, rooted in humanity, caring for human beings, not as producers, or consumers, or workers, or employers—but as human souls.

The Parsonage

BADER, G. E., (Editor), *I Married a Minister*. Abingdon, 1942.

GEBBARD, A. L., *Rural Parish*. Abingdon, 1947.

———, *Parsonage Doorway*. Abingdon, 1950.

JACOBS, K., *The Children's Choir*. Augustana, 1958.

LEACH, W. H., *The Making of the Minister*. Abingdon, 1947.

HEWITT, A. W., *The Shepherdess*. Harper, 1943.

PORTER, S., *Papa was a Preacher*. Abingdon, 1944.

SPENCE, H., *One Foot in Heaven*. McGraw-Hill, 1940.

URANG, G., *Church Music for the Glory of God*. Christian Service, 1956.

20 | THE MINISTER & HIS CHURCH

THE CHURCH-MINISTER RELATIONSHIP IS ONE OF MANY facets. There are certain legal obligations into which the two parties enter. They can be enforced by law if that becomes necessary, but the moral obligations are outside of the legal realm. In a "no man's land" are a hundred things which the minister is expected to do that are hardly definable by either legal or moral codes.

Basically the call of the church to the minister is a legal contract. The minister agrees to serve as an employee of the church, subject to certain terms and conditions, and the church agrees to pay the minister for his services. If a house is provided the church agrees to keep it in good condition and probably provides for an auto expense account and other sundries.

But in every church-minister relationship there is a moral and emotional tie. He becomes the pastor of the flock, its spiritual overseer; he strengthens the faith of his people and they sustain his morale by agreeing to work under him and with him. He agrees that he will keep his teaching true to the faith of his particular denomination. The congregation agrees to accept rebuke and instruction. These things are hardly a matter of law but they are very important in the life of the church.

The minister agrees that he will give his time to the work of the church. There are exceptions of course but in the normal situation this means that the minister will give his entire working time to the congregation he serves, subject to rest hours and vacation weeks. He should not seek other employment which will handicap his work as teacher and pastor.

The Minister Owes Time To His Church

Back in the twenties when ministers were drawing up ethical codes for the profession they were very insistent on this point. The local church as an employer was entitled to the full time services of its employee, the pastor.

> As a Christian minister controls his time he should make it a point of honor to give full service to his parish.
>
> It is unethical for a minister to engage in other lines of remunerative work without the consent of the church and its official body.
>
> When a Methodist minister becomes a member of the Conference, he promises to employ all of his time in the work of God. We again call attention to the fact that he is thus honor bound to give full service to his parish.
>
> He should be conscientious in giving full time and strength to the work of his church, engaging in avocations and occupations in such a way and such a degree as not to infringe unduly upon that work unless some definite arrangement for part time service is made with the church.

It does not take a genius to read between the lines in statements such as these and understand that the framers of the statement were aware that many ministers of the period were not keeping faith with their contract in this respect.

There are times when outside work by a minister is necessary. Perhaps if his church does not offer him a living wage, he seeks a part time teaching job or takes up a second church which will add to his income. He may have the gift of authorship and write for the papers and use the time he is supposed to give to the church. Perhaps he is a popular lecturer and accepts many engagements or he has a farm to which he gives a considerable amount of time. These give him some extra compensation and it is his right to do these things *providing he has the consent of his employer church.*

A minister may go to his official board and say frankly that he needs the extra income and ask that he be given permission to work part time. In fact, such an arrangement might be a helpful thing. He will become acquainted with business men and methods. He will learn to appreciate people. But this appraisal is based entirely on an understanding with his church.

There are some groups of Christians which have as part of their basic philosophy the idea that the minister should work with his hands. Saint Paul did just that and established the precedent. Some churches supply the facilities whereby he can learn to do the things which his neighbors are doing. But in denominations which require the full time services of the minister, he should not take on extra work without a definite agreement with the board of the church.

We appreciate, also, that there are some small churches which can hardly offer a satisfactory field to an able bodied and alert minister. I can think of no life more deadening than to be situated in a very small parish where the minister is under obligation to give full time service to the parish. The result is a "calling" where the calls develop a weak parish. These things should be so defined to promote understanding.

One can easily rationalize that any extra employment adds to a man's understanding of life. The lecture of the day at one meeting of ministers was on the duties of the pastor. The speaker was pressing upon the brethren very heavily to keep away from secular work for extra income. The lecturer had to cut his lecture short to drive a hundred miles to fill a speaking engagement at a convention. One minister, the pastor of a small church who ran a farm on the side, remarked: "At least, I put in my extra work in my own community and with my own people."

Customarily, the minister writing a book talks this over with his official board and explains the amount of time which it will take from his other duties. This is not alone good sense, but it is simple honesty. The problem is not so simple when the pastor of the church takes time from his local parish to serve his denomination. Both the church and the minister have a responsibility to aid the work of the denomination. The minister needs to attend the official meetings of the denomination and partake in its program. Even here, however, it can be overdone. Some very strong churches are not pleased to have their ministers away so much, even on denominational work.

Minister without Portfolio

In one church, one of the lay leaders talked of the pastor as their "minister without portfolio." Upon a question he explained that the minister was away from the parish so much that he had very few parish functions, hence had no portfolio.

Other churches feel that their minister has a definite contribution to make to denominational and interdenominational work. They gladly release him for that task. The Presbyterian Church in the U.S.A. and its sister denomination, The Presbyterian Church in the U.S., insist that no one should aspire to the moderatorship of the denominations unless his church is willing to release much of his time for the denominational work. Since the position pays no salary, the churches share their pastors with the denomination.

There are many good movements in every good community which should have the support of the minister and each asks for effort and time. These multiplied duties are taking too much time from the local parish which pays the bill. In recent years ministers have become conscious of this conflict and are more selective in the interests to which they lend themselves. Even the ministerial meetings are coming under fire these days. It has been pointed out that the men who get ahead are not those who jump at every chance to take on another job.

Good Use of Time

There are other ways to violate the contract on full time service. The codes mentioned earlier emphasize that the pastor should use a good part of the time for which he is paid for serious study "in order to thoroughly apprehend his message, keep abreast of current thought, and develop his intellectual and spiritual capacities . . . should make it a point of honor to set aside sufficient time for reading and study."

A man may give his full time to his parish and yet fail to use the time to the best advantage. Most employed men have their time defined by their employer or business practices. They arrive at the factory or office at a specified hour, leave at a regular time. The minister makes his own schedule and may find easy excuses for cutting work which is distasteful. There will be duties at home. The baby is ill and the good wife needs help. There needs to be a partnership in the minister's home. If the wife helps him with his social and parochial duties, she has a right to ask him to help her with the babies, the dishes, and the washing. What shall be taken out of the program to make up for this time?

As his own schedule maker, the minister may go to his study at eight A.M. and stay there until noon without getting in much real study. If he carries the newspaper with him he may give a half hour or more to that. Here are some suggestions from the pen of a good Presbyterian minister who some years ago left this world. He was James Elmer Russell.

> It is easier to do almost anything else than it is to study. We are all in danger of dawdling. One man can be tremendously busy in the study without getting down to hard work. . . . Many ministers waste time over newspapers and current periodicals. Alexander Maclaren advised young ministers to keep the newspapers out of the study until after dinner. . . . Another added: 'The later you dine, the better.'

Every minister has moments of dullness when his mind refuses to create. He puts his sermon ideas on paper but no thoughts fly up. The technique of getting started is hard, but one of the best ways is to select a theme. If the mind is not alert, pick up a book which discusses the subject. It is good priming which may start the thinking process.

Lay out a schedule of reading so that when dead moments come you can take in the thoughts of others. Make notes of course, but use the storage capacity of the subconscious. This treasure chest of ideas in the individual brings flashes of insight at the most unexpected times.

Every church expects the minister to give a great deal of time to pastoral work. Time is valuable and the program of visitation should be planned carefully. Take the sick and emergency calls first. Check the easiest route. Call ahead to see if the time is convenient. Next take the regular, parish-wide program. Call by streets or areas, changing only for particular cases. Limit the calls to twenty or thirty minutes.

There will be committee meetings, group meetings, individual consultations, luncheon clubs, and fraternities. All these should be worked into the schedule carefully and so planned that the minister can have some time during each day to play with his own children and help his wife.

But must the minister work twenty-four hours each day for seven days each week? No. That is hardly expected from any employee and the minister like everyone else needs time for physical refreshment. He probably should plan to take one day off each week to be used as he prefers. He may use it for rest and recreation with his family. He may play golf, fish, swim, play tennis, drive, or sleep. Let him not, however, make it so inflexible that he cannot respond to emergency calls if they arise. In a multiple ministry, the staff plans the week so that there will always be one minister on the job. The pastor of a three minister church tells of his trials:

> Each of my associates has a contract which provides for one day of rest each week. It does not specify the day. I do not have a contract with the church which regulates my time. Increasingly, I have found that these men are both taking their off days on Monday and I have all of the funerals and sick calls on those days.

Then there is the annual vacation. Churches are liberal and clergymen fare almost as well as teachers. They can make the most of this time for refreshment. The author was for fifteen years in the pastorate and two things were not fully appreciated until he left the church and went into a publishing house. The first was the real value in dollars and cents of a manse. Vacation periods of a month in length were the second. Neither was available in the years of business experience.

The church, however, will expect much more of its minister than time. It will expect cooperation and loyalty. The minister, in going to a church, has the unique experience of having a place prepared for him before he reaches the community. Those he has never seen become his friends and offer courtesies to him and to his family. He must respond with courtesy and loyalty.

Use of Parsonage

He will live in the parsonage, rectory, or manse and he owes the church careful treatment of the house which has been placed at his disposal. Neither he nor his family will abuse the property and they will see that the lawn is mowed and the yard kept clean. In moving from one community to another the minister will meet some conditions with which he is unfamiliar, but he will try to adapt himself to the local situation. When the family moves to another parish, the house and grounds will be left clean and neat.

Sometimes the family is disappointed with the house which the church offers. All complaints should be made before the family arrives and their remedying can easily be made a condition of the move. If left until the ministerial family is on the field, the necessary corrections are not easy to make.

The minister should seek to fit into the new situation through the pulpit and church activities. If he believes that the church organization should be changed for better service, let him lay the ground work but refrain from public comparison between his present assignment and the church he left. In one church of the Congregational system the new minister refused to take the chairmanship of the church and the several committees whose duties were specified in the constitution. This should either have been resolved before he accepted the call or else placed in a long range program. No minister should feel that he is above the law of the church which he has been called to serve.

He should at all times speak well of his church even though it takes great tolerance to do so. A pastor who constantly scolds his church is as unseemly as members who berate his sermons. He owes the church the best of his ability in his pulpit presentations and he should refuse to enter the pulpit unprepared for his task. He should avoid the negative habit of some men who turn the sermon into a critique of the church rather than a presentation of the great sacrifice.

In the relationship between the employer church and the employee minister, one other principle must guide the parties. The minister must be the final authority as to how he uses his professional time. He has a responsibility that few employees possess as no church is going to ask him to punch a clock or make out a schedule for his work. He must make many decisions as to the use of his time. The final judgment of the parish will be in the total effect of his services in the parish.

Things the Church Must Do

In a church in which the author was once installed, the minister who gave the charge to the people put the words in startling order. He had three points to his message. They were:

> The congregation owes the following obligations to its pastor.
> It should:
> Talk him up!
> Pray him up!
> Pay him up!

These are good injunctions. Those of us who remember the church of the pre-World War II days know that the third statement was almost as necessary as the first two. The church owes its loyalty to the minister just as the minister owes his loyalty to the church. The congregation can create a good reputation for their minister by telling the community in various ways that he is a good man and is doing a good job.

It is almost an adage that the first congregation a man serves gives him his direction for life. Recognizing that youth has its limitations, friendly counsel and understanding can help him develop his full qualities for the Christian ministry. We must admit that some ministers offer a severe challenge to their congregations. The responsibility to change the brashness of youth into constructive cooperative leadership rests with the congregation as well as with the minister himself.

In nearly every parish there are some people who feel that they can take personal control of the young man, direct his social life, tell him what organizations to join, how to vote, and whom to marry. This is not the kind of cooperation about which we speak. We are thinking of those who do not want to control the thought or life of the minister but who encourage him to be his best self.

The minister is the greatest single publicity asset which a church possesses. The church will thrive or falter depending on his leadership. A congregation given to minute analysis and criticism of the minister not only hurts him but itself. The church owes it to the minister to see that he has the equipment necessary to do his best work. Give him a good study and office. See that he has an automobile allowance sufficient to do the work of the congregation. Help protect his time for study. Encourage him to continue studying to broaden his knowledge. Introduce him to those people and organizations which will benefit from his help.

The church owes it to the minister to respect his judgment in the pulpit program and the administration of the parish. He is probably the best authority in the community on church methods and practices and he may be the only one in the parish who has done any research in church finance, building equipment, etc. Do not curb every suggestion with the words, "It won't work here." Many churches have strangled themselves by taking the attitude that no suggestion of new methods can be applied to the local situation.

The church should respect the minister's judgment regarding the use of his own time. In these days of pressing duties there will be complaints that the minister has failed to call on some family or has not been available for some requested service. Some in the congregation may be sure that he is doing some unnecessary things and neglecting some vital parts of the program. In such instances tolerance is the wisest course unless there is a flagrant violation of ministerial responsibility. There are usually ways provided in the constitution of the local church or the denominational practice to ask for an explanation. The Scriptures advise that when we find a brother at fault we take two or three and go to him and discuss the matter.

While the minister is the master of his own time, the congregation has the final authority over the program of the church. Let any minister be warned that the program should take precedence over ministerial personality. Occasionally a foolish minister feels that he should go ahead and organize a special group without consulting the official board of the church. He is on dangerous ground. Let him first lay his proposition before the proper board and have clearance on the matter. The minister is the servant of the church; he neither owns the building nor controls its program. The church should be the protector of democracy, not its enemy.

Unfortunately there are many instances of conflict between the local church and the minister. A feud may become very bitter if the congregation is split and public meetings are held to debate the matter. Whether or not the minister wins his point, he usually loses his church. After the conflict is resolved, his best friends will agree: "We have now vindicated our pastor but for the unity of the church, we feel it is better that he seek another parish."

The congregation, individually and corporately, has the responsibility to pray for its pastor. Prayers of faithful church members have made a success of many ministers. Occasionally

I visit a church where the minister and his board gather for a few minutes of prayer before the service. I am always touched when a lay voice, trembling with sincerity, prays that the pastor this day may be given words of wisdom. At times he should also request restraint. A famous evangelist of a generation ago, J. Wilbur Chapman, became the pastor of a church where the chancel was so planned that around him as he preached sat the elders of his church. It was as though the prophetic words had changed from "I say unto you" to "we say unto you." There is good precedent in the practices of the early church for such a chancel and it might be a good one to recover.

The third point in that installation address is also pertinent. The church owes the minister a living—not opulent, not extravagant, but a decent living for himself and his family. Any call or contract into which the church and minister enter should specify the terms of employment and the compensation to be paid. Any amount specified should be paid promptly on the date it is due.

The salary to be paid the minister and the compensation of other salaried members of the church staff should be the first obligation against the church budget. Many business and public utilities give a discount for cash payments. The minister should not be expected to do this, but every individual knows that a salary paid on the specified date is worth more than one paid at "some convenient time." We wish that it were true that a church which talks up its minister and prays up its minister never fails to meet its financial obligations to him, but there are instances where this rule does not hold.

The Minister as a Candidate for a Church

Here is one area in which the attitude of the minister is both sensitive and important. Ministerial placement varies according to denominational practices. The three parties, denomination, local church, and the minister, are all parties to the transaction. This cooperation should work for the settlement of the minister in a church where he finds the best opportunity for self-expres-

sion; one in which the church can realize its greatest strength
and one which will increase the strength of the denomination.

Despite the theory that the church should seek the pastor, the
wise minister will not remain passive. The clergyman has the
privilege, when the right time comes, to study the field to see
if he can find a church which offers him the advantages of
service which he thinks desirable. Yet nothing so disturbs the
minister's own services or the peace of his congregation as
rumors that he is looking for a new assignment. The study
should be made quietly and confidentially for the good of all
concerned.

The names of vacant churches may be secured from several
sources. Even churches of the Congregational system now have
regional offices which clear such information. The approved
technique is for the minister to approach the superintendent or
official in charge and inform him of his desire to make a change.
With the list of the vacant churches at his disposal this official
in ordinary circumstances is the proper intermediary.

Sometimes the minister prefers to by-pass this office. Then
the task becomes more difficult. He will secure his leads from
friends, the denominational papers, and the newspapers. There
is no reason why a minister could not subscribe to a newspaper
clipping service to get information of vacancies.

The intelligent minister is not just seeking a church, he is seeking the church where he can best serve. He needs to know a
great deal about the individual congregation before he decides
he should seek to serve it. In the meantime the vacant church
is, or should be, studying its own program to see what qualities
it needs in the next pastor. The minister may have friends who
live in the city of the vacant church and can supply information.
The denominational yearbook will give financial and membership reports. These of course are important but it is well also
to have information regarding the city, the location of the
church in the city, and the type of congregation served. With
this information, the minister will be in a position to submit his
name to the church.

It would be wise to have his name submitted by a minister friend. The better known this friend is to the church under consideration, the more impressive his recommendation will be. On the whole, a recommendation from a neighboring minister is worth more than one from a denominational executive. If the committee of the church is impressed, it will doubtless write directly to the minister. No church should be approached unless the candidate is sure that there is a vacancy or soon will be a vacancy. The church on its part should be sure that the candidate knows whether or not others are being considered for the post. A minister has a right to assume serious consideration when he is invited to visit the church either as a preacher or a visitor. It is customary for the church to pay the travelling expenses of the candidate and some churches will add to that an honorarium for the services.

If a call is extended and accepted, the minister should then notify the officers of his present church of his decision and prepare a letter of resignation which should be read to the congregation. This should include the date when the separation will be made. In many denominations the congregation must pass on the resignation before it becomes effective. Occasionally the request is met with a negative vote and the minister faces a dilemma. If he has been working on a contract, the church can require him to complete it before he leaves.

Any employment contract will probably specify the number of months to elapse before the minister can conclude his pastorate. If his contract does not specify the time he may indicate it in his resignation. It should not be less than one month and three months are preferable. To specify a shorter period implies that the pastor is anxious to hurry away from the parish.

21 | THE MINISTER IN HIS PROFESSION

THE MINISTRY IS AN OLD AND HONORED PROFESSION anchored in the ages of antiquity. Its members are supposed to be above the profit motive but they are subject to the same emotional reactions as all men. That they should try to state some code of conduct which would make it possible for them to work with others in the profession without jealousy or bitterness is natural. After family and church, the next source of cooperation should be the brethren, perhaps those in the local church.

Today thousands of growing churches have more than one clergyman on the staff. Ability to work together in the accomplishment of the program requires qualities of adjustment for a happy ministry. We have discussed this at some length in the chapter on the multiple ministry. There will always be one man who is designated as *the* pastor. There will doubtless be a considerable margin between the income of *the* pastor and his associate or assistant.

The Christian ethic would define very clearly what the relationship of the two or more men should be. The chief pastor may take a patronizing attitude which cannot help but lead to a misunderstanding with his associate. One way to avoid this is to have the responsibilities of each clearly defined as in the earlier chapter mentioned above.

A complaint of many men in the lower positions is that the minister takes the attitude of a superior individual. The associates may not sit in conferences at the higher levels. They are not permitted to take the weddings which will offer the higher fees. They are denied the coveted opportunities to preach from the pulpit. Their assignments of parish duties are often obviously the undesirable. Any minister knows the cure for this situation

371

372 THE MINISTER IN HIS PROFESSION

is simply for each minister to live in the spirit of New Testament fellowship with the men on his staff and to use their ability in helping to plan the services of the church.

In many local churches there will often be found a retired minister and his family. This man may have been a former pastor who continues to live in the community and desires to participate in the work of the church. In such a case it is hard for him to give up the pastorate and to accept the quiet life of retirement. He welcomes the opportunity to officiate at weddings of the children he has baptized and take the funerals of those he has served during his active years. Any minister of the Cross who has given his life in Christian service is entitled to recognition, especially in his old parish. The ethics of the situation require that he recognize that his successor is now the pastor and the responsibility of directing the parish work is no longer his. The retired minister should know that he can come into active work in the church only by the tolerance of the pastor. The pastor on the other hand should be courteous enough to use him for occasional vacation supply and some of the other duties for which he is qualified.

If the retired minister is not a former pastor of the church, but simply a community resident, the situation is more easily resolved. He attends services as a regular member, is available for teaching as the opportunity arises, and can serve into emergencies when the pastor is out of the city.

Predecessor and Successor

Most ministers have predecessors. The ethical code makes rather strict requirements, when a minister leaves a field and a new pastor is called, that the former pastor keep himself from the field. This does not mean that he should not pay an occasional visit to the community, but he definitely should keep himself apart from any pastoral situation.

Congregations are slowly being educated to the idea that any request for the services of a former pastor should be made through the resident pastor. If a dying person or a bereaved family wishes for any reason to invite the former pastor, they should first take this up with the present pastor and discuss the matter with him. The average pastor will usually be glad to extend the invitation. If the family should not be familiar with the amenities of the situation and extend the invitation directly to the ex-pastor, it is then the duty of the minister invited to ask if the present incumbent knows the situation and then make his acceptance conditional on the permission of the pastor. After a few instances of this kind the people in the parish will know how to act.

There have always been some ministers who have felt free to return to an earlier parish with or without an invitation and to visit the homes and to take upon themselves official duties. In the book *Ministerial Ethics and Etiquette* (Abingdon), edited by Nolan B. Harmon, a story is told of a one time bishop of the Methodist Episcopal Church. He was asking required questions of ministerial candidates.

> "Will you go where you are sent and that willingly and gladly?"
> He suggested that he would like to change this to:
> "Will you go where you are sent and stay away from where you have been?"
> Asked if John Wesley was the authority for this, he added:
> "No, John Wesley did not put that in, but if he had known what I know he would have."

The predecessor does have some rights in the situation. The present minister is building upon a foundation laid by another. He cannot entirely avoid the responsibility in the situation. These may be courtesy items but we think that they are moral obligations. An anonymous writer in *Church Management* (December 1956) lists these obligations.

> 1. A pastor owes to his predecessor the courtesy of replying to any letter which he addresses to him. Incidentally this is a courtesy a minister owes to any brother pastor. It probably is more necessary in the pastor and predecessor relationship.

2. He should put the predecessor on the mailing list for any church publications including the church calendar. The former pastor likes to see his former church prosper and the information the publication brings him will be helpful.

3. It would be nice if the predecessor would be invited back to fill the pulpit occasionally. Perhaps he can supply a Sunday or two in the vacation season and in this way see his old friends.

4. The minister has an obligation to see that any personal mail is forwarded to his predecessor at his new address.

The responsibility is two-sided. The parish is under the direction of the pastor, but courtesy should permit a former pastor to visit his old friends without any embarrassment. The guest, however, should observe the courtesies for the occasion. He definitely should not give advice to his friends as to the present minister or program. It would be well that he let his friends understand that he is not in a position to discuss the leadership of the church.

What the Minister Owes His Successor

The minister also has a debt to the man who follows him in his parish. If he has the success of the work at heart, he will want to see that the man who follows him has every help in continuing the program which has been established. Each man has his own personality and his methods of work and one's successor need not follow in detail the identical program. One advantage of a change of pastorates is that various phases of church leadership will be emphasized by different men.

One minister may be strong in Christian Education and give a great deal of time to the school and its work. The next minister may stress counselling and pastoral work. A third may have administrative strength; a fourth may be an accomplished theologian. The result is that over the years the local church has had a faculty of four members, each strengthening the church with his own specialty.

As each pastor must build on the foundation laid by his predecessors, so each minister must see the wisdom of his successor having the opportunity to build on his work. He owes this tolerance to the man who will follow him. It would be fine if every minister could sit down with his successor and talk over the program of the church emphasizing what he considers its strengths and its weaknesses. It requires a man of considerable objectivity to do this without revealing his own likes and dislikes so the success of such a conference may not be too serious a matter.

He does owe it to his successor to speak kindly of the man who has been called to follow him and to prepare the congregation to receive him as their pastor. Even if he knows that the man has some faults he can have brotherly restraint and mention only the good qualities of the man and his family. Some ministers feel that their congregations should be informed of any limitations of their successors. The desire to project themselves in this area is unfortunate and may handicap an entire ministry. Most ministers know they make mistakes which they do not intend to repeat in any new parish.

The minister who moves from a parish should leave for his successors orderly and accurate records. Any minister going to a new church will need these in planning his work. Membership records and calling lists should be brought up to date for his use. A portfolio on each family in the congregation will be a valuable asset.

While a minister is free to take from the files of the church office any personal letters, he should be careful to leave those which are the property of the church. Correspondence regarding purchases and considerations of memberships to and from denominational offices are usually the property of the church and help to assure continuity of progress.

The books on the shelves usually belong to the minister. They should be removed from the office together with his personal property before his successor arrives. If there are books he does not want, he may leave them in some conspicuous place so that the successor may claim them if he wishes; otherwise, he is free to destroy them.

All personal items and family property in the parsonage should be removed. The minister has the responsibility to leave the property of the church, including the house in which he lives, clean and orderly for the next occupant. Avoid leaving property with the note, "We will pick this up when we pass through next year."

His Brothers in the Community

Naturally there is a feeling of fraternity among all men "of the cloth." The fellowship of those in the same calling helps the average worker. He can feel at home with men who are doing the same work and facing the same personal problems. A congenial group of clergymen is an asset to any community. If there are bickerings and jealousies among ministers they make choice bits of gossip for tale-bearers. From the days of the apostles to the present time churches have been plagued by tale-bearers within their own ranks.

"How do our churches work together," one asked the minister of his church. The reply was: "How do you fight the devil?" At first the questioner was shocked thinking that the minister was speaking of a competing church as a devil. But the minister explained further. "There is only one way to fight the devil. Let every church and individual who wants to destroy him get together. Our churches work together to that end."

In most communities fundamental concepts differ. Some churches insist on an exclusive communion, others invite all Christians to the Lord's Supper. Even differences such as this are no excuse for the clergy of the community not to get together to discuss their mutual problems. The minister should plan to welcome the new minister who comes into the community. As soon as the new minister is settled, it is well to make a friendly call to tell him that he is welcome in the community. If there is a local ministerial association he should be invited to attend the next meeting and participate in the discussions.

If the newcomer is of your own denomination you will want to discuss with him the history of your group in the community and find ways of working together for the denomination. The same thought of cooperation should be given ministers of other groups. Any minister is ambitious to make his church as strong as possible. It is considered unethical to do this at the expense of a neighboring church. It is unwise to be put in a position of soliciting members who are affiliated with another church. Be cautious of receiving such members. The word "proselyting" is a bad word in church circles.

There is, however, a constant shifting of members from church to church. Sometimes a Methodist marries a Presbyterian. The family feels they should not be divided and must decide with which church to affiliate. When such a family comes to a minister suggesting that they would like to join his church, it would be well to ask if they have consulted the other pastor. If they hesitate, the minister himself should talk with the other pastor to make sure that he understands the situation. If possible, it is much better for the members themselves to make the contacts with the ministers.

In case of "split" churches, caution should be used. If a large number of people decide to leave the split church, it is well to discuss the matter very seriously to decide whether the Kingdom of God will be helped by this action. The minister has a right to know why they are leaving another church to join his. If such members are aggrieved without real cause he may want to discourage the move.

There are, unfortunately, some individuals who will never be happy in any church. They move from one to another. In one town the author visited, he found a church with the appellation "The Mad Church." It was explained that everyone in other churches who got mad joined this one. That is hardly a laudable commendation.

Dealing fairly with a neighboring minister means dealing fairly with his church as well. One certainly should not intrude in his neighbor's church program or the church itself. In his calls, he should respect the membership of his neighbor's church. If he has occasion to call in the homes of his neighbor's parish, he should make a point of saying a good word for his brother minister.

I recall a remark made of a certain minister who, retired from active service, was in demand as a supply preacher. Every Protestant group in the community welcomed him. Some wondered about his popularity. He gave this as the explanation: "I never serve a church without making an effort to strengthen the reputation of the pastor." Both clergymen and church members appreciated this attitude.

Ministers should not accept weddings and funerals from a neighbor's church unless the matter has been properly cleared. If called in for emergency service in case of sickness or death the minister should make it clear that the pastoral care is to revert to the regular pastor when he is available. The supply pastor should give an account of service and surrender all responsibility. If a fee is involved he should be permitted to keep it with the consent of the regular pastor.

The minister's home is often an open house for visiting ministers and evangelists. Hospitality usually places a burden on the hostess of the manse, and this she willingly assumes. At times, however, some guest overstays his leave and becomes too much of a burden.

We know of a Presbyterian Church manse which has one room set aside as a guest room, endowed and available for returned missionaries or ministers passing through the community. The care of the room and meal service, however, falls upon the wife. If the church is holding revival services the evangelist probably will enjoy this room as well as some ministers who seek such entertainment to reduce the travelling expenses for themselves and families as they travel through the country.

We feel that in some of these instances the wife is entitled to protest running a rooming house even for the travelling saints. The problem is not a new one. John Knox in his chapter in *The Ministry in Historical Perspective* (Harper) tells how the

Didache gives instructions for determining whether a travelling prophet is genuine or false.

> The prophet who orders a meal in the spirit shall not eat of it. If he does he is a false prophet. . . . Whoever shall say in the Spirit, 'Give me money' (or something else), you shall not listen to him, and if a visiting prophet stays as long as three days, he is a false prophet.

In concluding these three chapters on ministerial ethics, I recall an outline given by the late Dr. Albert W. Palmer of the Chicago Theological Seminary. Here are the captions which really tell the story.

Ten Commandments for Ministers

1. No sheep-stealing.
2. No tale-bearing.
3. Loyalty to predecessor.
4. Consideration for successor.
5. Play the game with ecclesiastical authorities.
6. Be a good citizen.
7. Devote full time to the job.
8. Serve regardless of compensation.
9. Remember the minister's special responsibility regarding women.
10. Make a success at home.

22 | THE PASTORAL MINISTRY

TRADITIONALLY, THE MINISTER HAS BEEN KNOWN AS the "shepherd of the flock." This intriguing picture too often leads to a wrong impression of the real character of a minister's work. Dr. Jowett pointed this out in his Yale lectures on preaching. He mentioned that the picture of sweet, fluffy, little lambs did not give a realistic vision of the flock. There are also plenty of obstreperous old rams.

Frank H. Ballard, the distinguished British preacher, describes the life of the minister in a small English community in the following words.

> In Linton, if you walk down the street not knowing where you are going, they know. They know what you have for breakfast and when you go to bed at night. Tell it not in Gath, but we do know too much about our neighbors' faults if we are not so well acquainted with their virtues. You must not be too surprised or upset if people stay away from services because something has hurt them, or the women's guild is suddenly split down the middle. Here is the problem—how to rectify the damage. If you leave it severely alone the breach will continue. If you make a fuss over them, that is just what some of them want and you are encouraging them to do it again. Happy is the minister, or the minister's wife, who has what is called tact. All that I can say is, that is what you need more than the wisdom of Solomon, and some country ministers have much more of it than I have.

On the other side of the picture the minister historically faces the responsibility to lead his people into the Christian way of life. He accomplishes this through the pulpit ministry, through the fellowship activities of the church, and through the pastoral program. The clergyman who will give himself wholeheartedly to the task will find that it not only builds and sustains congregations but that it brings to himself a rich and sustained reward.

Early in the nineteen hundreds, church attendance went into a slump and Sunday school attendances declined. A very definite relationship is evident between the lessening of church interest and the trend of those years to do as little pastoral calling as possible. The period followed an era of great preaching and students for the ministry were urged to do much reading but little doorbell ringing. The clergy needed little encouragement to persuade them that they had wasted hours of precious time doing an unnecessary routine task.

Perhaps the most often repeated story on preaching of the time was that of a Scottish minister who, when rebuked for lack of diligence in the pastoral work, raised his feet and put them on the desk. To the complaining committee, he said: "You can have my feet or my head but you can't have both." This attitude of the clergy in regard to pastoral work may have improved the quality of the preaching; it did contribute to the decreasing size of Sunday congregations of that era.

Many of the great preachers we honor were likewise great pastors. The noble Phillips Brooks was without peer as a preacher. His sermons are marvels of inclusiveness and revelation, but in his own Boston he is recalled through memories as a great pastor. The following picture of this side of his life is revealed in the chapter written by Charles F. Kemp in *Pastoral Care* (Abingdon, J. R. Spahn, editor).

> Phillips Brooks is remembered as one of America's great preachers; he also was one of our greatest pastors. He was extremely sensitive to human need and made constant study of human nature. Although the halls were not large enough to house the audiences that came to hear him, he never lost sight of personal needs. He refused to seclude himself, saying that the man who wanted to see him was the man he wanted to see. His house was a refuge for all who were in trouble. They came at all hours of the day and night, all types and all ages, from all denominations and from all levels of society. Each was met

with sympathy and understanding. Each person in his study was made to feel that he was the one thing of most concern to Phillips Brooks, as indeed at that time he was. A. V. G. Allen, his biographer, speaks of the strange power he seemed to carry with him in the hospital wards. A mysterious influence seemed to go forth from him for good, for strength and life, even when he sat down in silence by the bed side and no need was felt for words.

Harry Emerson Fosdick will long be remembered as a distinguished preacher. I was living in New York during the now historic controversy in the First Presbyterian Church when he, a Baptist minister, became the pulpit minister of that church. The church expected from him only the time of preparing and delivering the sermon, but he soon sensed that no man can serve a church without drawing himself into a pastoral ministry. From his experiences with that pastorate, he wrote his book on pastoral counseling.

As a very young man I served a church in Buffalo, New York, where I had the opportunity of sharing the confidences of Samuel V. Van Rankin Holmes, then pastor of Westminster Church. A theological and intellectual power, he influenced the city, but I saw some things the public did not share. I recall the afternoons he set aside for pastoral work. He owned no car but used a taxicab and early each afternoon on calling days the cab stopped at the church for him and he began his rounds. I doubt if anyone can sustain the thesis that pastoral work lessens pulpit ability.

Today pastoring has come back. We still have the conventional house by house calling as our fathers had. To this must be added the new emphasis on pastoral counseling which is so important a part of the ministry that few can ignore its responsibility. Like house to house calling, it has its temptations and its pitfalls but it is bringing people who are spiritually lost back to normal spiritual life. Thorough counselling takes a tremendous amount of time and this in itself becomes a problem.

Pastoral obligations must be organized to fit into the program of the busy minister.

A Department of Pastoral Work

The church must be so organized that the congregation will appreciate that "pastoring" is the responsibility not only of the pastor but of the congregation. Churches today, whether formally organized into departments or not, think of their work in areas such as Worship, Education, Finance, Fellowship, Missions, etc. Pastoral work should be recognized as having equality with these other activities. Parish visitation is not something the minister does because he has time on his hands. A committee or commission on "pastoring" should carefully develop programs in which laymen and women can participate helpfully. It is no longer the sole responsibility of the pastor and many opportunities arise for reference to local agencies and competent individuals. The techniques discussed in the chapter "Reaching the Congregation" all have a place here.

Home Visitation

This tradition of the pastoral ministry must be continued. The minister needs to make and keep contact with every family. It will probably be necessary to make out a visitation program in advance, leaving space in it for emergency calls. He will need a pocket record or some other method by which he can list the families by areas for convenience in making his calls. The reason for house to house calling is not merely that the people expect it, but that it gives the minister an opportunity to see his people which is denied to every other profession. The doctor does not see his patients until injury or disease comes upon them and one resists visiting the psychiatrist until his nervous condition requires it. The minister, on the other hand, has the privilege of dropping into homes at any time. He sees mental and physical sickness in their earlier stages and can start his treatment at an earlier period.

In the larger parishes the calling will probably have to be done by geographic areas planned in advance to fit into the annual program. Publicizing the area to be covered week by week will give the people in these areas a chance to change their own schedules to be at home when the minister calls. If he does not find them at home the responsibility for absence will be placed on their shoulders, not on his. Ministers are sometimes embarrassed by the comment, "You have been here a year and you have not been in our home." If he has rapped at the door several times and found no one home, this criticism will not go very far.

Many of these house by house calls will be made in homes where they are needed for no visible reason. These can be brief and informal and the minister probably profits more than the people. It does not take long to sense the situation. The conversation need not deal exclusively with church matters. The experienced pastor knows that the quickest way to get a parent to open up for free discussion is to ask about the children in the family. This is definitely a friendly opening. If the parents are dissatisfied with the work being done in the church school, the minister soon has that message whether it is spelled out or not.

If in any parish arise instances of dissatisfaction based on the personality of the complaining person rather than on the program or activities of the church, the pastor must be skillful in explaining the situation, not accepting every complaint as justified. He certainly must not "double-cross" his own workers in church or school. One cannot justify his own leadership by passing blame to another.

The minister will have to be his own judge as to whether he shall pray in the home that is visited. Usually if there is sickness a prayer will be appreciated. If the sickness is slight, prayers for health may border on the ridiculous. If a change is being made or a child is leaving for college, a brief prayer asking God's guidance will probably be appreciated. Sometimes a good shock treatment is necessary to impress on the host or hostess that his attitude toward the church and the minister is unfair. The pastor must deal kindly and tolerantly with the families to whom he ministers.

Dr. George Stewart, at one time president of Auburn (New York) Theological Seminary, once told of this experience. He had tried to cover the house to house visitation of a new parish in one year, but he had failed in this because of absentees. A week was devoted to revisiting these homes to become acquainted with the family. At one home he was met by a matron who did not respond to his friendliness.

"Why, Dr. Stewart," she said, "I had about decided that you did not know that we belonged to your church. This is the first time you have been in our home."

Dr. Stewart caught on quickly. He asked if the children were home from school. They were. He asked that they be brought into the house and several were called in. Next he suggested that since one of his duties was to train them in the catechism he wished to ask them questions to see what they had learned. Neither the mother nor the children knew many of the answers. Next he suggested that they have a prayer before he left. The mother agreed and he kept them on their knees for fifteen minutes.

Then, as he left he explained that he had been to the home before but found nobody in. For this he was sorry but he would try to visit oftener. The housewife reacted quickly to this:

"We appreciate the visit," she said, "but don't feel that you have to see us every few weeks. We are loyal members and you can count on us. It would be better for you if you gave most of your time to the sick and troubled."

The minister complains of course about the burden of this kind of calling. But the individual member who wishes some attention is not nearly so dangerous as the families in the inner circles who expect many calls a year from the minister. A few families who monopolize the time of the minister are far more dangerous for the work of the church than those who simply ask for occasional recognition.

There is nothing more dangerous in the pastoral procedure than for the minister to give an unfair portion of his time to one small group in the church. The explanation of the two circles is this: the larger circle represents the membership of the church. The small circle represents a small group of loyal people in the congregation. These people can be counted on for

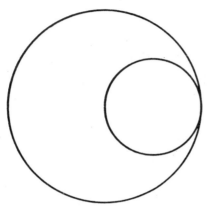

The tell-tale circles. Every church has two circles. The large represents the total membership. The small one represents the small, loyal group who are consistent worshippers, and sacrifice of time, effort, and money. The pastoral objective is to bring those outside the inner circle into it. The growth of a local church is measured not only by the size of its membership but by the size of its inner circle.

support in the services of the church and for leadership in voluntary activities and finance. As these people are the heart of the church, they should be able to get along without too much pastoral attention so that the minister can give his strength to those in the larger circle. In too many churches, the minister reverses this and gives much more of his energy to a small group. This in itself leads to a sort of religious inbreeding. The group gradually develops its own method of thinking and a private vocabulary of religious terms. Out of this group must come your workers, but it is slow death for the group to serve only itself. The ideal is that this circle should eventually coincide with the larger one. A constantly enlarging inner circle shows a church which is growing spiritually. A constantly narrowing inner circle reveals a church which is slowly dying.

This is important in many ways but especially in the program of successful pastoring. The aim of the pastoral call is to integrate the entire membership into the smaller circle. One reason why new sects show larger per capita giving than the old established denominations is shown right here. In the enthusiasm of newness there is no outer circle.

Help for the Minister

As the church grows in size the burden of house to house calling becomes very great. The minister will need help and there is always the possibility of adding to the ministerial staff and dividing the responsibilities. This does relieve the pressure.

One of the simplest ways to divide the calling list is to let each minister pastor the people in his own area of work. That is, the minister of Christian education would have pastoral oversight of the homes which are reached through the educational program. Even if a third minister is added to direct the pastoral program he will need the help of his fellow ministers to reach all the families. Another is to set up the entire list and alternate by years. In this way each of two ministers will visit each home during a two year period. The calls should be recorded very carefully so that there are accurate records. Unless this is done some will be missed. Very recently, a minister of a three-minister church assured me that with three pastors every home was receiving attention. About the same time a member of that church told me that not a minister of the church had called at his home since he joined the church five years before.

House by house calling of necessity misses many. Employed women are seldom home to receive visitors. The men of working age are in shops, offices, and stores. The minister needs to contact these. In an effort to do so he may plan group or individual meetings in the church in which he meets each one personally.

He also will make it clear that he can receive visitors in his study, preferably by appointment. One minister makes a practice of calling absentees by phone after many disappointments in trying to reach them at home and suggesting that they come to his study. The enlargement of these practices will relieve the minister from much travel time.

Lay Help in Pastoring

There are two ways in which lay organizations can help the minister in the program. The first, discussed at length in an earlier chapter, is the division of the parish into districts with a lay person or man and wife charged with each district. These leaders will make calls quarterly or semiannually at each home.

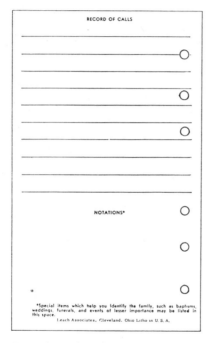
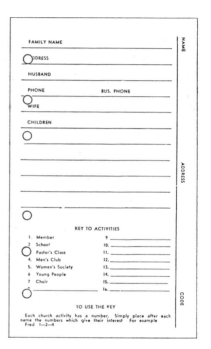

Pastor's calling list. Cards like these, kept in a loose leaf binder, give the minister instant access to record of his calls.

When these workers see need of pastoral attention, they notify the minister's office at once so he may render service. The second method is for the pastor to have a group of people about him on whom he may call for individual work. Preferably these have met with him to gain some knowledge of the purpose and techniques of pastoral work. They are selected both because of their interest in the church and individuals and because they have the most valuable quality of discretion and understand the privilege of confidence. This group can perform a most valuable service to the pastor and the congregation. Reports should be made directly to the pastor.

Emergency Calls

Emergency calls require special pastoral attention. They include serious accident cases, deaths, illnesses, disturbances in the families, in fact all the crises of life. Here no layman can function because the pastoral technique is necessary. Here again there can be no absolute division among the ministers of a multiple ministry church. We have known churches where the ministers have definitely agreed on dividing the lists for pastoral work; then tragedy comes to a family and they want the pastor. If an associate is embarrassed in such an instance, the minister must go into his associate's territory. An instance is recalled of a church which had a preaching minister. He was to be protected from any administrative or pastoral work, but before the new preaching minister had been on the job for six months the layman in the church who headed the committee which selected the pastor died suddenly. The family wanted the pastor to conduct the burial service. Should the man be consistent in division of pastoral duties and require that the associate take the task? Of course, he did not. The man was his friend and more than anyone else had persuaded him to become pastor of this church. He took on the task.

Calls in case of emergency have always played an important part in the ministerial profession. The technique differs from that of house to house calling. He comes on the scene for a special purpose and he must as the man of God give confidence and security so far as he can.

Hospital calls are almost a daily activity for the minister of our time. Many cases are not critical and in some instances the patient is just resting. Here definitely there is no need for carrying a prayer book or offering a bedside prayer. There is enough tragedy and death found in the average hospital without the minister adding to it with a morbid suggestion of his own.

There are other instances in which the realities of the situation must be met. Patients and families expect the minister to offer help and assurance. The author in his own hospitalizations was impressed with the advantage that the Roman Catholic priest has over the Protestant minister. A curtain is drawn around the bed of your Roman Catholic neighbor. Through the thin curtains you can see the little flame of the candle which has been set on the table. The patient is confident that the words of the pastoral adviser are bringing him into the presence of God.

The minister of course will be ready to kneel in prayer with his patient, but more often he will stand near the bed. He should not do this until he has first asked if it is desired. In many instances he could carry a compact communion service set and offer to give the patient the bread and wine which by blessing have become the body and blood of Jesus Christ. The patient is probably more reconciled to inevitable death than are his family or the minister himself, but psychologically the family is helped by this service. The same procedure may be followed in the visit to a home where there is serious illness.

Very effective in cases of accident and shock is for the minister to seek to bring peace from the distress by suggesting that the group kneel with him for prayer. None of the prayers in this instance should be long and use of the prayer book is more advisable than spontaneous prayer. The prayer book implies an authority larger than that of the individual minister. In many cases the minister is left on his own and must improvise a prayer which will fit the situation. Don't count too much on a dying patient understanding the spoken words.

Prayers in Emergencies

Some time ago *Church Management* asked fifty well known ministers if they were sometimes confronted with emergency calls which demanded prayers not found in the formal books. Most of them replied by sending copies of the prayers they used. These have been published under the title *Prayers of the Moment*. They seem to be prayers created in the urgency of the moment.

HER DADDY CAME HOME

An alcoholic after a "spree" came home to his family. He also returned to the pastor's counseling class for alcoholics. The family was happy and sent the little eight year old daughter to give six dimes to the church. Five of these were from the mother, one from her own piggy bank. Asked why she had brought the money, she said, "Because my daddy came home." The minister in the adjoining room heard her presentation and came into the office. With the little girl and the church secretary he kneeled in prayer. The prayer follows.

Jesus, we thank Thee that our daddy has come home. We love him as we know you love him! We pressed our faces against the windowpanes of life waiting for his return; and we pray we may be so happy and kind that he will always be glad to be with us. We also pray that you will forgive his mistakes and that he will always be with You. These things we pray in Thy name for Thou art our Father in Heaven. Amen.

HERBERT E. RICHARDS, MINISTER,

FIRST METHODIST CHURCH, BOISE, IDAHO

SETTING A LIMIT ON LIFE

The distinguished specialist had advised the patient's wife that he had but a few weeks to live. The wife was emotionally upset and called her pastor. The author suggested that no doctor had authority to place a limit on life—that belonged to God alone. He suggested that they talk to the husband and then take the matter to God in prayer. The husband was encouraged to fight what the physician thought was inevitable. The prayer is given below. The patient was able to return to his employment and lived for five years instead of a few weeks.

O God, we know that all the issues of life are in Thy hands and Thine alone. Help us to make a single resolution that we will remain here in this world, doing what our hands find to do, just as long as Thou dost want us to live. Help Mr. —

to carry out his resolve to live as long as possible and to serve
Thee as best he can as long as Thou dost let him live. Amen.

Calls in hospitals should be brief. Nurses and doctors have
their work to do. The patient is weak and tires easily. In cases
involving serious illness the minister probably should not even
be seated. Let him come with the appearance of strength when
his patient is weak. A few words to express his pleasure at being
able to see him, followed by the prayer and possibly communion, a smile, and away is a good technique. There should be no
sitting on the bed or leaning against it. Hospitals are stingy
with chairs and rightly so. The hospital room is for recovery
from illness, not a conference.

The Minister as a Counselor

Ministers have always done counseling work but it has been
only in recent years that the techniques have been formalized
into a definite procedure. Richard Baxter probably is the father
of pastoral counseling as it is done in the Protestant churches.
Pastoral counseling differs from house to house visitation in one
important way. The foregoing pages have shown that parish
visitation is not only a method of serving the individual but of
strengthening the church. Pastoral counseling is the technique
of helping the patient return to spiritual, mental, and physical
health through the use of psychological techniques which have
added to our knowledge of personality.

One minister in his parish visitation found in one home a
young lady who had been taking care of her sick mother. The
obligation of this care had kept her from the society of those
of her own age. She had no girl friends and had never had a
boy friend. She had developed the peculiarities so common to
those drawn away from society and she desperately needed
help. Her mother was a tyrant and demanded full time services
from her daughter, rebuking her if she left the house for a half
hour. When the mother died, the girl was left alone and the
minister felt the need to help her to a normal life. Following the

service he took the opportunity to talk with her about her future. He found that she really knew what the care of her mother had cost her and she wanted to become an active person.

The minister counselor is very fortunate in having an active institution which can help him in his pastoral program. He sought the aid of the institution here. He suggested to the young lady that she attend the morning services and join the young peoples' society which met on Sunday evenings. This she agreed to do, but the minister soon found that his remedy was far too simple. The morning services were very formal. She shook hands with several people who hurried on to their tasks. The young people had passed the girl by and she was not prepared to join in their interests. Her peculiarities even amused them.

The minister retreated for a fresh start. He asked two of the most active and popular young ladies in the society to his study. He explained the situation and asked if they would not as a special task take the new girl in hand and help her to feel at home in the society. This method proved more effective, but was not the end of the case.

The two young ladies were very helpful but their personal arrangements interfered with the pastoral work. The girl felt that there was discrimination against her and again the minister had to enter the picture. With the help of his wife he invited the girl and a few other young ladies to his home. In private conference he had to bear down very heavily to show her how much she had to gain personally to secure the fellowship she needed. With the assistance of others she was guided in her selection of clothes and the use of a hairdresser.

During the counseling periods the girl displayed an interest in foreign countries and this lead helped. The minister was able to arrange for her to join a travel study group. Here she found herself on a level with others. She began to develop and soon acquired friends. The friendships led her into a party which was spending several weeks in Europe.

This very simple case in pastoral counseling indicates how much of the minister's time is necessary to get one young

woman on the track to normal existence. The minister who goes
in for counseling must recognize that each individual is a personality. He must deal honestly with that personality as he seeks
to guide it to mental and spiritual health. In a half dozen cases
about every emotion in the human race is touched.

In the volume *Pastoral Care* (Abingdon), edited by J. Richard Spann, fourteen different classifications are given for counseling. These are Children, Youth, Young Newlyweds, Middle
Aged, Normal Church Members, the Church's Senior Members,
the Heavy Laden, the Sick, Alcoholics, the Mentally Ill, Church
Officials, New Church Members, Those Without a Church,
Those in Institutions, and College Students. These areas are
merely groups of people.

Within each area are found all the illnesses, fears, hopes, de-
lusions, jealousies, sex irregularities, meannesses, joys, failures,
accomplishments, embezzlements, loyalties, and emotions to
which the human race is heir. You can find them in the smallest
church. The minister who seeks to be a counselor takes on a
tremendous task, the most difficult part of which is to find time
to do a good job.

The minister who is willing to serve in this field realizes that
sin is not so simple a thing as our fathers supposed. To the old
divine there was a straight line between right and wrong, between honesty and dishonesty. Our modern interpretation has
destroyed that conception and we have learned that the line
is hazy and irregular. You cannot divide the people of the world
into saints and sinners. Life is not as simple as that.

Richard Baxter of Kidderminster, recognized as the father of
Protestant pastoral counseling, found that his own mind grew
and changed in this respect. In his *Autobiography*, he writes:

> I now see more good and more evil in all men than thereto-
> fore I did. I see that good men are not as good as I once
> thought they were but have more imperfections. And that
> nearer approach and fuller trial doth make the best appear
> more weak and faulty than their admirers at a distance think.
> And I find that few are so bad as either their malicious ene-

mies or censorious separation professors do imagine. In some, indeed, I find that human nature is corrupted into a greater likeness to devils than once I thought any on earth had been. But even in the wicked usually there is more for grace to make advantage of, and more to testify for God and holiness, than I once believed there had been.

I less admire gifts of utterance and bare profession of religion than I once did, and I have much more charity for many, who by want of gifts, do make an obscurer profession than they. I once thought that almost all that could orate movingly and fluently and talk well of religion, had been saints. But experience hath opened to me what odious crimes may consist with high profession; and I have met with divers obscure persons, not noted for any extraordinary profession or forwardness in religion but only to live a quiet blameless life, whom I have after found to have long lived, as far as I could discern, a truly godly and sanctified life, only their prayers and duties were by accident kept secret from other men's observation.

Preparation for Counseling

In preparation for effective counseling the minister needs training in many areas of modern learning. He needs to imbibe some of the knowledge of the medical practitioner—at least enough to help in his diagnosis of the spiritual needs. He must have some basic information in the area of sociology to understand the forces which shape personality. Since he must delve into the minds of individuals, he must be well informed in the modern concepts of psychology.

Theological seminaries are now offering introductory courses. The January 1957 issue of *Pastoral Psychology* lists twenty-five seminaries with longer or shorter courses. In addition the National Council of Churches and various state and city federations provide workshops and conferences in this area. The medical profession is cooperating and hospitals which offer pastoral internships for a summer or longer periods now number forty-five.

The minister must keep in mind that he is neither a physician nor a psychiatrist nor a professional psychologist. He is a minister of the church of Christ who believes that Christian faith is a potent factor in mental and physical health. Counseling is the method of his work.

No minister can cover this wide field. He must work with others. Occasional meetings between physicians and clergy are necessary because cooperation may be the key to health. The minister who would counsel must also learn to use the various social agencies which are found in every city and county in the country. In my own city the list of social agencies covering nearly every side of life—legal, physical, and home adjustments, employment, poverty, and many, many others—takes four columns of small print in our telephone directory. In larger cities, a local directory which describes the field of each of the social agencies may be purchased. The minister will save hours and hours of time and much agony if he will study these listings and learn how to refer cases which come to him to mature counselors, skilled in their respective areas.

For those who do not have local agencies covering these many phases of existence, the minister-counselor may secure literature in advance from national agencies. *Where To Go For Help* (Abingdon), by Wayne E. Oates has been written to give the addresses of these social agencies. For instance if a girl in your congregation becomes pregnant and needs help, to whom could you refer her? This book gives the lists of many institutions, some not too far from you, where hospital services are available and where it is not necessary to reveal the girl's identity. The volume also gives resources for reliable literature covering the problem areas of life.

In addition the minister should have contacts with physicians and psychiatrists who can help give direction to those who need their skilled services. He may know a banker who can give good advice on finance to those who need it so much. Counseling like pastoring is not a one-man job.

Pastoral Techniques

The minister who goes into the counseling field will need to adapt his pastoral techniques to make a successful change from house to house calling. The calling program has two motives, appraising the spiritual health of the members of the congregation and building participation in the church program. The

PARISH FILE CARD — HOUSEHOLD GROUPS													

Congregation:_____ Zone:_____

FAMILY NAME: ADDRESS: PHONE:

CODE: 1—Baptized, 2—Believer, 3—Member, 4—Active, 5—Attends S. S., 6—Shut-in, 7—Leader, 8—Worker, 9—Musical (V. or I.), 10—Active Supporter: C—Choir, M—Men's Work, W—Women's Soc., Y—Youth, S—Scouts

		Born	Occupation	1	2	3	4	5	6	7	8	9	10
HUSBAND:													
WIFE:													
OTHERS:	Relation												

PASTORAL CONTACT (CODE): S—Sick Call, B—At Business Address, O—Pastor's Office, L—Personal Letter, N—No Response, or out, C Other Chance Contacts, When no letter—Normal Pastoral Call in Home. NOTES

Yr.	Jan.	Feb.	Mar.	Apr.	May	June	July	August	Sept.	Oct.	Nov.	Dec.

Front (top) and back (below) of a parish calling-card.

counseling program is directed at the moral and spiritual health of an individual personality. The relationship of doctor and patient, of lawyer and client, is called for. That requires privacy.

If the church provides space for this service the room must be such that both he and his visitor may be assured that everything said is held in the strictest confidence. This is a far cry from the days when it was felt that the minister's wife should accompany him on his house to house visits and when the minister left his study door open so there would be no confidential information in his study conversations. Today privacy is one of the first requisites for good counseling.

The minister would do well to have a room provided for this purpose and list the hours he is available. His people should be persuaded to make engagements by telephone beforehand. The room itself should be near an entry so that clients can enter and leave inconspicuously. Of course counseling can be successfully given in the homes of the parish, but even in these instances it is necessary that the minister be alone with his patient.

Counseling can also be successfully accomplished during calls in professional and business offices, traveling in an automobile, train, or airplane, provided the necessary privacy is available. One minister states that he has had outstanding success on fishing trips, but here again the seclusion of consultant and consultee is essential.

The minister-counselor needs to keep a careful file showing the progress made from visit to visit. This is particularly important if the service involves many consultations or if the minister has made several consultations at the same time. The information in the reports is of course confidential. It may be written in a book, but a file for each client is better. Sheets of the progress report may be placed in the file following each consultation. In the chapter on "Integrating the Congregation" there is pictured a counseling file which also serves as a family church record.

Remember also that the time between consultations is important. In checking the client it is necessary to find out what his actions and reactions have been during the period between the meetings. There are some simple rules for the guidance of the counselor which it is well to keep in mind.

1. The aim of counseling is not alone to help the counselee but to direct the counselee to help himself. The late Fritz Kunkel said: "The more we want to help them, the less we are able to help them." Sympathy on the part of the counselor is necessary but too much sympathy may distort the objective point of view. One distraught woman said to her minister: "I appreciate your interest but you have become so deeply involved in my problem that we have two sick people now instead of one." A minister is easily caught in this trap. Setting himself as the judge of righteousness, he offers a cure for all problems of the human mind and soul. In the end, he may himself need a pastor to set him on the right track.

2. Resist any temptation to be overly interested in the problems of the client. Many rich morsels for the collector of off-color stories will pass in the counseling sessions. If the minister is tempted to be a gossip he has plenty of good material. These confidences are part of the information with which the counselor must work, but in no sense are material to satisfy his own curiosity or that of his family or others.

3. He should never take the attitude that he is the authority and that his advice is compulsory. He may settle the problems of his client but doubtless will find himself with another dependent who cannot move without first seeking his advice.

4. He should avoid relating how he recovered from a similar experience. The minister who has gone through the agonies of personal tragedy is undoubtedly a better counselor, but he must develop the resources of the counselee's experiences, not his own.

Finally the minister needs to do a very thorough job of diagnosis. In the old days, one minister limited every counseling visit to thirty minutes and always ended with a prayer. The devils which confuse people today can not be driven out in thirty minutes and they resist the formal prayer which is often used to get the client out of the room. Prayer has an important part but only the dishonest use it as a trick or miracle.

In one famous case of conversion to the Catholic faith a questioning individual visited, in succession, several Protestant ministers for help. The visitor's narration of her experiences reveals the weakness in some pastoral approaches. One minister listened briefly to her story and said: "There is nothing wrong here which cannot be cured by instruction in the principles of our faith. I suggest that you join my membership class which meets for six weeks on Tuesday evenings. I am sure that will clear away your doubts."

A second after a brief visit said: "Let us unite in prayer." After the prayer, the client was dismissed. A third assured the visitor that her troubled condition was the judgment of God of the things which had come from the visitor's pen. From these men she went to a Roman priest skilled in the art of counseling. Not long afterward the papers announced her conversion to the Catholic faith.

Pastoral power is great, but useless if applied without careful planning and skilled techniques. With the opportunities of training and literature available today, these can be acquired.

Pastoral Counseling

Bonnell, J. S., *Psychology for Pastor and People*. Harper, 1948.
Cabot, R. C. and R. L. Dicks, *The Art of Administering to the Sick*. Macmillan, 1930.
Cole, W. G., *Sex in Christianity and Psychoanalysis*. Oxford, 1955.
Dicks, R. L., *Pastoral Work and Personal Counselling*. Macmillan, 1949.
———, *Who Is My Patient?* Macmillan, 1941.
Fosdick, H. E., *On Being a Real Person*. Harper, 1943.
Hiltner, S., *Pastoral Counselling*. Abingdon, 1949.
———, *Religion and Health*. Macmillan, 1943.
Kamp, C. F., *Physicians of the Soul, A History of Pastoral Counselling*. Macmillan, 1947.
May, R., *The Art of Counselling*. Cokesbury, 1939.

OATES, W. E., *Where To Go for Help*. Westminster, 1957.
PIKE, J. A., *If You Marry Outside Your Faith*. Harper, 1956.
SCHERZER, C. J., *The Church and Healing*. Westminster, 1950.
WESTBERG, G., *Nurse, Pastor and Patient*. Augustana, 1955.
WISE, C. A., *Religion in Illness and Health*. Harper, 1942.
WYNN, J. C., *Pastoral Ministry to Families*. Westminster, 1957.

The Pastor

ADAMS, H., *The Pastoral Ministry*. Abingdon, 1932.
BAXTER, R., *The Reformed Pastor*. Many editions.
BLACKWOOD, A. W., *Pastoral Work*. Westminster, 1945.
DICKS, R. L., *And Ye Visited Me*. Harper, 1939.
DOLLOFF, E. D., *Maturing in the Ministry*. Round Table, 1938.
DOUGLAS, L. C., *The Minister's Every Day Life*. Scribner's, 1924.
HILTNER, S., *Preface to Pastoral Theology*. Abingdon, 1957.
KEMP, C. F., *Physicians of the Soul*. Macmillan, 1947.
LEACH, W. H., *The Making of the Minister*. Cokesbury, 1938.
WINTERS, G., *Love and Conflict*. Doubleday, 1958.

23 | THE MINISTRY OF MARRIAGE

WHEN A COUPLE, A MAN AND WOMAN, COME INTO THE study the minister senses that they want to talk marriage. They may be very young and very much in love or they may show the years of maturity and experience with marriage. Between these two extremes are many kinds and conditions. Some are teen-agers inspired by the marriage concepts of our day. Some belong to that great class of common law marriages who are now eager to legalize their relationship. Where there is evidence of pregnancy the minister sees social pressure forcing the couple. Another couple is accompanied by a small child, the pride of the widowed bride who is seeking a home for the child whose father was a casualty of war. In no other situation does the work of the minister offer more dramatic possibilities nor require so much careful thinking and honest counseling as in his ministry to those who would marry.

"Marriage," says the liturgy, "is instituted of God, regulated by his commandments, blessed by our Lord Jesus Christ, and to be held in honor among all men." The minister sees many other influences entering in. The Christian Church as a whole and the local church in its particular program seeks to lead its youth into ways of life which will be happy and rewarding. From the earliest years through maturity the injunctions from the pulpit, the lesson material in the church school, and the individual leadership try to implant the Christian concept of marriage and to encourage the companionships which will lead to satisfactory home relationships.

If the two who come for marriage consultation have been raised within the church family the minister already knows, fairly well, just what the individual concepts of marriage may be. The young people who have been participating in the church school, the youth organizations, and the summer camps have been fairly well grounded in the requirements for a successful marriage. With the others he must start at the beginning to trace their background.

The pastoral practice of requiring some kind of a consultation period before the wedding is a good one. More and more ministers feel that their responsibilities are such that they cannot respond to every request which comes. State laws and denominational regulations make it impossible to respond to all requests. Moral principles must guide the minister in other instances. Most states now require a license before the minister can officiate at a wedding. The presentation of a license duly signed should not be the final deciding factor in the matter. The state may sanction many marriages that the church cannot.

Churches which require the publication of marriage bans are in a very good position to enforce some kind of pre-marriage counseling. Ministers of churches which have no such regulations could insist that all couples who plan marriage should make arrangements for the wedding at least one week before the ceremony. For a church wedding this is almost a necessity to enable the church, organist, and minister to set a time which is mutually agreeable.

Ministers make their own programs for counseling. Some limit it to a single session, others ask for several. Probably a rigid rule is not desirable because each couple presents a different situation. The minister is required to ask certain questions. He must ask if the license is available at the present time or when it will be. He must ask if this is the first marriage for both or for either. If not a first marriage, are the parties widowed or divorced? If divorced, is the applicant the innocent party in the divorce? In either case how long ago did the divorce take place? Do either of the parties have children?

Next the minister needs to know about their religious background. Do they come as church communicants seeking a Christian marriage or are they merely seeking the blessing of the church upon the wedding? The minister here will become the evangelist and sense in many instances an opportunity to help the couple in the establishment of marriage by getting them interested in the program of the church.

The minister needs to know something of their ideals for the establishment of the home. Are both going to work? Do they wish a family now or later? He is now getting very close to the subject of sex. It is questionable just how far a minister should go in consultations in this field. He can and should make it clear to those before him that the sexual part of marriage is blessed by God as are other marriage relationships. If the discussion then leads into birth control, he can give his own and the church's attitude. Specific sex instructions probably are not in the province of the minister. He can very well at this stage of the consultations present to the couple a good book to guide them in sex relationship. Such books as *Harmony in Marriage* by Leland Foster Wood and *Sexual Harmony in Marriage* by Oliver M. Butterfield are available in inexpensive paper covers. The minister may prefer to refer this matter to a physician or to a city or county agency which has qualified consultants. We like the suggestion made by John Charles Wynn in his book *Pastoral Ministry to Families.* He suggests that if a minister feels he should give intimate sex instruction that he clear the matter with his own board before he does so that there will be no misunderstanding as to the purpose of such consultations.

The interview will of course cover the wedding ceremony itself. The minister should take a copy of the service he uses and read it paragraph by paragraph interpreting as he goes along so that no one will mistake this profoundly religious ceremony for a pleasing social custom.

The minister should plan to go over with the prospective bride and groom the details of the wedding service. The young applicants will be most interested in this. They will want information concerning the organization of their party, how the processional will be organized, where the families will sit, points at which they will join hands, when a kiss is permitted, if and when pictures may be taken, etc.

The minister must be patient at this point though he has been through the program time and time again. If the wedding is a large one, a rehearsal must be held so that every person concerned will understand the program. If the minister has some one on his staff who can supervise the rehearsals the task may be delegated. In some instances a church employee takes this on a fee basis relieving the minister from pre-wedding rehearsals. Nevertheless, the minister who officiates should go through the ceremony with the couple so that they may feel he is not only the officiating clergyman but a friend.

Some weddings are very informal, even held in gardens, but the formal church wedding involves many details. Careful preparation can make its memory very pleasant while unforeseen irritants can change the entire atmosphere.

Professional marriage consultants put much emphasis on the proper training of the ushers. More than pages, they are friends of the participants. They will meet the guests, offering the left arm to the ladies and escorting them to their seats. The male guests follow along but are given little attention by the ushers. Traditionally the bride's family will sit on the left of the church as you face the altar, the groom's family on the right side.

Some ministers and consultants have found that the best method for conducting the rehearsal is first to place every member of the party in his proper position before the altar. In this way they know where they will stand during the ceremony. Having placed them in the proper positions, the minister next asks the organist to play the recessional so that the party may leave in proper order. Having mastered this part of the ceremony, they can see the purpose of organization and more readily enter into the pageant. Next starting from the beginning, the ushers are given a chance to seat the guests (imaginary persons if necessary). Finally the bride's mother is seated. The ushers roll out the aisle carpet and the processional begins. If the church has a center aisle it is always used for this; if there are two center aisles, one may be used for the entry, the other for the exit.

The groom with his attendants enters from the altar end of the church, the bridal party from the narthex. The order of entrance should be as follows:

1. The master of ceremonies signals the organist to begin the march.
2. The organist begins the march.
3. The groom's party enters and takes its position.
4. When the groom's party is about half way to the position, the ushers start their march to meet them.
5. When the groom's party is placed, the first bridesmaid starts her march. She is followed by the other bridesmaids in order, each at intervals. Do not crowd or hurry. The maid of honor follows the last bridesmaid. The pace should be slow and dignified with a definite number of beats between the steps. The hesitation step so popular a few years ago is passing out of fashion.
6. The bride and her father start up the aisle. The bride and father may find it desirable to walk in rhythm (she starts with her right foot, he with his left), but not in step.
7. The ceremony.
8. The recessional.
9. The reception.

The reception is an important part of the formal wedding. Sometimes it is held in the church and many churches have a committee which provides refreshments at a stated fee. Otherwise, the reception is held in a hotel or club or in the bride's home. As soon as the invited guests have arrived, the reception line is arranged so that each may pass the line to extend congratulations. The usual order of the reception is:

Bride's mother.
Bride's father.
Groom's mother.
Groom's father.
Bride.

Groom.
Maid of honor.
Bridesmaids.

After the guests have passed through the reception line, the bride is customarily escorted by the groom to the table where the wedding cake reposes. The bride cuts the first piece from the lowest layer and shares it with the groom as the evidence of union in the new relationship. Following this is the informal buffet lunch, followed by the throwing of the bouquet.

Practically every cost except an honorarium for the clergy is paid by the parents of the bride. Such charges would include the organist and other musicians, the church custodian, fee for the church if one is charged or gift to the church if one is not, wedding counselor or master of ceremonies if one is employed, caterer, decorations and flowers, canopy to church door, aisle cloth, hotel accommodations for out-of-town guests, taxicab service, etc.

While there is a movement among ministers to officiate at weddings as a Christian service and on that basis to refuse an honorarium, most ministers still are glad to be remembered. The policy in churches may vary. Some feel that the ministry of the wedding is most important and will make no charge for the use of the building unless a reception is held in one of its rooms. Others have a fixed schedule of fees which are made available in the pre-marriage interviews.

In most instances the church requires that the officiating minister be one of the clergy of the church where the service is held and that the church organist be used. Guest ministers or organists must definitely be cleared before the ceremony takes place.

The use of a professional master of ceremonies seems to be growing. This individual assists the family with the entire program for the wedding. He helps them plan the program, aids in the selection of the invitations, gives publicity to the papers, makes suggestions for showers and public announcement, coaches the wedding party and in some instances supervises the church rehearsals, plans for the receptions, and takes care of many details, including advice on proper dress.

The music for the wedding is very important. There may be a clash here between the ideas of the professional master of ceremonies and the minister of the church who feels that many of the popular selections ordinarily used are offensive. The following are recommended by the ministers of the West Side Presbyterian Church, Ridgewood, New Jersey. This list, you will notice, omits many light and sentimental numbers often used at weddings.

ORGAN SELECTIONS

Bach, "Air for the G String"
Bach, "Arioso"
Bach, "If Thou Art With Me"
Bach, "Jesu, Joy of Man's Desiring"
Bach, "Sheep May Safely Graze"
Bach-Gounod, "Ave Maria"
Boellmann, "Suite Gothique"
Bonnet, "Elves"
Bonnet, "Song Without Words"
Franck, "Adagio" (*Fantasia in C*)
Franck, "Cantabile"
Handel, "Air" ("*Water Music*")
Karg-Elert, "Harmonies du Soir"
Karg-Elert, "Now Thank We All Our God" (excellent for Processional)
Liszt, "Liebestraum"
Liszt, "Les Preludes"
Lemare, arr. "Irish Air from County Derry" (Londonderry Air)
Mendelssohn, "Andante" (4th Sonata)
Mendelssohn, "Andante" (Violin sonata)

MacDowell, "Woodland Sketches"
McKinley, "Cantilene"
Nevin, "Will o' the Wisp"
Rubenstein, "Reve Angelique"
Schumann, "Traumerei and Romance"
Schubert, "Ave Maria"
Schubert, "Serenade"
Saint-Saens, "My Heart at Thy Sweet Voice"
Saint-Saens, "The Swan"
Wagner, "Dreams"
Wagner, "Minster Processional" (Lohengrin)
Wagner, "Prelude to Lohengrin"
Wagner, "Introduction to Act III" (Lohengrin)
Wagner, "Prize Song" (*Die Meistersinger*)
Wagner, "To The Evening Star" (*Tannhauser*)
Weaver, "Bell Benedictus"
Widor, "Andante Cantabile" (*Symphonie IV*)
Widor, "Serenade"

VOCAL SELECTIONS

Black, "The Pledge"
Bohm, "Calm as the Night"
Burleigh, "O Perfect Love"
Clokey, "Wedding Suite"
Diggle, "A Wedding Prayer"
Grieg, "I Love But Thee"
Handel, "Where'er You Walk"
Lovelace, "Wedding Benediction"

Malotte, "The Lord's Prayer"
Root, "Love Never Faileth"
Schubert, "Ave Maria"
Schubert, "Serenade"
Schutz, "Wedding Song"
Ward-Stephens, "Love Never Faileth"

Variations in the Service

Ministers will have many requests for variations from the liturgies of marriage which are offered in the historical services. Some of these are simple and can be added with little change in the program.

In the double ring ceremony, a ring is placed first upon the proper finger of the bride and the groom speaks the words of the gift, "This ring I give thee, in token and pledge of our constant faith and abiding love." The minister next receives the ring which the bride will give to the groom. She places it on his proper finger and repeats the same words which the groom has just uttered.

A Second Minister

Often there will be requests for a second minister to have a part in the service. In these instances the pastor of the church where the ceremony is performed should be recognized as the official pastor. The assisting minister may be given any part or parts of the service which the two ministers agree on with one exception. The pronouncement of marriage should be made by the official pastor and he should sign the return certificate. Both ministers, however, may sign the certificate given to the bride and groom.

A Minister Officiates at Wedding of His Daughter

A minister wishes both to give his daughter away and to officiate at her wedding. This can be accomplished simply. He marches to the altar with the bride remaining with her until he answers the question: "Who giveth this woman to be married to this man?" Having said "I do" he leaves the bridal party and takes his place before the altar, conducting the balance of the service.

Use of the Engagement Ring

As a rule the engagement ring is removed for the wedding ceremony. However, there is nothing sacred about the custom. One couple very much wished to have the engagement ring blessed in the ceremony. To do this, the hand of the bride was bare when she came to the altar. The wedding ring was placed in the usual manner. Then from the best man, the minister received the engagement ring. This he handed to the groom with the request that it be placed on the finger which now bore the wedding ring.

The groom said these words as it was placed.

"This ring, symbol of our engagement to marriage, is again placed on your finger to affirm the love expressed and to provide a guard for the vows of marriage just taken."

Local Church Check List

If a church can do so it is wise to publish a list of requirements for those who may want to use the church facilities for weddings. The following list was issued by the Lake Avenue Baptist Church of Rochester, New York. Notice that there is a schedule of fees.

1. DATE AND TIME. Check with the minister or church office as early as possible. Since there are about 50 weddings a year, be sure the time and date you want are clear before making any public announcement.

2. PLACE. Weddings are performed in: The sanctuary of the church, the Barrett Parlor, the Webster House Parlor, the Webster House Board Room, and the garden. The place will depend largely upon the number of guests expected.

3. INTERVIEW. Make an appointment with the minister whom you wish to perform the ceremony. He wants to know both of you personally before the wedding, and his experience gives him something important to share with you concerning Christian ideals of marriage. Allow an hour for this interview, and try to arrange it at least a week before the ceremony.

4. FLOWERS. In planning flowers be sure your florist is familiar with the arrangement of the room where you will have the ceremony, and that he is clear as to where the flowers are to be delivered and when. Check this with the church office or janitor. Also let the church office know how the flowers are to be disposed of after the ceremony.

5. REHEARSAL. For weddings where there is music and a bridal procession, it is necessary to have a rehearsal. This is usually arranged for some evening before the wedding. Allow an hour for the rehearsal. The bride and groom, their parents, their attendants, and ushers should be present.

6. MUSIC. Arrangements for music should be cleared with the minister. The church will provide the organist for all weddings in the sanctuary. The church will provide the pianist for other ceremonies if this is desired. Fees for these services are indicated on the next page. Guest vocalists may be invited by the couple or will be secured by the church if so desired. Check with the organist or pianist on any vocal solos and on any special numbers you wish played in the recital, so that the music may be secured if necessary. Arrange for your soloist to have a rehearsal with the accompanist possibly on the evening of the wedding rehearsal.

7. RECEPTION. Contributing members of the church may use church or Webster House facilities for a wedding reception, but must clear all arrangements carefully with the church office. A fee is charged to cover cleaning expenses.

8. PHOTOGRAPHS. Photographs may not be taken while the ceremony is in progress. The ministers will be glad to coop-

erate with you for photographs taken before or after the ceremony.

9. SCHEDULE OF FEES.

Sanctuary

For the use of the building	$20.00
Organist	10.00
Janitor	5.00
Rental of Crash for Aisle	4.00

Barrett Parlor

For the use of the building	5.00
Pianist (if secured by church)	5.00
Janitor	3.00
Rental of Crash for Aisle	4.00

Garden

For the use of the garden	10.00
Janitor	5.00

10. MINISTER'S FEE. The amount of the minister's fee is left to the discretion of the groom.

There is little uniformity in the practice of charging for the use of the church for weddings.

There are no general fees for small weddings at Webster House, unless the services of the janitor are necessary. There is no charge for the use of property for the ceremony in the case of families which contribute regularly to the church. Fees should be paid at the time of the rehearsal and a bill will be submitted if requested. The leaflet distributed by the West Side Presbyterian Church, Ridgewood, New Jersey contains this section on fees:

It is not the policy of this Church to look upon weddings as a source of revenue. There is, therefore, no charge for the use of the Church Sanctuary for a wedding.

1. For use of the Church School Auditorium or other rooms *for receptions*, the fees are as follows: $5.00 for utilities; $5.00 for dish rental; $10.00 for services of kitchen custodian; $10.00 for sexton service, and $5.00 for additional sexton helper, if needed to re-set rooms.

2. There is a fixed charge of $30.00 for the organist; this includes playing for the rehearsal and a program of music preceding the actual ceremony, as well as the wedding marches and accompaniment of soloists.

3. Soloists from the church quartet may be engaged for $20.00, which includes a rehearsal and singing at the wedding.

4. The church sexton is to be paid $10.00 for an average wedding as a minimum; in the event of special arrangements or unusual cleaning, it is expected that $15.00 will be the minimum.

Some churches feel that they have a definite mission to encourage church marriages rather than civil marriages so they offer the church without charge with the exception of music costs. Many churches which make charges have a provision that members of the church contributing regularly to the budget should be exempted from the charges. There are other churches which fear the invasion of marginal marriages, mixed marriages, and other questionable unions if they open their doors freely to all comers.

Informal Weddings

Not all weddings are celebrated in the church. Many are held in homes and garden weddings are very popular in certain sections of the country. Either the home wedding or the garden wedding can be very effective. The same type of organization should be used. In case of the garden wedding an altar constructed of boards and covered by a white cloth will serve. The groom and his attendants will approach from the right (facing the altar). The bridal party will progress through the center as in the church.

In the home wedding the processional is very limited and the bride and groom may well meet at the altar. The groom with his attendants will enter and take their place at the front (right) of the altar, the bridal party (which will need to be small) will come down the stairs and meet there.

Integration of the Communion Service

Some ministers have found it helpful to include a communion service in the wedding ceremony. Reverend Arthur M. Krueger while pastor of the Peace Evangelical and Reformed Church, St. Paul, Minnesota did this. The service was offered to the couple and the minister did not insist. In most instances the response was favorable. Immediately after the pronouncement of marriage, the couple was asked to kneel for communion. After a few words from the pastor explaining the importance of religious convictions in the family life, the couple were offered the bread and wine. This method definitely impresses every one present with the religious nature of the service.

Minister at the Reception

The officiating minister and his wife are always guests at the reception, but they need not stay through the entire hour. When they have passed the reception line and participated in the luncheon they may ease themselves from the scene.

The Post-Marriage Ministry

Marriage from the Christian point of view unites a man and a woman who will establish a family. The ministry of the pastor will continue many years. He will find that much of his counseling is in the marital area. Family troubles continue to take the pastor's time and these are discussed at greater length in the chapter on pastoral work and counseling. Here we wish to give some of the techniques which help the minister keep his contact with the family he has helped to establish.

The first step in the post-marriage ministry is to give a certificate of marriage which reminds the couple that marriage is ordained by God. Some ministers have found that a booklet certificate which contains the entire service is helpful.

Another (John Knox) has six short chapters for the couple to read while they are adjusting themselves to the new

Our Marriage Will Last

*"What therefore God hath joined together,
let not man put asunder"*—Matthew 19:6

We are in love. We love each other so much that we want to spend the rest of our lives together.

We are so much in love that we want to establish a home, where we may throw our protecting love about our children, and rear them in an atmosphere of love and tenderness.

We are so greatly in love that we want nothing to mar the beauty and lasting romance of our union. We believe our marriage will be a lasting one. But thousands of young couples equally in love have taken their sorrows and differences to divorce courts, where romance and bliss have ended in bitterness and recrimination.

We believe that to make our marriage a glorious success we shall need the guidance of God. Therefore we solemnly pledge ourselves

. . . to pray regularly for divine guidance in planning our home, our lives and our future;

. . . to attend as often as humanly possible the church of our choice;

. . . to go, together, to the minister who married us, or to some other minister, with our differences, before going to a lawyer.

. . . .
GROOM

. . . .
BRIDE

. . . .
MINISTER

"As for me and my house, we will serve the Lord"
Joshua 24:15

(This certificate, to be signed by both parties, was designed and written by Cecil G. Osborne.)

relationship. One page in the certificate should contain a second compact which the bride and groom may sign. The one shown here was planned by a Baptist Minister, Cecil G. Osborne.

The newly married couple will of course be given an invitation to attend services if they do not do so already. The ushers should be given instructions to watch for them and give them a good welcome to the church. The minister will follow this with a pastoral call when they are settled in their new home and seek in every way that he can to integrate them among the families of the church.

The minister will keep a record of the weddings at which he officiates. This list should be carefully protected so that on the anniversary of the marriage he can send cards reminding them that he was an important bond in their union. Often these records are helpful in legal and inheritance matters.

Some ministers with long pastorates plan to hold services in June of each year at which the couples married by these ministers come together for a special service to be held in the church. One of the compensations of a long pastorate is the opportunity to enjoy pastoral fellowship with the boys and girls who are the fruits of the marriages over which the minister has officiated.

The Golden Wedding Service

Anniversary services can be an important part in the ministry of the marriage. The minister will have some calls to officiate at the Silver Anniversary, but the Golden Anniversary (fifty years) service is the one usually sought. One of the favorite ways of conducting such a service is to use, if available, the identical service which was used at the original ceremony. The original ring will again be placed on the bride's finger.

The service may be enlarged with the use of appropriate verse and scripture and a few words of commendation. The following quotation from Robert Browning is always appropriate.

> Grow old along with me!
> The best is yet to be,

The last of life for which the first was made!
Our times are in his hand
Who said, "A whole I planned,
Youth shows but half; trust God; see all nor be afraid."

This from an unknown author.

God keep my heart attuned to laughter
     When youth is done;
When all the days are gray days, coming after
     The warmth of the sun.
God keep me from bitterness, from grieving,
     When life seems cold;
God keep me always loving and believing
     As I grow old.

Charles Kingsley's verse also offers a suggestion.

When all the world is old, lad,
And all the trees are brown;
And all the sport is stale, lad,
And all the wheels run down;
Creep home and take your place there,
The spent and maimed among;
God grant you find one face there
You loved when you were young.

For those who prefer a completely new service, we suggest
something along the line of the following which was created
by George W. Wiesen, while pastor of the Baptist Church,
Wayne, New York.

PRELUDE ("I Love You Truly").

THE PROCESSIONAL (Mendelssohn's "Wedding March"). The
party approaches the place selected for the service.

INVOCATION. We come, Our Father, seeking Thy presence on
this happy occasion when two Christian people come to re-
flect on the numerous blessings of a happily wedded life. We
trust that in Thy presence, they may find added joys to which

they can look forward. Together they have proven that wedded life can be a success in a day when divorce rates and broken homes are on the rise. They have proven that a wedded life carried out in proper relationship to themselves and to Thee, is a reward in itself for the effort. We ask Thy blessing upon the things we do here this night. In Christ's name we pray. Amen.

INTRODUCTION. When God created man to live on this earth, it is recorded that he said, "It is not good that man should live alone." He created woman to share the mutual blessings of companionship as well as to share the mutual burdens which each must bear, making the propagation of a human race possible. From that point on, history records the activities of men and women who worked together for the steady development of a better world.

Fifty years, no doubt, seem relatively long as we consider the many changes that have taken place in that time. But those same fifty years, no doubt, seem relatively short to you who have shared the mutual blessings as well as the mutual woes of your wedded life. Together you have weathered the storms of depression, severe epidemics of illness, the hard work of building a home and family life, never forgetting your vows to one another—that you were willing to unite your lives for better or for worse, through times of poverty and wealth, through sickness and health, never forgetting that you were forsaking all others to bring happiness to the life of each other.

Following this pathway has brought you to a new era of life. You have entered what has been called by many "the golden sunset of life," yet with just as great a faith and hope in each other as you had when it seemed like the dawn of a new life.

We would that you could live many, many more years with and for each other and so prove to a world that is now suffering from an epidemic of broken home life, that married life can be a blessing when carried out in proper relationship to each other and to God.

As you enter into this new era of life and renew your vows to one another will you join your right hands.

THE VOWS. ———, will you take ——— to be your wife, to live together after God's ordinance in the holy bonds of marriage, and will you promise in the presence of God and before these witnesses to love her and comfort her, honor and cherish her, in sickness and in health, in prosperity and adversity, and forsaking all others, remain faithful to her as long as you both shall live?

————, will you take ———— to be your husband, and to live together after God's ordinance in the holy bond of marriage, and will you promise in the presence of God and before these witnesses to love him and comfort him, honor and cherish him, in sickness and in health, in prosperity and adversity, and forsaking all others, remain faithful to him as long as you both shall live?

What token do you offer in pledge of your vows? (The wedding ring is proffered.)

Let this ring which has served as a symbol of the brighter band binding you together as one, continue to serve its intended purpose, and as the ring is without end, so may your joy and prosperity be unending.

May the blessing of God continue to rest upon the remaining years of your wedded earthly life, and may the blessings of this life go with you into eternity.

THE BENEDICTION. May the Lord bless thee and keep thee. May the Lord cause His face to shine upon thee and be gracious unto thee. May the Lord make the light of His countenance to shine upon thee and give thee peace, now and forevermore. Amen.

THE RECESSIONAL (from *Lohengrin*).

Marriage

ADAMS, T. F., *Making Your Marriage Succeed*. Harper, 1953.

BAILEY, D. S., *The Mystery of Love and Marriage*. Harper, 1952.

BRINK, F. W., *This Man and This Woman*. Association, 1948.

CADY, E. and F., *How To Adopt a Child*. Whiteside, 1956.

CHAPLIN, D., *Children and Religion*. Scribner's, 1948.

DUVALL, E. M. and R. L. HILL, *When You Marry*. Association, 1953.

DUVALL, S. M., *Men, Women and Morals*. Association, 1952.

LANDIS, J. T. and M. G., *The Marriage Handbook*. Prentice-Hall, 1953.

LEACH, W. H., *The Cokesbury Marriage Manual*. Abingdon, 1948.

WOOD, L. F., *Harmony in Marriage*. Round Table, 1939.

24 | MINISTRY TO THOSE WHO MOURN

THROUGH MUCH OF OUR LIVES WE LIVE AND WORK AS members of a group. We belong to a religious society, a political party, a labor organization, or a professional group. But in the crises of life, each of us is an individual. The value of any minister of the Gospel is his ability to help individuals in the days of such crisis. We come into the world as individuals, we leave it one by one. The help of the clergyman in the time of sickness and death is taken for granted. His responsibility is to aid those who suffer and mourn in adjusting themselves to the realities of life and to direct their minds to the eternal compensations of Christian faith.

The ministry to those who mourn will start of course many months and years before death visits the home. Through the ministry of the pulpit, personal contacts with the family, and reputation acquired in his professional work, the minister will be put in such a position that the family which mourns will have confidence in his methods and his words.

Sometimes one lingers in illness for many months before death finally closes his eyes; at other times, death is instantaneous. Sometimes the minister is called to give Christian burial to a saint well prepared to meet his God; at other times, the deceased has lacked the first credentials of faith, yet peace must be brought—if possible—to those who grieve. Sometimes he will stand at the casket of one whose physical life has been destroyed by a murderer; other times, he will be asked to pray over the remains of one who has murdered. In one home the person taken from this life has lived to a ripe maturity; in another, a youth is stricken down as his sun shines bright. Some

of these things were discussed in the chapter on pastoral calling
and counseling. This chapter will consider the pastoral methods
from the time of death through the burial, with some suggestions for a post-burial program.

In cases of a serious illness, the pastor of course has been
constantly informed of the health of the patient. He has seen
the suffering individual grow weaker. He may have discussed
the probability of death with him and it is not unusual for the
arrangements of the funeral to be discussed before death comes.
If the minister gets in touch with the family at the earliest possible moment, there will be no embarrassment about making the
plans for the funeral.

In other cases where the family or the deceased is a member
of the minister's church, the clergyman has the right to assume
that the spiritual part of the funeral and burial will be under
his supervision and he should contact the family as early as possible. In these cases the minister should telephone the home as
soon as the news is received, asking at what hour the family
will want to talk over the funeral arrangements. In some families a difference of opinion may arise on details, but these items
should be settled before the minister calls.

There are still other instances in which death comes to a
marginal family, one which has no official connection with the
church. The minister has no obligation to make the contact;
indeed, it might be embarrassing for him to do so. He is in the
community as a Christian minister to serve, but in this instance
the family or the mortician must call the minister to take the
service. When that call comes, he is free to offer his services
and ask for a time when he can talk with the family or the person in charge to see just what they expect of him.

A pretty clearly defined code of ethics describes the relationship of the minister and the members of his congregation in
time of death. The minister has the obligation to minister to the
people of his parish and the people on their part have the obligation to consult the pastor of their church regarding ministerial
services in the case of illness, distress, and death. If a minister

from outside the church is desired for the service the matter should be cleared with both pastors.

These obligations do not extend to those outside the parish. The minister should be careful about seeming to encourage a request for his services from any family who belongs to another congregation. If such an invitation comes, he should talk with the pastor of the church before he accepts. The pastor is not a free lance. He has his parish responsibilities and is expected to render definite services to his church. At the same time, he must respect the parish of his neighbor.

Outside of the parishes there are thousands of people who will be calling upon the clergy of their city for religious services. Non-Christians die as well as the faithful. The friends of drunkards, gamblers, and the morally unclean will come to the minister asking his help. This poses a moral problem. The minister would do well to accept these opportunities for service but in no sense does this imply that the minister is condoning the sins of the deceased. He is commending the spirit of the person who died to Almighty God. Who besides God can judge what good there may be in the soul of man?

The Pre-Funeral Conference

In most instances a pre-funeral conference with the members of the family is desirable. Keep in mind that there are several parties interested in the funeral arrangements. The mortician has charge of the physical arrangements. Often the family lawyer comes into the picture, particularly when large estates are involved. There are the various members of the family. Finally the minister as spiritual leader will be counselor and helper through the trying days.

The season of death has so many variations that it is difficult to devise a program which meets all cases. In these days of easy marriage a man may have an ex-wife or several ex-wives with children by each wife. In the case of the death of a woman, the situation is reversed, but there is always a possibility of estranged children coming into the picture.

Where grief is plainly evident, the minister feels that he must suggest a prayer for those who mourn. In other situations, prayer may be very much out of place. The family must make a decision on some very important items—the date and hour of the funeral, the funeral director, and the place of burial. The minister's chief interest is in the hour and the date, the place, and the family's desires as to the service to be held. He certainly should be consulted before an engagement is made for him.

Some families have a definite plan for the funeral, including the verses of scripture to be read and the music to be provided. The minister will listen courteously to all of these suggestions. Insofar as he conscientiously can, he will want to meet these requests, but often he finds it difficult or impossible within the confines of Christian conscience.

A certain clergyman asked that his funeral service be patterned after the morning service of worship with the congregation singing the hymns he loved. This seemed very appropriate and was followed. A musician's request for music by a string trio seemed appropriate. Some requests for special music are so atrocious that a sensitive minister will feel he cannot yield the point. More often than not, the family will say to their pastor: "You knew John, we will leave it entirely up to you." This is usually a good decision and will be appreciated by the minister.

Funeral Trends

Funeral customs vary in different parts of the country. In the large eastern cities the funeral sermon has pretty well passed out of use but is still common in rural and small town areas. A generation ago the home funeral and the church funeral were yielding to the funeral parlor. Today there is a definite movement back to the church funeral, especially in parishes which provide a chapel for that purpose.

Large funerals continue in the rural areas of the south but the trend is to smaller funerals in the north and east. Definitely there is a resistance to a long funeral. Twenty minute services are not uncommon and private funerals are on the increase. Cremation is more common. Music is provided in most funeral services but the soloist or choir is passing. Some ministers, seeing their inability to meet the needs of various funerals, take refuge and simply read one of the historic liturgies; some swing to the other extreme and use informal services.

Great floral displays are still a part of many funerals. However, many organizations including churches have noted the cost of these gifts and have sought to direct the expenditure into other channels. Note the obituary notices in the daily press. You will find many in which the relatives suggest that instead of flowers the money be contributed to the heart fund, a youth camp, a college, or local church in which the deceased was interested.

Some fraternal organizations have funeral liturgies for their own members. There has been much confusion and some bitterness among churches and lodges regarding these, but the trouble is gradually being resolved. Usually the fraternal service is held at a separate hour or at a time just prior to the religious service. If the fraternity also desires a service at the grave, it should precede the religious service. Ministerial associations in many cities have urged the discontinuance of Sunday funerals. Undertakers are cooperating in this and not many Sunday funerals are held at the present time.

Minister and Mortician

Close cooperation between the funeral director and the minister is very important. As these two professions meet together the individuals soon learn to know one another and establish a friendly and helpful relationship. The mortician soon learns the desires of individual clergymen. One wishes the lectern; others prefer to stand without it for the service. One likes the use of earth in the committal service; another prefers flowers; a third wishes neither.

The funeral director definitely wishes the minister to stay out of the discussions regarding caskets and burial costs; in return, he will not try to dictate the length of the service or the material used. Ministers are often troubled by the funeral costs borne by people of low incomes. Attempts to correct this through cooperative funeral organizations have made a very small dent in the whole practice. Funerals are expensive and both grief and pride play a large part. The minister can help to cure this in his continuous ministry, but little can be done if he waits until the crisis of death is upon the family.

The Funeral Service

The minister will plan to arrive at the place of the service ten to fifteen minutes before the announced hour. The family has probably gathered before this and the friends are assembling. He need not go to the family to greet them, he should, however, pass through the room so that they will have assurance that he has arrived. A nod of the head and a smile will assure them that he is meeting with them in this hour.

If the minister wears vestments in his church services, he will want to wear them for the funeral service. Many continue to wear them until the interment is concluded. Others lay vestments aside at the conclusion of the service and do not revest for the service at the grave.

If the minister prefers to read one of the great liturgies of the church, his program for the service is pretty well set, but not entirely. He still has the choice of Scripture and prayer. The selection must be made to fit the time that is available and the individual to be buried. Even a strict liturgist will depart from the prescribed form to use a prayer which might apply very clearly to the situation at hand.

If the minister prepares his own program, a heavier responsibility rests upon him. Before he does so he will want to read carefully three splendid liturgies, those of the Protestant Episcopal Church, of the United Lutheran Church, and of the Presbyterian Church in the U.S.A. In choice of expression, Scripture, and prayers these can be his guide. For the minister who wishes to create his own service, the following outline will be appropriate.

AT THE CHAPEL

1. Music (preferably organ).
2. Opening sentences.
3. Brief invocation.
4. Scripture.
5. Music.
6. Address or sermon.
7. Prayers.
8. Benediction.

AT THE GRAVE

1. Opening sentences.
2. Committal.
3. Benediction.

Two of these items, vocal music and the address, are questionable. The practice of preaching a sermon goes back a long way in the history of the evangelical churches. Ministers in the past have relished this wonderful opportunity to rebuke the sinful and portray to them the horrors of eternal punishment. The triumph of the evangelistic preacher was the funeral which he used for self-gratification.

The purpose of the religious funeral should be far different from that. Life and death are always mysteries in themselves. Christian faith becomes serene with a belief in the Fatherhood of a God who cares for His children. The purpose of the funeral should be to help those who mourn to adjust themselves to the new lives they must lead, to give them comfort in the assurance of the Father's love and care, and to assure them that they have strength for their heavy responsibilities.

The very words of the Scriptures bring assurance. Carefully intoned they will bring calm even if the words are not appreciated. Usually it is advisable to use the King James (authorized) version of the Bible. This surpasses all other editions in poetry. Listen to this noble quotation from the book of Job.

I know that my redeemer liveth, and that he shall stand in the last day upon the earth; and though this body shall be destroyed, yet shall I see God; whom I shall see for myself and mine eyes shall behold, and not as a stranger.

Can any words which the minister composes give more comfort than these from the Gospel of John?

Let not your heart be troubled; ye believe in God, believe also in me. In my Father's house are many mansions; if it were not so I would have told you. I go to prepare a place for you.

Many fine passages suitable for the burial service do not appear in the historical liturgies, but may be very effectively used. For instance, at the funeral of a physician read Ecclesiastes 38:1-8. At the funeral of a distinguished citizen, try Ecclesiastes 44:1-4; at the service of a good woman read Proverbs 31:1-30.

Music? Yes. Solos? No. Unless there is a definite request for vocal music, keep to the organ. Select music which breathes the atmosphere of eternity not of human emotionalism. I have forgotten the entire service held for a minister friend except for two items. One was the repetition by the organ of Mendelssohn's "Rest In the Lord"; the second, a personalized prayer which was used in place of an address. A portion of this prayer follows a little later in this chapter. Among suitable organ selections, the following would be included by most people:

Bach—"Arioso"
Bach—"Come, Sweet Repose"
Bach—"Jesu, Source of Man's Desiring"
Chopin—"Prelude in C Minor"
Dvorak—"Largo" (New World Symphony)
Cesar Franck—"Panis Angelicus"
A. R. Gaul—"Adoration" (The Holy City)
A. R. Gaul—"No Shadow Yonder" (The Holy City)
Handel—"I Know That My Redeemer Liveth"
Novello—"Like As the Hart"
Sibelius—"Theme from Finlandia"
Arthur Sullivan—"The Long Day Closes"

There are some improvisations on well known hymns which are worthy of use. Included would be:

Croft–Matthews—"Jesus Calls Us O'er the Tumult"
Croft–Matthews—"O God Our Help in Ages Past"
Marsh—"Jesus, Lover of My Soul"
Palestrina–Matthews—"The Strife Is O'er"

A short address is not out of place if it be brief, sympathetic, and imaginative. The minister will be speaking largely to the subconscious and only indirect personal references should be made. A Bible verse has power to create a picture by appropriate illustrations and rich verse. Knead these together in an address of ten minutes and it will be something worth while. Here are two examples in outline of such addresses:

AT EVENTIDE

When the even was come, he saith unto them, Let us pass over unto the other side.   Mark 4:35

I. LIFE SYMBOLIZED AS A DAY. There is a parallel between the day and a human life. Early morning represents the newborn babe. The early hours have the freshness of adolescence and youth. There is high noon, which corresponds with maturity. At that time come the heat and burden of the day. Then comes the even with its dusk, and, finally, comes the darkness of night. Night brings its sleep. But one sleeps to awaken refreshed for the new day.

II. THIS SYMBOLISM IS TRUE. When one has lived the allotted years of life, death is as natural as life itself.

As a fond mother, when the day is o'er,
  Leads by the hand her little child to bed,
  Half willing, half reluctant to be led,
And leave his broken playthings on the floor,
Still gazing at them through the open door,
  Not wholly reassured and comforted
  By promises of others in their stead,
Which, though more splendid may not please him more;
So nature deals with us, and takes away
  Our playthings one by one, and by the hand
  Leads us to rest so gently, that we go
Scarce knowing if we wish to go or stay,
  Being too full of sleep to understand
  How far the unknown transcends what we know.
                        —Henry W. Longfellow.

III. A DAY WELL SPENT MEANS PLEASANT DREAMS. When one closes his eyes at the end of day he expects to awaken refreshed. So also when one at the end of a long life closes his tired eyes in what men call death. The awakening will come. You may have confidence.

> So live, that when thy summons comes to join
> The innumerable caravan that moves
> To that mysterious realm, where each shall take
> His chamber in the silent halls of death,
> Thou go not, like the quarry-slave at night
> Scourged to his dungeon, but, sustained and soothed
> By an unfaltering trust, approach thy grave
> Like one that wraps the drapery of his couch
> About him, and lies down to pleasant dreams.
> —William Cullen Bryant.

HEAVEN IS A PLACE

I go to prepare a place for you.   John 14:2

I. IT IS A PLACE. We need have no illusions about it. It is but natural to expect that in the future life those who have lived here, in the ideals of Jesus, shall find a home where they may be near Him. That is not the result of arbitrary judgment but natural evolution.

Put on the light; I do not want to go home in the dark.
—O. Henry

I am on my way to heaven, and I do not intend to get lost.
—Bishop Edwin H. Hughes.

II. IT IS A PREPARED PLACE. Heaven is not an accident. It has been prepared by God for those who serve Him, and by the individuals who anticipate citizenship there. We help to prepare it through our expectancy and Christian living. Stepping from an earth place to a heaven place is but a transition.

Henry Ward Beecher was walking through a cemetery with a friend. Said Beecher: "I suppose that they will be bringing me out here before long. But, God knows, I won't stay here." "Where will you be?" asked the friend. "Somewhere doing business for God," said the preacher.

Christopher Morley, in writing about Heywood Broun, commented he always took an innocent pleasure in being what used to be known as a man about town; and little by little he discovered that the town that is the most interesting is the city of God.

III. IT IS A PLACE OF CHRISTIAN FELLOWSHIP.
More homelike seems the vast unknown
Since they have entered here.
We have loved, we love now, we shall love forever . . .
(Dying words of Robert Wilhelm Bunsen to his wife.)

Heaven is a prepared place of many rooms. Here, in an atmosphere congenial to the Christian, one continues to serve and grow in grace. The best of earth seems weak indeed as they face the future beyond the grave. Few of us are satisfied with our achievements. We ask the opportunity to grow in wisdom and in stature, to commune with our friends and to know our Christ.

The art of using personalized prayer is now coming into its own. All semblance to an address is avoided and even the personal references are included in the prayer. This is one of the brightest developments of the past generation. The portions of two such prayers which follow show something of the technique used.

PRAYER AT THE FUNERAL OF A MINISTER

More especially we offer our thanksgiving for this Thy servant now at rest. We praise Thee for the heritage of Christian conviction to which he was born, for the devout and inspiring men and women who touched his boyhood and youth, kindling a passion for Christ, whose memories he cherished in unfailing gratitude; for the many and large gifts with which Thou didst endow him, and his dedication of them all to his ministry—for the grace and charm of his presence, for his humor and contagious enthusiasm, for his outgoing nature, his keen interest in people and his zest in helping them, for his sensitive understanding, his tender sympathy, his readiness to spend and be spent in ministering to human sorrow, pain and bewilderment, for his civic conscience and his boldness and tact in combating social injustice, and for the devotion regardless of cost to his own strength with which he poured out himself for the congregations over which Thou didst set him as a shepherd and bishop of souls. We thank Thee for the vision, skill, and unfailing toil of his leadership in Thy Church, his delight in the worship of Thy sanctuary and the pains he gave to his preparation to guiding Thy people into Thy presence, for his breadth of thought and love restive under the outworn divisions of the Body of Christ, for his prayer and endeavor to do away with barriers which sunder Christians one from another, and for his eagerness to hasten the day when followers of Christ should be both in spirit and outwardly one.

—Henry Sloane Coffin

Prayer at the Funeral of a Good Woman

We lift our hearts and voices to Thee in thanksgiving for all the gifts of Thy spirit in her—for the tender and happy memories of Thy servant in the pleasant hours of social intercourse—for her zest of life, the keenness and variety of her interests, the vivacity of her temperament which added joy to hours of happiness. We bless Thee for the novel qualities of her character, for her patience and courage, for the brave and uncomplaining way in which she bore her illness. We praise Thee for her unwavering faith in her heavenly Father revealed in Jesus Christ her Saviour. We bless Thee for her wholehearted belief in the living word of God and in the power of the Gospel of Jesus Christ. We thank Thee for her love of Thy house, for her noble service to the church she loved. We bless Thee for the radiance she brought to every circle and every company. We praise Thee for the lovely memories of her as a wife and mother, the tender sympathy and kindly thought of others. And now, in the presence of all that is mortal of her, we praise Thee for her entrance into Thine everlasting kingdom.

O Thou who art the comforter of Thy children, Thou God of love and tenderness, we pray for those who mourn at this time. Bless and console Thy servant who was most precious to her, and unto whom she was dear. Bless and comfort the son and inspire him with knowledge that by the cultivation of the virtues and qualities of the mother who bore him, he shall best honor and perpetuate her memory. Comfort the absent sister. Amen.

—Robert B. Whyte.

The Committal Service

This service is usually brief and no further address is expected. The family group gathers around the open grave. The minister reads a few verses of scripture, then follow the committal words and the benediction. At the conclusion of the benediction the minister will go to the members of the family and taking each by the hand give a final word of blessing. The Scripture may be brief and some liturgies use lines from several parts of the Bible. The following reading is effective.

> Our help is in the name of the Lord, who made heaven and earth.
> Like as a father pitieth his children, so the Lord pitieth them that fear him.
> For he knoweth our frame; he remembereth that we are dust.
> As for man his days are as grass; as the flower of the field so he flourisheth.
> For the wind passeth over it and it is gone; and the place thereof shall know it no more.
> But the mercy of the Lord is from everlasting to everlasting upon them that fear him, and his righteousness unto children's children.

A good sample of a committal service is this from the *Presbyterian Book of Common Worship*.

> Forasmuch as Almighty God hath taken out of this world the soul of our brother (or soul of this child) we therefore commit his body to the ground, earth to earth, ashes to ashes, dust to dust, looking for the resurrection and the life of the world to come, through our Lord Jesus Christ; who shall change our mortal body, that it may be made like unto His own glorious body; according to the mighty working whereby He is able to subdue all things unto Himself.

For burial at sea this prayer from the *Book of Common Prayer* of the Protestant Episcopal Church will be meaningful.

> Unto Almighty God we commend the soul of our brother departed, and we commit his body to the deep; in sure and certain

hope of the Resurrection unto eternal life, through our Lord
Jesus Christ; at whose coming in glorious majesty to judge the
world, the sea shall give up her dead; and the corruptible bodies
of those who sleep in Him shall be changed, and made like unto
His own glorious body; according to the mighty working
whereby He is able to subdue all things unto Himself.

This from the *Scottish Book of Common Order* is frequently
used for the cremation of the body:

Forasmuch as it hath pleased Almighty God to take unto himself the soul of the brother here departed, we therefore commit
his body to be dissolved, ashes to ashes, dust to dust, in sure and
certain hope of the resurrection to eternal life, through our Lord
Jesus Christ.

The minister who wishes to develop his own liturgy should
get a pocket-sized, loose leaf notebook and use each page for one
entry of opening sentences, Bible readings, prayers, outlines of
addresses, committal services, etc. He can list many separate
items to fit various occasions. A few minutes spent in shifting
the pages will give him a complete service for the task at hand.
This sort of thing has been done commercially but one will
grow for the minister who wants individuality in his burial
services.

The Post-Funeral Ministry

The formal ministry to those who mourn is not completed
when the minister leaves the cemetery. Within a few days he
will again call at the family home. The family needs some time
to complete their plans before this call and usually a week is
long enough to wait. He will want to return to the family to
see how they are making their adjustment to bereavement. Are
the children going to continue their college work? Where will
the widow live? What disposition has been made or is being
made of the business? Questions like these always press upon a
family in the days of bereavement.

The minister never makes a charge for the funeral services,

except for actual expenses incurred. In many instances, the family will hand him a gift of appreciation, but the minister's salary is paid to cover ministries such as these. Many clergymen prefer not to accept the proffered gift, often to embarrassment of both the minister and the bereaved family. It is probably better to accept and then to write the bereaved thanking them for their kindness. In some instances the minister salves his conscience by placing such gifts into a particular fund—children's education, books, vacation, or what have you. This simple rationalization may pacify the minister's own conscience.

Some ministers feel they have a right to charge non-members a fee for services rendered in the time of death. Certainly they have that right and just as certainly non-members who call upon the clergyman should be willing to pay something for his services. The general feeling among men of the cloth is that it is better to accept a friendly gift than to name a definite fee.

We have pointed out that the purpose of the funeral is not evangelistic. However, contacts may be formed in these services which will bring lasting friendship for the man and new members for his church. If the service is placed upon a strictly professional basis it may weaken this friendship. The good pastor will always seek to avoid any suspicion of commercialism in his community or parish efforts.

The Funeral

BLACKWOOD, A. W., *The Funeral.* Westminster, 1942.
GRUBER, O., *If A Man Die.* Vantage, 1955.
HALSEY, J., *A Living Hope.* Abingdon, 1932.
HARMON, N. B., *The Pastor's Ideal Funeral Manual.* Abingdon, 1942.
LEACH, W. H., *The Improved Funeral Manual.* Baker, 1956.
WALLIS, C. L., *The Funeral Encyclopedia.* Harper, 1953.

Ministry to Those Who Mourn

DICKS, R. L. and T. S. KEPLER, *And Peace at Last.* Westminster, 1953.
———, *Comfort Ye My People.* Macmillan, 1949.

Irion, P. E., *The Funeral and the Mourners*. Abingdon, 1954.
In the Garden (Leaflet). Leach Associates, 1957.
Rogers, W. H., *Ye Shall Be Comforted*. Westminster, 1950.

Ministry to the Sick and Dying

Babbitt, E. H., *The Pastor's Pocket Manual for Hospital and Sick Room*. Abingdon, 1949.
Cabot, R. C. and R. L. Dicks, *The Art of Ministering to the Sick*. Macmillan, 1936.

25 | THE CHURCH & ITS YOUNG PEOPLE

THE YOUNG PEOPLE OF THE CHURCH HAVE THEIR RELA-
tionship to the church school and in many instances the school
period is supplemented with further activities. Because of the
importance of this age group, youth has become a most essential
area in planning the church program. The group can remain
entirely within the framework of the school and develop there
a larger program. Traditionally, the program has been two-
handed. One hand represents the church school where youth
classes function as the youth department; the other hand is
the organization of a young people's society for religious and
social activities.

Historically, the creation of the International Society of
Christian Endeavor in 1881 set the pace for the young peoples'
work. Born in a time of rising religious interest under the leadership of Francis E. Clark, it rose as a gleaming star above the
churches and local societies, rose up in thousands of communities
and tens of thousands of local churches. From this movement
the denominations caught a new vision of youth work possibilities and soon they began to set up their own youth programs.
The Methodists had the Epworth League; the Baptists, the
Young Peoples' Baptist Union; the Lutherans, the Luther
League, etc. Many local churches were sad to yield to denominational pressure and transform their Christian Endeavor Society to the denominational pattern. Though many years have
passed since the inception of denominational young peoples'
societies, the International Society of Christian Endeavor still
functions effectively.

At the present time little uniformity prevails in local church
practices serving youth. The International Society of Christian

436

Endeavor still maintains an active headquarters in Columbus, Ohio. The denominational tendency, however, is toward the Youth Fellowship. This includes all young people in the church from Junior High to ages twenty-two or twenty-three when the young adults take over. Some still preserve separate youth organizations. The United Lutherans have the Luther League; the Southern Baptists, the Training Union; some others maintain a separate youth organization.

The Youth Fellowship is an effort to unify and strengthen the work of teenagers, but experience reveals that there must be a division in the department. Juniors and high school students do not easily mix in social or educational work. The General Assembly of the United Presbyterian Church of North America sounds a warning to its churches at this point. After noting the commendable qualities of the Youth Fellowship idea, it added:

> Again the point of concentration seems to be in the senior high age. . . . As in last year's report, the warning must be sounded not to lower youth activities to children's ages because they give larger attendance with less effort. Senior high must have the church now or be lost.

In this chapter, we are not dealing with the Youth Fellowship in its broad sense but with the special needs of high school youth and the young people in the years which follow immediately after high school.

These years are critical and important. Young men and women are on the edge of maturity and they face problems of dating, marriage, home, vocation, and parenthood. The church does not dare to pass them by. Their needs and their instincts are quite apart from those of the Juniors who might be included in the church youth fellowship program. If the reader is interested in a church organized along youth fellowship ideas, he will have to interpret the suggestions as dealing with the young people in junior and senior high school and just beyond.

Protestant Evangelical forces of the United States and Canada have listed the following as the objectives of Christian education for growing people.

1. A consciousness of God as a reality in human experience and a sense of relationship to him.

2. Such an understanding of the personality, life, and teaching of Jesus as will lead to experience of him as Saviour and Lord, loyalty to him and his cause, and will manifest itself in daily life and conduct.

3. A progressive and continuous development of Christian character.

4. The ability and disposition to participate in and contribute to the building of a social order throughout the world, embodying the ideal of the fatherhood of God and the brotherhood of man.

5. The ability and disposition to participate in the organized society of Christians—the church.

6. An appreciation of the meaning and importance of the Christian family and the ability and disposition to participate in and contribute constructively to the life of this primary group.

7. A Christian interpretation of life and the universe; the ability to see that it is God's purpose and plan; a life philosophy built on this interpretation.

8. The assimilation of the best religious experience of the race, preeminently that recorded in the Bible as effective guidance to present experience.

Such a program means a real promotion. The first qualification is the availability of physical space in the church building which may be termed the youth center or the youth lounge. It is difficult to conceive of a good young peoples' program without physical facilities adapted to the purpose. For a class on Sunday a separate meeting place will be sufficient but a larger program will include study and social meetings and a portion of the building must be made available for that purpose.

In the chapters dealing with church building mention is made of multiple purpose rooms. These can have double, triple, or even multiple use. Rooms for youth work fit splendidly into this category. The most meager youth program will offer church school classes for the various church school grades. That is the very minimum youth program. The first extension will probably be some form of a Sunday evening meeting. This may be a general meeting under the formal young peoples' society, an extension of the church school work, or a part of the program of the youth fellowship of the church.

Churches which really seek to serve youth also plan their programs to include weekday activities. These take various directions but most require space in the church building and the youth center in the church soon acquires three uses; Sunday morning, Sunday evening, and weekday. Any quarters available for youth should take care of these needs. Not only classrooms but a youth center is needed to provide class facilities, social facilities, a refreshment bar, and recreational space. If dancing is included in the local church program, there should be a floor suitable for it. Television for entertainment and music will be helpful.

If the group has handcraft hobbies, space should be made available. Books available for those disposed to read is a good idea. There will of course be a piano and possibly a record player. Here is a place for fellowship and fun but also for good religious discussion and social projects.

As with all other parts of the church program, the building should be designed to fit the program. One tragedy to be avoided is to build for class work only and then try to incorporate the larger program into the classrooms. Another bad mistake is to build a youth center and then fail to have a program which utilizes the building. Frankly we do not see how the objectives listed above can be achieved unless the church building provides areas for the basic needs of the program which the parish wishes to carry on. In actual practice many churches do have programs much larger than their buildings could normally support, but as a rule the leaders will find that their efforts are more successful if they have the proper physical facilities.

The Program in Operation

Two of the six objectives belong to the Sunday morning program. A good school with classes for young people together with an adequate service of public worship will help them to learn of God and his church. Both the service of worship and the school have a part in this integration of the religious ideal. In no sense should the school and the service of public worship be competitive.

As we have insisted in the chapter on religious education, one of the limitations of the present church school is that the departmental worship services are too long and too broad. They not only take time needed for learning but in the older age group they definitely compete with the service of public worship.

There is need for a devotional service for the young peoples' department at the church school but it should be simple and direct with the emphasis on prayer. Let youth develop prayer habits rather than listen to adult prayers. Lengthy exhortations by the leaders are to be deplored. Instead place the emphasis on good lesson material and good teachers.

There are many evidences that your young people will cooperate with good leadership but deplore the practice which substitutes personality for knowledge. In a survey made among groups of youth to find why their leaders failed, two outstanding causes were found. The failures were those who either were too ready to criticize or who did not know enough about the things they were trying to teach. Young people do need counselors who are sympathetic and interested in the things which interest them but the matter of age was not mentioned in any of the replies.

The class hours on Sunday morning should concentrate on good lesson material and good teaching. Whatever text book is used, the basis of instruction should be Bible, church, or denominational history. The necessary mechanics of the hour should be taken care of as simply and effectively as possible but no one should be left with the idea that the main purpose of the class is to bring together young people for an hour of pleasant fellowship on Sunday morning.

Attendance at the morning service of public worship should be part of the curriculum for the church school youth department. There may be some reason to try to teach worship to children but young people should learn the art of worship through participation.

One way to get young people to attend the Sunday morning service is to give them some definite task in connection with the service. Included in the features which would interest young people are ushering, choir singing, checking attendance, addressing post cards to absentees, and parking supervision. But since the average church has few opportunities for service in these categories, this is hardly the answer to the needs of youth. Would not the real answer be to organize the church service itself so that it brings to the young people a real worship experience and leads them into the presence of God. Not every young man or young woman is a one hundred per cent extrovert who must find his God through showing people to their seats or displaying his voice from the choir loft. More young people are definitely interested in the worship experience than we sometimes realize. They are doubtless more mystically inclined than the previous generation.

In a survey reported by Nevin C. Harner in his book *Youth Work in the Church* (Abingdon) some interesting thoughts regarding worship were revealed. The survey sought to compare the experiences of young people who attended liturgical services to those of young worshippers in free churches.

1. Do you feel that you really worship God during the morning service?

Free Church Youth	Yes, 20	No, 4 ·
Liturgical Youth	Yes, 15	No, 0

2. Can you recognize a certain progression in your own worship experience as the service moves along?

Free Church Youth   Yes, 6   No, 9
Liturgical Youth   Yes, 11   No, 2

3. Are there any portions of the service which make you feel very keenly the sense of God's presence?
The young people from the Free service mention music, prayers and sermon most frequently. The young people from the Liturgical churches mention the confession and the absolution, and the prayers. Four of the latter groups mention the moments of silence, often with organ music in the background.

4. If you could make one change in the service of your church, what would it be?
The young people of the Free churches want more liturgy and more music. One, however, asked for less music. Several suggest shorter sermons. The young people from the Liturgical services asked for greater variety in the service.

One interesting fact in this survey is that not one mentioned the reading of the Scripture as an inducement to worship. On the whole this study is very interesting in showing that young people definitely do recognize that the purpose of the morning service is to worship God. They seem to recognize a progression in worship. The probabilities are that today's young people will be more eager for the experience of worship than they were when the volume which contains this survey was written. The recovery of worship has been one of the interesting developments of our day.

For the preacher this is very interesting. He should learn that the way to attract young people to his services is not by turning the morning service into a revival meeting or a campfire song fest. He must perfect the service of worship so that the techniques hallowed by history can be utilized to full advantage.

Young people like some liturgy, yet there seems to be a wearisome feeling if little variety is given. Some feel that prayers could have a little more personal meaning so far as they are concerned. They need to understand the purpose of worship. In the liturgical churches where they have received instruction in this they seem to understand that motion is a part of the service. Free churches need to give such instruction to their youth so that they also will see worship as movement or progression. Understanding the drama of the penitents coming to the church and the open acknowledgement of sin followed by the absolution, the period of instruction and consecration, and finally the benediction, gives that important quality to their worship. Yet how realistic is this drama in today's world?

Just what kind of sermons do young people like? A number say that they like short sermons. That probably means that they like interesting sermons. It surely does not mean that the sermon should be filled with popular stories or juvenile language. It surely means that the sermons should be vital and presented in such a way that the thought challenges the youth who sit in the service. It does not mean that the minister is to water down the content—rather, to express his thought in an orderly and appealing way.

Sunday Evening Program

The morning program has its emphasis on learning of God and the church. The evening program will normally turn toward society and the place of youth. Fellowship has an important part and there is always the danger of trying to make this meeting a second Sunday school or a second worship service. The old Christian Endeavor topics and those of other youth organizations were religious at the core. The church in its entire approach to youth emphasized religion. The program for a Sunday evening meeting might go like this:

6:00 P.M. Supper.
7:00 P.M. Brief worship.
7:30 P.M. Presentation of the subject of the evening.
8:15 P.M. Discussion.
9:30 P.M. Adjournment.

The program of this evening session is most important. There are several ways of approaching it. A program committee must decide what material is to be presented. The program adopted may be the study of a book on a vital subject. The world is so full of material today that making a choice is difficult. It could deal with war and peace, American democracy, social security programs, the rising East or any of many subjects; or, if the committee prefers, it may be a very personal program dealing with dating, marriage, children in the home, and kindred subjects. If a book is selected, the leader for the course should follow the text pretty closely. Copies could be purchased by the groups so they could be brought up to date for each week's lessons.

Again, the committee might decide to invite various speakers to the meeting to talk of their own specialities. From the civic agencies may come those who speak with authority on juvenile delinquency, city zoning laws, local relief work, new housing needs and purposes, city recreational program—and many other themes. Very valuable information can be brought in this way. This sort of a "pot-luck" may not provide the continuity of a text book but it usually produces much personal interest.

A third method is to select a text and have various members present the subject to the group. Of the three this probably produces the most effective leadership but mediocre instruction. A friendly spirit of informality should characterize the Sunday evening session. Boy friends and girl friends have the privilege of sitting together during the sessions. The personal discipline is a quiet kind and lectures on conduct are unusual. The counselor becomes a very important part of this session as he does at any weekday activity. His or her personality is most important in the whole scheme of things.

The Weekday Session

Nearly every church has classes for young people during the morning hour. Many add to this the Sunday evening session and a few provide a mid-week session. Some parents object to their young people staying out at night and competition with the schools is strong. With juvenile delinquency growing in many cities there is a feeling that a curfew should be enforced. But the biggest reason for few weekday activities is that churches have not sensed the need of supplementing their youth work.

The Sunday morning and Sunday evening gatherings have been given definite patterns but these do not begin to fill the needs of youth. There is still a whole area of class and individual projections which can be undertaken under the title "exemplifying Christianity."

Parishes which have set up church nights find it easy to include the youth in the dinner fellowship and then permit them to go to their own rooms. Churches which include in their winter program "The University of Life" naturally include a time for youth. In some communities, the churches and schools cooperate in a youth night. The evening is set in advance as part of a cooperative program and the schools agree to let the churches provide the program for the young people for that night. School assignments can be made appropriate for the activity. The denominations which stress youth fellowship programs insist that meetings be held between Sundays.

> Special weekday meetings of many types are an established part of the program of most Youth Fellowships. These include banquets and other social events, dramatics, 'song fests,' business meetings, work projects, service activities, coaching clinics, interchurch leagues, conferences, rallies, and retreats. These must be timed on the monthly calendar so as to avoid unnecessary competition, and to fit into the schedules of the young people who are in the group. The test of whether a Youth Fellowship is really functioning lies in the use it makes of weekday opportunities to express the ideas discussed on Sunday in practical life, in group fellowship, and in service projects. (Oliver deWolf Cummings, *The Youth Fellowship*. Judson, 1956.)

Those who insist that a weekday meeting is necessary are usually reluctant to set up a definite pattern for these meetings. Here the program must follow local practice. Where a church has achieved a comprehensive youth program through working with established organization, such cooperation may provide the basis for weekday meetings. The Y groups, 4-H, and hobby clubs may be included in the program while keeping their regional relationships. Some leaders would prefer to discontinue relationships with these groups and to take control of the entire program.

The between Sunday program is not a study period but a time for fellowship. One program may be much different from another. Possibilities include banquets, dramatizations, hobby sessions, handcraft experiments, interchurch youth rallies, and retreats. Here is an opportunity for the young people to use their ingenuity. There are of course many areas for personal and collective projects. In a broad sense the between Sunday program is one of action. Religious discussions should not be barred and prayer and expression services can have a place, but youth should seek its own solutions.

Young people often undertake projects such as painting walls, mending hymnbooks, and developing a library. A workshop meeting can be held for instruction in the use of projectors, recorders, and other electronic equipment so vital to church programs. The meetings can provide opportunities for mission study or visits to the city mission or county jail. If desired, visits to churches of other faiths can easily be arranged.

The group might want to visit the various social agencies of their own city to see how the Community Fund is spent. It can visit interracial groups and Christmas baskets for the needy are always a worthy project. In other words, the best program for between Sunday work is one of expression—simply putting Christianity into action.

The many activities which bring Christian fellowship and experience to youth include the summer camp, retreat, or training school. Young people are natural prospects for these. The experience of meeting with others in worship, play, and project work can be personally rewarding and stimulating. Such camps are available to most churches today and many of them are denominationally owned and directed.

The Leadership of Youth

Youth work requires good leadership. Some teachers and superintendents are qualified for this, but others are more efficient in the teaching hour than in the leadership of weekday activities. Still others may be needed for personal counseling which is the most difficult task of all. The denominations which have official youth fellowships suggest that each age group fellowship have (a) a superintendent for the departmental session; (b) a sponsor for the evening meeting; (c) an adviser to the weekday club groups; and (d) a chief counselor to the cabinet.

In actual practice the same person may assume two or even more of these duties. As the meetings are usually coeducational, many churches try to find a married couple to take over the duties of the adviser. In each of these areas a program is worked out in advance so the duties can be clearly stated. Both the Presbyterian and Methodist handbooks on youth fellowship suggest that teachers of high school groups may also serve as advisers in program activities.

Where clubs such as the Y or 4-H or other groups are included in the youth program they should be tied to the church through the appointment by the Board of Christian Education of an adviser and counselor. Outside of formal counseling in helping to set up programs and to direct the progress falls a mass of individual counseling. Here the pastor of the church can best serve the youth of his church. Fortunate is the pastor to whom the young people turn for direction in their problems.

The pastor, however, need not be the only individual available for this personal counseling. Not every person is qualified, but in the average church there will be some person or perhaps a married couple, who will be glad to accept the assignment. The late Norman E. Richardson produced the following test by which an individual can check his own qualities. It looks like a long chart but it is an effective one.

Qualifications for a Youth Counselor

The items in this check list are classified under the following ten headings:

   I. PERSONAL FITNESS.
  II. INAUGURATING THE CONFERENCE.
 III. OBJECTIVES OF THE CONFERENCE.
 IV. ESTABLISHING AND MAINTAINING RAPPORT.
  V. GETTING AT THE FACTS.
 VI. INTERPRETING THE FACTS.
VII. EFFECTING A TURNING POINT.
VIII. DETERMINING REMEDIAL MEASURES.
 IX. ENLISTING CO-OPERATION IN REMEDIAL PROCEDURE.
  X. BRINGING THE CONFERENCE TO A CLOSE.

In measuring the efficiency of your current practice as a counselor, place opposite each one of the 150 items listed below a figure which represents your estimate of your own degree of efficiency with reference to that item. Use either 0, 1, 2, 3, 4, or 5. Let 0 stand for failure and 5 for superior excellence. Let 3 stand for average or fairly good. Then 4 may be used to designate above average or very good; 2 will stand for below average; and 1, for very poor. Take the sum of these 150 numbers and divide them by 750. This will give you the percentage rating of your efficiency.

PERSONAL FITNESS

1. Can I be trusted with confidences?

2. Am I the kind of person whom people in trouble seek out and to whom they like to come?

3. Do I have broad and varied personal interests—do I contact human life at many different points?

4. Do I maintain a wholesome outlook upon life; am I free from serious emotional defects such as chronic resentment, grouchiness, anxiety, frustration, crankiness, loneliness?

5. Is my record one of square dealing and true friendship with all who have sought my counsel?

6. Do I have sufficient social imagination and sympathy to put myself in the place of the one who comes to me for help and to give that help no matter how inconvenient or costly to myself?

7. Can I keep a proper distance between myself and the one seeking counsel; am I sufficiently deliberate and objective to understand his problem?

8. Can I identify such attitudes as remorse, penitence, grief, regret, shame, repentance, sorrow, bewilderment, and other mental characteristics of persons suffering from problems that baffle or agitate them?

9. Do I have a sense of humor?

10. While counseling, do I maintain sufficient self detachment to keep from getting emotionally involved beyond the point of genuine sympathy; can I be gentle and firm?

11. Am I free from morbid curiosity and indelicate inquisitiveness?

12. Do I find deep, personal satisfaction in helping others solve their personality-adjustment or social-adjustment problems; do I feel the worthwhileness of it?

13. Do I know how to cross-examine people so as to get at the facts—how to formulate and ask questions that lead directly and honestly to the real problem?

14. Can I expedite an interview without leaving the impression that I am merely a "professional listener" or one who dallies along without a clear purpose?

15. Am I patient; can I keep from premature interpretation or classification of the problem under consideration?

16. Am I trying to become increasingly intelligent and skillful in helping others to lift repressions and to dissolve harmful tensions, thus aiding them to secure release, naturalness and spontaneity of self-expression?

17. Am I ambitious to excel as a counselor or personal consultant, and am I doing all I can to improve myself in regard to this kind of service?

18. Is my counsel regarding religious matters backed up by a wholesome, vital, and developing religious life?

INAUGURATING THE CONFERENCE

19. Are my talks to groups often the forerunners of conferences with individuals?

20. Am I alert to discern the influence of immediate surroundings upon the procedure and the outcome of conferences with individuals; do I realize the difference between a street car and a study as a place for holding a conference?

21. Can I talk on the subject of personality adjustment so as to awaken interest and confidence?

22. Do all sorts of people consider me approachable; am I easily available for counseling, capable of being informal or formal, as the occasion demands?

23. Am I able to control conversation so as to make a transition from casual to serious matters, thus inaugurating the consideration of the personal problem to be discussed?

24. Do I appreciate the natural reticence or hesitation of people to enter into a conference in which they may have to expose their minds, their personal affairs, or their life histories?

25. Do I understand the values and the handicaps, when beginning a conference of catching people off guard, of getting unpremeditated answers?

26. Am I able to make a shrewd guess whether to do the talking or to let the one seeking counsel talk freely?

27. Am I sufficiently well informed to identify the symptoms of various kinds of mental and personality problems and thus start the conference in the best way?

28. Am I alert and firm in avoiding responsibility for the treatment of mental diseases that cannot be cured by counseling?

OBJECTIVES OF THE CONFERENCE

29. Do I really understand and appreciate the value and beauty of a strong, sound, released, and useful personality?

30. Do I have a clear understanding of what personal counseling can accomplish in facilitating the orderly development of personalities toward increasing strength, soundness, spontaneity, and usefulness?

31. Am I convinced that I have a moral right and responsibility, under certain conditions, to make the resources of my personality available to others and thus to help improve or salvage human life?

32. Do I try to arrive at an immediate alleviation or solution of particularly acute problems?

33. Do I take full advantage of the specific opportunity presented in each conference?

34. Do I appreciate the invio-lability and intrinsic value of human personality, no matter what are its needs, scars, or limitations?

35. Do I know how far to go in order to get the maximum, useful results out of each conference?

36. Do I follow through to a definite outcome—tactfully overcoming all obstacles?

37. Do I let the one seeking counsel work out his own salvation in so far as he is able to do so, after having received my counsel?

38. Do I distinguish between an immediate and an ultimate or remote objective; do I keep from trying to do too much, all at once?

39. Do I differentiate between the particular aim of an immediate conference and the general or comprehensive needs of the one seeking help?

40. Can I recognize and differentiate situations in which the need is dominantly intellectual or cognitive, emotional, or habits of living?

41. Am I able to help the one seeking counsel, personally to appropriate and make use of the help given him?

42. Can I visualize or picture the personality of the one seeking counsel, after his needs shall have been met, his problem solved, and he has been made whole—has become capable of

living what, for him, is the abundantly useful and satisfying life?

43. If I am unable to handle the situation do I refer the one seeking counsel to another person who will be able to help him?

44. Am I deeply interested in helping people to find in religion as well as in science, the unfailing source of a sound, strong, released, and useful personality?

ESTABLISHING AND MAINTAINING RAPPORT

45. Am I versatile in making use of the social attitudes of domination, inducement, compliance, and submission?

46. Am I alert to detect a general attitude of insincerity or an attempt to "put something over" on me?

47. Am I skillful in stimulating or motivating cooperation on the part of the one seeking counsel; can I make him feel at ease?

48. Do I keep the conversation on the level of the experience and intelligence of the one seeking counsel?

49. Do I respect the point of view expressed sincerely by the one seeking counsel, even though it is wrong?

50. Do I avoid unprofitable argumentation or clash of opinions?

51. Do I avoid putting the one seeking counsel on the defensive or forcing him to argue his case or become entrenched in a wrong attitude?

52. Do I avoid procedures that might lead to subsequent personal embarrassment or loss of confidence?

53. Do I sensitively avoid the unnecessary uncovering of tender or embarrassing factors in the mental furnishings of the one seeking counsel?

54. If severity is necessary, is it employed deliberately and not in a hot-headed manner?

55. Am I particular to keep from unnecessarily humiliating the one seeking counsel; from depriving him of the power of recovery?

56. Do I give the one seeking counsel a square deal making sure to take no unfair advantage of him?

57. Do I carefully avoid the professional, "wooden," it's-all-in-the-day's-work attitude?

58. Do I avoid any punitive or threatening attitude that might injure the cooperative or spontaneous spirit on the part of the one seeking counsel; am I free from a false superiority that tries to cover up a sense of fear or a feeling of incompetency?

59. Do I safeguard the bond of sympathy or cooperative fellowship throughout the counseling period,—do I avoid arbitrariness

or dogmatism as the conference proceeds?

60. Am I alert to avoid the use of scientific or technical language that is unfamiliar to the one seeking counsel?

61. Am I sure that all questions asked are within the comprehension and clear understanding of the one seeking counsel; do I try to prevent hazy or fuzzy answers?

62. Am I careful not to proceed faster than those who seek counsel can assimilate and apply?

63. Do I give abundant opportunity to the one seeking counsel to state his case frankly and without feeling that he ought to safeguard himself or protect his personal interests?

64. Can I justify the expectation of the one seeking counsel when he looks for constructive suggestions, new insights, moral support, or some other form of real help?

GETTING AT THE FACTS

65. Do I go after the facts in a straightforward, tactful, but persistent manner?

66. In making the diagnosis, am I careful not to use dishonorable or shady methods?

67. Do I go through the motions of getting at the facts even when I think I know what they are?

68. Am I alert to identify errors in judgment, false inferences, lapses of memory, misunder-standings, and other unintentional errors on the part of the one seeking counsel?

69. Do I maintain a matter-of-fact or strictly fact-finding attitude during the process of getting at the facts; do I encourage straight thinking?

70. Am I alert and firm in checking any tendency on the part of the one seeking counsel, to depart from the facts, to evade them, to cover them up, or to falsify them in any way?

71. Do I check any tendency on the part of the one seeking counsel, to substitute inferences, private opinions, or personal interpretations for the facts?

72. Do I watch out for the use of "artful dodger" tactics or purposeful indefiniteness on the part of the one seeking counsel?

73. If a bad start has been made, do I skillfully make a new approach?

74. Do I give enough guidance and encouragement to keep the fact-finding process moving until it has been completed?

75. Am I skillful in formulating and asking questions so as to draw out needed information?

76. Do I make sure that my questions and suggestions are clearly understood and applied to the situation in hand?

77. In getting additional information, do I make skillful use of the information which the one

seeking counsel provides readily or has already given?

78. Am I alert to study the reliability of answers given to my questions or suggestions?

79. Am I careful to scrutinize any answer which the one seeking counsel may make, even if he did not understand the question?

80. Do I avoid posing as having more information than I really possess?

81. Do I avoid getting involved in rationalizations or in wishful, sentimental thinking?

82. When uncertain about it, do I check up on the reliability of what has been offered as fact information; do I consult supplementary sources of knowledge?

83. Am I alert to detect misrepresentation of the facts whether intentional or unintentional and every other mode of crooked thinking?

84. Am I undeceived by the ability of the one seeking counsel to appear frank, open faced, sincere, and honest while covering up important information or even being untruthful?

85. Do I keep the conference on a sufficiently objective or impersonal basis to prevent embarrassment in getting at and facing the facts?

86. Do I avoid interruptions or distractions while the one seeking counsel is honestly trying to get at the facts and to relate them?

87. Do I make a clear distinction between relevant and irrelevant matters; do I cut out wandering, meandering thinking?

88. Do I pass over trivial or inconsequential matters as quickly as possible?

89. Do I avoid suggestions that might deflect the conference from its primary purpose or outcome?

90. Am I alert to discern the "protected area" and to keep the fact-finding activity directed toward it,—possibly by the use of varied approaches?

91. Do I refrain from insisting upon or suggesting unnecessary or irrelevant exposure of the personality or the life history of the one seeking counsel?

92. Do I avoid impertinent curiosity or irrelevant inquisitiveness?

93. Am I careful not to prejudge or to decide prematurely the pertinency of facts under consideration?

94. Am I alert to observe emotional conditions on the part of the one seeking counsel, that make it prudent to discontinue the conference for the present?

95. Do I keep at the fact-getting task until all the pertinent facts are brought to light, in spite of the difficulties to recall them?

96. Just as soon as all the facts are out "on the table," do I proceed to their interpretation?

INTERPRETING THE FACTS

97. Do I realize that matters that seem trivial in themselves may be of great consequence when intimately related to a life history?

98. Do I interpret the facts in the light of the personality traits or general constitution of the one seeking counsel?

99. Am I careful not to draw hasty or superficial inferences from the facts as presented?

100. Am I alert to take into account the cultural or family background of the one seeking counsel?

101. Can I differentiate between a sincere desire for advice and a request for confirmation, validation, or approval?

102. While the conference is progressing, am I alert to take into account the personal bearing of the one seeking counsel, thus getting hints concerning the meaning of the facts?

103. As soon as I have all pertinent facts in mind, do I deliberate carefully and independently in an effort to reach a decision as to their meaning?

104. In reconstructing the situation, do I realize that the narrative to which I have listened may have been presented in the wrong chronological or logical order?

105. Do I realize that the interpretation given by the person seeking counsel may be biased —reflecting his own delinquency or defeat or the projection of his own problem?

106. Do I distinguish between confusion as to what is right or wrong and intentional misbehavior?

EFFECTING A TURNING POINT

107. Do I place squarely up to those seeking help the necessity of and responsibility for making decisions in line with the outcome of the conference?

108. While the conference is in process, am I alert to observe and to take immediate advantage of opportunities to press home the suggested solutions of the problems?

109. Do I express reasonable confidence that the conference will be brought to a successful issue?

110. Am I concretely, specifically helpful to the one seeking counsel as he tries to make up his mind concerning the nature of the problem and what to do about it?

111. Is my counsel convincing; does it inspire confidence?

112. Do I take plenty of time to let the one seeking counsel discover for himself all that is implied in his adopting the suggested solution of his problem?

113. As far as the situation demands it, do I drive home all that is involved in the hearty, personal appropriation of the counsel as given?

114. Do I distinguish between superficial or impulsive reactions to proposed solutions and those that are the result of sober reflection and deliberate intention?

115. Do I make sure that false interpretations of the problem are fully surrendered before the new suggested solutions are adopted?

116. Is my own sincerity and moral earnestness so contagious that it helps to start the one seeking counsel on the road to recovery?

117. If the one seeking counsel lacks confidence in his ability to apply it to himself or seriously to take it to heart, do I help him to find and appropriate adequate resources outside of himself?

118. Do I distinguish between solutions that involve new personal adaptations to existing conditions and those that involve the necessity of breaking with them and seeking a new environment?

119. Whenever a new moral attitude is necessary, do I guide those who seek my counsel through a complete and thorough-going act of repentance?

120. Am I able to engender faith and confidence in myself before offering specific counsel?

DETERMINING REMEDIAL MEASURES

121. Is the counsel which I give clearly applicable and useful to the one seeking it; is it free from the influence of my own predilections; am I capable of doing a real job?

122. Do I make sure that stock phraseology does not get in the way of clear understanding of what is involved in the recommended attitudes or conduct?

123. While the diagnosis is going on, do I watch out for hints that are helpful in coming to a conclusion concerning remedial suggestions?

124. Do I avoid the use of "specifics," making sure to understand the uniqueness of every person's personality-adjustment problem?

125. Do I help clear the mind of the one seeking counsel, of reliance upon stock remedies?

126. Do I make it very clear where reliable sources of personal help may be found, either privately or from some other source?

127. Do I refrain from giving information that would do harm or would interfere with effecting a solution of the problem?

128. If new information is needed from the one seeking counsel, in addition to what is immediately available, do I make adequate provision so that he can secure it?

129. If new attitudes are to be assumed, do I make sure that

they are clearly understood and cherished?

130. If new habits are to be formed, do I follow through until they are well established?

ENLISTING CO-OPERATION IN REMEDIAL PROCEDURE

131. Do I put squarely up to the one who has accepted counsel, his responsibility for doing all in his power to solve his own problem and live a new life?

132. Am I able to give sound specific counsel concerning the remedial values of faith in God?

133. Can I give good, practical advice concerning the value of prayer, corporate or common worship, the devotional study of the Bible, participation in the sacraments, and other sources of religious help?

134. Do I awaken reasonable expectation and confidence with respect to results, provided the counsel given is heartily adopted?

135. Do I safeguard the self respect of the one seeking counsel —helping him to see the difference between his true self and the defect in his personality?

136. Do I help the one seeking counsel to see himself and his relation to his problem, objectively?

137. Am I careful not to force or to superimpose my own opinions upon the one seeking counsel but rather, to guide him as he thinks through his own problem to a sound solution?

138. Do I improve morale and enliven hope on the part of those who have received and adopted my counsel?

BRINGING THE CONFERENCE TO A CLOSE

139. Am I careful to make a thorough job of it, before bringing the conference to a close?

140. Do I bring the counseling period to a close as soon as it has achieved its purpose and has reached the point of diminishing returns or of negative results?

141. After the turning point has been reached, do I concentrate attention upon bringing the conference to a fitting close in which life is seen again in its wholeness?

142. After I have exhausted the vital possibilities of the conference, do I express personal interest in the remaining task of transforming the counsel into personality or character traits in the one who has sought my help?

143. If it becomes clear that the problem cannot be cleared up in one conference, do I make adequate preparation for a subsequent conference or a continuation of this one?

144. If another conference is needed, do I make definite plans concerning its place and date?

145. As the conference comes to an end, do I, by intercessary prayer, the gift of a book, or in some other definite way, show genuine, personal interest in the one who has sought and received counsel,—is he justified in assuming that he can rely upon me for further help as he takes up the recommended, creative activity?

146. Am I on my guard against abnormal or unnecessary expressions of gratitude or appreciation on the part of the one who has received counsel?

147. After the conference is over, do I keep in vital touch by correspondence or personal contact with the one who has sought counsel?

148. Am I free from an unwarranted desire for appreciation of or expressed gratitude for any service I may have rendered?

149. Do I encourage those who have personality-adjustment problems to make the solutions of those problems the objects of prayer as well as of study?

150. In bringing the conference to a close, do I suggest strongly a wholesome balance between self reliance and reliance upon God or upon friends: Do I point out the dangers of unwarranted self reliance and excessive reliance upon God, the sacraments, and the ministry of friends?

Youth Work

BOWMAN, C. M., *Ways Youth Learn*. Harper, 1952.

BURKHART, R. A., *From Friendship to Marriage*. Harper, 1937.

———, *Understanding Youth*. Abingdon, 1936.

CONVIS, L. A., *Adventures into the Church*. Harper, 1951.

CUMMINGS, O. De W., *Guiding Youth in Christian Growth*. Judson, 1955.

———, *The Youth Fellowship*. Judson, 1956.

FERRARI, E. P., *Its Worth Your Life*. Friendship, 1956.

FINEGAN, J., *Youth Asks About Religion*. Association, 1949.

GESELL, A., *Youth, the Years from 10 to 16*. Harper, 1956.

HARNER, N. C., *I Believe*. Christian Education, 1950.

———, *Youth Work in the Church*. Abingdon, 1942.

LUTZ, P. H., *The Quest for God Through Understanding*. Bethany, 1937.

OVERTON, G. S., *Living with Parents*. Broadman, 1954.

SPAULDING, H. F., *Youth Looks at the Church*. National Council, leaflet.

STOCK, H. T., *Church Work with Young People*. Abingdon, 1929.

TANI, H. N., *Ventures in Youth Work*. Judson, 1954.

WITTENBERG, R. M., *How to Help People*. Association, 1953.

26 | WOMEN IN THE CHURCH

FROM THE FIRST CENTURY WOMEN HAVE BEEN ACTIVE
in the Christian church. Since women gathered around the empty
tomb on Easter morn they have been serving the church. Every
New Testament reader knows of Lydia, the seller of purple;
Dorcas who was healed by Peter; Priscilla, wife of Acquila
who was a Christian disciple and teacher; Mary, the mother of
Mark who opened her home for the Last Supper; Eunice, the
mother of Timothy; and Phoebe, the servant (deaconess) of the
church at Cenchrea.

Whether Paul was a bachelor may be debatable but it is
evident that he had much respect for these women who were
leaders in the local churches and wrote of them in the highest
terms. Deaconesses appeared in the early centuries and the
"widows" were given positions of honor in the local churches.
The historic Roman church gave women a prominent place and
many are the names of saints and leaders who showed splendid
administrative qualities in the running of the convents.

The Protestant churches have been reluctant to yield the
higher ordinations to women. Some churches including Baptist, Disciples of Christ, and United Brethren have for years
ordained women to the ministry. The Methodists now give
them ordination and the Presbyterian Church in the U.S.A.
has recently given to women the privilege of ordination. The
Episcopal churches do not grant it at this time nor do the
Evangelical and Reformed nor the Lutheran bodies.

During the last half of the nineteenth century the women of
the church found expression for professional religious work
through service as deaconesses. During the years between 1885
and 1900, an estimated one-hundred fifty institutions for the

training of deaconesses were organized in the United States. The functions of the deaconess were somewhat pastoral. She made regular calls on the homes of the parish, had responsibilities in the training of youth, and similar duties. She usually wore a specialized garb which identified her and her work. The Episcopal, Methodist, and Lutheran Churches in particular emphasized this type of full-time service.

Do not confuse the professional deaconess mentioned in these paragraphs with the office of the deaconess in the local church. Many denominations make provision for a board of deaconesses which somewhat parallels the board of deacons. The women who hold this office are in no sense a part of the ministry of the church but are a group to which is assigned certain charitable and other functions. It is a secondary board used largely to integrate the women into the work of the parish.

The Lambeth Conference of 1930 definitely recognized the deaconess as belonging to the ministry of the church. "The order of Deaconess is for women the one and only order of the ministry which we can recommend to our branch of the Catholic Church to recognize and use." Powell Mills Dawley in his volume *The Episcopal Church and Its Work* says:

> The traditional means of ministerial activity of women, apart from religious orders, has been through the office of the deaconess. This revival of a primitive office in the Church's life came toward the end of the nineteenth century when associations of women for the purpose of serving the Church had become numerous. In 1889 canonical recognition of such vocations was made in the provisions of canon law governing the ministry of deaconesses.

In the Methodist Church the deaconess was not given any ordination but rather consecration for her task as a special lay function. During the past two generations the number of institutions training women for this work has lessened and the number of women taking up the work has decreased. This may be because of new opportunities opening up for women to serve the church in other ways.

In the denominational organizations women are now given prominent positions of authority. Some denominations have boards entirely sponsored by women and usually staffed entirely by women. The profession of "Director of Religious Education" has provided employment for thousands of women in denominational work and in local churches. As the training schools for deaconesses declined, the number which train women for educational work has increased.

In addition to the educational work, local churches still use women as parish visitors and in many churches they serve on secretarial and clerical staffs or as hostesses and dining room supervisors. The Church probably has never had as many women in full time employment as it has at the present time.

The future status of women in the ministry of Protestantism remains problematical. With the growing importance of women in many social and professional areas, the pressure upon the denominations to ordain women to the ministry is tremendous. Some women who have served as pastors have distinguished themselves and done splendid work. To this date very few, if any, of the larger churches have called women to their pulpits. Maude Royden, a communicant of the Church of England, could not receive ordination in that church but was ordained into a Congregational Church in England, serving for a while as associate minister of The City Temple, London.

We should point out that the Protestant Episcopal Church does recognize religious orders for women and there are at the present time fifteen connected with that church. These orders set up institutions and give themselves to relief of the poor, teaching in needy areas, and training women for active life in the local parishes. Requirements for entering these institutions parallel, to a degree, those specified by Roman Catholic orders.

While women will find it difficult to secure recognition for pastoral work there will be undoubtedly a growing opportunity for them to serve in the field of religious education. Churches are increasing in size and resources. The larger churches have not only a general director of Christian Education but departmental directors. Every such position filled by a woman releases a man who may be valuable as a pastor for a local church.

One who aspires to the position of educational director should plan to take courses on religion in college and then supplement this with work in a graduate school of Christian Education. Some schools still train at the collegiate level but future requirements will demand more specialized training.

The woman who aspires to a secretarial position needs a dual preparation. She should know very well the history of the denomination in which she plans to serve and also its ecclesiastical organization. In addition, she needs to be a proficient stenographer and typist and understand orderly business procedures. As a rule the equipment in a church office will parallel that of a business office, so business training will be helpful. The same rules of conduct will apply. She in addition must have sense to appreciate the need of keeping her eyes open but her conversation cautious. This of course applies to a business organization as well as a church office.

Women's Organizations in a Local Church

Officially and unofficially, women have always been important in the local church. In fact so many of the lay tasks were left to women that when the every member canvass was introduced, churches found it difficult to secure men to assume the responsibilities for the work.

The women discovered that chicken pie suppers could bring in money to help pay the local church expenses and their leadership filled the basement dining rooms of churches pioneering in the new America. We do little justice to this contribution by laughing it off as unimportant. The social virtues in the program went unrecognized at the time. The church suppers became the big social events of the church year. Families drove for miles to participate; they became acquainted with their neighbors. Local young men and women found opportunities for quiet talks and the long rides home provided a means for courtship. In the eyes of history the monetary contribution of the church supper may have been small, but its social contribution was significant. And many a minister's son knows that the dollars which came from these activities helped to provide shoes and food for growing families. This pioneering activity has been changed, but not eliminated from our churches.

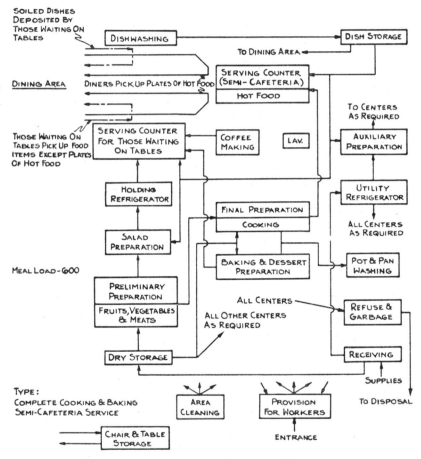

A well-organized church kitchen. The kitchen is still an important part of the women's work in the church. One organized such as this is the pride and joy of those who supervise food service. (From Clarence W. Schroeder, *Food Service*. Published by the Hotpoint Company, Chicago. Used by permission.)

The leaders became conscious, however, that the women's work of the church should be more than raising money by providing meals. The evolution of the program was a three-pronged organization of the women of the church: (a) The Bible Class; (b) The Ladies Aid; and (c) The Missionary Society.

The Women's Bible Class has been and still is important in the life of the local church. It has its Sunday meeting under a competent leader. Usually an evening meeting is held sometime during the month stressing fellowship, with a discussion, a light lunch, and a business session. The fully developed class needs officers and especially a calling committee to keep contact with its members. The class fits into the program of religious education and is subject to the educational board of the church. Often, however, adult classes fail to appreciate the entire program of education and refuse cooperation in the use of space and equipment. This will limit the service which the class might render.

The second prong of the organization of this historic evolution was the Ladies' Aid Society. This consisted of the women who felt a love of the church and believed that they could best serve by raising money to help build the budget of the church. They were the Marthas of the church. They could easily pray to the "Lord of pots and pans and kettles." As we have mentioned above they made their contribution.

The third prong was the Ladies' Missionary Society. This organization had a dual purpose. Its members studied the foreign mission work of the church and raised money which was sent to a board to help the cause. Many societies have had their own projects. Often they took the lead in packing food and clothing to be sent to some home mission field. For some reason or another the missionary societies found it difficult to sustain vitality and the individual societies began to dwindle in numbers and works. We must be fair and acknowledge that they were a sustaining force for missionary interest.

This change was probably inevitable as we entered an era when local churches, conscious that they needed more unity in their program, sought to bring order out of confusion. Instead of classes, they wanted a program of education; instead of several women's organizations, they needed a department of women's work. Instead of many collections, they needed an all-inclusive budget.

The transition from the several women's program to a united program under an auxiliary, guild, or women's association has not been as difficult as one might suppose. The method has been to combine the various activities in a general organization inclusive of the entire adult female membership of the church. At first it may have been merely a federation. Where the earlier groups went by separate names these were continued. The purpose of the single organization is to eliminate duplication and plan an over-all program for that department of church work.

A pattern for the society depends on the heritage of the local church, but the constitution must be broad enough and inclusive enough to include all groups. For instance the Methodist Church at Winter Park, Florida, some years ago decided to unite all of the women's activities into a guild. They found that they needed the following departments to carry on the work of the various organizations: Missions, Literature, Mite Box, Parsonage, Program, Social, Stewardship, Visitation and Membership, Welfare, Worship, and Junior Work. Each of these departments has to have a secretary. The members are divided into circles. Once each year the membership of the circles is determined by the chairman drawing names from the entire membership of the church. There is a good scriptural basis for this.

The constitution and by-laws provide for monthly meetings of the association and, in addition, monthly meetings of the circles. Each circle has its own chairman, secretary, and treasurer. The executive board consists of the president, vice-president, recording secretary, and corresponding secretary; the secretaries of each of the departments; and the chairmen of each of the circles.

This plan for a unified organization for women is now recommended by all denominations and probably more than half of the local churches are set up on such a basis. The Women's Auxiliary to the National Council of the Protestant Episcopal Church issues a little booklet to the churches of that denomination describing it in detail. For smaller churches it recommends an organization with departments to fit local needs. For the larger churches it

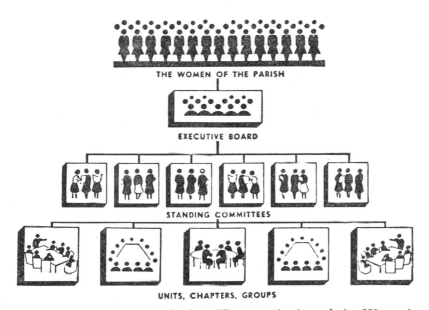

THE WOMEN OF THE PARISH

EXECUTIVE BOARD

STANDING COMMITTEES

UNITS, CHAPTERS, GROUPS

The unified women's organization. The organization of the Women's Auxiliary, as recommended by the Women's Auxiliary of the Protestant Episcopal Church.

recommends a general organization with departments and also groups or circles as in the plan proposed above. Where a unified organization seems to be impossible, a step in the direction would be the federation of the various women's activities. The booklet says in part:

> The success of the unified plan depends to a great degree upon the program which should be comprehensive enough to include projects in all fields from the parish to world-wide mission. The elements of a well balanced program are worship, study, service and fellowship. Service and study go hand in

hand. Since the Woman's Auxiliary does not set up a definite program to be followed by all groups, each parish must study parish, community and diocesan needs. A parish inventory and. a community survey are helpful devices for this purpose.

In the recommended plan the assembly or general meeting which includes all women of the parish meets once a month or once a quarter or when called, but preferably at stated intervals. This meeting emphasizes worship. Group members are drawn by lot from the total membership and the composition of the groups should be changed at least every two years. Meetings should be held once or twice a month. Membership of each circle should not exceed twenty-five. Programs stress fellowship, handwork, and business. Meetings will be informally conducted by the chairman.

The finances of the organization should be placed on a budgetary basis set up in advance. The funds are raised by pledged contributions by the members and supplemented with any income from money raising enterprises. The program of the women's organization is left to the local society. In some instances it may be confined to the church, at home and abroad. In others, social and political subjects are included.

Organizing the Program

The following is taken from the report of a program chairman of a women's society. Since most programs will be created locally and will include references to local personalities we have left these items as they were in the presentation.

Note that the chairman covers five areas of work: Planning, Education, Work Projects, Money Raising, and Budgeting.

Planning

Programs for the year will be definitely planned in advance and printed in booklets, three inches by five inches, entitled "Women's Society Year Book."

Date of Meeting.
Leader.
Music (Name of woman in charge of music for meeting).

Speaker.
Hostess.
Luncheon committee.
Reporter.

The membership will be divided into ten lists, each headed by a captain whose business it is to remind the women on her list of the meeting, to be an enthusiastic booster for the program, and to arrange transportation of those who require it.

An up-to-date filing system to record addresses, attendance, etc., will be an improvement on the old random sheets of paper. All the women of the church are automatically members of the Women's Society, no fees are set. The membership will be divided into four groups, each with two co-chairmen. Each group will raise seventy-five dollars in addition to the money raised by the society as a whole.

Educational Program

SOCIAL SERVICE. A member of our church who is working with the Children's Aid Society will deliver this address.

WOMEN'S PLACE IN THE WORLD TODAY. This will be a panel discussion with six women taking part, two from our society and two from each of two societies in neighboring towns.

WORLD FRIENDSHIP. A college classmate who is a missionary on furlough from Africa will, no doubt, impress us with her enlightening talk.

DO PARENTS UNDERSTAND YOUNG PEOPLE? This will be a discussion led by one of our members.

WHAT OTHER SOCIETIES ARE DOING. Reports will be given by three members after they have gathered fresh ideas from other societies.

CURRENT MISSIONARY NEWS. The most important and up-to-date missionary news will be collected and presented by one of our members.

ILLUSTRATED TRAVEL TALKS. An excellent speaker from the

468   WOMEN IN THE CHURCH

Canadian Pacific Railway will illustrate his talk with beautiful slides, all gratis. No doubt one could secure the same from the Union Pacific Railway.

BOOK REVIEW. A worthwhile book will be chosen and reviewed by one of our members.

RECENT GAINS AND LOSSES IN THE CRUSADE FOR PEACE. One of our members who is particularly acquainted with this subject will bring us up to date in this matter.

WHAT ARE THE STANDARDS OF THE IDEAL HOME? A discussion on this topic will be led by one of our members.

THROUGH THE WINDOW. A distinguished woman who has just returned from a visit to the mission fields of China and Japan has many vitally interesting facts to tell us. She will show her gorgeous foreign costumes by having some of the women model them at the close of her talk.

RECENT TRENDS IN EUROPE. This will be given by an able guest speaker on current events.

THE UNDERPRIVILEGED. A member of our church who is now working in the Social Settlement, Chicago, will familiarize us with her work.

HIGHLIGHTS. Delegates to the State Conference and to the Adult Training Institute will give their reports.

Work Program

The work program will be the charge of a definite committee with special committees working under this general committee.

ARTICLES FOR CHURCH FAIR. Church Fair committees will be in charge of making fancy and work aprons, bridge covers, quilts, pot-holders, towels, dolls, baby clothes.

GOWNS FOR INTERMEDIATE CHOIR. Gowns for the senior choir and the Congo Singers are kept in repair by the gown committee. They will also be responsible for making new gowns for the intermediate choir.

CANE CHAIRS. Many of our chairs require recaning. A committee of women blessed with the ability to do this are taking on the arduous task of caning these chairs.

SUPPLIES FOR MISSION HOSPITALS AND SCHOOLS IN THE SOUTH. The work committee will be in charge of making pillow cases, layettes, tablecloths, etc., and of collecting the essential donations for this work.

PACKING THANKSGIVING AND CHRISTMAS BASKETS.

Money-Raising Plans

CHURCH FAIR. The outstanding event of the year, the church fair in November will engage the time and attention of all the women. As a novel way of arranging the setting we shall have an enchanted cottage with rooms well filled with attractive things to sell. In the cottage may be purchased articles appropriate to each room. Thus one may buy towels, wash cloths, etc. in the bathroom; cushions, fancy work, ornaments, books, etc. in the living room; things to tempt the appetite, home cooking, fruit, pickles, as well as breakfast cloths, dish towels, etc., in the kitchen; and white elephants in the attic. In the dining room the famous turkey dinner will be served.

HOBBY SHOW. What man or woman isn't puffed up with pride when invited to display his or her hobby? Knowing this to be human nature we will artistically arrange an exhibition of diversified hobbies around the dining room. Collections run all the way from old coins to pipes; from china dogs to elephants; from army medals to pictures of movie stars, souvenirs of foreign ports, old glassware, stamps, shawls, and antique furniture. A live mink from a dentist's mink ranch has already been promised.

PAPER PLATES. Instead of mite boxes we plan this year to use picnic paper plates. Each plate will be decorated around the outside with the names of the holidays for the year; for example, Washington's Birthday, Lincoln's Birthday, Christmas. In the center a suitable envelope will be attached. Each member will be given one of these plates and will be urged to celebrate each of the fifteen holidays by placing ten cents in the envelope. From each of these we hope to receive one dollar and fifty cents.

MOTHER AND DAUGHTER BANQUET. For novelty perhaps you

will be more interested in attempting a mother and son banquet, and a father and daughter banquet. Many of our women who have no daughters and who desire to parade their stalwart sons are insisting on this arrangement.

MID-WINTER SPECIAL. This new feature, when the past presidents will be honored, promises to be a success. A special dinner and program will require effective planning.

VALENTINE LUNCHEON. Spring flowers and appropriate decorations will make the dining room attractive, and a postman to deliver valentines will make the occasion a happy one, we trust.

MEMORIAL CANDLE LIGHTING SERVICE. The Women's Society plans to take charge of this for a vesper service. People in the church now and those who have moved away will be contacted and invited to pay one dollar to have a candle lit in memory of some dear one.

BIRTHDAY GARDEN TEA. This will be a June activity on the beautiful lawn of a country home.

MUSICAL TEA AND HOME COOKING SALE. We plan to have two or three of these in the course of the year.

DINNERS AND LUNCHEONS. The society makes money on dinners for various occasions and has proceeds from the Thursday twenty-five cent luncheons.

Budgeting Receipts

The proceeds from endeavors will be used as follows:

Pledge to Missions.
Pledge to Church.
Expenses of Delegates to Summer Conference.
Decorate Church Dining Room.
Finance Vacation Church School.
Materials for New Robes, Chairs, and Dining Room Drapes.

The president of another women's society informs me that for their annual meeting they arranged the room as a railway station with information desk (literature on table), newsstand (books and magazines), first aid (exhibition of White Cross work), telegrams (reports sent in the form of telegrams which two red caps delivered), and placards about the room bearing other information.

The constitution of the Woman's Association of Lakewood Congregational Church, Cleveland, Ohio, which follows is a good example of organization which includes the various features mentioned in this chapter.

Constitution for Women's Association of Lakewood Congregational Church

ARTICLE I—NAME
The name of this society shall be The Women's Association of Lakewood Congregational Church.

ARTICLE II—PURPOSE
The purpose of this society shall be to enlist the women of the Parish in a fellowship of worship, education, service and giving, to undergird the program of the Church as it serves the cause of Christ in the community and throughout the world.

ARTICLE III—MEMBERSHIP
Any woman of Lakewood Church or community who subscribes to the above purpose may be a member of the Woman's Association and shall be entitled to vote, and to all its privileges. Each member of the Association is also a member of one of the Circles into which the membership is divided. Each Circle shall annually choose from among its members (or the Association shall elect) a Leader who by virtue of her office shall be a member of the Executive Board of the Women's Association.

ARTICLE IV—OFFICERS AND ELECTION
SECTION 1. The officers of the Women's Association shall consist of: President, three Vice-Presidents, Corresponding Secretary, Recording Secretary, Treasurer and two Key Women. The officers and chairmen of standing committees and three of the five members of the Nominating Committee shall be elected by the Association at the Annual Meeting.

SECTION 2. The term of office shall be one year. No officer except Treasurer and Key Women shall be eligible for the same office for more than two consecutive terms.

SECTION 3. The Nominating Committee shall consist of five members, three rotating members, one elected each year for a three year term, and two members elected for a one year term nominated from the floor by the Association. The Committee shall make its report at the Annual Meeting of the Association, the report having been posted one week in advance.

SECTION 4. Election of officers shall be held at the Annual Meeting and shall be by ballot, except when the number of candidates does not exceed the number to be elected, in which case the election may be by acclamation.

ARTICLE V—EXECUTIVE BOARD

SECTION 1. The Executive Board of the Women's Association shall consist of the Officers, the Chairmen of Standing Committees, Leaders of Circles, Wives of the Pastors, Special Appointees, such as Historian, Parlimentarian, Sales Tax Chairman, and such others as the Board may designate.

SECTION 2. The duty of the Executive Board shall be to administer the affairs of the Women's Association, increase the efficiency of the work, make recommendations to the Association, fill vacancies except Leaders of the Circles, call special meetings.

ARTICLE VI—MEETINGS

Regular meetings of the Women's Association shall be held the first Wednesday of each month except July and August. Fifty members shall constitute a quorum. Regular meetings of the Executive Board shall be held each month, prior to the meeting of the Women's Association. One half of the members of the Board shall constitute a quorum. The Annual Meeting of the Association shall be held in May. Special meetings of the Board may be called by the President or any three members.

ARTICLE VII—COMMITTEES

Chairmen of Standing Committees are elected. Other members of committees shall be appointed by the President in consultation with the respective chairmen, using a plan of rotation (see page 476) (one new member each year for a committee of three, or two each year for a committee of six to serve three years). The Committees shall be: Devotional and Family Life, Program, World Fellowship Education, Public Affairs, Friendly Service, Finance and Stewardship, House, Hospitality and Membership, Publicity, Flower, Nominating, Ways and Means, and such others as the Board may designate.

Article VIII—AMENDMENTS

This Constitution may be amended at any Regular Meeting of the Association by a two-thirds vote, provided there is a quorum, notice of such amendment having been given at the previous regular meeting or written notice ten days before the meeting.

PARLIAMENTARY AUTHORITY

Robert's Rules of Order shall govern all deliberations of this Association. The Parliamentarian shall advise the presiding officer in question of procedure and parliamentary law.

STANDING RULES

Rule 1—Duties of Officers.

President. The President shall preside at all meetings of the Association and of the Executive Board, and shall appoint all committees, unless otherwise directed. She shall be a member Ex-officio of all committees except the Committee on Nominations, and have general supervision of the work. She shall represent the Women's Association on the Board of Trustees.

First Vice-President. The First Vice-President, shall, in the absence or at the request of the President, preside and perform all other duties required of the President. She shall serve as Chairman of the Program Committee.

Second Vice-President. The Second Vice-President shall in the absence of both the President and the First Vice-President, preside and perform the other duties of the President. She shall be Chairman of the Devotional and Family Life Committee.

Third Vice-President. The Third Vice-President shall be Chairman of the World Fellowship Education Committee, and shall have charge of the World Fellowship programs of the Association.

Recording Secretary. The Recording Secretary shall keep a correct record of the proceedings of all meetings of the Association and of the Executive Board, reading them in their respective bodies.

Corresponding Secretary. The Corresponding Secretary shall assist the President with the correspondence of the Association and shall send or telephone messages at the call of the President.

Treasurer. The Treasurer shall receive all moneys and shall disburse the same upon authority of the Executive Board, approved by the Association. The Treasurer shall see that the books of the Association are closed at the end of the fiscal year and ready for the annual audit.

KEY WOMEN. The Key Women, one denominational, the other interdenominational, shall be the contact persons between the local group and the district and the State. They shall bring to the group information sent to them by the district chairman and state officers, make reports to the Association, promote attendance at denominational and interdenominational meetings, and be responsible for such other duties as will promote the interests of the denomination.

HISTORIAN. Shall make a permanent record of the outstanding events and accomplishments of the Association.

THE DEVOTIONAL AND FAMILY LIFE COMMITTEE seeks to advance the spiritual growth of the members of the organization through devotional services, distribution of Devotional and Family Life literature, encouragement of personal and group devotions, and by stimulating church attendance and giving assistance to the Circles.

THE PROGRAM COMMITTEE is responsible for the program for the meetings of the organization and may advise with the Circle Chairmen about their programs. The Committee shall consist of six members, three following the rotating system. The chairmen of the Devotional Life, Public Affairs, and World Fellowship Education Committees shall constitute the remainder of the Committee.

THE WORLD FELLOWSHIP EDUCATION COMMITTEE shall be in charge of World Fellowship programs and for the obtaining and distribution of such information to the Association and for the promotion of World Fellowship interest.

THE FINANCE AND STEWARDSHIP COMMITTEE is responsible for stewardship education, for preparing the budget to be submitted for approval to the organization. The Treasurer shall be a member, in addition to the rotating members.

WAYS AND MEANS COMMITTEE shall suggest and supervise all money-raising projects of the Association. All such projects must be approved by the Executive Board and Association in advance.

THE FRIENDLY SERVICE COMMITTEE shall study the needs of the community and the mission institutions which may be met by work projects, secure the cooperation of the organization or circles in meeting these needs, and keep the members informed about the institutions. Friendly Service quotas for mission stations and information about them are to be secured from the state or district Friendly Service Chairman.

THE PUBLIC AFFAIRS COMMITTEE is responsible for the presentation and promotion of study of any matters of public interest in a Christian society, local, national or world wide. The Chairman shall be a member of the Public Affairs Committee of the Church.

THE HOUSE COMMITTEE shall consist of two divisions:

1. *The House Maintenance Division* shall cooperate with the House Committee of the Church in proper maintenance of the building.
2. *The Food Service Division* shall have supervision of the kitchen and dining room.
   a. It shall procure a Housekeeper, subject to the approval of the Board.
   b. It shall be directly responsible for the formulation of the luncheon and dinner calendar.
   c. It shall be responsible, directly or indirectly as occasion demands, for the planning, purchasing, preparation and serving of all food. Church organizations may assume this responsibility for food they are serving if they so desire, provided they first check with the Food Service Chairman.
   d. It shall consist of a *Chairman of the Division,* who alone supervises the Housekeeper, and who is member ex officio of the committees which comprise her *Food Service Division;* and of five chairmen of the following committees:
      1. The Purchasing Committee
      2. The Menu-Planning Committee
      3. The Dining-room Service Committee
      4. The Dining-room Decoration Committee
      5. The Pantry and Table-setting Committee
   e. It shall formulate such rules governing the use of the dining-room and kitchen and their equipment, as seem necessary, and upon adoption by the Board, shall implement their enforcement.

THE HOSPITALITY AND MEMBERSHIP COMMITTEE shall seek to enlist every woman in the parish as an active member of the organization, shall promote friendly visitation, shall arrange for a welcoming committee at all meetings, and shall seek other ways of encouraging friendliness in the church and community.

THE PUBLICITY COMMITTEE shall be responsible for Columns, newspaper and poster publicity for all Women's Association meetings and activities.

THE FLOWER COMMITTEE shall supply and arrange flowers for church services and assign them to the Circles for distribution to the sick and shut-ins.

THE RED CROSS COMMITTEE shall have charge of all Red Cross work and Sewing.

Rule 2—CIRCLES.

Circles shall be entitled to:

1. A seat on the Executive Board.

2. Cooperation of the Women's Association for all functions.

3. Access to denominational material, and services of standing committees.

4. Services of Housekeeper.

Circles shall be responsible for:

1. Taking a proportional share in the Association budget.

2. Taking part in the dinner work.

3. Organizing their work along the lines of the standing committees.

4. Encouraging attendance at Association meetings.

All Circles organized in 1950 or later, shall be mixed every two years, beginning in 1953.

Rule 3—AMENDMENTS.

These Standing Rules may be amended at any regular meeting of the Women's Association by a two-thirds (⅔) vote, provided there is a quorum.

ROTATING.

The senior member (one having served two years) of any committee would normally become chairman, but this is not mandatory. It is the duty of the Nominating Committee to make the decision and so recommend in their report, as the Nominating Committee presents a nominee for all elective positions.

This rotating plan cannot apply to the three Vice Presidents, as they are elected as chairmen of their respective committees. The three rotating members of their committee are in addition to the elected chairman.

An Installation Service for the Officers of the Women's Organization

The past president addresses the minister, presenting in turn each of the officers to be installed.

PAST PRESIDENT: Reverend Sir: The members of (use the proper title, guild society, auxiliary, union or other name) have indicated their trust and faith in these women by electing them as officers for the coming year. On behalf of the —————— I present to you —————— elected to be the president.

MINISTER: ——————, do you accept this responsibility placed upon you by your fellow members?

PRESIDENT ELECT: I do.

MINISTER: For the sake of your own spiritual growth, and the force of your example, will you be constant in your attendance at the services of the church and the ——————, and faithfully seek to perform the duties of this office?

PRESIDENT ELECT: I will.

MINISTER: By virtue of my authority as minister of this church, I install you as president of the —————— for the coming year. I present you with this gavel as a symbol of your authority and leadership and with this Bible which shall be a reminder that you shall lead your fellow women in the spirit of worship as well as deliberation and service. May God give you grace to fulfill the duties of your office.

PAST PRESIDENT: I present to you ——————, who has (have) been elected vice-president (presidents), secretary, and treasurer.

MINISTER: Will you accept the responsibilities placed upon you by your fellow members, and will you endeavor to discharge your duties to the best of your ability?

OFFICERS ELECT: I will.

MINISTER: By virtue of my authority as the minister of this church, I install you as leaders in your respective areas of the ——————, reminding you of the responsibility you have for moral and spiritual leadership in this society. May God give you grace to fulfill the duties of the several offices.

PAST PRESIDENT: May I now present the persons who have been selected to be the group (circle) leaders for the ——————. They are ——————.

THE MINISTER: (naming each person in turn). Your work is a most important one for upon you depends the loyalty of those in your group. Do you accept this responsibility and agree to serve according to your ability?

GROUP LEADERS: I do.

MINISTER: By authority given to me as the minister of this church, I now install you as group (circle) chairmen of the ————. May God give you grace to fulfill the duties of your several offices.

INSTALLATION PRAYER BY THE MINISTER:

O Lord, Jesus Christ, who in the days of thy flesh didst accept the services of the faithful women who ministered unto thee, be pleased to call upon these thy servants, called to serve thee in the work of this church, thy grace and heavenly benediction. Help them to walk before thee in humility, yet with a high sense of the duties of their positions. Give them carefulness, unselfishness, faithfulness, wisdom, and zeal in the affairs committed to them. Grant that through their labors the spiritual life of this parish may be quickened and uplifted, to the glory of thy Holy Name. Amen.

Women in the Church

BLACKWOOD, C. P., *How To Be An Effective Church Woman*. Westminster, 1954.

BROWN, A. C., *Handbook for Group Leaders*. Woman's, 1952.

CAVERT, I. M., *Women in American Church Life*. Federal Council, 1948.

KIRK, J., *Group Activities for Women*. Harper, 1954.

NOVOTNY, L., *Women in the Church*. Standard, 1941.

PROHL, R. C., *Women in the Church*. Eerdmans, 1957.

WALLACE, H. K., *Stewardship in the Life of Women*. Revell, 1928.

WYKER, M. A., *Women in the Scheme of Things*. Bethany, 1953.

27 | EVANGELISM IN THE LOCAL CHURCH

THE BASIC PURPOSE OF THE CHRISTIAN CHURCH IS TO evangelize. The great commission given by Jesus Christ is: "Go ye into all the world to make disciples of all nations." The pew worshipper is so badly informed about the purpose of the Christian church that he thinks of evangelism as a minor arc in the entire circle. Instead, evangelism is the circle and the arcs are worship, education, finance, church building, preaching, missionary education, music, pastoral calls, etc. This entire book on church management is a treatise on evangelism, for every technique discussed is part of the program which leads to that end.

Yet, the responsibility for the confusion rests on the clergy of the church rather than the members. The minister who announces a week of evangelistic services increases the confusion. By making the announcement that he is planning evangelistic services he has unconsciously implied that his regular sermons are not in that category.

The clergy also share in the responsibility of classifying evangelism as the preaching and exhortation which secure decisions for the Christian life. Evangelism in this respect becomes a ritual and the minister reduces evangelism to the status of the revival meeting. If he feels that he cannot do so, the church may employ a man who uses the terminology of the revival. The revival meeting is a specialized form of evangelism and any church that feels that that is a complete program in itself is making a big mistake. The revival meeting is not a complete evangelistic program, and likewise a church which does not sponsor revivals may have an effective evangelistic program. In this chapter our hope is to show the evangelistic program of the local church in an all inclusive sense.

Pastoral Evangelism

This subject should be placed ahead of all others because the pastor as the head of the church will influence the entire program of evangelism. The minister's personal techniques include:

1. The regular pulpit ministry.
2. The special evangelistic ministry.
3. His personal counseling ministry.
4. The communicant or confirmation ministry.

Should the regular Sunday morning or evening sermon be produced with the evangelistic purpose in mind? If by evangelism is meant the deepening of the spiritual life of the individual, yes; if it means that each sermon should be followed by a public invitation for people to declare their intentions to become followers of Jesus Christ, the answer is "at times, perhaps."

That the only evangelistic method of preaching asks for personal commitment is one of the errors too frequently made. The purpose of the sermon and the entire service of worship is to deepen the spiritual experience of the individual. That most of those who sit in the pews have previously pledged their discipleship is an indication that they have made in many ways their profession of faith in Jesus Christ and are asking to be fed with the bread of life. The service of public worship is for the feeding of the flock.

The entire atmosphere of the service of worship is quite contrary to the spirit of a revival meeting. A hymnal is used rather than a song book. The tempo is that of reverence rather than one of enthusiasm. To close a service of worship with the language of the revival invitation seems incongruous and the reasoning that makes this necessary is difficult to follow. If the minister makes himself available so people may speak to him or make an appointment to see him in his study, that should be sufficient.

Every sermon, whether the words reveal it or not, should have within it the appeal for a fuller consecration to the things of God. If this presentation is effective, it is good evangelism whether or not an invitation for confession is given. There must be some compromise position between the aesthetics of the service of worship and the tempo of the revival meeting where the two may meet. For the person who appreciates the worship service, the use of revival hymns in the morning service is absurd; to the person who likes revivals the quiet of the sanctuary of work is not inviting.

The minister may find himself in a difficult position when he announces a series of evangelistic sermons. Must he use the revivalist language which he dislikes to conduct evangelist meetings? Can a church hold a successful revival without the songs of invitation ringing in the ears of the worshippers? Must there always be a movement of the converts to the altar? Is the signing of cards a necessary technique of evangelism? Must the minister who in his Sunday morning service presents a sane, rational appeal for Christian living resort to the tabernacle style of emotional presentation and the revival hymns to promote evangelism in his church?

One will say that the technique of the revival meeting has been developed through many years of practice. Men such as Billy Sunday, Billy Graham, and others have found it necessary to place around them the circus atmosphere, the call to the altar, the emotional gospel hymn to get results and there must always be a crowd. The English evangelist, Bryan Green, does not do so. He uses the church. In the place of altar confessions, he uses the counseling room; instead of gospel hymns, he uses the historic hymns of the English church and he gets results. But there is a general feeling that to hold a successful evangelistic service the revivalist atmosphere of music, marching feet to the altar, and the hymn of invitation are necessary.

The weeknight mission in which the minister tries to present the dogmas of the church in an orderly, sensible way has not been too successful in Protestant churches though it seems profitable for the Roman Catholic. Bishop Roy H. Short of the Methodist church insists in his book *Evangelism in the Local*

Church (Abingdon) that the best evangelistic preaching is not the noisy kind. Rather it is characterized by conviction, truth, confidence, and urgency. He further says that the method for making conversions is by influencing the judgment, influencing the emotions, and thirdly securing a response of the will.

My own observation after thumbing through several volumes of evangelistic sermons is that they usually are based upon a Bible text, are saturated with humble illustrations given in the first person, and that they always close with an appeal for action. When this appeal is omitted, they lack the evangelistic force.

There is a small volume of sermons by the still famous evangelist, Dwight L. Moody. Let's see how the catch line follows the sermon theme.

SERMON TOPIC: "Thou Fool."

TEXT: *Thou fool! This night thy soul shall be required of thee.* Luke 12:20.

CLOSING APPEAL: Am I speaking to mothers here, today, whose children have gone? If these children could call back from that world of light, it would be: "Mother, Come this way." Am I not speaking to fathers, today, whose children have passed the river? I don't believe that there's a man or woman in Tremont Temple but has some one—it may be a sainted mother—gone. Isn't she beckoning you away from this world of sin, woe, wretchedness, and misery? We have got an elder brother. Nineteen hundred years ago, the Son of God crossed the river. May God help you to come to him today!

SERMON TOPIC: "How Backsliders May Return."

TEXT: *Go and perform these words, and say, Return thou backsliding Israel.*   Jeremiah 3:12.

CLOSING APPEAL: The Lord turned and gave him one look of love, and bitterly broke Peter's heart, and he went out and wept bitterly. My God loves you. Do as Peter did. Come back to the Lord and he will bless you a thousand times more than he ever did in the past.

SERMON TOPIC: "Working For Christ."

TEXT: *Which of the prophets have not you persecuted? And they have slain them which showed before the coming of the just One, of whom ye have been the betrayers and the murderers.* Acts 7:52.

CLOSING APPEAL: Now friends, I am talking facts, and you know them to be facts. You know of men who have fished all night and caught nothing, because they didn't cast the net on the right side of the ship. . . . Where are they now? Go and hunt them up. I'd like to have you find them. You don't get afraid when you take the man—Jesus Christ. No man with the Holy Ghost has ever failed; I'll challenge you to find a heaven-sent man that ever failed. When God sends a man, there's no failure.

Preaching for decisions is a certain type of salesmanship. But there are other methods—some of them long range—which are likewise effective. In business, the methods of salesmanship have changed in the past two generations. Large corporations count their gains by the years, not by the days. Sales are preceded by advertising and contacts and the same methods have been taken up by the church. Direct emotional salesmanship has been supplemented with educational and pastoral methods until the revivalistic appeal no longer carries the entire burden. The salesman must keep in mind that when the right time comes, he must close the contract. For the church, that is the time of ingathering.

In the business world personal salesmanship has in most instances supplanted the mass salesmanship. Mass presentations are still used, but the larger and more important sales are landed by a good salesman in direct contact with the principal in the case. The use of the word "ingathering" implies a bringing in of a group or crowd of people, but the best evangelism will probably be accomplished through heart to heart talks.

Where churches still maintain evening services, the minister may find a weekly opportunity for revival in that service. The evening service will probably bring the transients and the unchurched and a different approach is needed. Some years ago the Lutheran Church of the Messiah in Philadelphia recognized the special nature of the evening congregation and so constructed its chancel that the morning service would be rich in liturgy while for the evening service the center pulpit was restored and the emphasis placed on the evangelistic message of the minister.

The Pastor's Personal Evangelism

If the minister has the instinct of the pastor, he finds opportunities for evangelism every day of the week. He uses techniques to find who the strangers are in the Sunday services and during the week he makes a contact with them. The men he meets socially or in a business way are keenly appraised by him to learn of their religious interests. He knows how to ask the right questions to find if any are troubled in spirit. This is very important. Otherwise he may cripple his entire work by speaking at the wrong time. In his house to house calling he may find many adults and youth who need to be brought to the foot of the cross. The fields are definitely white for the harvest and the pastor must know how to use the scythe. The wrong word spoken may destroy weeks of planning, but the right word at the right time can change a man's life.

The pastor needs a long term program and in some individual cases needs an extended campaign. One pastor has told me of his efforts to convert the football coach of a college in his town. This man was a good influence and moral in every respect but was neither a churchman nor a professed Christian. The minister tried carefully to find the way to approach him. He visited his home but never could find time alone with him. He visited the gymnasium but there were always students around him. To get him alone, he finally decided to ask him to come into town and have luncheon with him. There over the table the minister pointed out the tremendous influence he had and suggested that he owed it to these young men and women to consider seriously becoming a Christian. Otherwise, he pointed out, many future citizens might pass by the opportunity being offered to them. The coach was visibly moved; he admitted that he had often been at the point of making his confession but had kept putting it off. His open confession was made at the church which he joined within a few weeks.

Christian F. Reisner, a Methodist minister of a generation ago, was a natural pastor. He was responsible for the building of the Broadway Temple in New York City. When he saw unchurched men whom he thought would be helpful in his church, he planned a program to bring them to a Christian decision. To show how far he would go to win a convert he told me this story. There was a man of Methodist heritage who had showed some interest in his church. He studied this man not only to bring him to Christ, but as an addition to his official board. He decided that the best way was to visit him at his office. He made an appointment. The morning he was to make the call the man's secretary called to say that he had been unexpectedly called out of town. The next time he decided to go into the office without an appointment and take his chance. "I wish that I had time to see you," said the man, "but I have an engagement in five minutes. Do call again."

He tried several times to make an appointment but each time the man was unavailable. One morning after much thought and some prayer, he made his way to the office. There was confusion in the outer office. The man looking out said: "I am sorry that I can't visit with you today, Dr. Reisner, I am off to Canada for a fishing trip." There was a pause, then he added: "How would you like to go along? One of our party can't make it. We have his train and lodge reservations. The expenses are all prepaid. If you like hunting, here is your chance to enjoy a week. We even have the rifles; you do not need to bring one."

Reisner decided right there that he needed a week's vacation. He rushed home, packed, and got to Grand Central Station before train time. He really knew very little about hunting and he suspected that when his friend mentioned rifles that they were not going after rabbits. The next day he found himself

486 EVANGELISM IN THE LOCAL CHURCH

hunting for deer and moose. He stalked with the other men, though he hardly knew why; when anyone pointed out the deer, he shot whether he saw the game or not. He brought some tasty venison back home with him, but he brought something else more valuable. He brought back a man who had yielded himself to Christ and asked to be of service in his church.

How petty the methods of some seem compared with these well thought out campaigns. We hear of a preacher who sits down by a man in the train, immediately turns to him and says: "Are you a Christian?" That is petty salesmanship. Evangelism is worthy of a better approach.

But individual instances do not make a program of pastoral evangelism. The minister needs to have a workable system for securing prospects, listing prospects, and contacting prospects. He needs listing forms to supplement his own thinking. The old evangelist kept a prayer list. The transition has been to a prospect list containing the names, addresses, and information about each person. Next, the minister must find some way to make contact with them. A portion of his calls for each week should be on the "prospects."

They come from many sources. Parents of children in the Sunday school offer a fertile source. Neighbors of present church members offer a field which should be developed. Each organization in the church has marginal members who can be pulled across the border into active service. Letters from ministers in other cities offer him ideas. The method combines the pastoral call and personal counseling. These two features work together well. A good system of securing prospects and listing them is essential in orderly pastoral evangelism.

The Communicant Class

The fourth method of pastoral evangelism is through the confirmation or communicant class. The term *confirmation* is an old one in ecclesiastical history, coming from the denominations which practiced infant baptism. At baptism the children are too young to speak for themselves. The parents or the godparents present them and promise to bring them up in the "nurture and admonition of the Lord." There comes a time in adolescence when the child has reached sufficient maturity to speak for himself. At that time the pastor takes the child into a special class to instruct him in the doctrines of the church. At the end of the instruction the child may, if he has the desire and qualifications, "confirm" the vows given in his infancy by his parents or godparents.

The churches use for this instruction their catechisms, a system of questions and answers prepared for the purpose. The technique is instruction is simple. The pastor reads the question and the child memorizes the answer. The pastor enlarges upon the answer so that the answer would not be merely parrot-like repetition. Many churches provide that the final examinations should be public. This method of instruction for church membership has been in use for many generations.

While still an effective system, the modern minister wishes to go deeper into the mind of the child and seeks to implant an understanding of the answers. Assent does not seem to be quite enough. Numerous books with lesson material for adolescents are now available. But occasionally a minister having tried the information method prefers to go back to the catechism because he has memory as his helper. Once thoroughly learned, the catechism is not soon forgotten.

The catechism needs to be supplemented. The child should be taught to pray if he has not already learned to do so. He needs to know more about the modern church than is available in the catechism. More complete instruction is now given in most instances.

The term "confirmation" assumes that the child has previously been presented for baptism. He is now a baptized member. When he completes the course of study, he confirms the vows taken for him by his parents or God-parents. Some denominations do not practice infant baptism. For them this instruction class is know as a "communicants' class" or a "membership class."

These classes are sometimes conducted concurrently with the church school. The pastor, perhaps, takes the children from the junior department for a number of weeks for this special instruction. In other churches, the class is conducted separately from the church school. The pastor takes the group a weekday after school or Saturday morning. The trend today seems to be in favor of the release from church school on Sunday morning for the instruction class.

Some ministers have found an opportunity to offer an instruction class for adults. The purpose is the same, indoctrination into the principles of the Christian faith and the responsibilities of church membership.

Lay Evangelism

More and more churches believe that evangelism is the task of the entire church rather than having the pastor take the entire burden. Lay evangelism of one kind or another has an important place in the life of the church today. Geographical parish organizations such as the Good Shepherd plan or the Centurion plan are splendid for lay evangelism. Much more common is visitation evangelism in which laymen and laywomen from the church go out on a certain day or week to call on every prospect.

Like pastoral evangelism, the program of visitation evangelism is based on a prospect list. Without definite prospects and definite assignments, the results are sure to be disappointing. We have noted that the minister gathered his prospects in a rather informal way; when the entire church goes in for visitation evangelism that basis is hardly broad enough.

The Community Survey

A community religious survey in which every home is reached for basic religious information is the only sure method of getting a complete list for the evangelistic effort. In the average community this survey must be a cooperative venture among the various denominations. The set-up of the survey program would go like this.

1. At a meeting of the local church federation or ministerial association the plan is presented for consideration. One thing will be immediately noticed; there are churches in every community which will not cooperate. That is the first stumbling block. It probably will be impossible to get complete cooperation. The next effort would be to get partial cooperation. A committee should discuss the matter with the non-cooperating ministers explaining what the program is. These ministers should be assured that whenever a family preference is expressed for that church that the cards will be turned over to it whether or not it cooperates. That assurance usually will create a good feeling. It may go so far as to receive from the objecting pastor an assurance that he will advise his people to receive the survey visitors in a friendly way.

2. A general committee representing all the cooperating churches should be set up. Among the decisions to be made is the date for the survey; the geographical districts; the size of the teams; whether a church should be given territory around its own parish to survey or whether its members should go to other territories. Usually it is well that all of the visitors from one church be in the same unit. It is also desirable that they be sent to an area away from their own church so they get a brief picture of the home life in other areas of the city.

3. An outline map of the city should be prepared to show every street. The zones finally agreed on should be indicated on this map. Church locations should be shown. Smaller copies of this map should be given to each church. Zone leaders need a good map showing housing units in their respective zones.

4. Early in the effort church members should be asked to volunteer for the survey work. The Sunday on which the work starts will be set and the request explained. If possible, no team of workers should have more than ten calls. These cards should go to the general chairman. He in turn will hand them to the canvass committee.

5. The general committee should divide the responsibility into several groups.

a. Publicity and preparation. This committee will handle all public announcements and make contacts with the local churches to get their cooperation.

b. Literature committee. This committee will have charge of the production of the maps and all card and report forms used.

c. Canvass committee. This committee will decide on the zones, the division of the workers into teams, the detailed methods of the work. The churches of each zone are represented on this committee and a resident member should be chairman of the zone group.

d. Assignment cards should first be distributed to the chairman of each zone; next by the zone chairman to individuals of his group. Cards should be returned to the zone chairman where they will be divided by church preferences and then passed on to the general chairman. A zone committee of from three to five persons should head each zone.

e. Preferably the survey should be consummated on a Sunday. Where that seems impossible start on one Sunday and conclude on the next.

f. Training of callers should be by zone rather than city-wide.

g. When cards have been segregated by churches they should be so listed and returned to the general chairman who, with the help of his committee, will distribute them to the churches indicated.

h. The calls of the workers may be brief. In most instances, providing that the effort is made in warm weather, it will not be necessary to go into the house. The information can be taken down standing at the door. The following card is a good sample to be produced for the effort.

The Evangelistic Visit

Now that the lists of prospects are available we can move on to the second step—the campaign of visitation evangelism. This also may be a community effort, or it may be conducted by a single church. In the latter instance a list will be made up of those who have indicated that this is the church of their choice. Visitation evangelism is better fitted to a local church program than to a community program. Denominations differ on the term evangelism and in some communions the practice is to leave the task of winning souls to the minister. Certain churches may cooperate in the survey, but find it necessary to withdraw from the evangelist effort. In either case, the program will be largely the same. The steps would be these:

1. PREPARATION. Here is found the decision to have such an effort, the selection of the workers, the selection of the date or dates, and the training of the workers. The cards resulting from the survey give the basis for the program. To these should be added the names of young people in the church school and other organizations who should be reached individually for a decision.

2. BETTER TRAINED WORKERS MEAN BETTER RESULTS. At least two evenings should be given by all those who elect or are selected to do the visitation. The preparation should include prayer—the program should be steeped in this. Also the method of the program should be explained starting with the survey which is now past. Let the workers see how much preparation has gone into the program before they begin their work.

Explain to the workers that the calls they are to make will be quite different. The survey workers were advised to secure information at the door. The evangelistic workers should make their visit in the house. They have with them the card which gives information about the family.

A good introduction is something like this:

"Good morning. We are from the First Baptist Church. The community survey groups gave us the card with data about your family. It indicates that you might be interested in our church. We have come to get acquainted with you to see if there is any way in which we can be of service to you."

If a reticence is obvious the workers can go further by asking a few questions.

"Have you belonged to a Baptist Church?" If so, "Where?"

If they indicate they have never belonged to such a church, ask:

"Have you attended and participated in one?"

By questions such as these, they can be led to give you their religious experiences.

Sometimes families and individuals will give untrue answers just to hurry workers on their way. If the family does not respond to cordiality, the visitor should gradually ease himself from the house and move on to the next call. One can easily sense whether the family is interested or not. The kind of reception received should be indicated on the card returned to the committee.

If the family is receptive it will fall into one of two classifications. The first will include those who are interested but whom the caller may not think ready for church membership. They can be invited to attend the various services of the church. Special attention should be given to the children in the family and each worker should carry with him the list of classes in the church school, together with the names of the teachers. If there is a boy of twelve, one can say:
"George is just the right age for Miss Kendall's class. She will certainly be pleased to see him."
Informational bits of this kind can help to make the call profitable for the family. The teacher might be given the information so she may follow up the call.

Where the family reveals a satisfactory religious experience the worker may suggest that the minister secure a letter of transfer to the local church. If no letter is available the members of the family may present themselves for baptism and membership. If they are agreeable, the worker can so indicate on his card and see that the minister gets the information.

Here is the place to give a warning: the minister must get this information. Sometimes the general committee will be working with the cards for a period of weeks. When a family is ready for church membership or seriously needs the services of the minister, return the card in the usual way but prepare a special memo for the pastor that he may give an early follow-up to the matter.

In both the religious survey and the evangelistic campaign there is always a debate as to whether the workers should go singly or in pairs. Teams of two are preferable but both need not be present for all calls. In the survey two can secure information from two houses at the same time. In the evangelistic campaign the two should enter each home unless an individual feels he can do his best work while alone.

One must not set too rigid a pattern for this type of call. Versatility is necessary. The reception will vary from open resistance to any suggestion of religious interest to cordiality. In one survey in New York, large numbers of people asked that their names not be turned over to the committee as they were unable to assume the financial burdens of church membership.

In some homes the visitors pay merely a social call; other visits will tax all of their spiritual experience to help with the problems which are brought to them. They should be prepared when the occasion arises to pray with those who need the strength which comes from prayer. There are other times when prayer is the worst approach that could be made.

An important and helpful part of the visitation campaign is the opportunity for the visitors to get together and share their experiences. They will usually agree that regardless of how acceptable their services have been to others, the campaign is a deepening experience for each of them.

I recall an instance in which two men called on a third—a prominent man in the community—who had not been active in church. They started in a very casual way to tell their story. He stopped them.

"Just why did you come here to talk with me?" he asked.

They explained the program.

"Let's get to the deeper facts of life," he said and began to pry deeply into their own experiences. In the end he said: "I had been hoping I could discuss with someone the things of this nature. I have had some very strange religious experiences; would you let me go along with you?"

The callers agreed that he could make the calls with them.

During the conversations, he gradually worked to their side of the question and was very convincing in his suggestions and arguments. He sold himself so that he immediately identified himself with the church. One beautiful thing about visitation evangelism is this very fact. Callers who enter the program with diffidence receive a spiritual blessing for their efforts. They will have some difficult experiences but there will be many compensating ones. In no other work is the assurance of Jesus, "Give and it shall be given unto you," better verified.

Sunday School Evangelism

The use of evangelism in the church school parallels the situation in the church. The lesson material used by all denominations is planned to lead the child into a religious experience, but it may fail in obtaining definite decisions. If the minister has a communicant class, the decision time comes either when the child enters the class or when the course has been completed. This seems to be the natural situation. There have been many instances of special evangelistic services for children. Sometimes they are conducted in connection with organized religious revivals; sometimes they are especially organized to bring the children an opportunity to accept Jesus Christ.

The question of a children's revival is a difficult one. Some question the wisdom of subjecting children to the emotional strain of the open appeal. Others insist that it is legitimate and openly encourage the practice. The logical solution is to place any evangelistic effort to win children under the direction of the educational committee of the church. They understand the objects of Christian education and ensure that the program is integrated into the revival and does conflict with it. If the church is anxious to have decisions for Christ, the invitation could be given at stated intervals to the various classes and departments by the teacher, the pastor, or some one who is qualified to do that work. Historically churches have recognized the right of a child in his teens to make decisions of this nature. If the program can be integrated into the church school program, it will probably be more productive and will avoid contradictions which may arise under separately conducted campaigns.

The Place of the Revival Meeting

In the foregoing pages we have often mentioned the religious revival as a specialized form of evangelism. That is just what it is. Any assumption that the revival method is a complete program of evangelism is unrealistic. Revivals have played an important part in the life of the Christian church. Mass evangelism built our churches and our denominations and it still has a place in the church of today. On the day of Pentecost a sermon by St. Peter brought decisions from three thousand that they would follow Christ.

In pioneer America revival meetings offered the method of recruiting for churches. Revivals on the frontier brought many thousands of people together. There was great preaching by enthusiastic ministers and out of these meetings came our churches, but there were many excesses. Emotional pressure was high; converts were afflicted with strange manifestations. They fainted, talked in incomprehensible tongues, shook as if palsied, and displayed other physical disturbances. The inadequate housing of the camp meetings helped to encourage intimacies which often led to illicit relations. This part of our heritage we might wish to disown but we cannot.

Two things can be said for the old evangelistic meetings. They did create churches and they did bring spiritual convictions. The some good things are true about visitation evangelism, with one slight exception. Visitation evangelism definitely escapes the criticism of too much emotionalism, but the revival produced convictions that the visitation program cannot. Too often visitation evangelism is simply a friendly visit with a cordial invitation for the family to attend church. Revivals bring a realization of sin which causes men and women to fall on their knees and cry for mercy; mercy which is granted to them.

The revivals naturally divide themselves into two classifications. First would be those which are conducted by the local pastor or a pastor brought in to help him. The second would be the meeting conducted by a professional evangelist.

Whether to hold a revival or not depends upon the local situation. If unconverted people can be reached for Jesus Christ and other methods have failed, a revival may be the answer. If, on the other hand, there are no masses of unconverted people in the community, the revival probably is the wrong answer. In the great cities there are thousands and sometimes hundreds of thousands who are unfamiliar with the voice of God. Here is the opportunity for the revivalist.

Sometimes a minister gets discouraged. He finds little evidence of religious conviction in his own church. Someone suggests that the church hold a revival. People need to be born again. The diagnosis may be right; the church members may have lost their religious enthusiasms and convictions but a revival is not the solution. The answer is found in other pages of this book, for the time has passed when a good revival would answer every church ill.

I recall one downcast individual who came to me. He had enjoyed his monthly alcoholic binge and had finally come to himself.

"The only thing which can save me is another revival," he said. "Let me come to the altar again. That keeps me away from liquor longer than anything else." That may have been the inherent philosophy in the old gospel song, "Revive Us Again," but it is not the answer to alcoholism.

On the other hand in a church surrounded by non-church people who have resisted all invitations to participate, the revival meeting may be the answer. Many rural people are moving into urban areas to find profitable employment. The liturgical services of the city church are strange to them. They long for the evangelistic music and emotional appeals. They may be won by this method.

If the minister desires to conduct these special services, he has three alternatives. First, he may plan to conduct the services himself; second, he may prefer to invite a neighbor minister; and third, he may prefer to put the revival in the hands of a professional. If the last alternative is chosen, he will have to adapt his work to the program which the evangelist recommends. He owes that much to any man whom he believes to be qualified to lead his church in this effort. If he decides to conduct his own revival or to invite a minister neighbor, the local pastor will be in charge of the program. We suggest that any plans which are adopted include the following:

1. AN EXECUTIVE COMMITTEE. Make it a church affair rather than merely a pastoral effort. Secure the help of some good laymen and laywomen who can give respectability to the movement. The committee should be large enough to give leadership to the various committees to be appointed.

2. ADEQUATE FINANCING. Even the simplest formula requires money. It may be suggested that the expense be covered by free will offerings. Such offerings seldom are sufficient unless they are stimulated by other means.

One way is to have sponsors guarantee the costs. The persons who do this sign a card showing the limit of their responsibility. The total sponsorship should equal the anticipated expenses for speaker, music, public utilities, advertising, etc. Each offering taken reduces the actual amount pledged by the sponsors. The intent is that no sponsor will be called upon. If the offers seem too small, a committee may be put to work to take pledges to assure the amount needed is raised.

3. ADEQUATE PUBLICITY. Use banners, posters, newspapers, direct mail, radio, television and every other resource to get wide and intensive coverage. This will cost money but will produce results.

4. PLEDGED ATTENDANCE. You have noticed that Billy Graham uses this method in the opening weeks of his meeting. The community churches individually guarantee that they will bring a definite number of people to the meetings on the given nights. A revival must start out big. A small attendance on the opening night will set back the entire program.

5. SKILLED USHERS. Train the ushers for their task. It is important to seek the people, but more important to see that inquirers are directed to the right place. The ushers who do this must be sensitive and sympathetic.

6. ADEQUATE HOUSING. Make sure that the building which houses the meetings, whether it is church or hall, offer sufficient room for individual counseling. Today's revival does not end its services with a prayer and handclasp. The inquirers must definitely be assigned to competent people who will help guide them in the first weeks of Christian living.

7. CORRECT INFORMATION. Be sure to get the correct name and address of each person who makes a confession. This will be used for an early follow-up. The seed has been planted but it must be watered and fertilized to grow. That definitely is the responsibility of the church which sponsors the revival.

8. PROMPT FOLLOW-UP. See that the cards are given to the pastor of the church which is indicated as the choice of the inquirer.

9. FINAL ACCOUNTING. See that the finance committee makes an adequate accounting of the financial situation. Each sponsor is entitled to this.

It is not our purpose to go into the technique of preaching or the music of the revival. The sermons must be simple, biblical, and direct. Sprinkle them with plentiful illustration. Don't curb the emotional appeals; they are part of the effort. Select music which has proven its worth in revivals. Pray for a freedom from the inhibitions of sophistication; try to include personal references and humor. Keep in mind that you are not in the Sunday morning service; you are in the midst of a revival meeting the success of which depends upon using all the legitimate tricks of the trade to bring decisions for Christ.

Evangelism

ALLAN, T., *The Face of My Parish*. Abingdon, 1957.
BADER, J. M., *Evangelism in Changing America*. Bethany, 1957.
———, *The Message and the Method of the New Evangelism*. Round Table, 1937.

BLACKWOOD, A. W., *Evangelism in the Home Church*, Abingdon, 1942.
BRYAN, D. C., *A Workable Plan of Evangelism*. Abingdon, 1945.
DOBBINS, G. S., *Evangelism According to Christ*. Harper, 1949.
ELLIS, H. W., *Evangelism for Teen-Agers*, Abingdon, 1958.
JORDAN, G. R., *The Emerging Revival*. Abingdon, 1946.
KERNAHAN, E. A., *Adventures in Visitation Evangelism*. Revell, 1928.
MOTT, J. R., *The Larger Evangelism*. Abingdon, 1944.
MURRAY, A. L., *Reaching the Unchurched*. Round Table, 1940.
PATERSON, W. P., *Conversion*. Scribner's, 1940.
SHORT, R. H., *Evangelism Through the Local Church*. Abingdon, 1956.
STONE, J. T., *Winning Men*. Revell, 1946.
TEMPLETON, C. B., *Evangelism for Tomorrow*. Harper, 1957.

INDEX

Absenteeism, 249
Accounting, 228
Administration:
    check list, 181
    church finances, 208
    church-minister relationship, 358
    church school, 291
    court interference, 46
    establishing parish, 71
    facilities, 190
    membership records, 67
    methods of organization, 22
    office equipment, 199
    official board, 171
    place of minister, 10
    principles, 5
    program for official board, 181
    program making, 169
    public relations, 243, 256
    relationship of study and offices, 207
    validity, 1
    youth program, 436
Advertising, 252
Air conditioning, 140
Audio-visual aids:
    church school, 310
    public relations, 254
    radio and television, 255

Bells and carillons, 140
Budget making, 210
Bulletin boards, 247
Business manager, 102

Calendar, 249
Canvassing:
    capital funds campaign, 117
    evangelist survey, 488
    every member planning, 219
    instructions to solicitors, 224
    mailing addresses, 69
    new construction funds, 115
    organization of solicitors, 221
    professional, 117
    publicity, 222
Centurion Plan, 74
Chair specifications, 314
Choirs:
    building requirements, 138
    director, 279
    enlisting members, 287
    entry into chancel, 282
    necessity for rehearsals, 288
    personnel, 285
    place in processional, 272
    placement, 280
    preparation for worship service, 271
    rehearsal rooms, 281

Church school administration, 291
Classroom equipment:
    audio-visual aids, 315
    bulletin boards, 313
    chairs, 314
    chalk boards, 313
    cupboards, 313
    maintenance, 315
    pianos, 315
    purchasing, 315
    storage, 312
    tables, 315
    toilet facilities, 314
Construction:
    administrative requirements, 190
    air conditioning, 140
    assembly rooms, 145
    basic building plans, 129
    bells and carillons, 140
    building codes, 43
    choir facilities, 138
    contracting architect, 114
    educational facilities, 142
    finance committee, 112
    kitchens, 149
    location, 52
    maintenance checklist, 151
    obtaining mortgages, 122
    orderly arrangement, 147
    organization, 108
    parking facilities, 141
    public relations, 246
    recommendations committee, 109
    site selection, 112
    space requirements, 137
    toilet facilities, 148
    worship requirements, 130
    youth lounge, 149
    youth program requirements, 438
Counseling:
    aims, 399
    diagnosis, 399
    marriage, 402
    modern techniques, 392
    pastoral evangelism, 484
    post-marriage ministry, 414
    preparation, 395
    records, 398
    rules, 399
    youth problems, 448

Denominations:
    funds for new churches, 49
    inflexibility, 8
    methods of organization, 12
    publications, 254
    records requirements, 65
    women's organizations, 460

Dewey Decimal System, 194
Disestablishment, 27

Education:
  administration, 291
  adult indoctrination, 488
  assembly rooms, 145
  audio-visual aids, 310
  building requirements, 142
  catechism instruction, 487
  classroom equipment, 312
  communicant classes, 486
  departmental organization, 143, 301
  director, 297
  divided sessions, 309
  equipment, 148
  evangelism, 479
  graded pictures, 316
  history, 292
  official board, 297
  primary, 304
  religious drama, 318
  summer camps and conferences, 319
  Sunday school movement, 294
  vacation school, 318
  women in the church, 467
  worship services, 309
  youth program, 436

Established religions, 26
Establishing new churches:
  changing populations, 50
  denominational funds, 49
  location, 49
  membership application, 72
  parish organization, 72
  parking facilities, 62
  subnormal communities, 60
  zoning restrictions, 60
Ethics:
  ambition, 337
  church-minister relationship, 358
  family relationships, 351
  fraternity of clergy, 376
  guests, 378
  intellectual growth, 340
  ministerial discounts, 344
  ministerial fees, 345
  ministerial placement, 368
  obligations to minister, 365
  outside employment, 359
  personal finance, 342
  professional codes, 336
  professional relationships, 371
  social relationships, 348
  ten ministerial commandments, 379
  use of time, 339
Evangelism:
  catechism instruction, 487
  Christian responsibility, 479
  communicant classes, 486
  community surveys, 488
  emotionalism, 495
  lay help, 488
  pastoral, 480
  personal, 484
  personal visits, 491

Evangelism (Cont.):
  revival meetings, 479
  techniques, 481
  worship services, 482
  youth program, 494
Executives:
  business manager, 102
  check list, 181
  lay staff, 93
  minister, 10, 165
  organization, 16
  procedure, 9
  techniques, 175

Finance:
  accounting, 228
  budget control, 230
  budget making, 210
  building insurance, 157
  capital funds, 115
  every member canvass, 219
  functional sheets, 232
  fund raising, 210
  ministerial discounts, 344
  ministerial fees, 345
  ministerial salary, 368
  music budget, 286
  new construction, 112
  obtaining mortgages, 122
  operating principles, 235
  personal, 342
  publicizing the budget, 215
  purchase of classroom equipment, 315
  sources of support, 208
  tithing, 209
  wills and endowments, 235
  women's contribution, 469
Funeral services, 420

Guests:
  pastoral greeting, 273
  received in church office, 207
  registration, 71

Heating systems, 156

Incorporation:
  corporation sole, 29
  membership, 30
  legal forms, 28
  legal liabilities, 33
  trustee duties, 31
  trustee responsibility, 28
  voluntary religious society, 29

Lay staff:
  bookkeeper, 97
  business manager, 102
  compensation, 368
  conditions of employment, 104
  custodian, 93
  director of food service, 101
  meetings, 103
  ministerial secretary, 94
  office secretary, 96
  records secretary, 98

Liabilities:
  building codes, 43
  negligence, 44
  special assessments, 37
  taxation, 33
  workmen's compensation, 44
  zoning laws, 41
Liturgy:
  associated with music, 285
  committal services, 432
  evangelist services, 482
  funeral services, 425
  Golden Wedding service, 416
  of catechisms, 269
  of faithful, 269
  prayers in emergency, 390
  wedding ceremonies, 409
Location:
  changing populations, 50
  selection principles, 52
  subnormal communities, 60
  techniques, 50
  traffic considerations, 62
  zoning restrictions, 54

Mailing:
  addressing machines, 205
  change of address, 69
  classes, 67
  folding machines, 206
  Form 3547, 69
  returned, 67
  stampers and sealers, 207
Maintenance:
  air conditioning, 156
  books, 193
  building insurance, 157
  check list, 151
  classroom equipment, 315
  educational unit, 154
  exterior, 153
  fellowship units, 154
  fire prevention, 162
  floors, 160
  heating, 155
  nave and chancel, 153
  office and study, 155
  out of doors, 151
  parsonage, 156
  preparation for worship service, 260
  washrooms and toilets, 154
  wiring and lights, 156
Management:
  business manager, 102
  check list, 181
  church finances, 208
  democratic procedures, 8
  executive duties, 104
  executive techniques, 9
  facilities, 190
  food service, 101
  lay leadership, 6
  maintenance check list, 151
  membership records, 105
  office equipment, 199
  personnel, 106
  property and equipment, 106

Marriage:
  ceremony check list, 411
  church-state cooperation, 26
  compensation of family love, 356
  Golden Wedding service, 416
  integration of communion service, 414
  ministerial, 348
  pastoral counseling, 402
  post-marriage ministry, 414
  wedding ceremonies, 405
  wedding music, 408
Membership:
  application forms, 72
  change of address, 69
  checking attendance, 249
  evangelism, 479
  fund raising canvass, 219
  incorporation, 30
  instruction, 79
  integration, 65
  personnel file, 79
  records, 9
  statistical records, 65
  women, 458
  youth, 436
Ministers:
  administrative check list, 181
  ambition, 337
  charging fees, 345
  church relationships, 358
  commercial discounts, 344
  compensation, 368
  compensation of family love, 356
  counseling, 392
  consultation facilities, 198
  dismissal, 46
  division of work, 83
  education, 90
  emergency calls, 389
  entertainment in parsonage, 355
  ethics, 335
  evangelism, 479
  executive, 10
  executive calendar, 330
  executive duties, 165
  executive techniques, 175
  exemption from military service, 26
  family conduct, 351
  Federal Old Age Insurance, 47
  fraternity of clergy, 376
  funeral services, 420
  guests, 378
  home visitation, 383
  hymn selection, 279
  intellectual growth, 340
  lay help, 388
  multiple, 81
  obligations of church, 365
  obligation to church, 359
  outside employment, 359
  parish, 87
  pastoral assistance, 387
  pastoral ministry, 380
  personal contact, 65
  personal finance, 342
  place in processional, 272
  placement, 368

Ministers (Cont.):
prayers in emergency, 390
predecessor and successor, 372
preparation for worship service, 271
privacy, 353
professional status, 371
public relations, 245
records, 198
relation to choir, 289
relations with official board, 171
residence, 364
seeking a new church, 369
social relationships, 348
staff problems, 92
study facilities, 191
ten commandments, 379
use of time, 339, 361
wedding officiation, 404
without portfolio, 361
wives, 348
Mortgages, 122
Mourning, 420
Multiple ministry, 81
Music:
associated with liturgy, 285
choir organization, 284
director, 279
financing program, 286
funeral, 427
minister's responsibility, 279
organist, 279
organization, 278
wedding, 408

Newspapers, 253

Office equipment:
addressing machines, 205
desks, 199
duplicating machines, 201
filing cabinets, 200
folding machines, 206
stampers and sealers, 207
stationary, 200
typewriters, 199
Organization:
Centurion plan, 74
church school, 143
commission type, 18
Congregational, 15
denominational differences, 12
departmental, 20
division of work of clergy, 83
Episcopal, 13
establishing new churches, 48
establishing parish, 71
every member canvass, 219
executive procedure, 16
geographical, 74
historical, 3
incorporation, 28
multiple ministry, 81
music, 278
new construction, 108
New Testament influences, 2
pastoral ministry, 383
Reformed, 14

Organization (Cont.):
religious education, 296
Shepherd plan, 74
women in the church, 461
worship service, 258
youth program, 436

Parking:
safety measures, 62
space requirements, 141
Parsonage:
entertainment, 355
family conduct, 351
guests, 378
maintenance, 156
ministerial use, 364
privacy, 353
social relationships, 348
tax exemption, 37
Pastoral ministry:
committal services, 432
counseling, 392
counseling youth, 448
emergency calls, 389
evangelism, 480
funeral services, 420
home visitation, 383
lay help, 388
marriage, 402
mourning, 420
organization, 383
post-marriage counseling, 414
post-funeral, 433
prayers in emergency, 390
staff assistance, 387
traditions, 380
Procedure:
executive, 9
executive organization, 16
ministerial placement, 368
parliamentary, 9
pastoral counseling, 392
pastoral ministry, 380
wedding ceremonies, 405
worship service, 259
youth program, 440
Publications, 250
Publicity:
budget, 215
canvass, 222
Public relations:
advertising, 252
bells and chimes, 247
church paper, 250
community newspapers, 253
denominational publications, 254
impact on community, 243
literature rack, 248
media, 246
ministers, 245
new construction, 246
pastoral call, 248
pastoral letter, 249
periodicals, 252
radio and television, 255
Sunday calendar, 249

Radio and television, 255
Records:
 application for membership, 72
 attendance registration card, 249
 card index, 197
 change of address, 69
 commercial forms, 67
 denominational requirements, 65
 financial, 210
 guest registration, 71
 management, 105
 membership, 9
 membership statistics, 65
 ministerial, 198
 pastoral counseling, 398
 personnel file, 79
 talent ballot, 77
Religious drama, 318
Revival meetings, 495
Ritual of friendship, 249

Seasons of the church year:
 Advent, 323
 Christmastide, 323
 Eastertide, 323
 Epiphany, 323
 fixed festivals, 327
 fixing church calendar, 322
 Lent, 323
 ministers executive calendar, 330
 movable festivals, 327
 special days, 327
 use of seasonal colors, 328
 Whitsuntide, 323
Separation of church and state:
 American contribution, 25
 disestablishment, 27
 established religions, 26
 tax exemption, 26

Taxes:
 church exemptions, 26
 dedicated property, 36
 endowment income, 40
 meals, 41
 parsonage, 37
 rules for exemption, 36
 sales, 40
 Social Security, 47
 special assessments, 37
Tithing, 210

Trustees:
 check list of responsibilities, 181
 duties, 31
 election, 31
 interpretation of office, 13
 legal responsibility, 28
 relations with minister, 180

Women in the Church:
 budgeting, 470
 constitution, 471
 education, 467
 installation of officers, 477
 money-raising, 469
 organization, 461
 traditions, 458
 work program, 468
Worship:
 benediction, 273
 building facilities, 258
 building requirements, 130
 check list for service, 273
 church school services, 309
 committal services, 432
 evangelist services, 482
 funeral services, 425
 hymn selection, 279
 liturgy of the faithful, 269
 order of service, 267
 place of music, 285
 progressive service, 271
 seasons of the church year, 322
 timing, 259
 ushering techniques, 261
 wedding ceremonies, 409
 youth program, 441

Youth program:
 building requirements, 149
 counseling check list, 448
 evangelism, 494
 facilities, 439
 leadership, 447
 objectives, 438
 organization, 436
 religious education, 291
 summer camps and conferences, 319
 Sunday evening, 443
 weekday, 444
 worship services, 441

Zoning:
 protective, 45
 restrictive laws, 42

C